THE EMERGENCE OF BROADCASTING IN BRITAIN

THE EMERGENCE OF BROADCASTING IN BRITAIN

Brian Hennessy

Edited by John Hennessy

Southerleigh

Published by
Southerleigh
Church Road
Lympstone
Devon EX8 5JT

southerleigh@btinternet.com

www.emergenceofbroadcastinginbritain.co.uk

Published by Southerleigh, 2005

Copyright © Brian Hennessy 2005

The Executors of Brian Hennessy assert the moral right of Brian Hennessy to be identified as author of this work

A catalogue record for this book is available from the British Library

ISBN 0-9551408-0-3
ISBN 978-0-9551408-0-8

Printed and bound in Great Britain by
Antony Rowe Limited
Chippenham
Wiltshire
SN14 6LH

www.antonyrowe.co.uk

All rights reserved. No part of this publication may be reproduced, stored in a retrieval system or transmitted, in any form or by any means, electronic, mechanical, photocopying, recording or otherwise, without the prior permission of the publisher.

In mid-1999, having gathered his facts, Brian learned that he had cancer. Over the remaining 18 months he wrote the book which is before you, asking me to round it off and see it into publication. To the memory of my brother I dedicate this book.

John Hennessy
May 2005

Contents

List of Illustrations ix
Acknowledgements xv
Preface xvii

INTRODUCTION 1

1 THE DAWN OF WIRELESS TELEPHONY 7
The Triumph of Telegraphy 9
Groping For Telephony in a Telegraphic World 13
British Voices in the Air 17
The Confraternity of Early Experimenters 28

2 WIRELESS TELEPHONY IN THE GREAT WAR 33
Telephony Revolutionised by the Oscillating Valve 35
Wireless Telephony for Fighter Aircraft and Civil Aviation 38
First British Wireless Concert 42

3 CHELMSFORD TESTS OF 1920 47
The Marconi Works at Chelmsford and its 'Studios' 49
Speech, Music and the First Soprano 56
Melba Broadcasts 61
Wireless Telephony and the press 67

4 BROADCASTING BY THE BACK DOOR 73
Radio Hams Clamour for Telephony 75
2MT Writtle, Chelmsford 81
2LO - The Experimental London Station 104
Initiating the Public into the Mysteries of Wireless 126

5 ELECTRICAL GIANTS ENTER THE FIELD 139
Electrical Giants form a British Broadcasting Company 141
Broadcasting Commences 156
2LO at Marconi House, London 165
The 2ZY Station at Trafford Park, Manchester 190
The 2WP/5IT Station at Witton, Birmingham 205

6 THE BBC TAKES OVER ... 217
The First BBC Appointments ... 219
'Head Office', Magnet House, Kingsway ... 232
The BBC Makes its Debut ... 240
No. 2 Savoy Hill ... 249
The Savoy Hill Studio ... 261
The BBC Reaches Out to the North, Scotland and Wales ... 269
Simultaneous Broadcasting Creates 'One Nation' Broadcasting ... 279
Growth and Change at Savoy Hill; 1923 ... 283

7 PROGRAMMES ... 293
Organising the Programmes ... 295
Music ... 304
Talks ... 311
Children's Hour ... 317
Drama, Features ... 323
First Stars Of Radio ... 328
Outside Broadcasts ... 336
The Radio Times ... 341

8 BBC TRIUMPHS AGAINST ADVERSITY ... 345
Collapse of the BBC's Initial Financial Structure ... 347
Growth and Change at Savoy Hill: 1924 ... 353
New Main and Relay Stations ... 360
Technical Development: 1924 ... 363

9 FOUNDATION FOR THE FUTURE ... 369
Reorganisation at Head Office ... 371
Royal Charter ... 376
Reith's Vision Shapes the Future ... 381
Pioneers Recall The "Great Days" ... 383

PLANS ... 389

BIBLIOGRAPHY & SOURCES ... 415
Bibliography ... 415
Specialist Magazines ... 423
Archive Collections ... 424

List of Illustrations

1. **THE DAWN OF WIRELESS TELEPHONY**
   British Voices in the Air
   - *Guglielmo Marconi*
   - *The Ditcham Multi-microphone used at Letchworth, 1913.*
   - *Site of Northampton station*
   - *Site of the Letchworth station*
   - *Grindell Matthews at the transmitter/receiver, Letchworth 1913*
   - *Grindell Matthews's wireless telephone station, Letchworth 1913*
   - *The Ditcham quenched spark wireless telephone transmitter and receiver at Letchworth, 1913*

   The Confraternity of Early Experimenters
   - *B L Davies of Reigate, Surrey*

2. **WIRELESS TELEPHONY IN THE GREAT WAR**
   Telephony Revolutionised by the Oscillating Valve
   - *Marconi valve telephone transmitter/receiver, 1914*

   Wireless Telephony for Fighter Aircraft and Civil Aviation
   - *Use of wireless to check position of aeroplanes in flight; Imperial Airways, Croydon Aerodrome*

   First British Wireless Concert
   - *Arthur R Burrows*

3. **CHELMSFORD TESTS OF 1920**
   The Marconi Works at Chelmsford and its 'Studios'
   - *Marconi's New Street works, 1913*
   - *The works outbuildings in 1920 showing the studios used at that time.*
   - *Marconi's New Street Works 1920, showing the studios to which the above plan refers*
   - *Sketch plan drawn by Round in 1958*

   Speech, Music and the First Soprano
   - *W T Ditcham at the 6kW transmitter used in 1920.*
   - *Winifred Sayer, the world's first woman broadcaster and first soprano; February and March 1920.*
   - *Mrs Winifred Collins (née Sayer), in 1982, and the microphone used by Melba on 15 June 1920*

Melba Broadcasts
Nellie Melba, left, with G Isaacs, Marconi General Manager, and Mrs Isaacs. Chelmsford, June 1920
Dame Nellie Melba, posed before the microphone, Chelmsford, June 1920

Wireless Telephony and the Press
Melchior at Chelmsford, 30 July 1920. G W White at the piano, W J Ditcham on left.
Passengers on the SS Victorian, in mid-ocean, listening to a wireless broadcast, July 1920
The first ship newspaper to contain news received by radio, July 1920

4   BROADCASTING BY THE BACK DOOR
  2MT Writtle, Chelmsford
    P P Eckersley
    The Writtle team, Chelmsford, summer 1922
    Writtle hut, Chelmsford, with some of the team, 1922
    Writtle Hut 1922 – Home to 2MT
    Transmitter at 2MT Writtle, Chelmsford, 1922
    Nora Scott with Kirke broadcasting songs for 2MT Writtle, 1922
    The Writtle hut in 1955

  2LO - The Experimental London Station
    Marconi House, The Strand, London; home of 2LO, 1924
    Franklin's 1.5kW transmitter (Mk1) installed in Marconi House, London, May 1922
    Marconi House Studio Layout, 1922
    A Co-Optimists theatrical programme. 1921
    2LO Broadcast schedule sent to listeners by postcard, 1922
    2LO broadcasts from the first All-British Wireless exhibition, 1922

  Initiating the Public into the Mysteries of Wireless
    The first practical wireless magazine to be published, 3 June 1922
    Advertisement for Wireless Receivers. Modern Wireless, May 1923.
    Statement of payments to artistes, 2LO London.

5   ELECTRICAL GIANTS ENTER THE FIELD
  Electrical Giants form a British Broadcasting Company
    The BBC was incorporated on Friday 15 December 1922
    Share certificate No. 11 signed by Noble, Binyon and Anderson, 8th March 1923

2LO at Marconi House, London
BBC (2LO) accommodation plan; seventh floor, Marconi House, London
2LO Mk2 transmitter, 1923
2LO aerial on Marconi House, London, 1924
Arthur Burrows playing the tubular bells with Stanton Jefferies, 1922
Stanton Jefferies at Round's moving coil microphone, Feb 1923

The 2ZY Station at Trafford Park, Manchester
2ZY studios, Metropolitan-Vickers Works, Trafford Park, Manchester
The original 2ZY transmitter at Metropolitan-Vickers Works, Trafford Park, Manchester
2ZY transmitting aerial supported by a water tower at Metropolitan-Vickers Works, Trafford Park, Manchester
Isolde Menges with horn microphone in 2ZY studio, Trafford Park, Manchester
The Wireless Trio playing into the flared horn, March 1923
Sydney Nightingale, with Jessie Cormack, using the conical microphone in the 2ZY studio.

The 2WP/5IT Station at Witton, Birmingham
Instrument room at 5IT, Witton, Birmingham
The original studio of 5IT at Witton, Birmingham, 1922
Percy Edgar (left) and A E Thompson – Station Director and Chief Engineer respectively – who began Children's Hour, 1923

6 THE BBC TAKES OVER
The First BBC Appointments
Reith's Letter of Application and CV (following page) to the British Broadcasting Co
Magnet House, Kingsway, London, 1922
John Reith

No. 2 Savoy Hill
The original control room at Savoy Hill, 1924
Enlarged control room at 2LO, Savoy Hill, 1927
The Institution of Electrical Engineers, 1923
Proposed BBC Room Allocation, Savoy Hill, July 1923
No. 2, Savoy Hill: the West Entrance of the Institution of Electrical Engineers

The Savoy Hill Studio
  Layout of Studio suite, May 1923
  Waiting in the artistes' reception room, 2LO, late 1923
  Marconi-Sykes magnetophone (i.e. moving coil microphone), 1923

Simultaneous Broadcasting Creates 'One Nation' Broadcasting
  The first Simultaneous Broadcasting 'room', Savoy Hill, 1923
  Staff on the steps of Savoy Hill, 1922.

7 PROGRAMMES
  Organising the Programmes
    Simultaneous Broadcasting programme board, October 1926

  Music
    Crowded into Studio 3: the BBC Wireless Orchestra conducted by Stanford Robinson, December 1923

  Children's Hour
    Aunt and Uncles in the 2LO studio
    Hullo Girls! annual, 1924

  Drama, Features
    Sound effects room, basement of Savoy Hill Mansion

  Outside Broadcasts
    Outdoor broadcast equipment, 1925: Capturing the song of the nightingale
    Outdoor broadcast equipment, 1925: Broadcasting the song of the nightingale

  The Radio Times
    First issue of the Radio Times, Volume 1 No. 1

8 BBC TRIUMPHS AGAINST ADVERSITY
  Growth and Change at Savoy Hill: 1924
    Reith's sketch for accommodation on floor 2, south wing, IEE building, November 1923
    The original plaque still on the pair of doors leading to the studios: 'Notice Please walk quietly when red light is on'.
    Savoy Hill Mansions, October 1926

  New Main and Relay Stations
    Studio at 6BM, Bournemouth Station, 1925

Technical Development: 1924
   Master clock, synchronised to the Greenwich time signal, and the tuning note apparatus, May 1927
   Studio 4: Variety Studio with Silence Cabinet, 13 April 1929

9   FOUNDATION FOR THE FUTURE
   Reorganisation at Head Office
      Messenger boys sorting the mail
      Enlarged Simultaneous Broadcast Switchboard, Savoy Hill, January 1927
      BBC Head Office Staff, November 1924

COVER: *Guy Lipscombe cover for The Broadcaster, September 1922.*

ACKNOWLEDGEMENTS

Grateful acknowledgement is given to those who granted the author an interview or who wrote to him:

George Day, holder of a transmitting licence 1912
Eric Hart, founder member of the Croydon Wireless Society in 1913
Edward Backhouse, who built and operated a wireless receiver in 1914
Winifred Sayer, the first soprano, and first woman to broadcast, 1920
Sir Christopher Cockerell, who, in World War 2, was in charge of the 'Writtle hut'
Evdokya Dmitrievna ("Doushka") Williams, former wife of Cecil Lewis who was appointed by the BBC in 1922 as Deputy Director of Programmes.
L E (Len) Newnham, wholesaler of radio components, c1922, and former President of the Radio Society of Great Britain
Mr J Herring, employed in the IEE Basement's Works Store, 1927.
Hilary Vincent, daughter of Caroline Banks, long serving General Office Supervisor from 1923
Mr W R Wilson, nephew of the owner of a Northampton transmitter site
Dudley Shearman, Northampton Site Secretary 1945 to 1980
Alan Burman, Northampton historian

Before he died in 2001 Brian wrote the following expression of thanks:

I would like to thank those who have kindly given permission for access to and the reproduction of photographs, plans, and written material, in particular:

Mrs. Leonore Symons; Archivist to the Institution of Electrical Engineers.
Mrs. Jacqueline Kavanagh, Head of the BBC Written Archives Centre.
Mr Roy Rodwell, Archivist to GEC Marconi.

Mrs Symons and her assistant, Mrs Janet Smale, conducted me round the Institution building and adjoining Savoy Hill Mansions (now 'Savoy Hill House') on more than one occasion and allowed me access to all surviving plans of the building. While few of the plans showed details of the BBC occupation, they enabled the process of 'piecing together' to begin.

This process was made possible by three documents supplied by Mr Neil Somerville of the BBC Written Archives Centre, namely a staff list for 1926 with room numbers; a detailed summary of the space occupied by the BBC throughout the Savoy Hill years and two sketch layouts for 1923, showing how the rooms then in use were to be allocated. In addition, Mr Somerville let me see invoices relating to the conversion of space for studio and other uses.

Mr Rodwell drew my attention to a Marconi booklet of 1924 called The Art and Technique of Broadcasting which includes information on equipment in use at Savoy Hill. He provided photographs and other relevant material from the GEC-Marconi Archives. Many other photographs are from the BBC Photographic Library and Archive and I am grateful to Bobby Mitchell for her help.

Mr J Herring gave me details of the BBC's occupation of the basement of the Institution of Electrical Engineers.

Brian Hennessy

Preface

When I asked Brian why he was writing this book, he replied that the beginning of any great enterprise should be recorded for posterity.

The enterprise that was to evolve into the BBC was the work of many individuals. Brian describes the struggles and frustrations of some of those individuals in developing innovative equipment and who, at the end of their day's work, broadcast night after night, becoming household names; 'Uncles' Arthur, Jeff and Caractacus of Children's Hour would rise to become Assistant Controller, Station Director and Organiser of Programmes at the BBC. Brian tells of the great John Reith who drew the existing main stations together, who battled with the press, the Government, the major receiver manufacturers and who brought the BBC from a staff of four up to a Chartered Corporation of several hundred in an extraordinarily short time.

This book contains much that is original, gathered over many years. Brian's meticulous detective work, visiting sites and seeking out people from those early days brings life to his book and a measure of detail that would otherwise have been lost for all time.

There are almost 100 photographs and plans and we have endeavoured to obtain copyright clearance and give credit to originators of work, much of it from the distant past. We shall be happy to put right any omissions drawn to our attention.

In money matters, it may help to know that, in 1923, a provincial station director was paid £250 per annum, there were 20 shillings (20s0d) to the pound and 12 pence (12d) to the shilling. There were also (and still are) 12 inches to the foot and just over 3 feet to the metre.

In the last 18 months of his life my brother formed his work into a book which transports us graphically into an era long gone. Mine is the privilege of editing and seeing it into publication. I am grateful to family members for help to that end. In particular I thank Brian's wife Giuliana, my wife Catharine and daughter Jane for their invaluable help over a number of years.

John Hennessy, FIEE
September 2005

INTRODUCTION

Our story unfolds with the development of wireless telegraphy, used for Morse code, in the years leading up to the Great War in 1914. At that time, telegraphy was used extensively for long-distance communication and was an invaluable method for ship communication. Amateur enthusiasts, also well-versed in the Morse code, could tune in to transmissions from ships and mainland Europe; for them the world was brought right into their homes. The author was fortunate in being able to contact two pioneers of those pre-Great War years, Edward Backhouse and George Day, who were able to bring alive once more the thrill of those times. George Day still remembered the astonishment with which he first heard, among all the Morse, a human voice - wireless telephony.

The initial development of wireless telephony was left largely to individuals. Lieutenant Crawford was one. In 1907, by adapting his ship's wireless telegraphy equipment, he broadcast a concert to neighbouring ships. Another was Grindell Matthews, a consulting engineer, who between 1910 and 1912 experimented with broadcasting to aeroplanes and cars. As his work developed he employed, as a wireless engineer, W T Ditcham. Ditcham had plenty to do. He had to find a way of generating and transmitting radio frequency power; he also had to overcome the problems of the microphones overheating because they had to carry the transmission current. Then there was the problem of determining a suitable detector for reception. Ditcham would later become chief engineer of the Marconi station, call sign MZX, at Chelmsford.

Initially, the burgeoning number of amateur experimenters was considered by major manufacturers to be a passing phase. However, within those Companies were individuals who believed there was a future. Captain Peter Eckersley is a name that will recur throughout our tale. He and his small team at Writtle, near Chelmsford, had built a telephony transmitter for Croydon Airport about a year earlier; he was now permitted by his employer, Marconi, to develop public broadcasting equipment.

With no appreciable funds, Eckersley and his team had to make do with what was around. The Croydon airport transmitter circuit was adapted and the first public broadcast was on 14 February 1922 using the call sign 2MT. The performance was muffled, valves badly overheated and the transmission was weak. But it was a start.

Funds for artistes were non-existent, so Eckersley and other engineers had to do the broadcasting. Marconi Head Office in London decided the form these experimental broadcasts would take - stereotyped announcements, records and the like. However they had reckoned without Eckersley. Following an exhausting day's work, he and his team would meet at the Cock and Bell to decide the evening's broadcast. Then back to the hut where Eckersley, the entertainer, was star of the group, spontaneously funny and receiving much fan mail. So was the 2MT Writtle legend born. Within a year our entertainer would be chief engineer of the BBC.

By its nature the story of this evolution is both a human and a technical one, the roles of its engineers intertwining with the human story of ingenuity and struggle in dealing with problems of engineering, premises and looming bankruptcy. To omit technical development would unbalance this great tale and the author, my brother Brian, has not been faint hearted in writing of this. He has, however, limited himself to a description of the technology and its attendant difficulties; that will serve as a starting point for further reading.

In early 1922, after a visit to the USA, Isaacs, managing director of the Marconi Company, returned to the UK full of enthusiasm for the building of radio receivers and transmitters throughout the country. He spurred on 2MT Writtle, but was not going to have a clear run. Other manufacturers were pressing the Postmaster General for permission to broadcast.

Rather than a multiplicity of applications and discussions, the Postmaster General restricted the building of wireless receivers and transmitting stations to existing British manufacturers of wireless equipment. He made the novel suggestion that the manufacturers, although in competition with each other, should form a decision making committee, subject to his overall approval. This was done and the committee came to be called the 'Big Six' - although in addition to representatives of the six major manufacturers there was also one representing all the smaller companies. The Big Six first met on 25 May 1922 and later became known as the British Broadcasting Committee. In turn, this Committee decided that it would form a Company known as the British Broadcasting Company, which later evolved into the British Broadcasting Corporation. But back to May 1922.

The race was on. Much to the dismay of Isaacs, his assumption that Marconi would end up building the transmitters and other manufacturers would be limited to the building of receivers was not shared by the rest of the Big Six! Certainly, only Marconi had any significant experience in this field but, undaunted, others would give it a run for its money. They gave the go-ahead to their research staff to produce something - in blissful ignorance of the enormity of what they were demanding!

Metropolitan-Vickers was one such challenger and sharing its enthusiasm was their head of research, Arthur Fleming. 'Metrovick' had done little to show that it was a realistic contender when it learned, in July 1922, that the Postmaster-General was about to decide the Companies that would be allowed to build the transmitting stations. Their research engineers quickly built a 50 watt transmitter of a type that any amateur could have built, a boardroom was taken over as a studio and quickly hung with sound absorbing cloth. They obtained a record player, borrowed records from staff and engineers became announcers. Thus the Manchester station, call sign 2ZY, started experimental testing on 27 July 1922. What impression it gave is not known, for there were parallel struggles within the Big Six that affected the issue; however, they were still in the running. The next problem to hit them, in October, was the commitment to build and run a 1.5 kilowatt transmitter and provide a broadcast service every evening, including live performers - by mid November! How they met their deadline, the reader will discover!

Apart from the problems of acting during the evenings (as with Writtle, money was tight) the engineers had intractable problems by day as they struggled to improve their equipment. The problem was that the USA was ahead of Britain and solutions that had been found there had been patented and were unavailable. In the UK, Marconi was ahead of the field and guarded its patents jealously. Nevertheless, Manchester 2ZY engineers persevered and, among other achievements, produced an excellent (but quite ungainly) microphone.

Western Electric had left it even later in developing its station, Witton 5IT, on the outskirts of Birmingham. With its production capacity fully committed to the manufacture of radio receivers it was not until early October 1922 that it began to design its own transmitter, in its London laboratory - with a deadline of 15 November! The equipment was packed on to steam lorries on 11 November, was held up by fog and arrived on the following afternoon. Under the direction of A E Thompson the studio was built and furnished, the aerial was erected and the station was operating three days later. However, once again, money and therefore artistes were in short supply and initially Thompson and his installation engineers had to entertain.

The pressure and stress on all engineers was unbelievable. Music placed yet new demands, not only on the quality of the microphone but also on studio acoustics. Very little was known about acoustics in 1922, even in concert halls, as witness the Albert Hall, London at the time! Microphones that could deal with music, amplifiers of unprecedented power, efficient aerials – all had to be designed as matters of extreme urgency. The frustration when new ideas did not work, the overwork, the looming deadlines, the quick meal snatched before entertaining the public … time was always short. When the great Dame Nellie Melba, accompanied by top brass, came to sing at 2MT Writtle, the engineers did put a small piece of carpet on the concrete floor in front of the microphone. This she kicked away and proceeded to sing into a microphone on which the engineers had fabricated a cone out of an old cigar box. Little did she know that in the middle of her performance the transmitter failed!

But the strength lay with the Marconi Company. It not only had a lead, thanks to development work at Chelmsford but, as it was to build six of the eight stations, it could justify a greater financial commitment. Furthermore, one of these six was the central London station, 2LO, into which it put its main effort, allowing 2MT Writtle to become technically static. Under the guiding hand of Arthur Burrows, 2LO grew rapidly. It was close to theatreland, enabling artistes to perform (*gratis*) before their evening show, and it was close to the decision-makers. 2LO continued apace, introducing Londoners to radio by inviting them to halls where they could 'listen-in'.

A mainstay at 2LO was the young and energetic Stanton Jefferies, who, interviewed for the post of conductor, found himself immediately *de facto* musical director and soon rose to Station Director. Overworked and overcrowded like everyone else, Stanton Jefferies would have auditions by day, become Uncle Rex for Children's Hour and then dash off to a nearby pub with Cecil Lewis to prepare for a Covent Garden evening. Jefferies would not forget the occasion when a celebrity was to broadcast and he had managed to persuade the press to sit outside. One obedient person he did not recognise; he inquired as to his name:

"My name is Reith."

Reith was appointed Managing Director by the newly formed British Broadcasting Company (formerly Committee) in mid-December 1922 and a small room was found for him and his few staff in Magnet House, London. His personal office was described as a cupboard. From that 'cupboard' he controlled the eight stations which the Big Six had created - plus Writtle, Chelmsford; each of these continued to operate with its individual call-sign.

An immediate task was to find premises big enough for his 2LO engineers who were bursting out of their space in nearby Marconi House; premises also big enough to hold his office staff who had to liaise with all eight stations. Just before Christmas 1922 Reith and three of his senior staff went around central London premises-hunting. They needed somewhere quiet, large enough to allow for expansion, close to theatre land and sufficiently presentable to receive persons of power and influence. They settled on the Institution of Electrical Engineers, next door to the Savoy Hotel and overlooking the Thames.

The tall, autocratic and demanding John Reith fought on all fronts. He won his battles against a hostile press, he demanded and won a good financial basis on which to develop the BBC, he undertook building works and expanded beyond the Institution of Electrical Engineers as his staff swelled to about 300. He alone decided the types of programme suitable for the listening public. He was even instrumental in having his employer, the British Broadcasting Company, with its links to manufacturing, replaced by a Corporation, the British Broadcasting Corporation, basically as we know it today. The effect of this man on his staff can be imagined but they were young and keen and as our story closes they recall those dynamic days with fondness; the start of a great enterprise. We present the story of their enthusiastic struggle to you. Auntie was young once.

John Hennessy
October 2005

1

THE DAWN OF WIRELESS TELEPHONY

The Triumph of Telegraphy

By 1914, wireless had become a large-scale and almost universal means of communication. It served the needs of ships at sea, commerce and administration, as well as having enormous military significance. Wireless could span oceans, link distant countries and penetrate inhospitable areas. The scale and effectiveness of wireless telegraphy, with its Morse code, had transformed the world in a remarkably short time. Following the vital earlier work of Maxwell, who developed the electromagnetic wave equations in 1873 and Hertz, who detected these waves at radio frequency in 1888, the first practical apparatus for wireless communication using these waves was only demonstrated several years later when in 1896 young Guglielmo Marconi arrived in England. Yet by 1914, a mighty industry had grown out of those first, tentative beginnings and many countries had contributed to major technical advances.

In all this, Britain was at the forefront. Wireless could link ship to shore and was vigorously developed for this purpose, particularly by the Royal Navy. By 1905, over eighty ships were equipped, many with long-distance receivers which kept in touch with England through the Marconi station at Poldhu, on the Cornish coast, even when they were far out in the Atlantic. The Gibraltar station performed a similar service for ships in the Mediterranean. For the North Sea and the Channel, the navy built stations at Cleethorpes and Portsmouth. In 1911, further stations were completed at the Admiralty in London and at Aberdeen, Ipswich and Pembroke. By the end of 1913, 435 ships had wireless; there were 30 shore stations, and direct control of the fleet from the Admiralty was an accomplished fact (Dowsett, H M, *Wireless Telephony and Broadcasting, vol I*, p5).

The British Mercantile Marine was not far behind. Already, by 1901, ships had begun to be equipped and the Marconi Company had coast stations at Holyhead, Caister and North Foreland. By 1910, all ocean-going vessels were equipped and the Marconi and Lloyds stations had been taken over by the Postmaster General. Without exception, they employed spark transmitters. These were devices that used sparks across a gap as the source of radio power. Due to the intermittent nature of the sparks they were satisfactory for the transmission of the dots and dashes that formed the Morse code but not for speech transmission which requires continuous radio waves.

Wireless, with its lower costs, was also successfully challenging cable for international commercial communication and a trans-Atlantic service was open to the public in 1908. The service received a boost with the completion of the high-power station at Caernarfon in 1914. One could send a 'Marconigram' across the Atlantic at 8d (3p) per word, messages being accepted at all Post Offices fitted for telegraphy, and also at Marconi House, London, which was open for this purpose day and night.

Stationed amid all this telegraphic activity, a man could spend a pound or so on wireless apparatus and tune-in to cities far away. He could intercept messages from coastal stations and ships at sea from the comfort of his own home. Powerful machinery generated messages that could be picked up by radio 'hams' on home made equipment. These messages came through as 'Morse' into the earphones at 20 to 25 words a minute. The radio ham had to be as familiar with Morse as with letters of the alphabet in order to read these messages.

The author knew one of these hams. He was Mr Edward Backhouse who, in 1914, was living in York. Backhouse had attached a mast to his chimney from which he stretched a three-wire aerial to a high tree. He built his own receiver paying only for the headphones. After dinner, he would tune in at 8pm to hear the press news being sent nightly from Paris to Algiers. From 8.30, he would hear Paris communicating with Toulon, Brest, Dunkirk and other French towns. After that, there would be chance messages from ships out in the North Sea and from coastal stations. In the mornings too there were time signals and weather reports from Paris and, from Poldhu, the news at noon or on one occasion an appeal for the blind. Backhouse was thus in instant contact with much of Europe; even the distant Nauen station near Berlin came through on his phones.

Though remarkably enterprising and proficient, Edward Backhouse was not a lone pioneer. Other amateur wireless enthusiasts went further and not only received but also transmitted signals from their own homes, primarily to one another over short distances. For this they had to be licensed by the Postmaster General, and were granted their licences 'for experimental purposes' (*Experimental Licences,* 1912, Post Office Archives).

Both old and young became skilled in operating wireless apparatus. In 1909, a Northampton schoolmaster described his success in teaching wireless principles to his pupils. In one relatively small area of Derbyshire, no less than three schools held licences to transmit (Clarricoats, John, *The World at their Fingertips,* p5).

The story told by George Day, a schoolboy at Bishops Stortford College, is quite remarkable. George received his first licence in 1912; a beautiful four-page document signed by the Postmaster General himself. It authorised him both at his home in Tufnell Park, London, and at his school, to operate a transmitting station with a wavelength of 350 metres and range not exceeding 30 miles. The licence also covered his receiving apparatus. This had a T-shaped aerial made up of two wires separated by 6ft spreaders and about 50ft long. The inductor consisted of black enamelled copper wire wound round a rolling-pin with a sliding contact to tune to the wanted station. His fixed capacitor, part of the tuning circuit, was made from old glass photographic negatives interleaved with tinfoil. He used a GEC crystal detector purchased for five shillings. The 2000 ohm headphones were a birthday present. Across the headphone leads was placed a capacitor (made of tinfoil interleaved with waxed paper) to bypass residual radio frequencies. The set was installed at George Day's school (letter from Dr Day to author).

Nearly 70 years later, George Day wrote to the *Radio Times*:

> 'In those pre-war days, there was nothing to be heard but Morse, which usually went too fast for me to transcribe. But one hot summer afternoon in 1914 I heard what must have been the first voices in the air. It began with an unearthly screech which went higher and higher until it was inaudible, and then came a man's voice followed by an unaccompanied contralto. The performance lasted only a few minutes, and, accustomed as I was to hearing buzzes and grunts, I was staggered. Apparently experiments were proceeding with a 'singing arc' circuit - probably at Marconi's in Chelmsford, but they have no record of this activity.' (*Radio Times*, 13 November 1982).

There is clearly something of a mystery as to who was transmitting telephony (necessary for voice transmission) instead of telegraphy on that hot summer's day in 1914. There is a further mystery as to the means used for this purpose. Only one thing is certain; for wireless telephony the sending station must have employed apparatus capable of transmitting continuous waves. The spark oscillations normally used for telegraphy were quite incapable of transmitting the human voice.

Continuous waves comprise electromagnetic waves of uniform amplitude produced without interruption. The development of continuous waves transmitters in the pre-1914 period represented a major advance in wireless telegraphy, for they were capable of much greater ranges than spark transmitters. In addition, sharper tuning was possible. A continuous waves transmitter would therefore cause less interference to other operators using a similar waveband. By contrast, conventional spark transmitters spread their energy over a wide band of frequencies.

The practical use of continuous waves dated from an invention in 1902 by Valdemar Poulsen of Denmark, based on generating the spark of the spark transmitter in an atmosphere of hydrogen or certain hydrogen compounds. By about 1906 he had developed this 'oscillating arc' apparatus into a fairly reliable continuous waves system, achieving a frequency of several hundred kilohertz, albeit at a low power output. The system was further developed in the USA and used for about a decade. At about the same time, Fessenden in Canada, Alexanderson in America and Goldschmidt in Germany developed special types of alternators capable of generating continuous waves, but these alternators, run at high speed, were subject to excessive wear (*Poulsen arc system,* 1907 – 1913, Post Office Archives).

In 1914, a third method of generating continuous waves by means of the thermionic valve seized the attention of a handful of the world's most brilliant engineers. Two of these were Marconi men working in Chelmsford and London. One, H J Round, had a particular interest in wireless telephony and undertook several experiments using the newly developed valve oscillator for telephony. Dr Day may therefore have been correct in supposing the brief 'concert' had its origin with the Marconi Company at Chelmsford, Essex but, if so, it was the valve, not the 'singing arc' that was employed.

However, as a most successful business organisation, the Marconi Company saw no future in telephony. The march of progress still lay with telegraphy. Powerful transmitters would soon provide an 'Imperial Wireless Chain' encompassing the empire. High-speed military and commercial telegraphic messages could be sent to all parts of the globe at minimum cost. Elaborate machinery had already been developed for this purpose. Marconi telegraphy had achieved almost a world monopoly and the Marconi Company was determined to continue to exploit its lead to the full. In this scheme of things, telephony had no place.

Groping For Telephony in a Telegraphic World

The 'concert' heard by George Day was probably not intended to entertain listeners so much as to test the equipment and get a response from those who picked up the transmission. Wireless telephony was seen simply as a specialised form of wireless communication. No one had yet foreseen broadcasting for mass entertainment.

For wireless telephony there were a number of principal requirements. At the transmitting end was needed, first, a source of continuous waves and, secondly, a means of varying the intensity of, i.e. modulating, these waves so that the modulation corresponded to the air vibrations of speech or music. Thirdly, at the receiving end a detector was needed whose rectifying action would give an output to the headphones which was proportional to the intensity of the incoming waves.

The first problem, continuous waves, had been dealt with during the first decade of the century. The third problem likewise presented no insuperable difficulties. The piezoelectric crystal and other detectors used for telegraphy were equally suitable for telephony.

The main difficulty throughout the years leading up to the Great War lay with the second requirement, that of modulation. With telephony, precise amplitude modulation over a range of 200 to 5,000 times per second (200 to 5,000 hertz, the main part of the audio range) was needed compared with imprecise amplitude modulation over a range of few hundred hertz for telegraphy. Carbon microphones similar to those used in normal telephone work were used. However, these had to be modified to handle the large currents and pressures necessary for transmission by wireless. These would otherwise cause the carbon granules to overheat, 'pack' or set together and, as a result, fail to respond to the vibrations of the diaphragm.

One 'solution' was to use several microphones in parallel, switching from one to the next as soon as overheating occurred. Another approach was adopted when, in 1908, Majorana employed a liquid microphone in conjunction with an arc transmitter. In 1912, another Italian, Vanni, used a similar method with some success. But even to an expert observer the fact that they worked at all was 'almost unbelievable' (Fortescue, C L *Wireless Telegraphy).*

Most famous amongst the telephony pioneers were R A Fessenden and Lee de Forest, both working in the United States. Fessenden was the first to achieve 'telephony without wires' with his Christmas broadcast of 1906. For this, he used a carbon microphone with a water-cooling jacket, covering the whole thing with asbestos. A small hole was left in the front for sound waves to enter. An alternator produced the necessary continuous waves, this having been designed by Fessenden to work at 70,000 hertz. The story of the subsequent broadcast has often been told. From Brant Rock near Boston, Fessenden's solo performance, aided by gramophone records, was heard by ships of the United Fruit Company, which had been equipped with Fessenden's wireless telegraphy receivers and notified in advance. Within months, Fessenden's work was published by Ruhmer in Germany and a translation by Dr Erskine-Murray made Ruhmer's book available to British experimenters.

Lee de Forest's experiments were carried out in New York and Paris in the years 1907 to 1909. For continuous waves, he used the Poulsen arc. His microphone took the form of a battery of four microphones arranged in a sound chamber, funnel shaped so as to have a small mouthpiece into which the speaker could shout. The microphones were connected in parallel. For his initial tests, gramophone records were played. To his surprise, radio operators in the New York area in which he was operating became greatly excited, none more so than George Davis, Chief Electrician at the Brooklyn Navy Yard. Perhaps he was the first to see the possibilities of broadcast entertainment as opposed to point-to-point, private communication.

This enthusiasm encouraged de Forest to attempt to relay from the stage of the Metropolitan Opera House. The stage microphones' output led to a receiver that in turn was pressed against the microphone of the transmitter in the attic. The attic microphone was placed in the ground lead of the transmitting apparatus and carried the full transmitted energy. Not surprisingly, much time and money was spent replacing microphones. As de Forest confessed later: 'Our attempt at picking up the stage performance was far from satisfactory. The microphones were crude and we had no amplifying means at our disposal'.

Nevertheless, de Forest was not yet ready to throw in the towel. He conceived the idea of bringing the artiste to the microphone rather than the other way round. A studio was fitted out at 103 Park Avenue, New York, the transmitter and aerial being on the roof. By negotiating with Oscar Hammerstein, he arranged for Madame Mazarin, a noted French contralto, to come to the studio where she sang 'Habanera' from 'Carmen'. But again, de Forest concluded he was groping for success with equipment that could never provide it. Apart from the microphones, the arc generator was 'crude, inefficient and unreliable'. 'And so,' he later wrote 'I was forced to abandon my efforts until the day when better technical means could be placed at my disposal' (*Telegraph and Telephone Age*, 16 November 1928, pp511/512).

Another pioneer to try his hand at telephony was H J Round who later did so much to create the essential apparatus for BBC broadcasting in its early 'Company' years. Round, an Englishman, joined the Marconi Company in 1902 and was sent to the United States where he worked at Babylon, Long Island. In his spare time he constructed one of the first arc radio telephones, in 1906. From a small transmitter near the Battery, New York, speech and gramophone records were transmitted to various places in New York including the Times Building and ships in the docks. On returning to England, Round continued with his 'arc' experiments and several sets were made in an attempt to provide a means of commercial communication.

These sets were used both in England and Italy. They incorporated an arc that burned in an atmosphere of hydrocarbon vapour enclosed in a cylindrical chamber fitted with a mica observation window. One of the electrodes was kept turning by a clockwork mechanism in order to improve the steadiness of the burning. A gas reservoir was provided. The transmitter was fitted into a mahogany case and finished with ebonite panels and brass fittings.

For some reason, the 1910 transmitter/receiver never went into production. But it did have a brief moment of glory. A test was arranged between two sets, one at Marconi's Hall Street Works, Chelmsford, and the other at Broomfield a few miles away. The great Marconi came especially to Broomfield to speak over the wireless and heard Prince (later Major Prince) replying from Chelmsford. Fortunately, one of the two sets survives in the Marconi museum at Great Baddow, a priceless example of 'steam' radio.

One of the last examples of the 'primitive' era of wireless telephony was the station built at Laeken, near Brussels. Though the last of the line, it was probably the first to undertake broadcasting in today's sense. Raymond Braillard, who was later a leading figure in European broadcasting co-ordination, set it up in 1913. A 'Moretti arc' was employed, which used electrodes of massive copper, one with a plain surface and the other with a longitudinal perforation through which a steady stream of water was pumped. The arc was complemented by the 'Marzi microphone'. To prevent overheating of the carbon grains, these were fed as a stream through the microphone, falling finally into a cup. At regular intervals, the operator emptied the contents of the cup into the feed reservoir.

With this extraordinary equipment, wireless concerts were broadcast in late-1913 and 1914. The concerts were heard as far away as Paris. The transmissions took place every Saturday between 5pm and 6pm. After starting with gramophone records, artistes were soon persuaded to appear at the microphone, the latter being fitted with a large paper trumpet. Unlike Edward Backhouse of York, the amateurs of Brussels and Paris could occasionally enjoy music as well as the basic diet of Morse emanating from Poldhu, Norddeich and the Eiffel Tower. Broadcasting had begun. However, the clouds of war were fast gathering. Laeken's destruction was imminent (Braillard, Raymond, *World Radio*, 30 March 1934, p446)

Guglielmo Marconi

British Voices in the Air

There was little scope or need for wireless telephony in Edwardian England. The whole country was already equipped for telephony by means of a network of trunk lines under the control of the Post Office, the local exchanges being mainly in the hands of the National Telephone Company. In 1912, the Company was itself taken over by the Post Office along with its 1,565 Exchanges. There were at this time over half a million subscribers. By the eve of the Great War, most rural areas were connected to the national system. Subscribers could even listen-in to theatres, music halls and concert halls by means of the 'electrophone'.

Against this background, it is perhaps not surprising that experiments in England into wireless telephony appeared to have little commercial future and were largely left to lone individuals. Their resulting 'voices in the air' went largely unrecorded, sometimes only emerging in the form of brief reminiscences a generation later. For example, it was only in 1928 that the work of Captain Q C A Crawford, R.N., received any publicity. Back in 1907, Crawford had been a Lieutenant on HMS Andromeda lying at Chatham and by some unexplained means he had adapted the ship's wireless equipment for telephony. On 6 February, with the help of several signalmen, he put out a 'concert' which was duly heard by other warships in the vicinity. The range of the broadcast was about three miles. Little more is known today about this venture (*Daily Mail*, 15 June 1928, *Morning Post*, 24 July 1929).

Another reminiscence took the form of a letter in 1932 to *Wireless World* (11 May 1932). This was from a wireless amateur named Anthony Hankey who recalled his telephony test back in 1907, arranged for the benefit of the War Office. Hankey used a portable Poulsen arc transmitter powered by a dynamo connected to a petrol engine. With this set he transmitted telephony some eighteen miles from Aldershot to Midhurst where General French and his staff were regaled with a sequence of songs and monologues, Hankey being their sole entertainer. As with Crawford's efforts, Hankey's came to nothing.

In the following issue of *Wireless World* (18 May 1932), P Denison of Sowerby, Yorks, recalled hearing a transmission from Cullercoats, Newcastle, in June 1909. The operator was attempting to communicate with the Poulsen telephony station at Lyngby, Denmark, by voice but 'a bad cough appeared to be troubling him'. Again, this appears to have been an isolated experiment.

But most remarkable of all were a series of tests carried out by a lone inventor named Harry Grindell Matthews. Unlike Crawford and Hankey, Grindell Matthews's tests did attract publicity but in the popular rather than the technical press. In consequence, no details are available of the equipment used for his initial experiments undertaken in the 1910/1912 period.

Born in 1880, Grindell Matthews was apprenticed to an electrical firm in 1896 and, in 1902, became consulting engineer to Lord de la Warre in Bexhill, Sussex. One magazine described Matthews's apparatus as small, portable and effective over seven miles. With this set, Grindell Matthews attempted a telephone link-up with an aeroplane flying at 700 feet over Ely Racecourse, Cardiff. This was in 1911 and anticipated an obvious application for wireless telephony - that of communicating with aircraft in flight.

But it was the 'Voice of the North Sea Ghost' that caught the public's imagination. Songs, and the sound of a man whistling, had been picked up by the North Foreland coastal station as well as by a number of ships in the North Sea. A wireless amateur named Ross had heard the same sounds in his headphones at his home in Dalston, London on 25 January 1912. The incident was reported in the *Daily Mirror* (31 January 1912). 'Who is he?' asked the Mirror. Grindell Matthews came forward. But Ross, unconvinced, insisted on a demonstration. This was duly agreed, and on 5 February despite a blizzard blowing, Ross heard Matthews' voice in his headphones: 'Hello Ross. Hello Ross. Matthews here. Can you hear me? One, two, three ... ten. Have you got it Ross? Matthews calling'.

Some remarkable demonstrations followed, using cars fitted with telescopic poles that could be raised to a height of 60ft. These were later described by Matthews's biographer, E H G Barwell in Death Ray Man (For a summary see Wander, Tim, *2MT Writtle, The Birth of British Broadcasting,* pp137/143).

The various reports in the papers paint a picture of unqualified success for Matthews, his equipment conveying speech and music with, for the time, remarkable clarity over considerable distances. Yet, when it came to putting his system on a more permanent footing with purpose built stations, Matthews backed away and engaged an experienced wireless engineer, W T Ditcham, to start from scratch. After much experimenting, Ditcham came up with his own solution. Ditcham was to prove that wireless telephony in the pre-valve era was not so readily achieved as reports in the press seemed to suggest.

The story begins in the early part of 1912 when Ditcham was employed by Grindell Matthews 'to experiment with a view to producing a practical wireless telephone system'. The choice of Ditcham was a sound one. He was steeped in every aspect of wireless. Back in 1906, he had worked for the de Forest Wireless Telegraph Syndicate. The Syndicate had stations at Oxford and Cambridge capable of transmitting over an enormous 100-mile range. De Forest had acquired the Poulsen arc patents and began to experiment with telephony. By 1908, Ditcham had taken charge of the two English stations and of a third at Shoeburyness. He made trips to the United States and China to demonstrate the Poulsen field telephone. By 1909, the Syndicate, now known as the Amalgamated Radio Telegraph Company, was wound up and Ditcham joined the British Radio Telegraph Company. In later years, Ditcham was to play a key role in the development of wireless telephony working with Round at Marconi following the cessation of hostilities in 1918.

Strangely, one of the first things Ditcham did was to abandon the Poulsen arc transmitter and seek another method of generating high frequency continuous waves The method he chose was that of the 'quenched spark' transmitter used by UK shipping for telegraphy from 1911. The quenched spark transmitter gave a steadier frequency and power output than the spark transmitter; however, it was driven by an alternator of, typically, 1 kHz and this resulted in a note of 1 kHz at the receiver – useful in Morse transmission but unacceptable for telephony. Ditcham had set himself a difficult task.

Much effort went into the design of the arc discharger. Initially, in accordance with work by others in the field, this constituted a gap, the cathode of which was aluminium and the anode of copper, the discharge between 10mm discs taking place in a chamber of hydrogen. However, the results were not good and Ditcham tried experimenting with combinations of other metals, and various gases, ending with hard copper cathode/anode electrodes and carbon dioxide in the chamber. Four such gaps or 'dischargers' were used in series. Above and below were cooling fins and, at the top of each, a handle to adjust the gap.

Compared to the discharger, designing a multi-microphone was relatively straightforward. Basically, Ditcham employed a readily available product, the carbon granule microphone. The problem of overheating and packing of the carbon granules was dealt with in three ways. First, one spoke into two microphones simultaneously, these being inclined towards the mouth. Secondly, there were four such pairs of microphones mounted on a holder. After speaking for two minutes or so, a quarter turn on the wheel fixed to the holder would bring the next pair of microphones to the mouth. Finally, the holder included an arrangement for periodically agitating the granules.

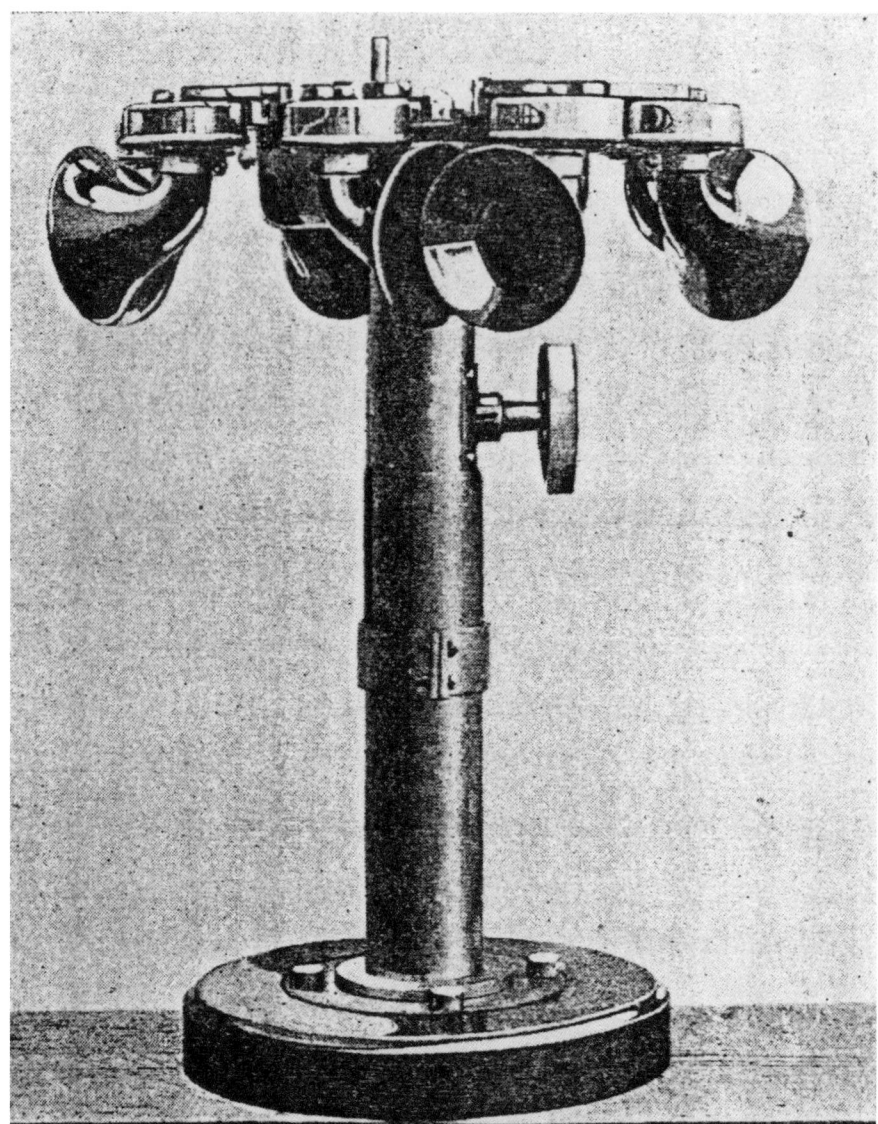

The Ditcham Multi-microphone used at Letchworth, 1913.

For reception, Ditcham employed Pickard's silicon-arsenic crystal detector purchased from a New York supplier.

Grindell Matthews was now ready to construct Britain's first wireless telephony stations. Two sites were chosen, the Post Office archives naming these as at the 'Pixmore Factory, Letchworth and Abington Park, Northampton'. The Letchworth station, in Hertsfordshire, was the first to be

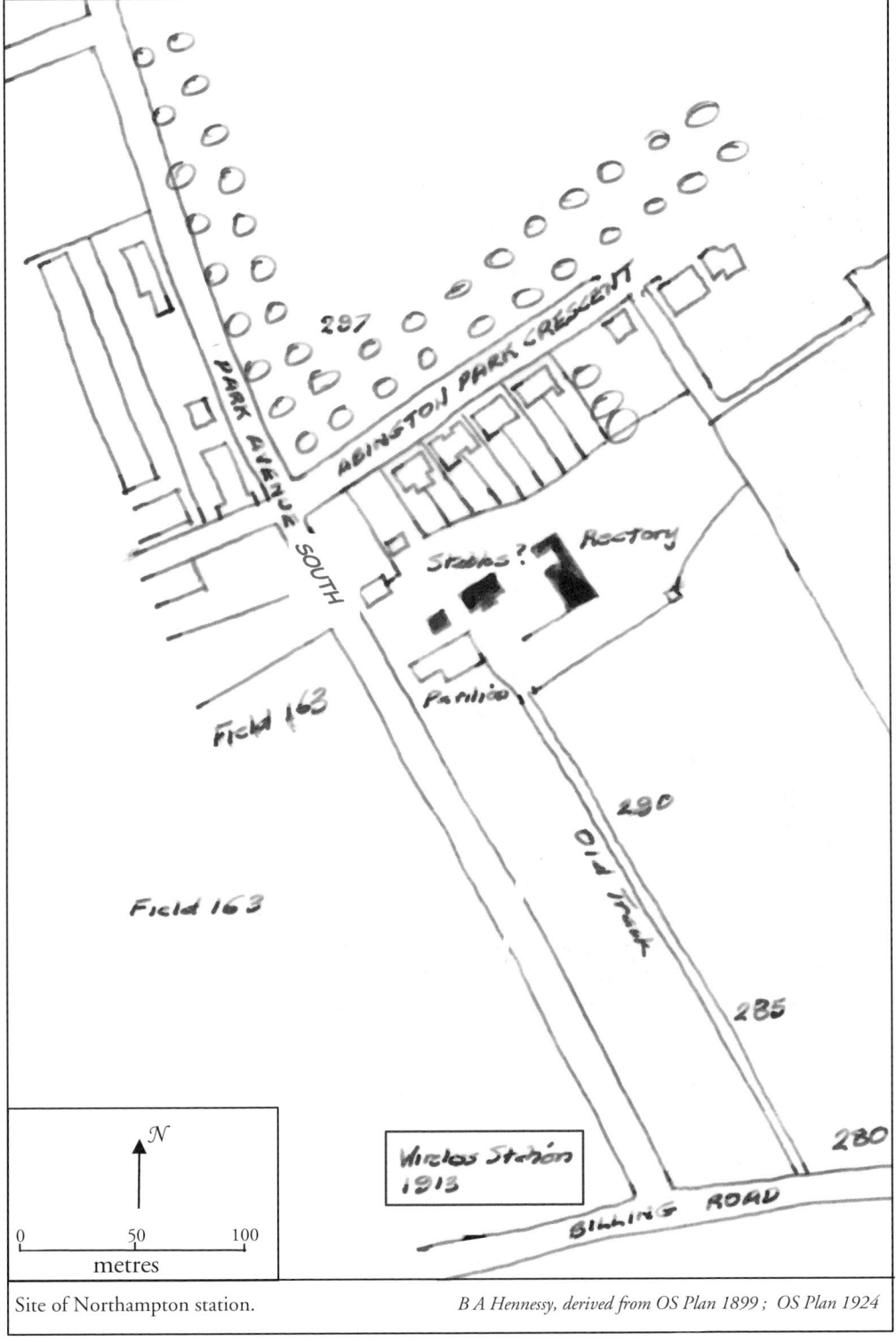

Site of Northampton station.   *B A Hennessy, derived from OS Plan 1899; OS Plan 1924*

Site of the Letchworth station. *LGC development map, 1914.*

built and, according to a local paper, was constructed early in July 1912 by J T Openshaw and Company 'on the old football ground behind the works of Kinora Ltd, Pixmore Avenue'. Immediately to the north lay the Letchworth Garden City industrial estate whilst to the east the site was bounded by a country lane (*Letchworth Citizen*, 11 July 1912).

The aerial was of the inverted L form and consisted of four wires suspended between masts set 200ft apart using 16ft spreaders. At the station end the mast was 110ft high; at the distant end, 70ft. The aerial pointed due west. The power plant was in a little wooden cabin well away from the operating hut. Power was generated by rotary converters working from the mains supply. The operating hut was constructed of vertical boarding on a timber frame, a small circular window providing the only light. All the equipment was mounted against one wall, this comprising the apparatus cabinet on the left with the aerial ammeter fixed to its side; in the centre was the microphone holder and, on the right, the control key and bell. Within the cabinet, the four dischargers occupied the top shelf; on the shelf below, tuning inductors and a relay; while on the bottom shelf was the receiver and apparatus for calling up other stations. This was done by means of a long musical 'dash' of appropriate pitch.

With the Letchworth station complete, tests could now occur between Letchworth and Grindell Matthews' office at 5 London Wall Buildings in the City. These were deemed successful enough for the next step to be taken. This was to construct the Northampton station to the same specification as Letchworth.

The site of the Northampton station can now be pinpointed, as a local historian, Mr Alan Burman, on being consulted by the author, found a picture of the station under construction in an old scrapbook. The illustration, too poor for reproduction here, was from the *Northampton Independent*. In the background are buildings, which still exist - the Priory Old People's Home that, in 1913, was a rectory. The station was constructed at the southern end of Park Avenue South. It was a logical site, for it is on the ridge overlooking the Nene valley with a clear view southward for many miles. The report accompanying the picture explained that the 'wireless telephonic station' was built on land owned by Mr Alfred Cockerell. Construction was undertaken by Messrs J G Pullen and Sons of Northampton. The short article referred to the 'latest wireless wonder' and the secrecy surrounding the project (*Northampton Independent*, 8 March 1913).

The Grindell Matthews wireless stations at Letchworth and Northampton exert a special hold on the imagination. Unlike the portable sets employed by

THE DAWN OF WIRELESS TELEPHONY

Grindell Matthews at the transmitter/receiver, Letchworth 1913.

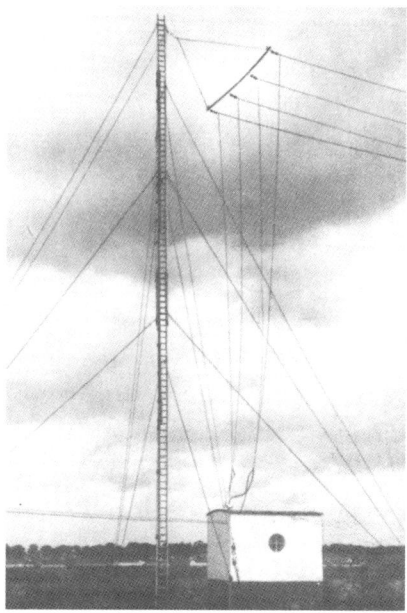

Dorsett

Grindell Matthews's wireless telephone station, Letchworth 1913.

The Ditcham quenched spark wireless telephone transmitter and receiver at Letchworth, 1913

earlier experimenters, there is something solid and substantial about stations with huts, masts and aerials. We can visit their sites and study pictures of the equipment. During the period of the author's research, the Letchworth and Northampton stations still had a place in living memory. They communicated with each other only over a brief interval, their lives being truncated by Government restrictions imposed on wireless activity at the commencement of the Great War. But in the brief interlude between creation and destruction, as if by magic, 'Mysterious voices were heard at various points in the Midlands' (Burrows, Arthur, *The Story of Broadcasting*, p44).

According to Ditcham, the Northampton station was completed in March 1913, enabling tests to commence between Letchworth, Northampton, and London. A switching system meant that a controlling key allowed either transmission or reception to occur according to its position. The Northampton aerial pointed due south giving it relative advantage over Letchworth as far as communication with London was concerned. The licence to transmit and receive was duly granted by the Postmaster General on 9 June, the two stations being authorised to transmit on 550m and 850m between 9am and 10am and 6pm and 7pm, power being limited to 1 kilowatt at each location.

Ditcham reported that, in the ensuing tests between the stations, lengthy conversations on general subjects had frequently taken place along with 'rapid cross talking in the form of questions and answers'. Messages had also been dictated and very seldom had he asked for a repetition. He went on to claim that 'the characteristic timbre of the voice is very accurately reproduced. The speaker, if familiar, can be immediately recognised' (Ditcham, W T., *Quenched Spark Wireless Telephony,* The Electrician, 9 January 1914).

Ditcham did, however, admit that 'in speaking a certain amount of practice is necessary as distinct enunciation is essential and it is desirable to speak in as loud a tone as possible'. This fact of life became all too apparent when Grindell Matthews demonstrated his system to officials representing the Postmaster General. On Tuesday, 14 July 1914, one of these officials, L B Turner, joined Matthews, Ditcham and three others in the little Letchworth hut, whilst the other official, a man named Addey, joined Mogridge who was in charge at Northampton. Turner reported to his chief, E H Shaughnessy, a week later:

'The speech between the two stations was not good. A continuous loud rustling sound was heard. Occasionally a few words were heard quite clearly but (only) for a few seconds at a time. In addition to changing the microphones frequently, it was necessary to tap them continuously while in use.'

The officials found that they could neither understand the operators' speech nor communicate between themselves. They saw no future prospects for the system and certainly no commercial future. It was a far cry from Matthews's extravagant claims 'to begin the race to link-up the world by wireless telephony' (Post Office Archives).

A few days after the demonstration, Matthews was requested to dismantle his stations. The War had begun. As it happened, he was in France. On his return, he found Post Office engineers had taken down the aerials and sealed the doors of the huts.

The Post Office was right. There was no future for the Grindell Matthews/Ditcham system. Already the Marconi Company was using a (thermionic) valve to generate continuous waves and so had the future for wireless telephony firmly in its grasp. Yet Matthews fought a long drawn-out battle for substantial compensation, still appearing to imagine that huge commercial opportunities had slipped away as his equipment and huts deteriorated. In the end he received nothing; what remained of his equipment, after it had spent years in Post Office hands, was delivered to his home in 1921 (*Grindell Matthews Wireless Patent Syndicate Limited,* 1915).

There is a sequel to this sad story. A journalist, Alan Burman, decided to write an article on the Northampton station as part of a series he was already contributing to a Northampton paper under the title 'County Tales'. His piece drew a remarkable response from a Mr W R Wilson, nephew of Alfred Cockerell on whose land the station had been built. Mr Wilson had been close to his bachelor uncle; he acted as his uncle's guardian in later years and, in due course, inherited his land. Mr Wilson, who was in his nineties when the author contacted him, had been almost a son to Cockerell. Not surprisingly, Wilson remembered visiting the wireless station in the field adjoining Abington Park Avenue as it was then named. Mr Wilson even recalled its construction:

> 'Pullens had the job, Pullens of Bridge Street. Higgins of Cogenhoe used a traction engine for the masts which had concrete block anchors. My uncle was invited to have a talk (with Letchworth) and said it was as clear as speaking on the phone. (They) wanted him to put some money into it. I'm afraid nobody got paid here. Pullens got nothing.

The governor got the two huts (in lieu of rent owed). Used to keep chickens in one of them.'

Mr Wilson then surprised the author by offering to show him the hut. 'It's eighty years old and the roof is rusty'. It turned out to be the generator hut, moved some way from its original site and damaged by 'gypsies' but still largely intact (Taped interview by the author with W R Wilson).

One of the aerial insulators was found in the ground by Mr Wilson and later given to the author. It is of a type generally employed at the time the station was constructed and is still in common use. Made by hand by Messrs Taylor Tunnicliffe, it is of hard vitrified porcelain; the furthest points of the loop of each rope overlap so that, should the insulator be fractured, the two loops will not part company (This type of insulator is described in *Wireless World*, April 1914).

The trying events surrounding the Letchworth/Northampton stations and their contents during the Great War and after is set out in documents in the archives of the Post Office. Also included in the archives are papers relating to Grindell Matthews's claim for compensation. Looking back with hindsight, we have to accept that the Matthews/Ditcham approach was doomed to failure. Inherent problems with the dischargers and with microphone overheating remained weak points in the system, as indeed they had been with all earlier attempts in this country and abroad.

The Confraternity of Early Experimenters

The first generation of experimenters in Britain was very short-lived. Most were granted their one guinea licences in the three year period 1912 to 1914, numbers rising from 258 at the end of March 1912 to 942 a year later and 1,963 by the end of March 1914, 326 licences having been issued in the first quarter of that year (Clarricoats, John, *The World at their Fingertips*, pp14, 33). But on 1 August, with war imminent, all were ordered by the Postmaster General to remove their aerials and dismantle their apparatus. In many instances, the equipment in those 2,000 homes up and down the country would never be used again. But among the amateurs were men who would play leading roles in wireless telephony development after the War, men like Scott-Taggart, McMichael and H S Walker. The seeds had been sown.

Those first amateurs became surprisingly well organised in their brief period of existence. From May 1910, all those transmitting were allotted call signs by the Postmaster General. It was decided to base these on three-letter combinations with X as the second or third letter. A directory of these transmitting stations was published in July 1913 by Gamages, the London department store that specialised in small wireless accessories. With its deep blue cover portraying one of these stations, the directory is now a very rare document. It included not only 405 transmitting stations but also a further 360 receiving stations. In March 1914, an updated version was published (The transmitting portion is reproduced in Jessop, G R., *The Bright Sparks of Wireless*, pp72, 88).

With this directory at their elbow, the wireless confraternity could now make contact with one another - at least with those within their working range. For half of them, this range amounted to no more than 10 miles. Younger operators could learn from those older hands how to improve their apparatus. For example, 17 year-old Eric Hart (HXE) who lived in Addiscombe near Croydon was able to contact Leslie McMichael, who lived in Forest Hill, and arrange to visit his station, MXA. McMichael's transmitter used a six-inch spark coil, the receiver consisting of a large inductor with a slider for tuning and a Perikon crystal detector. It had a remarkable 40-mile sending range and a power of 150 watts compared to Eric Hart's 40-watt set (Jessop, G R., *The Bright Sparks of Wireless*, pp11, 17).

The amateur wireless community was not limited to one-to-one contact but could meet, share their experiences and attend talks, for wireless clubs were springing up in all the larger towns; after Derby, in 1911, came Liverpool, Birmingham, Northampton, Newcastle on Tyne, and others. McMichael was one of the four men who established the London Wireless Club in July 1913, the others being Klein, Fogarty and Morgan. The objects of the Club were set out in an impressive document printed in blue ink (Jessop, G R., *The Bright Sparks of Wireless*, p13). Suitable accommodation in central London was provided by Gamages in the firm's premises at 107 Hatton Garden. In October 1913, the Club's name was changed to the 'Wireless Society of London'. The WSL soon attracted eminent scientists into its ranks and became a much-respected mouthpiece for the amateur wireless community in its dealings with the Postmaster General.

Despite being still in his 'teens, Eric Hart was also active in the club movement, having been a founder member of the Croydon Wireless Society in 1913. Eric also shared his knowledge not only in the club but by describing his equipment, much of which was home-made, in *Wireless World*. His licence of 31 March 1914 was an imposing document of eight pages signed and sealed on behalf of the Postmaster General. It replaced an earlier one of 11 February 1913. Seventy years later, Eric Hart could still read Morse at speed and could claim an unbroken string of licences from 1919 to 1982 quite apart from those issued before the Great War (*Radio Times*, 13 November 1982). During these years, Eric closely followed developments in wireless telephony, radio and also television broadcasting, visiting in each case the pioneer commercial and BBC stations. He had memories of many of the events and broadcasts described in this book (letters from Hart to the author).

The wide distribution of amateur stations up and down the country meant that many towns had at least one wireless pioneer (Jessop, G R., *The Bright Sparks of Wireless*, p10). In the author's home town that man was B L Davies (DWX) of Corra Linn, Cockshot Road, Reigate. His transmitter comprised an ordinary one-inch spark coil and accessories, the set having a range of 10 miles. Davies operated his station from 8pm to midnight. Reigate people were so amazed at his 'wonder of modern science' that they queued at his door just to catch a glimpse of the mysterious instruments. We can share their experience, for a contemporary postcard shows Mr Davies, with headphones on, sitting at a table loaded to overflowing with 'state of the art' apparatus.

The Gamages directory of transmitting stations declares that amateur stations had a transmission range rarely exceeding 20 miles. But in practice reception was often considerably more. Moreover, to the ranks of those equipped with transmitters/receivers can be added the almost equal number of

B L Davies of Reigate, Surrey.

those able only to receive. The wireless hams as they liked to be known, were the ears of Britain, picking up anything the ether had to offer. If, on very rare occasions, the brief sound of a human voice was transmitted among the welter of Morse, someone, somewhere, was bound to pick it up despite all the background hissing and crackling which generally accompanied it. René Klein, of the London Wireless Club, described to a reporter cases which had set the amateur wireless community in London talking. Not only had speech been heard but also snatches of music. 'It's a little uncanny to sit in one's room and suddenly to hear, from the depths of space, the sound of laughter or a man's voice slowly counting figures' (*Daily News*, 9 July 1913).

As we have seen, men like Ross and Treadwell not only picked up unannounced telephony but took the trouble to notify the press which then astonished its readers with the news: 'From out of the silence of the night there have wafted scraps of melody and tantalising fragments of conversation picked up by amateur wireless sets intended for messages in Morse' (*The Standard*, London, 28 December 1912).

Inevitably, there was much speculation as to where the sounds came from. Klein thought that the Admiralty was experimenting with voice transmission - they had in the past tried the de Forest system. W J Shaw (TWX), a leading amateur experimenter in 1913, attributed the music to a commercial wireless station at Stroud, in Gloucestershire, where the Lepel, and more recently, the Goldschmidt systems were thought to have been in use. Vague references were made to telephony experiments from a station in the North Tower of the Crystal Palace. Strangely, no one seemed aware of the Letchworth tests.

It was not long before the wireless hams were seeking a clear technical exposition for what seemed like magic to their ears. One of the first to enlighten them was the physicist George G Blake. At a meeting of the WSL on 26 May 1914, he described the use of the arc as a generator of high frequency alternating current and went on to demonstrate its use for the reproduction of the human voice. A few weeks later, on 30 June, the final WSL lecture prior to the outbreak of war was given. It described how continuous waves could be produced by high frequency dynamos. The speaker was Basil Binyon who, after the war, played a major part in establishing broadcasting in Britain (Clarricoats, John, *The World at their Fingertips*, p33). For the benefit of those who could not attend, these and similar WSL papers were published in technical journals such as *Wireless World*, *The English Mechanic*, *The Model Engineer* and *The Electrician*.

If the amateur community had nursed any ideas of seriously indulging in transmitting telephony, the papers presented in these periodicals would quickly have put paid to any such notions; complex arc machinery and high frequency dynamos were hardly on a par with the home-made equipment normally cluttering wireless hams' bedrooms! The know-how was too new, the equipment described too elaborate, and the War too imminent. They would all have to wait for George Blake to return and when, in June 1920, he would tell them how to build a simple wireless telephony transmitter using valves. Then nothing would stop them (Clarricoats, John, *The World at their Fingertips*, p51).

2

Wireless Telephony in the Great War

1914-1918

Telephony Revolutionised by the Oscillating Valve

The valve spelled ultimate doom to the spark and the arc as wireless transmitters. The valve was invented in 1904 by Ambrose Fleming, consultant to the Marconi Company, for use as a diode rectifier in the detection of radio waves. In 1910, the Marconi Company employed it in their Marconi-Fleming receivers for the detection of continuous waves. By then the Fleming diode valve was being edged out in favour of Lee de Forest's triode valve, patented in 1907. The triode, with its three electrodes, served initially as a rectifier; in 1910 its use in an amplifier circuit was developed.

The discovery had particular relevance to wireless telephony, making it at last a practical proposition. At a stroke, it overcame the old problem of overloading the microphone as the latter could be placed in a low current part of the circuit where it would not overheat. The signal output could then be amplified to bring it up to the strength required.

Then the epoch making breakthrough came with the discovery, that the triode valve could also act as an oscillator capable of generating continuous waves. This revolutionary method of generating continuous waves was first demonstrated by Meissner of the Telefunken Company in a test between Berlin and Nauen (about 20 miles, 35km) in June 1913. The test was witnessed by C S Franklin of Marconi. He hurried back to England to notify Round, his colleague who had a particular interest in telephony.

Meissner's circuit was not ideal. The valves were used at such high outputs that they tended to disintegrate rapidly (Goldsmith, Alfred N, *Radio Telephony*, p155). Round set to work and soon devised a circuit that avoided excessive anode current, with its blue glow and valve breakdown. Out of this emerged a small telephony set capable both of transmitting and receiving. It employed two types of valve developed by Round in 1913, namely a Marconi 'C' type valve (MC) for high frequency generation and amplification, and a Marconi 'T' type valve (MT) for transmitting. The receiver also used a crystal detector (Dowsett, H M, *Wireless Telephony and Broadcasting, vol I*, p153).

Round later recalled, in an article he wrote for the BBC journal '*World Radio*', the tests which followed:

> 'Some of these were carried out in England in 1913, both at Chelmsford and Marconi House (situated in the Strand, London); and there may be readers who still remember the transmission of

speech and music from Marconi House in the latter part of that year. The range of transmission was steadily extended and, early in 1914, we had succeeded in transmitting up to distances of 100 miles' (*World Radio*, 21 October 1932, p923).

Reproduced by permission of the Marconi Co. Ltd

Marconi valve telephone transmitter/receiver, 1914.

Apparently the aerial at Marconi House was used for a great many experiments at this period, involving speech and music, but these were conducted with only a few watts - perhaps 50 watts - in the aerial. Nevertheless, in a way this anticipated the role of Marconi House as the source of the 2LO broadcasting transmissions that were to come.

One complete outfit was sent to New York and telephonic communication was established between Aldene, New Jersey, and Philadelphia. The apparatus was also tested by the Italian Royal Navy at Marconi's specific request. Wireless telephone tests between two warships on the high seas some 20 miles apart resulted in perfect reception. Even ships either side of an outlying stretch of land had no difficulty in communicating. By means of a simple adjustment, the set could be used for telegraphy, doubling its range (*Wireless World*, April 1914). Another demonstration with warlike implications occurred on 4 May 1914; this time it was to Russian (Tsarist) army officers at the Savoy Hotel. They were in Britain to buy equipment.

The British military were also showing interest. In May 1914, a historic demonstration was given to representatives of the Navy, Army and Post Office. Round's assistant, C E Prince, helped him by making his house available and the tests took place between the Marconi Works at Chelmsford and Prince's house some 7 miles distant (*Faraday House Journal*, Vol. XIV, No. 5).

All this military interest was a portent of what lay ahead. One hopes the top brass were spared the engineers' standard test, the nursery rhyme 'Mary had a little lamb'. Round's assistant Tremellen got so tired of repeating this as he sat in Round's office in Room 110 at Marconi House, that he made a dictaphone record and played this into the microphone. But rather more severe tests of the equipment were to come during the forthcoming war, when the sets were carried aloft into the skies and used to convey vital information.

Wireless Telephony for Fighter Aircraft and Civil Aviation

For the military, the value of wireless telephony to the war effort was probably not fully apparent in 1914, however much they may have been impressed by Round's demonstration. It was Charles Prince, a seasoned Marconi engineer, who first showed the contribution telephony could make, namely for aircraft communication. Prince was working alongside the Royal Flying Corps at Brooklands, Surrey and soon realised that Morse sent from a plane was not only a difficult undertaking for the pilot but even more difficult for those on the ground who had the buzzes to decipher against the roar of the engine and the wind noise.

Prince had no official status and no money to spend. But he did have the moral support of General Sir David Henderson, then commanding the Royal Flying Corp (RFC). Prince's first aircraft telephone, developed amid great secrecy, was adapted from Round's 1914 set. The aerial was loose-coupled to the valve circuit, which oscillated continuously as a microphone modulated the current. It operated on 300 metres and, using a trailing wire aerial, achieved an air to ground range of 20 miles. The set was amazingly compact, about 13in x 8in by 5in. Prince tested the 'Mark I' at Brooklands, impressing even some of his own engineers, one of whom, Peter Eckersley, would follow in his footsteps after the war in developing wireless telephony for civil aviation.

Prince then took his 'Mark I' to St Omer, France, to demonstrate it to a party of senior officers including Lord Kitchener. Captain Dowding, later Lord Dowding of 'Battle of Britain' fame, took part in these early experiments.

The 'Mark I' left much to be desired but at least the work was seen to justify having its own facilities and a Royal Signals Experimental Establishment was set up at Woolwich. It was here that Prince designed his 'Mark II' set. With the formation of the Royal Air Force in 1918, Prince took charge of experimental work at Biggin Hill, Kent. He was able to gather round him a group of outstanding engineers and was rejoined by Eckersley who had been shot down while flying in France and hospitalised. At Biggin Hill, the main effort went into solving the difficult problems of ground to air communication and of communication between one aircraft and another (Prince, C E, *Lecture as President of FHOSA*, 1932).

One of the problems arose from the vibration of the airframe. This affected the contact between the 'cat's whisker' and the crystal. Crystals of carborundum were found to give a strong signal. The introduction of balanced crystals gave a 'push pull' effect, similar to that used in today's valve and transistor push pull circuits. This reduced the vibration problem but still left the other problem, that of wind and engine noise drowning the ground messages.

The truth of the matter was that until 1918, for the average pilot the wireless telephone was no part of his equipment. In *Sagittarius Rising*, published in 1936, and in his later autobiography, Cecil Lewis describes how he was taken aback when a Wireless Officer was posted to his flight. The man arrived with a 'small black box which he stuck in the locker behind my (cockpit) seat, keeping the second one on the ground for himself. He alleged I should be able to hear him, even five thousand feet up and a couple of miles away.' Apparently, 'it didn't work very well' though 'to speak to the ground was easy'. Lewis also tried to speak, again not very successfully, from machine to machine. Perhaps the surprising thing is that it worked at all.

Despite these shortcomings, aircraft at last began to be equipped. The pilot of 1918 would typically have stowed, in his cockpit, a 2-valve 20-watt telephony transmitter made by the General Electric Company USA, along with a 3-valve receiver from the Automatic Telephone Manufacturing Company, London. By the end of the war, 600 aeroplanes had been equipped along with 1000 ground stations (Hill, Jonathan, *Radio! Radio!* pp28/29).

With the cessation of hostilities Prince rejoined the Marconi Company and persuaded Eckersley to work with him in the new 'Aircraft Department' along with Furnivel, Van de Velde, Whistlecroft, Price-Smith and Trump, most of them his old colleagues from Biggin Hill and RFC days. The new team was concerned to continue the wartime work, only now the emphasis was to be on civil aviation, an entirely new form of travel. This was before the days of Imperial Airways when tiny companies working on shoe-string budgets and using ex-military aircraft sought to establish regular services from London to Paris and London to Brussels with additional flights to Cologne, and to carry officials and mail to the British Army of Occupation. Initially these companies were all dogged by bad weather and the unserviceability of aircraft. One pilot force-landed 33 times and took two days to reach Paris. Not surprisingly the three pioneer companies - Aircraft Transport and Travel, Handley Page and Instones were all desperate for navigation equipment, linking their aeroplanes to the new 'London Airport' at Croydon.

The Marconi Aircraft Department under Prince occupied a couple of small offices at Marconi House, London. To build their prototypes they were allowed a corner of Round's workshop. Here Prince designed the first set for civil use. But it was difficult to develop airborne wireless in the heart of the capital and so a move was made to a temporary site in a field at Writtle, near Chelmsford, Essex. Here the only building was a long ex-army hut. The site was very primitive. 'There was no electricity supply, little sanitation and for a while no direct water supply. Heating was by an ancient coke stove. The hut was dark and spartan with long trestle work benches' (Paper by E H Trump in *Marconi Archives*). To the hut came Eckersley, Trump and Ashbridge and, in 1920, Harry Kirke, who had served with Ashbridge in the Royal Engineers during the War.

P G Luck

Use of wireless to check position of aeroplanes in flight; Imperial Airways, Croydon Aerodrome.

Perhaps it was all too spartan for Prince who promptly handed over his job to Eckersley. The team soon produced results. By the end of 1920, Croydon Aerodrome had been equipped with a 1.5 kilowatt transmitter and with a double cage aerial 270ft long; a new 'AD' series of airborne radio equipment was also being designed and tested. For this purpose the team had the use of a DH6 aircraft (Registration mark G-EAAB) acquired from Air Transport and Travel, in March 1920. Van de Velde fitted it with the first completely screened ignition system. The plane often operated from the Writtle field, Chelmsford, on the other side of London.

For the listening wireless enthusiasts able to hear Croydon, the human voice had joined company with the world of Morse; phrases like 'Over Biggin Hill and winding in' were heard from the pilots of Instones and Aircraft Transport and Travel. (The 'winding in' referred to the trailing aerial). For many, if not most, British amateurs in 1920 and 1921 it was their first experience of telephony.

In a curiously British and almost offhand way the Writtle team were to be asked to play a crucial role in experimental broadcasting. It was not broadcasting as such, but a service to wireless experimenters, a service provided entirely by the team in the army hut as an adjunct to their legitimate workload of improving communication between aerodromes and airliners in flight.

First British Wireless Concert

The advent of the Great War hardly afforded fertile ground for the concept of using wireless for entertainment. The only individuals with apparatus for telephony were totally pre-occupied with its use for prosecuting the war. Telephony, like telegraphy, was for communication. But one man, in a very limited and localised way, nevertheless used the medium for entertainment for a few fleeting weeks in 1917. His name was Captain H de Alva Donisthorpe - 'Donny' to his friends.

Donisthorpe had been a pre-war experimenter with the call-sign DKX. During the war, like so many other former experimenters, he took on the vital task of training wireless operators. In 1917, he was attached to the Army Wireless Training Centre at Worcester, where special receivers were employed on which to train men in the interception of German signals. These receivers used valves. At that time, valves were notoriously unpredictable in their behaviour and had to be teased into life by warming the 'pip' with lighted matches. The valve proved so difficult to handle that considerable time had to be spent training operators in its use, particularly as breakages could be very expensive. Donisthorpe tried to get the officers and men to see the valve as a friend and devised a remarkable way of doing so.

In his spare time Donisthorpe built a wireless telephone transmitter and, in order to test the set, he set up two bell tents, one in a field and the other on a river bank about a mile away. While he manned the transmitter in one tent his wife manned the receiver in the other and sometimes their roles would be reversed. Mrs Donisthorpe later recalled sitting on a sugar box in front of the transmitter, a bath of oil now being used to cool the valve. It was usually night time and she would play records and talk to her husband over the wireless. As part of their test she had to repeat again and again: 'A wonderful bird is the pelican, its beak can hold more than its belly can'. At other times she took her place in the receiving tent and, if she heard nothing over the phones, would mount her push bike and pedal to the other tent to let her husband know all was not well (Mrs Donisthorpe, *Breaking Silence*, tape recording issued 19 June 1991; also Baily, Leslie, *BBC Scrapbooks*, vol. 2, 1918-1939 pp76/77).

Following the success of these tests, Donisthorpe, with the help of his wife and of Mr Eliot Macintosh, instituted the first wireless 'concerts' (Mr Macintosh later became Principal of Glasgow Wireless College). Three times a week, outside normal hours of duty, they transmitted gramophone records and recitations to army wireless training units in the area such as those at Droitwich, Malvern and Norton. None of the men there had ever before heard telephony and the wireless 'concerts' became very popular.

After the Armistice, Donisthorpe remained seized with the idea of using wireless for entertainment. He felt he could do better than relaying home-made programmes. Already the normal phone subscribers were able to hear performances from the stages of the London theatres by means of a service provided by the Electrophone organisation and its special exchange. Incurring only a modest extra charge, hundreds of Edwardian homes had been linked up and demand grew rapidly during the war and after. Whether Donisthorpe was inspired by the Electrophone service is not clear but he approached one of the theatres with a view to broadcasting the last night of a musical that had been running for several years. This would be for the benefit of the several hundred wireless amateurs that existed at that time. Alas it came to nothing. Donisthorpe would not be lifting the curtain on broadcasting in Britain (*Magnet Magazine*: date unknown to the author, but probably about 1935).

In mid 1922 Donisthorpe wrote a small booklet which he described as 'Everybody's Guide to receiving wireless news, concerts and messages'. But even at that date the amateur community had to await the advent of BBC broadcasting and what was on offer in the way of telephony generally amounted to little more than what Donisthorpe had himself provided for his men back in 1917 (Donisthorpe, H de A , *Wireless at Home*).

Donisthorpe was not the first to think of using wireless telephony for entertainment. That idea went back to the beginning, with Fessenden's work, with that of de Forest in America and with Braillard's in Belgium. But the idea of broadcasting as mass entertainment with sets in every home was another matter. Perhaps the first man in Britain to have any vision of what might be was Arthur Burrows.

Although a Marconi man, Burrows' professional background lay in journalism, not in electrical engineering. But as early as 1912 he had become obsessed with the idea of voices in the ether, heard miles away from their source. It was the latest wonder of science and he became one of the pre-war band of wireless amateurs (call sign VGX).

Like Donisthorpe, Burrows found himself called upon to train wireless operators in the interpretation of enemy messages and propaganda. But he performed his vital role from within Marconi, working at their Head Office in the Strand. Towards the end of the war, Burrows began to turn his mind to peaceful applications for wireless telephony; first, its use in the field of journalism and secondly, its potential for mass entertainment and information. In short, for broadcasting in the literal sense of the word.

Burrows suggested having concerts from the Albert Hall or Queens Hall and also other recitals relayed into the home. He even foresaw a means of covering the cost and avoiding listeners having to pay a subscription to the musical agencies. 'There would be no technical difficulty in the way of an enterprising advertisement agency arranging for the intervals in the musical programmes to be filled with appeals in appropriate tones on behalf of somebody's soup or tomato ketchup.' (*Yearbook of Wireless Telegraphy and Telephony, 1918,* p958)

At every stage in subsequent major telephony experiments and broadcasting development in Britain, Burrows was always there like a fatherly presence to guide and inspire and to set his high standards on the fledgling medium. Before Reith came on the scene, Burrows had already created the BBC ethos.

Foulsham and Banfield

Arthur. R. Burrows

3

Chelmsford Tests of 1920

The Marconi Works at Chelmsford and its 'Studios'

Until about 1880, Chelmsford had been a sleepy little market town, centre of a rural area since the time of the Normans. The town then gave birth to the 'clean' industrial era which we associate with the 20th. century, with firms like Christy and Norris, Crompton Parkinson, Hoffmann and the firm that was to change the world - Marconi. The association of Marconi with Chelmsford has lasted to this day. The works where the great telephony tests of 1920 took place look much the same today as then except for the loss of the gigantic masts, formerly a feature for miles around. These works, situated in New Street, were constructed in 1912 within 17 weeks of the plans leaving the drawing board.

But the Marconi Company's first home was a warehouse opened in 1898 in Hall Street, Chelmsford, now a protected historic building. Initially, about 50 persons were employed, the men working their lathes and other machines on the ground floor alongside the carpenters, whilst on the first floor women were employed in winding, insulating and lacquering the induction coils for the spark transmitters. The premises included a transmitting station with a wireless mast 187ft high and constructed of tubular steel. In 1905, main production transferred to Dalston, London and Hall Street was for a while used for research, with brilliant engineers like Round and Franklin playing the lead roles.

But Hall Street could never meet the needs of such a dynamic new industry as wireless. The New Street site by contrast was vast allowing for almost endless westward expansion behind the main front. The new two-storey building facing New Street included offices, reception space and a showroom with the Directors' luncheon room, offices and drawing office over. In a separate frontage block were placed canteens and a clubroom for the staff. Behind, was the factory proper. Working backwards from the frontage block, were the test room, mounting shop, capacitor/winding shop and machine shop. Alongside the latter was the carpenter's shop and, coming towards New Street, were the raw stores, a packing area with loading docks, finished stores and power test room. The packing area had the convenience of an adjoining rail siding that ran the length of the factory on its north flank. On the far side of the rail track was a powerhouse and reservoir.

But the dominant feature for miles around were the wireless masts. The tubular steel design replicated the Hall Street masts but on a totally different scale, rising 450ft and being set 750ft apart. Though needle-like in appearance, each was, in fact, 3ft in diameter. Five sets of insulated stays connected each

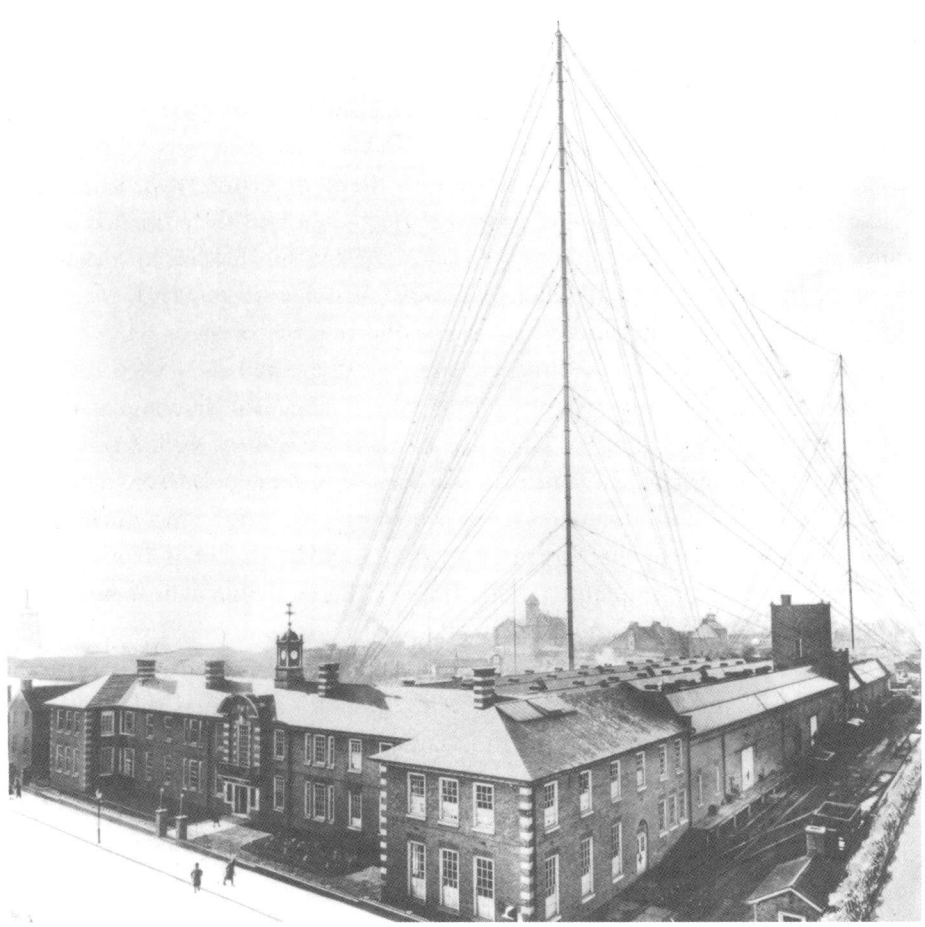

Reproduced by permission of the Marconi Co. Ltd

Marconi's New Street works, 1913

mast with its four steel anchors. The anchors were set in 100-ton concrete blocks. During 1915, the aerial was blown down in a gale and Mr Post, the engineer responsible, scaled one of the masts, finding his footing on the heads of the bolts that fastened the sections. On his back was fixed a wire cable for picking up the fallen aerial. Mr Post reached the top, within one hour it is claimed, fixed a pulley to the mast and the aerial was duly hauled up (*He climbed our mast*, 1944).

These were the masts used for the long-distance high power tests of 1920. Later they were used for the BBC's high power long wave 5XX station, the experimental precursor of Daventry. Still later, they were used for the experimental short wave Empire broadcasts. There are still (1999) people in Chelmsford who remember the masts which until 1935 dominated their town and which reflected its close association with the Marconi Company.

Although the last word in planned factory layout in 1912, it was not long before further development occurred. By 1920, a sequence of outbuildings had appeared on the far side of the rail siding. On this narrow strip of land was erected, first the Field Station, secondly, a long shed, probably used as a valve store, and thirdly the Research Laboratory/Transmitting House It was in this group of buildings that the dramatic transmissions of 1920 occurred - dramatic, not only for their range but for the star performers who appeared before the microphone, above all Melba, the great operatic prima donna.

In his review of inter-war history in Britain, Leslie Baily summed it up: 'To broadcasters, this back end of a factory at Chelmsford had the significance that a place where Caxton used his first printing press would have had for any printer or publisher today - the cradle of it all!' (Baily, Leslie, *BBC Scrapbooks*, vol. 2, 1918-1939 p.77). Alas the buildings are no more; the shed had been replaced by a brick building by 1928; the other two buildings were demolished about 1990, shortly after the author visited them.

By 1958 the Melba broadcast (Ch. 3: *Melba Broadcasts*) had become legendary in wireless history and the Marconi archivist of the day, G G Hopkins, sought to establish from the engineers the 'studio' used on this historic occasion. The engineers most closely associated with the arrangements for the telephony tests were Round, Pettengill and in particular Ditcham, who had joined the Marconi Company in 1915 (from Grindell Matthews) and had rejoined in 1919 after a spell in the navy. He was in charge of the enormously powerful 15-kilowatt transmitter.

In 1958 Ditcham was sure of only one thing; Melba did not sing in the Transmitter Building where he was in charge. Fortunately, Round remembered the occasion rather better. 'Melba sang in the little building situated near the big valve transmitter house. She sang about a yard from the microphones, not like the photo of her holding it. I had a bit of difficulty placing her as she told me she knew all about it. She had made a number of recordings. I let her do what she wanted to. She was interviewed by a crowd of reporters after the show standing outside the door.'

In his letter to Hopkins, Round added a sketch plan. This showed, alongside the site boundary, the Transmitter House; a small yard separated this from the 'little building' in which he indicated the positions taken by the microphone, Melba and the baby grand piano. The author's plan (drawn from

CHELMSFORD TESTS OF 1920

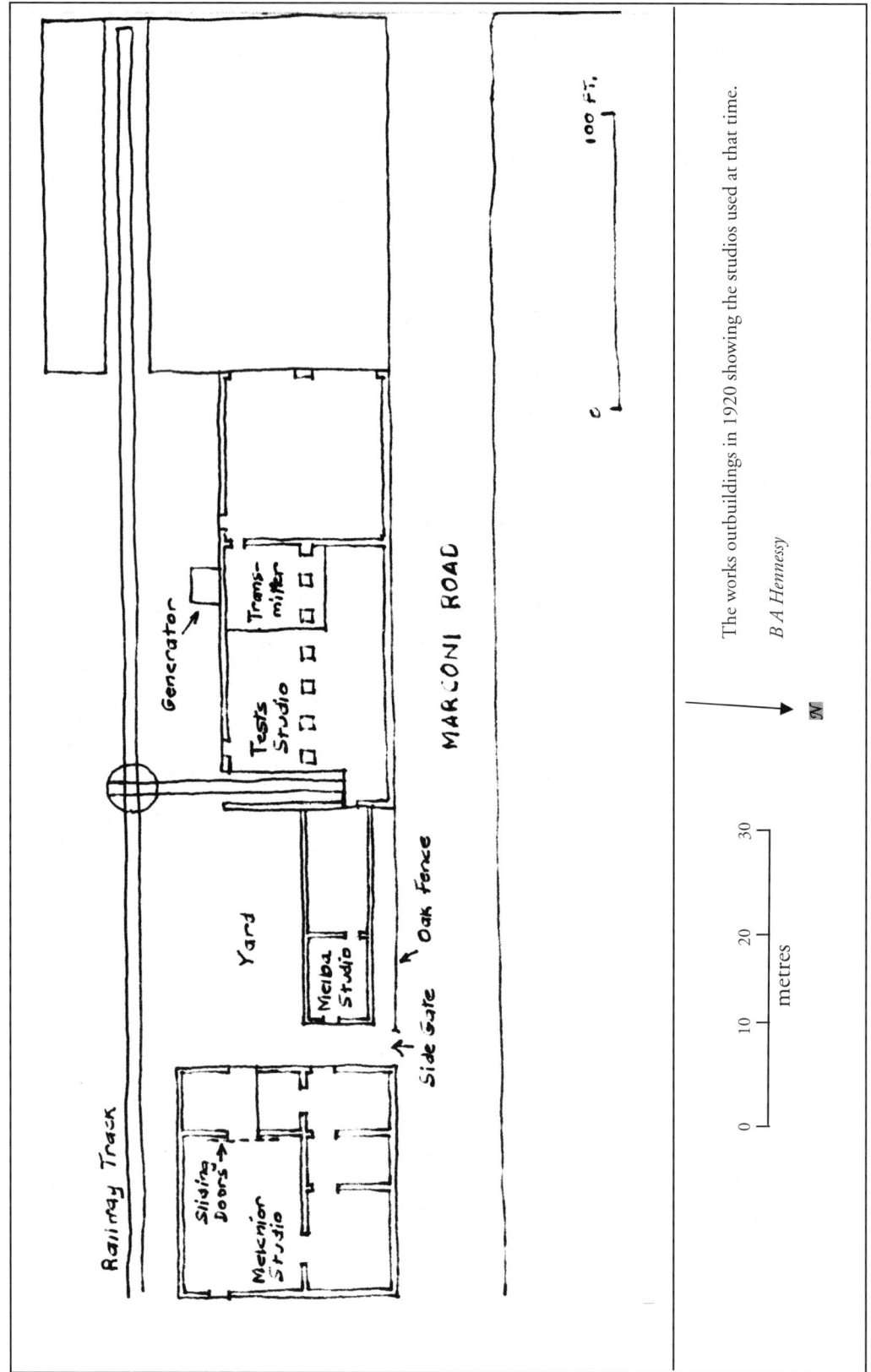

The works outbuildings in 1920 showing the studios used at that time.

B A Hennessy

Reproduced by permission of the Marconi Co. Ltd
Marconi's New Street Works 1920, showing the studios to which the above plan refers

a Marconi Company plan of the 1920 buildings) and the 1920 photograph above, differ in showing a linking building rather than a small yard. Round also marked the spot where he stood in the yard listening with a wavemeter to ensure all was well. A crowd formed in the road alongside the little building, listening to Melba (*Marconi Archives*). This then was the 'little building' used by Melba. The studio measured 30ft by 23ft and was entered by a door in the end wall. A gate in the works' boundary fence afforded direct access from Marconi Road.

When asked by Hopkins where Melba had sung, Ditcham had admitted he was unsure as to whether Melba sang 'from the dining room of those days or

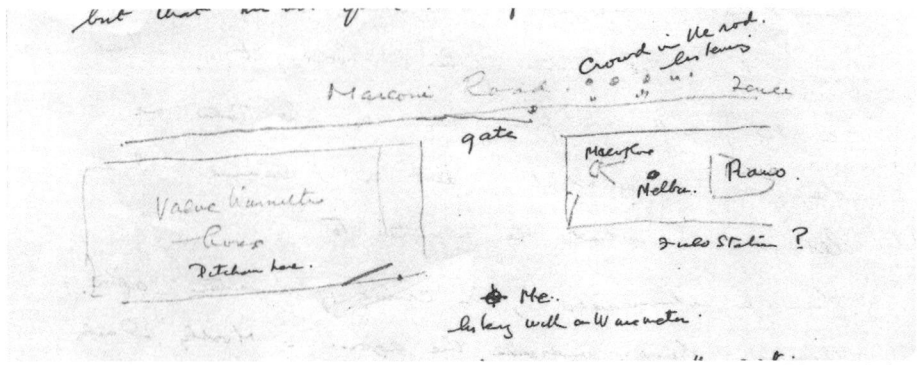

Sketch plan drawn by Round in 1958.

Marconi Archives

from the works out-building adjacent to our railway line' (letter of July 1958 in Marconi Archives). The Dining Room was for Directors and Senior Staff and was on the first floor at the southern end of the main frontage building. This, indeed, is where Melba should have sung! Round explained the confusion:

'It was laid down that Melba had to be received in, and to sing from, a very nice studio - and our laboratories in which the gear was housed were a very long way from being a room suitable for receiving the great lady. We undertook to put down a long landline (from the Dining Room), to bring the microphone current to the transmitter. However, at the last moment this turned out to be a failure as the line we had erected picked up so much of the high-frequency current from the aerial that it put the modulating valves out of action. What is now (in 1932) quite an easy problem to solve was in those days quite a difficult one, and Melba had to be content with singing in a shed near the apparatus in the laboratory. The place was made as comfortable as possible with a few mats and a piano, and the microphone was suspended.' (Round, Capt. H J , *Broadcasting Reminiscences,* World Radio, 21 October 1932).

Melba was not the only great singer to perform at Chelmsford in that series of tests. Five weeks later the great Danish tenor, Lauritz Melchior, came down under somewhat similar circumstances. Again for Hopkins the question of the 'studio' arose. Round's memory was of him singing in the Dining Room and placing the tenor a long way from the microphone on account of his powerful voice and the consequent danger of microphone blasting. Ditcham disagreed.

Melchior sang in the 'works out-building'. Pettengill backed this. 'The studio then in use was situated in the old Field Station'. This building had become the top end of the High Power Test building by 1958 but without any change in its appearance.

Fortunately, photographs were taken on the occasion of Melchior's performance. This time Ditcham was right. The photographs clearly show the main room of the Field Station, or High Power Test as it became, with its distinctive metal fire doors in the background. Against the spartan factory setting of bare brick walls and steel truss roofing the grand piano and its accompanist look totally out of place, but at least the 'studio', being 53ft by 40ft, must have afforded room for Melchior to stand well back from the microphone!

Shortly after Melchior's broadcast, another great singer came to the Marconi works. This was the famous contralto Dame Clara Butt. She was accompanied by her husband - himself a renowned singer - Kennerley Rumford. Round felt sure that they had used the Dining Room as their studio but, as with Melba and Melchior, that may simply have been what everyone had in mind.

Finally, what of the little band of workers who volunteered to take part in the initial tests of 1920? They included men from the works - one played the clarinet, another the oboe; and there was a man in Round's laboratory who played a one-string fiddle. Then there were the singers who were 'dragged in to help' one of whom, Mr E Cooper, had a very nice tenor voice. And one must not forget Miss Winifred Sayer, a soprano, who came over from the Hoffman works to make the 'concerts' more appealing to listeners. Round remembered them performing 'in close proximity to the running machinery which sometimes interfered with the musical character of the concerts.' In later years Mrs Collins, as she had become, in an interview with the author, recalled seeing the enormous valves glowing blue in the background as she sang. So the noisy 'studio' in this case was the Transmission Room itself, with its adjoining Crompton motor and generator. Fortunately, five months later Round had the sense to place Melba 50 yards away in the hut!

CHELMSFORD TESTS OF 1920

Speech, Music and the First Soprano

When Hopkins, archivist to the Marconi Company, was pursuing his enquiries about the 1920 tests, the 'studio' used by Winifred Sayer, the actual first soprano, was known as 'Marine Test'. But much earlier, it had been the Research Department's Laboratory. It was here, in 1919, that a 6kW transmitter had been built using MT2 transmitter and MR2 rectifier valves along with MT4 low frequency amplifying valves.

Reproduced by permission of the Marconi Co. Ltd
W T Ditcham at the 6kW transmitter used in 1920.

A photograph of the valve panel, with its associated aerial tuning inductor, shows Ditcham seated at a small trestle table speaking into the microphone and holding a newspaper. Ditcham's repertoire at the time of the photograph had clearly been extended to readings from newspapers, always of course those of the previous day for copyright reasons. Ditcham's normal routine had initially been even more prosaic, not to say downright boring:

'MZX calling; MZX calling. This is the Marconi valve transmitter at Chelmsford, England, testing on a wavelength of 2500 metres. How are our signals coming in today? Can you hear us clearly? I will now recite to you my usual collection of British railway stations for test purposes. The Great Northern Railway starts at Kings Cross, London and the North Western Railway starts from Euston; the Midland railway starts from St Pancras; the Great Western ....'

Following a successful Chelmsford to Madrid test, the set was increased to 15 kilowatts using MT4 and MR4 valves made at the Marconi-Osram works in Hammersmith - Round, Ditcham and Mogridge were all involved with the design.

For many years the Marconi station at Poldhu had used the 2500 metre wavelength and this was chosen for the Chelmsford tests as few other stations were using wavelengths in that neighbourhood (Frank P Swann, *Wireless World*, 1 May 1920). Ditcham's 'news service' was transmitted for two weeks in January 1920.

It was at this point that one of the engineers assisting in the tests started to organise short transmissions of musical items. The engineer, Mr G W White, was himself a brilliant pianist and was joined by Mr A V Beeton, oboe, and Mr W Higby, clarinet, both being from the works. Some vocalists, likewise from the works, were called in to help, including Mr Edward Cooper, who had a good tenor voice which transmitted easily. Mr Cooper performed with a local band and knew a young soprano, Miss Winifred Sayer, who was in the same group. He suggested she be invited to take part in the Marconi concerts. Although Miss Sayer was on the clerical staff of the neighbouring factory, Hoffmanns, and so would have to be paid, this idea was approved and a programme of concerts began to be prepared.

The transmissions were to be twice a day at 11 am and 8 pm, beginning 23 February and finishing 6 March 1920. The news would once again take up 15 minutes leaving time for perhaps three short musical items. On 20 February Round sent a memo to the Chief Engineer announcing the series of musical tests. He asked the Chief Engineer to inform all Marconi land stations, requesting them to report back if they heard the transmissions.

Years later, in 1991, the author visited Miss Sayer, or Mrs Collins as she had become, at Chelmsford, to obtain a first hand account of the concerts.

She had been announced by Ditcham, sitting by the transmitter panel, its valves flashing blue and close to overloading:

'MZX calling. This evening for a change we have a vocalist; a lady vocalist too, you'll be glad to know, so I will now ask her to start on her first song. Will you start now please?' (Baily, Leslie, *BBC Scrapbooks*, vol. 2, 1918-1939, p78)

Nothing could have been more incongruous; standing on a stone floor strewn with packing cases and nervously holding the 'telephone' to her lips she commenced her refrain:

> 'Sometimes, between long shadows on the grass,
> The little truant waves of sunlight pass,
> My eyes grow dim with tenderness, the while
> Thinking I see thee, thinking I see thee smile.
> And sometimes, in the twilight gloom apart,
> The tall trees whisper, whisper heart to heart,
> From my fond lips the eager answers fall,
> Thinking I hear thee, thinking I hear thee call!'

It was from the Marconi Archives that I had discovered the song she had sung. It was an Edwardian ballad with the title 'Absent'. I presented Winifred Collins with a copy obtained from Boosey and Hawkes; her eyes lit up:

> 'That was the song I sang - the only song I did. I didn't know what they wanted so I thought it best to choose a short piece. Then Eddie Cooper sang. I said to Eddie Cooper, 'What do we do now?' Then we had a duet. There was no piano, Eddie Cooper had a tuning fork and hit it and off we went. They gave me ten shillings each night. I sang three nights. When it was all over I went home and my father said, 'What did you do?' I told him (about the microphone) and said it seemed a bit daft to sing into something like that. It only took twenty minutes. We just came away; never thought anymore about it.' (Taped interview, by author, 14 January 1991).

But as she left 'a gentleman' (Godfrey Isaacs, Managing Director, Marconi), told her she had made history. Miss Sayer still remained mystified. The full impact of what she had done only struck her when she received a copy of the Marconi Company's 'Souvenir of an Historical Achievement' (1920, Marconi Archives) with the Company's compliments and thanks for her services inscribed on the back. The little booklet listed all who had heard the broadcasts and had written to the Company. 145 amateur experimenters in all parts of Britain and

Ireland were listed. Typical was Eddie Gage of Gloucester who sent a one penny stamped postcard with the message; 'Wireless speech received here. Hearty congratulations.' In addition, 68 reports were from ships at sea, eight being 1000 miles or more from Chelmsford. Other reports came from land stations in Ghent, Lisbon and Norway. The amateurs' receivers had included both crystal sets and valve sets in roughly equal numbers but with crystal type 31 sets predominating among the ship installations. An astonished but now fully convinced Miss Sayer turned to her father: 'Well, they couldn't make that one up could they!'

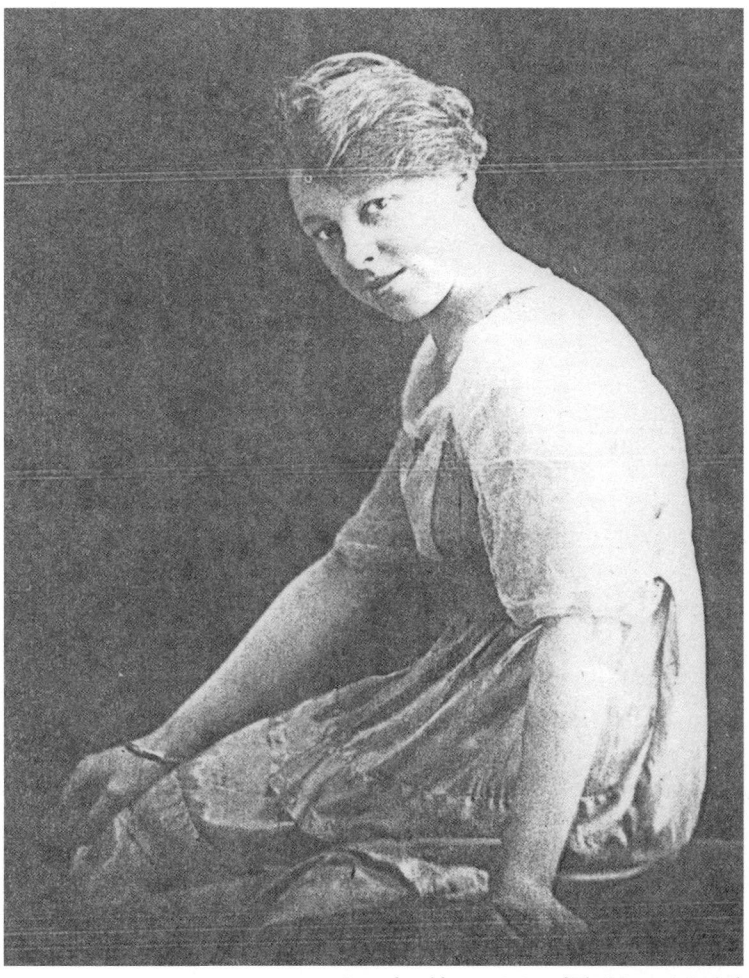

Reproduced by permission of The Marconi Co. Ltd
Winifred Sayer, the world's first woman broadcaster and first soprano; February and March 1920.

Others too were astonished. At Burlington House, Piccadilly, a committee meeting of the Royal Society was adjourned by its Chairman in order that members might witness 'a rather interesting experiment.' They entered an adjoining lecture theatre where two small bits of apparatus were positioned. They then heard a programme of songs, piano and speech 'radiating' from Chelmsford, some thirty miles away. Their bewilderment was not alleviated when the demonstrator said musingly: 'I'm afraid the sound is harsh.' (Hadow, Sir Henry, *Preface to New Ventures in Broadcasting*). At least the Marconi Company was a little more gracious. On the back of the 'Souvenir' it referred to the vocalists having no accompaniment other than the powerful hum of a fifteen kilowatt motor generator and having to sing 'amidst surroundings which only an experimental building can provide.'

Some idea of what amateurs and ships wireless operators heard back in 1920 exists in the BBC Sound Archives as, years later, Winifred once again sang her song over the air (*Scrapbook for 1920,* BBC Home Service, 31 January 1956).

B A.Hennessy

Mrs Winifred Collins (née Sayer), in 1982, and the microphone used by Melba on 15 June 1920

Melba Broadcasts

For many years, Dame Nellie Melba had triumphed in the opera houses of Europe and America. She had first sung at Covent Garden as far back as 1888. She maintained her supreme position for quarter of a century, perhaps the leading prima donna in the golden age of opera. Who could have guessed that the great Melba would ever leave the bright lights of the London stage to spend even one evening journeying to an Essex factory so that she could sing standing on the hard floor of a storage shed? Could anyone who witnessed works hands performing, or who saw the girl from Hoffmanns looking bewildered and feeling daft when asked to sing into a telephone mouthpiece, have predicted that the world's greatest operatic prima donna would, within five months, take up much the same position and sing into the same mouthpiece. Still more unlikely, considering she had sung with the great Caruso back in 1902, was Melba's description of the event at Chelmsford as being 'the most wonderful experience of my career'.

Melba's live audience, apart from the 'official party' of ten or so from London, consisted of a crowd of local people standing in the road outside and one young lady hovering nervously at the door of the hut and peering in at the 'toffs' - Winifred Sayer. There was of course the wider audience, the wireless amateurs at their equipment, concentrating on getting the best adjustments, headphones clamped on. And in a paper warehouse in the Blackfriars Road, London, sat Melba's secretary beside Tom Clarke of the *Daily Mail*. In Walthamstow a tense audience waited, its members including two schoolboy wireless hams. And out at sea were the Morse professionals - the ships' Wireless Operators. A greater contrast to the glittering audience of a normal 'Melba night', with its feel of being a great Society occasion, could hardly be conceived. But the scattered listeners awaited Melba with an equal sense of expectation and she would not disappoint them. Amid an unlikely setting, the strangest 'Melba Night' of all was about to unfold, one where there was no stage, no cast, no orchestra, no habitués, no society ladies with flashing jewels; just scattered listeners, few of whom had ever been to an opera, but most of whom had undoubtedly heard of the legendary diva.

How had it all come about? Arthur Burrows and Tom Clarke should probably share the credit for the idea. Burrows was then publicity officer for Marconi and, as we have seen, one of the few men with any vision of broadcasting. He could see the huge publicity value for Marconi of radiating a voice such as Melba's to the world.

Tom Clarke knew Burrows from earlier days. As News Editor of the *Daily Mail*, Clarke was steeped in what the *Mail* had always offered its readers under the driving force of its far seeing proprietor, Lord Northcliffe. Northcliffe catered for working people - 'people in a hurry'; for vast numbers of average men and women who were curious about every aspect of life - sports, fashion, books, the latest idea, the new sensations of science. Ten years earlier, the *Daily Mail* had promoted aviation; now it was to be broadcasting. Northcliffe was ready to back the idea of the Melba broadcast with an offer of a £1000 fee.

When first approached the singer remained adamant that her voice was not a matter for experimentation by young wireless amateurs and their 'magic playboxes'. It is reputed to have taken all the persuasive talents that Lord Northcliffe could muster to change her mind (Wander, Tim, *2MT Writtle, The Birth of British Broadcasting*, p21). A contract was thereupon prepared, even down to the menu for the meal Melba would expect on arrival. Melba signed.

On 15 July 1920, she travelled down by train from London, attired in a black dress with white trimmings and white hat. Accompanying her were her son, George Armstrong, together with his wife and Melba's two accompanists, Frank St. Leger and Herman Bemberg, one of whose songs she was due to sing. Also with her were Burrows, acting as official escort, and Godfrey Isaacs and his wife representing Marconi. Lord Northcliffe and his friend Sir Campbell Stuart completed the party.

On arrival, Melba enjoyed her meal of chicken, champagne and her favourite unleavened white bread in the Directors' luncheon room and the official party were led by Burrows and Ditcham through the works to see the masts and the transmitter house and so to the substitute studio. Here a photograph was taken of a rather dour Melba standing outside the shed with Mr and Mrs Isaacs. On the left, one can make out the 5ft 6 in boundary oak fence. On the far side of this, but not visible in the picture, a crowd had begun to assemble with a policeman or two to keep them in order should the need arise. The official party now threaded into the 'studio' and took their seats. A rather posed picture of Melba holding the microphone was now taken after Melba disdainfully kicked away the carpet mat under her feet exposing a bare concrete floor. In reality the microphone was not held but had to be suspended to allow the powerful singer to stand back several feet. A hat stand was adapted for this purpose. Following established gramophone recordings practice, the microphone was fitted with a horn but, in the usual Marconi makeshift way, an old cigar box was broken up and re-assembled for this purpose. The microphone with its horn has lasted to this day as a prized exhibit in the Marconi Archive collection.

St. Leger now prepared his music ready to accompany Melba at the piano. Ditcham, following a slight but annoying last minute hitch, ensured the technical side was in perfect order and ready to transmit. The Marconi announcer (Burrows?) stepped to the microphone:

> 'Hello, Hello, Hello! Dame Nellie Melba, the Prima Donna is going to sing for you, first in English, then Italian, then in French.'

He apologised for Marconi's having no control over the 'atmospherics'. A chord was struck and listeners heard the first fleeting notes as Dame Nellie ran up and down the scale. This preliminary check brought a flurry of adjustments, the engineers tapping meters and adjusting capacitors for tuning. The distance between microphone, singer and the piano were all critical (Wander, Tim, *2MT Writtle, The Birth of British Broadcasting*, p24). Melba intervened at this stage

Reproduced by permission of the Marconi Co. Ltd
Nellie Melba, left, with G Isaacs, Marconi General Manager, and Mrs Isaacs. Chelmsford, June 1920.

CHELMSFORD TESTS OF 1920

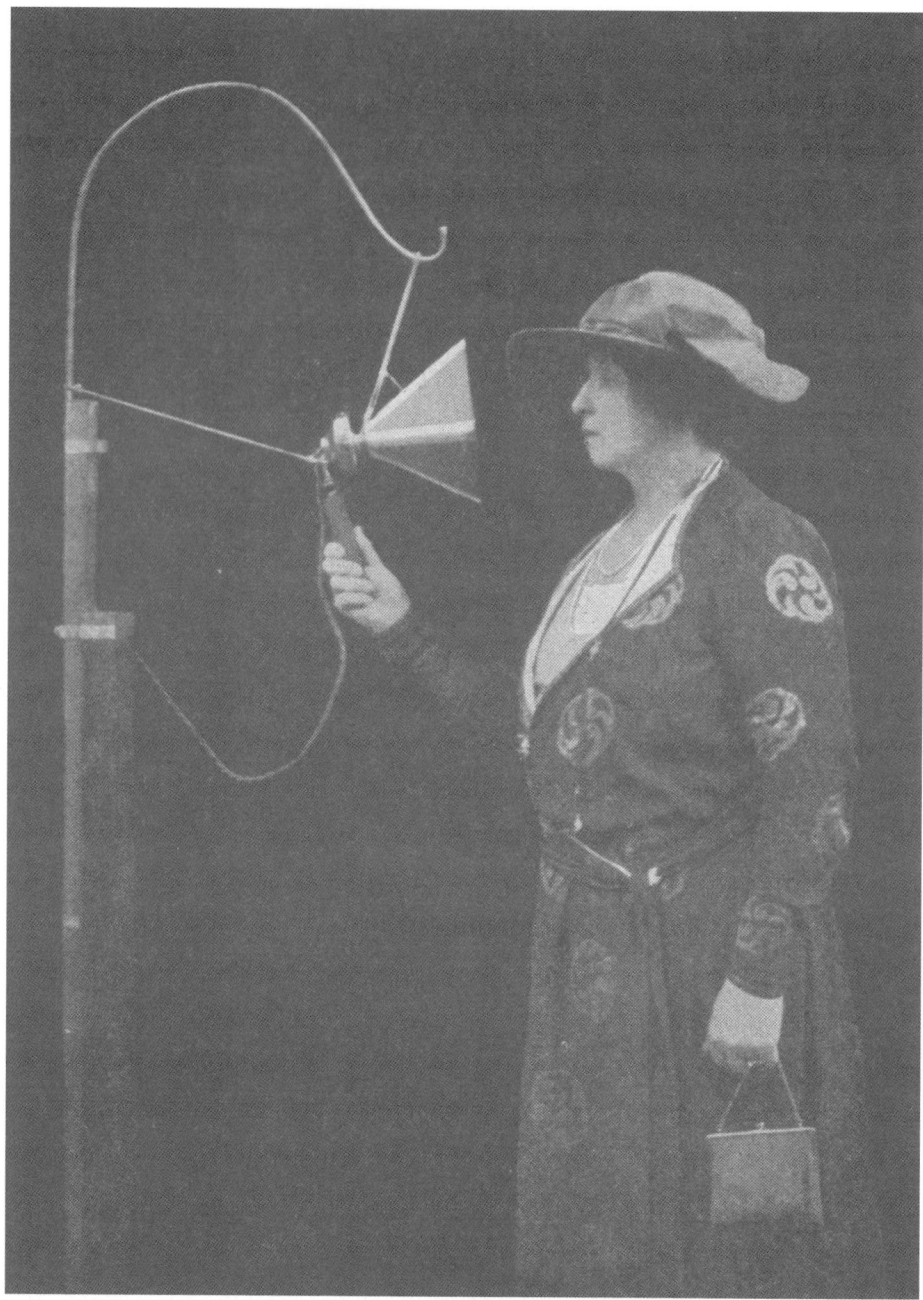

Reproduced by permission of The Marconi Co. Ltd
Dame Nellie Melba, posed before the microphone, Chelmsford, June 1920.

saying she knew all about the gramophone recording business and she was going to sing before the microphone in the way she thought was right. Round wisely realised this was one battle he had lost; he was soon to have another in which he would have more success. Meanwhile, he took to the yard outside to listen on his wavemeter.

Then the great moment came, Dame Nellie's voice singing the old favourite, 'Home Sweet Home' was radiated by the powerful transmitter loud and clear across Britain and the Continent and out to sea. Puccini's 'Addio' from 'La Boheme' then followed. It too went off without a hitch.

St Leger now left the piano so that Bemberg could accompany Melba in the last item, a piece of his own composition called 'Nymphs and Sylvain.' This had already commenced when one of the valves on Ditcham's panel started to misbehave itself and finally broke. Ditcham stopped the machinery and all went silent except in the 'studio' shed where there was nothing to suggest anything was amiss. Round rushed from the yard to the transmitter house. The repair would not take long but the concert had had an abrupt ending as far as listeners across Europe were concerned and the third song had been all but lost. Round then went through to the shed where he found Melba still singing 'Nymphs and Sylvain' blissfully unaware of what had happened. He let her finish and, as though nothing had gone wrong, and knowing all was now well with Ditcham, addressed her with the words: 'Madame Melba, the world is calling for more.'

Imagining that he had been receiving messages of appreciation from all over the world through the magic of radio, she responded: 'Are they? Shall I go on singing?' Bemberg was still at the piano and so Melba sang his 'Chant Vénétien'. As an encore, she then repeated 'Nymphs and Sylvains.' Listeners therefore missed nothing of the planned programme. Melba finished with the first stanza of the National Anthem. Amid applause, the announcer stepped to the microphone. 'Hello, Hello. We hope you have enjoyed hearing Melba sing. Good Night!' (H J Round, *Broadcasting Reminiscences,* World Radio, 21 October 1932).

In the *Daily Mail's* paper store in Blackfriars Road, Tom Clarke and Melba's secretary had to share the headphones. Tom passed these to her so she could hear the second song. As she heard Melba commence 'Addio' her eyes nearly came out of her head. 'It is Melba!' she cried in astonishment. She had not really believed Clarke up to that moment (Clarke, Tom, *My Northcliffe Diary 1931,* p149).

Winifred Sayer went home disillusioned. Invited at her own request, she belonged neither to the official party inside the shed nor to the crowd out in the street. She heard the slightly muffled sound of Melba without the excitement of hearing her either direct or by wireless. She felt overlooked especially when Melba and her party emerged after the concert. 'She just swept past, a most peculiar looking woman'. This was her verdict; and it was one still fresh in her mind seventy years later.

But for everyone else it was a night of jubilation - for Burrows and Clarke whose idea it was; for Round who had saved the programme by quick thinking and only regretted not being able to hear Melba's voice; for Ditcham whose equipment had performed well, if not perfectly; for Isaacs whose company had achieved enormous publicity at no great cost; for Northcliffe whose paper ran the story for the entire week; for all the amateur listeners across the country and abroad for whom the first 'quality' broadcast had been laid on like a banquet; for ships and commercial stations; and for Melba herself for whom the broadcast of July 1920 was thereafter a source of great personal pride.

Wireless Telephony and the press

Despite the success of the Melba night, Marconi made no attempt to institute a broadcasting service or to commence the manufacture of crystal or valve sets for home use. Their main concern throughout 1920 and 1921 was to establish a telephony service for the press both here and abroad. Pettengill, one of the engineers most involved with the tests, remembered the Melba follow up when engineers were sent to major towns all over Britain armed with receivers so they could demonstrate to members of local newspaper staffs how wireless telephony could be used for gathering and transmitting news. He was himself sent to Glasgow; others to London, Birmingham, Manchester and other towns. As a result, during July and August, receiving stations consisting of 4ft frame aerials with multi-valve amplifiers were erected in newspaper offices at Sheffield, Preston, Newcastle and Belfast and the press Association conducted experiments in the broadcasting of news items.

On 23 July 1920, a *Daily Mail* reporter, walking across Hampstead Heath carrying a portable telephone receiver, received a message from the news editor of his paper (Tom Clarke) transmitted from Chelmsford. His receiver was mounted in a dispatch case, 17 ½ in by 13 ½ in by 7 in. The aerial, a small loop 16 ½ in by 13 ½ in, was positioned under his coat. The case with its six valves, tuning capacitor and accumulators must have been heavy to say the least! (Dowsett, H M, *Wireless Telephony and Broadcasting, vol I,* pp56/57). A few days earlier, another *Daily Mail* reporter, carrying a similar set, had received a message from his office via Chelmsford while he was travelling in a train between Bromley and Bickley (*Daily Mail,* 20 July 1920).

It was by no means the first attempt to interest the press. In the spring of 1919, a party of British journalists were able to take a motor-bus ride between Chelmsford and Colchester and listen to talk from Marconi House, London, between thirty and forty miles away. Whilst on the bus they also heard wireless-transmitted music. And in the Spring of 1920, another party of journalists had been taken on a flight over the Eastern Counties; during the flight, they were able to transmit to their newspapers (Burrows to Miss K Shackleton, 1 January 1921: *Marconi Archives*).

More ambitious were the transmissions to the Continent. On 23 March 1920, the *Daily News* sent messages to Rome using as their agent the London correspondent of *Il Messaggero* who was stationed at Chelmsford for the purpose:

'I am standing in a corner of a large compartment of a shed packed with queer goods. I am alone here, leaning against a heap of cases having under my hand a frail folding table, on which two small telephone mouthpieces lie, hanging loose from an ordinary telephone wire. In the next compartment of the shed a dynamo has been set in motion, the tungsten wires have been kindled and the whole shed is filled with the buzzing of the engine. The engineer, who acts as operator, has been shouting meaningless words and phrases into the mouthpiece: 'One, two, three, four ... Monday, Tuesday, Wednesday ... January, February ... The Great Eastern Railway starts from Liverpool Street, the GWR starts from Paddington ...' etc. All is ready. The engineer goes to watch the dynamo, and I can talk to Rome. It is a strange sensation. The men who are listening to me are people I know. I throw my voice into the mouthpiece and I tell them they should recognise my voice. Will they really hear me?'

Confirmation that Signor Cassuto had got through soon came. His editor simply sent a Marconigram. The *Il Messaggero's* London correspondent had unwittingly also got through to Iceland, the Azores, Poland, Greece and to ships in the mid-Atlantic. Hardly private, though on this historic occasion the messages were of a formal character addressed to the Italian Premier, Signor Nitti, the President of the Italian Association of Journalists and, of course, Signor Cassuto's editor (*Daily News*, 24 March 1920).

On 30 July 1920, a similar event was arranged, this time the London correspondents of Norwegian, Danish and Swedish newspapers transmitted messages to their papers from Chelmsford, and there was a special message from Queen Alexandra. Afterwards, Lauritz Melchior, the Danish opera tenor, sang a number of items, including the National Anthems of Norway, Sweden, Denmark and Great Britain.

Mr David Charles, FRPS, took photographs of Melchior. As with the Melba shot, also taken by Mr Charles, the picture of Melchior close to the microphone is posed; in reality, he stood four or five yards from a suspended microphone. The gentleman on the far right is probably his accompanist; it is the Marconi engineer G W White who is at the piano. Ditcham lolls against the piano looking distinctly unexcited. The other man is Olaf Trost, a Marconi mast engineer and friend of Melchior. A second photo (not shown) again shows Melchior, Trost and White - also a young lady, name unknown. From these pictures we can tell exactly the setting in which Melchior stood; the scene had not changed when the author visited it seventy years later. A few months afterwards, the building was demolished.

Reproduced by permission of the Marconi Co. Ltd
Melchior at Chelmsford, 30 July 1920. G W White at the piano, W J Ditcham on left.

But the supreme challenge remained. Burrows was determined to include for the press a demonstration of wireless telephony across the Atlantic Ocean. As it happened, the Imperial press Conference was to be held in Ottawa, Canada and the UK delegates sailed on the S.S. Victorian on 20 July 1920. The Marconi Company threw themselves into the arrangements with enormous energy and imagination. First, temporary 6kW telephony stations were set up at Poldhu, Cornwall, and Signal Hill near St. Johns, Newfoundland. A 3-kilowatt set in a special cabin on board the 'Victorian' allowed communication with these stations and also with Chelmsford.

On the second day Burrows, who was on board the liner, full of press people, offered to let them send messages back to England to their papers. He tried to call Poldhu without success. 'Hello, Poldhu!'… 'Hello, Poldhu!'… 'Hello Poldhu!' Eventually he got a reply from Chelmsford where Round heard him by chance and offered help. It turned out that Poldhu had been requested not to transmit; a French ship had gone aground and a rescue operation involving wireless was underway.

Reproduced by permission of the Marconi Co. Ltd
Passengers on the SS Victorian, in mid-ocean, listening to a wireless broadcast, July 1920.

Chelmsford continued to provide news and music up to its maximum range of 1600 miles. Burrows used this news to issue the *North Atlantic Times* 'Special Empire press edition'.

On 25 July 1920 the 'Victorian' contacted Newfoundland, 650 miles away where Mogridge was stationed. Soon there were distinguished voices welcoming the delegates.

Whilst at sea, gramophone records were broadcast to ships within 800 miles radius. The task of DJ fell to Temellen and Allnut, the Marconi engineers on board, with Burrows also doing his bit. Ships' wireless operators scattered across the ocean telegraphed their appreciation and put in requests. High on the list was Harry Lauder's 'I Love a Lassie,' along with Kreisler's 'Caprice Viennois' and Cobb's 'On the Road to Mandalay' (Burrows, Arthur R, *Looking Backwards: 10 years;* also Burrows, Arthur R, *The Story of Broadcasting*, pp 49/51).

Though generally a success as far as speech was concerned, the live concerts sent out from Chelmsford by the Station Works hands left much to be desired. Beeton's oboe solos did not sound well on the wireless 'the tone varying according to the note'. Burrow's verdict on the vocal duets was 'awful'. But the piano solos and many of the songs by male voices were 'excellent'.

The 'Victorian' experiment was very much Burrows' idea (Correspondence in *Marconi Archives*). It formed part of the experiment aimed at providing, both

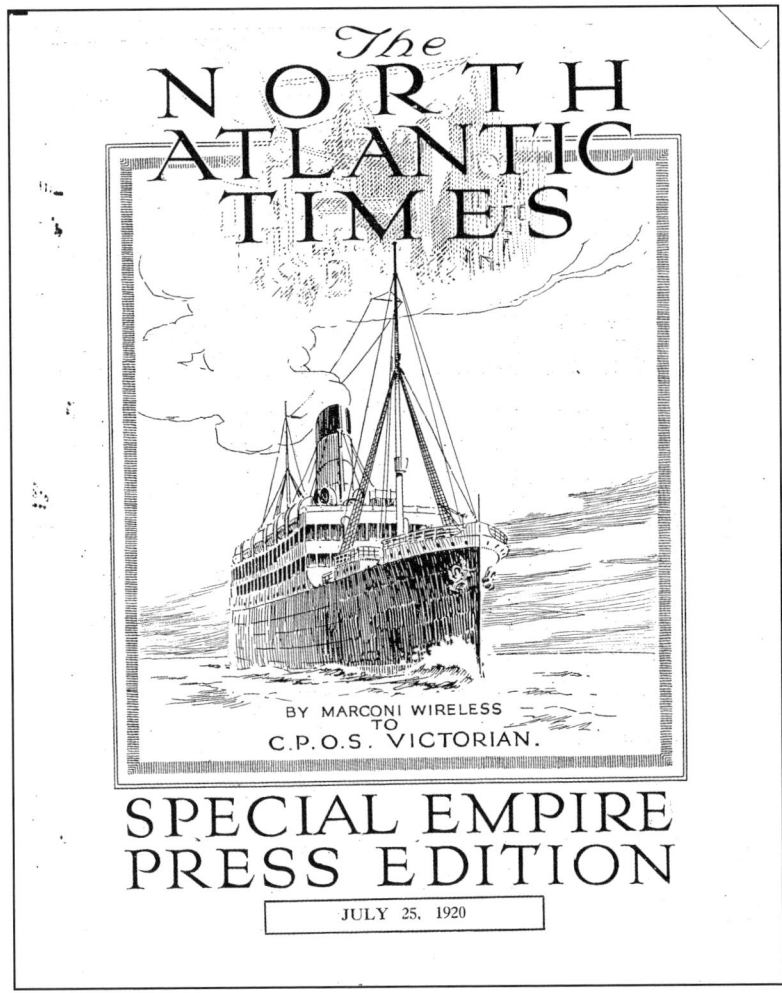

The first ship newspaper to contain news received by radio, July 1920.

for this country and internationally, a service to the press. Despite Government opposition, Burrows attempted to pursue this goal throughout 1920 and into 1921. Yet even he had to admit that, in Britain, 'reception was found to be difficult in many newspaper offices owing to the abundance of electrical machinery generally in use.'

Marconi was not enthusiastic, seeming to see little future in a wireless telephony service for the press. On 9 August 1920, orders were given that special tests should cease forthwith. The Chelmsford transmissions would be limited to quarter of an hour, Poldhu's likewise. Apparently, a Major Hamilton of the Royal Air Force had 'complained bitterly of jamming by Chelmsford.'

In any case, it was international communication by high-speed telegraphy that was considered to provide the way forward. The high power station at Caernarfon had been completed in 1914 for transatlantic services. European services would soon be centralised at the Ongar Station for transmission to Paris, Berne and Madrid, reception from these European locations being at nearby Brentwood. Full co-ordination and two-way working for the Ongar and Brentwood stations (both close to London) was planned, using Radio House, Wilson Street, London.

The Government therefore did not meet with much opposition from Marconi when it sought to curtail the Chelmsford telephony transmissions. The Postmaster General regarded them as liable to interfere with more essential services such as those from the Post Office's Leafield arc station, which served Cairo and India. The matter was not helped when reports of actual interference started to land on the Postmaster General's desk. The new and struggling civil aviation companies soon provided an example. The pilot of a Vickers Vimy 'machine' was crossing the Channel in thick fog and was trying to obtain weather and landing reports from Lympne. All he could hear was a musical evening from Chelmsford. The Melchior broadcast itself was castigated for jamming aircraft communication. Even the Melba night came in for criticism as a 'frivolous' use of the airwaves. The Post Office felt the Marconi broadcasts had more to do with publicity than scientific development. The writing was on the wall. By autumn of 1920, Chelmsford had been silenced (Briggs, Asa, *History of Broadcasting in the United Kingdom:* Vol I, pp 49/50, 1961).

It was not only the end of press experiments in telephony; it nipped in the bud any possibility of broadcasting taking off. If there was one lesson to be learnt by those who had listened enthralled to Melba, it was that broadcasting could never be launched in this country with a 'big bang'; it could only emerge by a long and tortuous process of negotiation.

On Chelmsford's close down its equipment was transferred to Poldhu and the old Marconi station at Clifden in Ireland.

4

Broadcasting by the Back Door

Radio Hams Clamour for Telephony

The amateur experimenter in wireless, otherwise known as a 'radio ham' had been around as long as his professional counterpart. The number of amateurs rose rapidly in the two years preceding the Great War and wireless clubs began to appear in the larger towns. Predominant was the Wireless Society of London (WSL). Highly qualified speakers ensured the membership kept abreast of the latest developments and their talks were published in *Wireless World*.

The War quenched all this activity. Inevitably, many of the 'old brigade' with their three-letter call signs failed to take up their hobby again once peace came. But a solid core of serious experimenters did resume as soon as permits allowed. They were joined by a new breed of men who had learned their trade serving in the signals units, the Royal Flying Corps, or at sea. They were probably not as well-heeled as their pre-war forebears but they could make a start, constructing sets from equipment left over from the War, some of it relatively new and unused.

But all this enthusiasm for wireless was held firmly in check by the Postmaster General. He had control over the release and manufacture of equipment and he also controlled the use of any such equipment. As before the War, radio hams wishing to undertake wireless work had to be licensed. This applied not only to those who wished to transmit but also to those who merely wanted to receive signals. The Postmaster General had to balance the interests of the amateurs against the demands of a military still obsessed with the need for wireless vigilance in the face of possible threats to the nation's security. Furthermore, wireless was vital for commercial and international communication and for civil aviation. To preserve these essential services free of interference strict control over amateur activity would be needed. The simplest course for the Government would be for the Postmaster General to retain the wartime restrictions in force and then to relax these, proceeding cautiously, step by step, as the need arose. This, then, was the course adopted.

For example, when the green light for amateurs was given on 21 October 1919, it was in respect of receiving apparatus. To qualify, 'experimenters' had to submit evidence of British nationality and a satisfactory reference. They also had to provide details of their apparatus and of any suppliers. In return they were granted an Experimenters Licence, the annual fee being ten shillings. The pre-war licenses had been cancelled on 5 July and so even the old hands had to resubmit their credentials.

To strengthen its hand in negotiating with an over cautious Postmaster General, the WSL advocated affiliation with the ever increasing number of local clubs at its meeting in October 1919. By February 1920, 15 out of 20 wireless societies expressed their willingness to affiliate. By December 1921 when the WSL was still locked in a struggle with the Post Office, no less than 63 societies had become affiliated. The WSL could speak for thousands of amateurs across the nation.

Experimental transmitting licences were finally granted on 1 August 1920 but were still hedged round with restrictions. Typical was McMichael's licence. This rejected the power and wavelengths he had applied for, insisting on 10 watts and 180 metres. Transmission would be limited to two hours a day and communication limited to three specified stations. McMichael's call sign was to be 2FG. Issued alphabetically, the number of call signs extended to 2NZ within a year. *Wireless World*, 20 August 1921, listed 127 of the 250 stations (Clarricoats, John, *The World at their Fingertips*, p55).

Of the 127 stations listed, the majority was licensed for 1000 metres and 180 metres, power in general being limited to 10 watts. Many were equipped for telephony rather than telegraphy; this, for the amateur of 1921, represented a new frontier and a new challenge. Interference on 1000 metres led to change, later, to 440 metres.

So, dotted about Britain, low-powered private stations, normally concerned with communications in Morse, were beginning to communicate by the spoken word. At least twenty stations in the London area transmitted speech and music daily and sometimes nightly on 440 metres (Clarricoats, John, *The World at their Fingertips*, p68). Among the well known 'London broadcasters' were Jack Partridge 2KF, Harry Walker 2OM and Bill Corsham 2UV. Their broadcasts were a regular Sunday morning feature (Jessop, G R., *The Bright Sparks of Wireless*, p37). Walker's music programmes had a considerable amateur following; they could be picked up over most parts of West London and were always introduced with 'This is Brentford calling!' Walker's favourite tune was the latest hit - 'Three o'clock in the Morning'. The two pioneers in the wireless trade, Burnham and McMichael, , both transmitted programmes. Burnham and Co. offered a 'complete receiving set' as early as March 1921 and invited purchasers to 'listen-in on Fridays at 9.40pm for 2FQ'. To go with their high quality and expensive sets they offered a highbrow programme.

Bill Corsham, 2UV, not only offered gramophone records but also live programmes by budding local talent. We can hear the authentic sound of these early programmes of the pre-BBC era, or can certainly come very close to doing so, for Corsham replicated and recorded them in later years for the Derby Wireless Club Library, using his original equipment and records. A half-hour programme transmitted by 2UV early in 1922 provides a good example:

> 'Skaters' Waltz' (Strauss)

> 'This is 2UV amateur station 2UV situated at Harlesden, London, NW10, transmitting records on 440 metres. I would be glad for any reports on the strength and quality of the signals. Please stand by. I have commenced with the 'Skaters' Waltz' by the Metropolitan Symphony Orchestra'.

Corsham then played the following records:

> 'A dream' sung by Enrico Caruso.
> 'Light Cavalry' played by the Band of His Majesty's Coldstream Guards.
> 'A Perfect Day' (woman singer, not identified by Corsham).

> 'This is 2UV, 2UV! Amateur Radio Station 2UV transmitting a test programme from 104 Harlesden Gardens, Harlesden, London NW10 in England. I would be pleased to receive reports on this transmission. All reports will be gratefully acknowledged. This is 2UV transmitting and closing down, I hope you enjoyed notes of 'A Perfect Day.'

With much loud clicking as the microphones were switched over, listeners heard the closing notes of 'A Perfect Day.'

Corsham used to put on similar programmes in connection with lectures at local libraries and clubs. Many such lectures, linked to telephony demonstrations, were authorised in 1921 and attracted record numbers. The public was beginning to get wind of what wireless was all about and what it could offer. 2UV was just one of many stations transmitting telephony in the London area; they included 2DD, 2DF, 2DX, 2JA, 2KF, 2KT, 2LI, 2NH, 2NM, 2ON, 2OM, 2PX, 2QQ, 2SH, 2SX, 2TI, 2VN, 2VU and 2VW. Robinson of 2VW even made recordings of some of these transmissions using an Edison Bell cylinder machine. Reports on the amateur programmes appeared in *The Star*, one of the London daily papers.

Both the broadcasters and their radio ham listeners were working men so all this activity tended to be confined to week-ends. Apart from anything else, the little 10-watt transmitters would probably have been swamped by Morse stations during the working week. Corsham captured the kind of interference heard in the 'phones in his later reconstruction of the 1921/22 period. First there were the coarse scraping sounds of Morse; then the more tolerable sounds of high note Morse; and finally, worst of all, the new and immensely powerful Morse arc transmitters - Leafield was an example. These filled all frequencies with a 'rushing' or hissing sound like that of an engine getting up steam through which the sound of muffled Morse could just be distinguished. For most of the burgeoning army of amateurs, these were probably the only sounds ever heard on their crystal sets in 1921. Only the elite amateur experimenters equipped with highly selective valve receivers could expect to pick up telephony - and valves, according to Corsham, 'could not be had for love nor money.'

Nevertheless, those fortunate enough to possess multi-valve receivers had the additional advantage of being able to pick up continental stations, one or two of which were providing 'concerts'. Most notable was the Dutch station, call sign PCGG, transmitting from the Hague and run by Hanso Idzerda.

This station had links with 'Burnham' – Britain's top wireless manufacturer, and programmes were partly aimed at a real or supposed British audience. But with a modest power of only 250 watts and a need to reach listeners on the limits of its range, PCGG was not well placed to serve Britain. However, PCGG could be received 'even on a one valve set with a carefully adjusted reaction circuit; but for good readable speech two or more valves were desirable'; this was the advice given to 'HCE' of Willesden - reaction consists in feeding part of the amplifier output back to its input so as to increase the effective input.

'BHM' of Ilford received much the same reply when he wrote to the editor of *Wireless World*: 'Yes, you can get PCGG on one valve provided reaction is used. But the results are not loud and would be greatly improved by additional amplification.

Gilbert White, a schoolboy, remembered being invited with other boys to the home of his science master one Sunday afternoon for the express purpose of listening in to PCGG. The master, Mr Waite, had a single valve set. Dead silence was enforced as Mr Waite, with a Woodbine cigarette in his mouth, succeeded in getting the station. The cigarette ash increased to about two inches as he sat motionless, hardly daring to touch the tuning capacitor in case he lost the fragile contact with the Dutch station's concert (*Breaking the Silence*; a video compiled from earlier interviews issued on 19 June 1991; no longer available).

For the most part, only well-equipped hams could expect to pick up PCGG and this could easily be upset by interference from Croydon airport. The truth was, Britain needed its own PCGG.

With this in mind, the Wireless Society of London began negotiations with the Postmaster General in the spring of 1921. The case put for the amateurs was hedged round with arguments of a somewhat sophisticated nature. They needed a central, reliable and independent transmitter of Morse and telephony against which to judge the quality and performance of their apparatus. Experimental work on apparatus could then be based on a scientific footing. This in turn would further wireless development generally.

It was four months before the WSL received a reply from the Postmaster General. On 15 August 1921 F V Brown, Assistant Secretary at the Post Office, wrote to say the Postmaster General agreed with the WSL proposal to transmit signals for a period of half an hour per week but this could not include telephony. He did not give any reasons for this decision but doubtless he was aware that in 1921 the 'experimenters' were increasingly becoming 'constructors' and the demand for telephony was increasingly becoming a demand for 'broadcasting.' Already, by the end of March, 4000 Experimental Licences had been issued and 1700 more had been applied for and were being processed. Representatives of the WSL, however respected and knowledgeable, hardly constituted the right body with which to discuss what could amount to broadcasting by the back door. The Postmaster General was again determined to proceed one step at a time.

Marconi had shown readiness to help so the Postmaster General authorised it to establish a station in the Chelmsford area with the call-sign 2MT subject to the following conditions:

> Half an hour a week for transmissions, these being 7pm to 7.30pm on a weekday.
> Maximum 1 kilowatt on 180 metres and 450 metres for spark and continuous waves. Also on 1000 metres for continuous waves, some transmissions to be on a power of 500 watts and some on 250 watts.
> Every seven minutes transmission was to be followed by a three minute interval during which a qualified operator was to listen to check if interference with Government or commercial stations was occurring. If a call came to say this was happening 2MT was to cease its transmissions at once.

So a very limited service of Morse calibration signals was launched in the autumn of 1921. But the WSL returned to the attack with a petition supported not only by its 395 members but also by 63 affiliated wireless clubs. This called again for telephony even if it meant operating on reduced power on the shorter wavelengths of 200 to 300 metres to minimise any possible interference. Telephony would help the development of good receiving apparatus, including loudspeakers. But the main reason was simply that this was what amateurs were 'chiefly interested in at the present time'.

The Postmaster General finally relented. In January 1922 he authorised Marconi to extend their Morse service to include 15 minutes of speech and music, the power being limited to 250 watts. He had not instituted broadcasting as we know it - general entertainment for the home on an economically sustainable basis. But he had made a move that would build up an overwhelming demand for broadcasting during the crucial months of 1922.

2MT Writtle, Chelmsford

So it was over to the Marconi Company. Like the Postmaster General, they had their own reasons for keeping the service within bounds. First, of course, this big company had to keep on the right side of the Postmaster General; secondly, they could expect no significant financial support from the amateur community; and thirdly, they could not afford to let the service disrupt normal work. So it was decided the content of the programmes would be determined at Head Office in the Strand, the task falling to Arthur Burrows, their Publicity Officer. It wasn't so much that Burrows and his team of seventeen had any spare capacity; the decision simply reflected Burrows' familiarity with, and enthusiasm for, wireless telephony.

The task of building the transmitter would fall, not surprisingly, to Eckersley's team at Writtle, near Chelmsford, Essex, which had built the telephony transmitter used by Croydon Airport a year or so earlier. The relative isolation of Writtle resulted in the engineers having to take on a second task; that of undertaking the actual transmissions. As though aware of the chaos that might ensue, Burrows made sure the programme presentation would amount to little more than stereotyped announcements, the playing of records provided and 'holding the hand' of occasional artistes sent from London. In short, the broadcasts would not be so very different from those the amateurs were capable of putting out for each other. But unlike these, they would be generated by a single powerful transmitter. Useful comparisons could therefore be made as amateurs sought to improve their transmitters or as they listened-in on other receivers in their neighbourhood. Any variation in quality from Writtle would probably be due more to the receiving apparatus and atmospherics than to the transmitting apparatus.

From such tightly reined beginnings, few could have foreseen that 2MT Writtle would be destined to go down in history for its spellbinding humour, informality, imaginative variety and spontaneity. For some months, the programmes did indeed go out as planned by Head Office, though with the more highbrow records discarded by the engineers at their programme planning sessions in the 'Cock and Bell'. At this stage Eckersley was in the habit of leaving others to get on with the transmissions, going home to listen to the evening's programme on his own receiver. But one summer evening he decided to see the transmission through after joining the others at the 'local'. Returning with them to the hut, he took over the presentation and became 'more exuberantly informal than (he) had intended,' failing to play all the records and ignoring the 'shut down' periods. 'I went on talking and talking, convincing myself that I was being very funny', encouraged in this by Kirke's broad grin and Wynn's chuckling. The staff held a post mortem. 'I did not say much except "Did I say that? Really? Good Lord!". But fifty or more postcards from listeners testified that 'a good time was had by all! The reaction of these was, do it again, we like it' (Eckersley, R., *BBC and All That*, p42). Despite a reprimand from Burrows, an unrepentant Eckersley made many more such broadcasts. And so the 2MT Writtle legend was born. 'Our star was Eckersley. He'd go up to the microphone and apparently without effort be spontaneously funny for ten minutes at a time. He talked to our listeners as if he'd lived next door to them for years, and they loved it' (P Wynn, quoted in *London Calling*, 10 October 1946).

P P Eckersley

This kind of imaginative informality, mixed at times with almost anarchic humour, would not return to broadcasting until the 'Goon-Show' in the early fifties. It grew out of a unique combination of circumstances. The isolation of the hut gave a sense of being insulated from Post Office bureaucracy and from Head Office fussing. The engineers were highly intelligent, full of youthful fun, none more so than their chief - a born entertainer. Conformity to convention did not go down well at the hut and any hint of such would quickly be lampooned. Broadcasting provided a relatively undemanding sideline, one for which, moreover, the duty engineers each received £1 a time from the Wireless Society of London. Perhaps most importantly, they knew they had a lively, responsive audience whose enthusiasm jumped across all normal social barriers, making them a united and cheery confraternity. Anything innovatory or hilarious in the way of telephony resulted in instant fan mail and the call to 'do it again, we like it.'

For the Writtle engineers, that initial association with broadcasting was to be by no means transitory. Within a year, Eckersley would be appointed Chief Engineer of the British Broadcasting Company and later, of its successor, the Corporation. Within the next three years, all but one of the engineers would have left Writtle for the British Broadcasting Company, Ashbridge and Wynn in turn rising to become BBC Chief Engineer and Kirke, Head of BBC Research. In this sense, Writtle was a seedbed for broadcasting technique in Britain. So, before examining what was actually transmitted from the hut, a word about the team, and about the hut in which they worked at the time of the memorable 1922 broadcasts.

For this purpose, we have the perfect guide - Rolls Wynn. Years later, in the mid sixties, Wynn recorded his reminiscences of Writtle as though they still were fresh and recent. For this he employed a small Marconi portable recorder and some tapes which Geoffrey Goodship, then a BBC Liaison Engineer, had left at Wynn's retirement home in Worthing for this purpose (Wyne, R T B, *Memories of Writtle*).

Wynn makes it clear that Writtle did not do basic research, only development. This nevertheless entailed design, installation, testing and demonstrating. The team, in Eckersley's words, 'taught one another, cursed Head Office, and screamed good-natured abuse at the works for not following (their) specifications' (Eckersley, R., *BBC and All That*, p39). Wynn remembered Eckersley as brilliant and full of creative ideas. He was by nature open, approachable and spontaneous. Except possibly for one or two who, now and then, were the butt of his sense of humour, he must have brought much

Reproduced by permission of the Marconi Co. Ltd

The Writtle team, Chelmsford, summer 1922.
Back l to r: B N MacLarty; H L Kirke, The Hon R T B Wynn, H J Russell
Front l to r: F Bubb, N Ashbridge, Capt P P Eckersley, E H Trump, Miss B Beeson

hilarity and amusement to those working under him in the dreary conditions of the hut.

In overall charge, though rarely there, was R D Bangay. He was already seen as a veteran of the sparks era, having joined Marconi back in Edwardian days. Bangay had provided the standard textbook on wireless telegraphy much used during the Great War. At that time, he had headed the Field Department. In 1921 this was merged with the Aircraft Department to from the Designs Department which Bangay now took over. In doing so, he found himself responsible, among other things, for Eckersley's experimental work. All the indications are that he found it quite impossible to keep up with the bright young men and the new telephony developments. He spent most of his time at Chelmsford revered as a splendid representative for Marconi; he was very much what was then termed 'a topper.' What with one thing and another, Bangay provided the perfect target for Eckersley's barbed humour.

> Riding down to Bangay
> On my Norton bike,
> Got some drawings with me,
> Which I'm sure that he will like.
> Though I shall explain them,
> He'll never understand,
> But he'll send them to Head Office
> Who are sleeping in the Strand.

Noel Ashbridge was Eckersley's 'number one'. He 'turned Eckersley's ideas into ironmongery.' 'Ash' designed small transmitters including those capable of duplex working; that is, simultaneous two-way working. As the prospect of 'proper' broadcasting grew closer, he designed suitable receivers including the RB1, RB2 and the prestigious two-valve V2 receiver. Ashbridge was a foil to Eckersley in every way, a kind, sagacious, cautious man totally lacking the ebullience of his chief and the sense of the ridiculous portrayed by other members of the team, particularly by Wynn himself. Though still only 33 years old, 'Ash' was already showing signs of baldness. He possessed a Villiers motorbike, which he always had some difficulty starting; the team usually ended up pushing him off amid great hilarity:

> It was a Writtle evening
> And Ash's work was done.
> His RB1 and RB2
> Were on production run.
> A clever cautious man was he
> Who knew an awful lot
> Strong legs to start his motor bike
> But getting thin on top.

Ashbridge had his own quarters in the 'Broomfield Hut' in the north west corner of the field. He worked there with Wynn as his assistant. Here too, for a short time, was an 'amusing little devil', Jock Stewart.

On his tape, Wynn reveals little about himself. But he had worked with Eckersley and Prince at Biggin Hill and Woolwich during the War. Subsequently he studied at Cambridge, joining the team after graduating in 1922. Wynn was remembered by Eckersley as a 'natural happy man, racy, his conversation punctuated by sporting allusions.' This doubtless reflected his background as 'The Honourable Rowland Tempest Beresford Wynn' - 'Rolls' or 'Rolly', popular with all his colleagues, equally at ease with Eckersley and Ashbridge and very much valued by both. He could certainly be counted on when there was any opportunity for innovatory or amusing broadcasting or to team up with 'Eckersley' for a little versifying.

> Hey diddle dodrode
> Two grids in one quadrode
> The outer one forming the plate.
> The electrons got muddled
> With so many grids,
> But the final M valve was eight
>
> Four and twenty B valves standing on a shelf
> Ash couldn't find one so I had to go myself
> When the circuit opened the phones began to sing,
> Don't you think I was right to smash the beastly thing?

Edward Herbert Trump is always counted as one of the team. In reality he was usually abroad, dealing with variations to standard equipment which Marconi customers wanted. Like Wynn, Trump had served with Prince and Eckersley during the war. Alone of the Engineers, Trump withstood the temptation to gravitate to the BBC. He became even more closely associated with the aircraft wireless work of the hut, taking over from Ashbridge in 1926 just as Ashbridge had himself taken over from Eckersley in 1923. Trump stayed rigidly single-minded in his role through to 1960 when both he and the hut finally left Writtle, the hut to become a school sports pavilion, Trump to enjoy a well-earned retirement.

The hut dated from 1914 and was relocated after the war to Lawford Lane, Chelmsford. Made from standard timber sections it had a length of 66ft and a width of 16ft. When the author visited the Marconi site shortly before its closure in the early nineties, the hut's brick foundation was still visible as a kind of footprint in the grass.

The workshop had its own external door on the lane side. The main entrance was on the field side and that led straight into a laboratory with benches down each side and a stove at one end. This was Kirke's domain. Kirke was a valve expert and dealt with aircraft sets. A brilliant engineer, he

Reproduced by permission of the Marconi Co. Ltd

Writtle hut, Chelmsford, with some of the team, 1922.

possessed uncanny insight. 'I say, Eck,' he would say, 'don't you think we could try this?'

To the left of the entrance, one turned into an office about half the size of Kirke's laboratory. It had two desks, one for Eckersley, the other for his secretary Betty Beeson. She was a placid even-tempered young lady in her mid twenties and good at her job. She must have heard some frightful language when the engineers got electric shocks but would immediately respond with concern.

Beyond the laboratory, and of similar size, was the power plant room. It occupied the middle portion of the hut. This was MacLarty's territory. Here he built and tested his 1½, 3 and 6 kilowatt transmitters to the accompaniment of various explosions and clouds of smoke. Wynn remembered him 'mucking around with pots of oil, stirring them like witches over their brew'.

Next came the workshop with a store, again corresponding in size to the laboratory. The workshop had benches against the walls with machinery

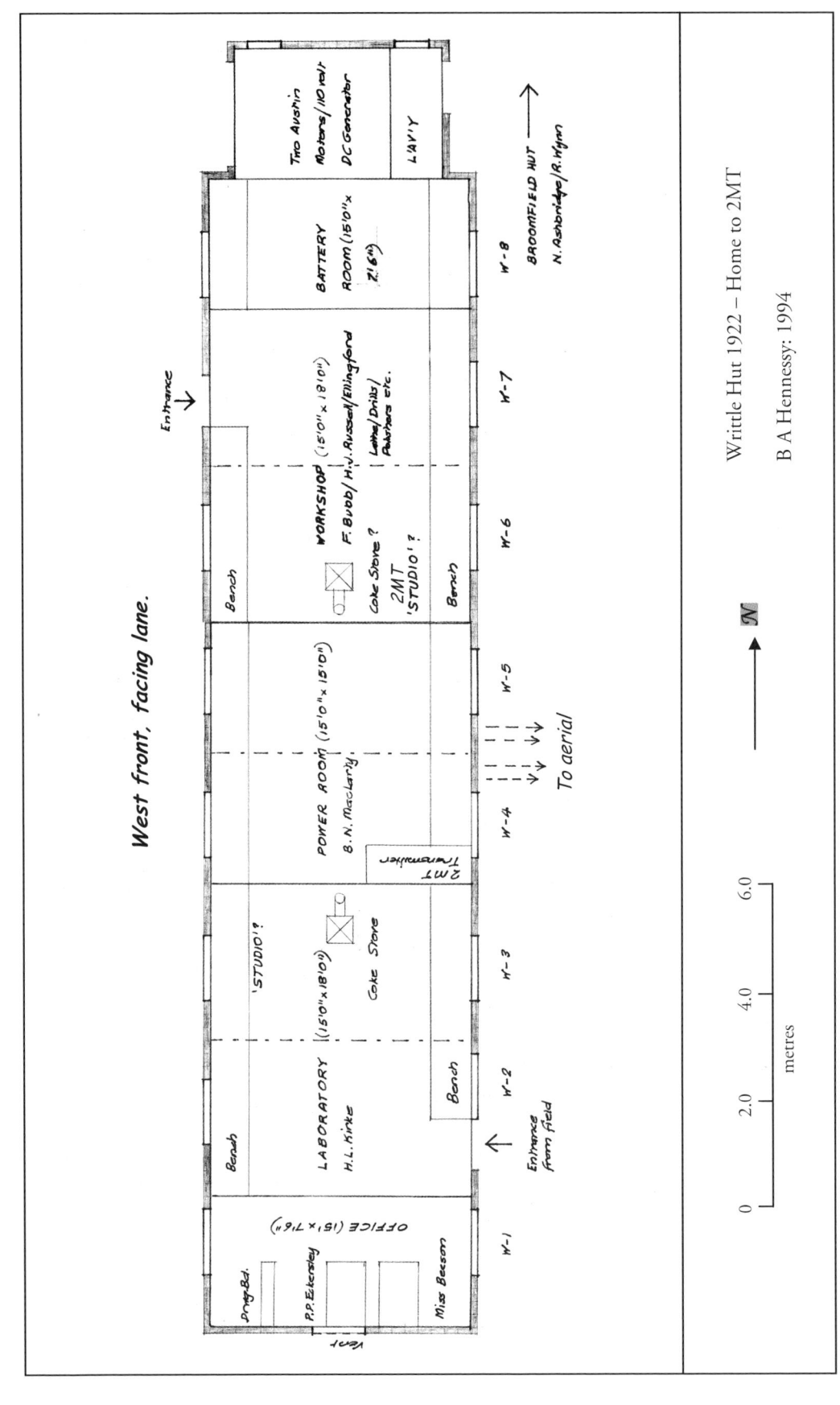

such as the lathe, drills, and the polishing machine in the centre of the room. Bubb, an old hand, was in charge. Freddy Bubb was a great character and responsible for mechanical development work. He was 'quite a toughy' with a hiss to his voice and a slight facial twitch. Wynn's memories were of his 'amazing capacity for drinking beer' and of his breaking the hearts of a number of local girls. Russell, his assistant, had hair dropping over his eyes which he would flick back with a toss of the head as Bubb commented reprovingly on his work - 'some day you'll learn, laddie'.

Here too was Ellingford, a labourer and general factotum, who cleaned and made the tea. He summoned Ashbridge and Wynn from the Broomfield hut by Morse with one long buzz - the Morse for 'T'. One hopes it was worth it. Wynn was convinced he laced the tea with Shellac. Unlike the others, Ellingford was a country man, quick to spot birds of interest; he kept a goat tethered to one of the masts; not surprising that he had his leg pulled constantly.

At the far end of the hut lay the Battery Room, where the generator was also located, under the care of Russell. The generator was driven by two four-cylinder Austin petrol engines. Smoothing of the output voltage was provided by a large capacitor and an iron cored choke. This system also supplied light for the battery room.

An extension was added to this end of the building, containing the generator - and an earth loo. When Ash put in a plea for loo paper to replace the old newspaper scraps, he found, on his next visit, a swatch of sandpaper!

It is clear that each member of the team had a specific role and place in the hierarchy. Each had his own work area. The hut was not run as a jolly collective. If anything, social rapport only developed after the working day was done. MacLarty, Trump, Jock Stewart and Russell all put up at the 'Cock and Bell'. Mr Beeson was landlord there for 40 years from 1892. Here too lived his daughter, Eckersley's secretary, Betty Beeson. The pub's backyard was, for generations, the site of horse stabling and watering, right next to the village pond, shaded by a willow tree. Beeson's wife kept order and prepared the evening meal. 'I don't know what yer going to have for supper tonight Mr MacLarty. We've nothing for yer. Yer can have a bit of fish if yer like!' She would then produce an excellent meal.

As there was no room at the inn, Wynn took digs in 'Deodora', a house on the corner of Lodge Lane just across from the 'Cock and Bell'. It was in the care of the three Smale sisters. They were seamstresses or dressmakers and would sit sewing in their window, which overhung the path. They took in a string of local curates, all young bachelors. With his charm and background, Wynn would have seemed a highly desirable lodger. Ashbridge soon joined his assistant Wynn, again a nice respectable lodger for the three spinster ladies to have in their house.

Unlike all the others, Eckersley was married. His wife Stella could be described as 'county'. She had found a house to her liking in Witham about ten miles from Writtle. Here she could enjoy riding and keeping chickens with Mr Bones to look after the garden.

Thus, except for Eckersley, the requirement to conduct a broadcasting service presented little disruption to the engineers' private lives. They could get back to their digs within minutes to tidy up and enjoy supper. A quick stride got them back up the lane to the hut in time for the half hour programmes, and they were back in their digs by eight. They may have seen transmitting to the amateurs not so much a chore as an interesting diversion. For his part, Eckersley tended to leave things to Ashbridge but eventually, as has been told, he took it into his head to stay on and make things decidedly more diverting.

Back in February 1922 the first broadcasting job was to build the transmitter. To economise, the engineers would use the materials to hand even if this meant the transmitter being partly assembled before each weekly transmission and dismantled on each programme's completion. It is said to have been designed by MacLarty and Kirke and built by Bubb and Russell. But Ashbridge wrote to Wynn in December 1961 refuting this. It was he who built the first 2MT transmitter and, he claimed, MacLarty 'did nothing but grumble'. In support of Ashbridge's claim we need to note that the circuits were identical to those of the Airport transmitter. The latter had been built before MacLarty's time but with Ashbridge in attendance to oversee things.

But MacLarty was involved with the subsequent development of the transmitter, which was located on the file side of his room. It was housed on two tables at right angles to each other. On the left hand table were placed the variometer (a variable inductor) and a Morse key. The other table supported, from left to right, the primary circuit inductor, a variable capacitor and a panel on which were mounted three MT4 valves - the output valve and below it the modulator and amplifier valves. On the smaller panel to the right were mounted two MR1 high tension (HT) rectifying valves with the HT transformer below. Directly on the table was the HT choke and, on the edge of the table, a filament choke. Details of the transmitter were given by MacLarty decades later in *Wireless World*, January 1963.

Reproduced by permission of the Marconi Co. Ltd

Transmitter at 2MT Writtle, Chelmsford, 1922.

The aerial took an L-form and was made up of four parallel wires on 12-ft spreaders. The masts, which were portable, were each 110ft high and 200 feet apart. The aerial feeder was run out of a window behind the transmitter to the nearer of the two masts.

The Peel Conner carbon granule microphone, then the only one available in Britain, was designed for speech. In no way could it faithfully transmit the full range of musical frequencies. This was a problem throughout 2MT's one year of life. The studio occupied a corner of the workshop where there was just room to place an upright piano and soloist. The external workshop door doubtless provided access for the piano.

The new transmitter was first put to the test on 14 February 1922. This was to be the first night of telephony and an opportunity for the engineers to show what they could do. For the amateurs it was a long awaited day and most prepared to listen-in with high hopes. Ernest Blake, technical assistant to H W Allen, Joint General Manager of Marconi, had drawn up the programme, which would include artistes. Accordingly, a piano was hired from the nearest shop, three and a half miles away, and elaborate tests in positioning the microphone were carried out (Baily, L and Brewer, C, *The BBC Scrapbooks*, p257; also *Marconi Archives*). The usual calibration signals were to be given from 7pm, finishing at 7.25pm. Telephony would commence at 7.35pm and finish about 7.55pm. Records would be played on the 'Cliftophone'. Burrows had been at great pains to secure this for these 2MT transmissions. As a result of his efforts, the Chappell Piano Company of New Bond Street agreed to supply the gramophone at half price - £13 15s 0d instead of £27.10s.0d - provided the word 'Cliftophone' was mentioned whenever the title of the record to be played was given. The 'Cliftophone' had been duly delivered from London, in a special protective box which Burrows had had made for it, since the 'Cliftophone' was not to be permanently housed in the hut but returned by train after each weekly transmission.

After so much planning, everybody expected a good 'First Night.' But it was not to be. In the hut, the transmitter was just being 'warmed up' when with only minutes to go a horrid crackling, followed by a complete cessation of signals, heralded trouble. Kirke managed to spot the problem - a broken down capacitor; he quietly substituted another. Signals came on again (Eckersley, R., *BBC and All That*, p40). In due course, the well-known baritone, Robert Howe, sang 'The Floral Dance' and then a dialect ballad. This was followed by a cello rendering of 'The Lost Chord,' and then the records.

But all was not well as Ashbridge, listening in at the Broomfield hut immediately realised. In front of his unsuspecting seniors in the hut, Eckersley put on a brave face but knew there would have to be an inquest once the top brass had gone. The whole performance had been 'muffled' and the valve anodes were blushing more deeply red than was their wont. The *Times* reporter, who had listened in at the home of Leslie McMichael, Secretary of the Wireless Society of London wrote 'from a medley of spasmodic noises a baritone voice, singing, detached itself. It grew stronger until the song 'The Floral Dance' was clearly, though only faintly, audible. The piano accompaniment between the verses was more audible than the voice.' Most of Mr McMichael's friends considered the transmission weak. By the end of the transmission, all sounds seemed to be entirely wiped out.

The other reports that came in next day were fair but far from enthusiastic. McMichael wondered whether the powerful arc transmitter at Leafield was to blame; Burrows suggested the next transmission should start with telephony, leaving the calibration signals to follow as this would lessen the chance of

Leafield causing trouble. But the results were no better that week nor indeed the next. It was Kirke who finally realised the trouble. The capacity of the hurriedly substituted capacitor was a hundred times greater than it should have been. From then on, the Writtle transmissions were no longer the subject of pungent comment but were voted 'OK, old man' by the growing audience of amateur enthusiasts (Eckersley, R., *BBC and All That*, pp40/41).

The transmission of Tuesday 21 February was the first of the standard concerts based entirely on a supply of records from London. The 'Cliftophone' having been returned to London, it was again despatched on Monday by train to Chelmsford. Ashbridge was to arrange its transfer thence to the hut. Burrows expected it back Wednesday morning, asking the engineers this time to use the protective box which they still had somewhere in the hut. With the gramophone, Burrows had packed four records:

> Kashmir Song' (Clara Butt)
> 'The Swan' (flute solo)
> 'The Angel's Serenade' (cello solo)
> 'Il Bacio' and 'Softly Awakes my Heart' (cornet solos)

In writing to Eckersley to confirm those arrangements, Burrows asked for the concert to begin at 7pm and reminded Eckersley of the rule about intervals every 10 minutes during which one of the staff would listen for possible messages from the authorities; also, the need to refer to the Cliftophone as each piece was announced. He suggested putting the microphone right inside the sound box with the doors left open (letter of 20 February 1922: *Marconi Archives*).

That second concert saw a new routine firmly in place. At 6.00pm, after the day's work was finished, the bits and pieces needed for the transmitter - capacitors, chokes, inductors - were all put back to recreate the transmitter. A quick check was made to ensure that it was modulating. If OK, it was up the muddy lane to the 'Cock and Bell' for high tea - fish, marrow jam and an immense amount of gin. There would be a discussion as to what to do. Then it was back to the hut, Ashbridge and Kirke walking to the far hut to switch on the receiver and put on their headphones. They would immediately hear Eckersley's voice with its characteristic ebullience:

> Hello CQ! Hello CQ!
> This is Two Emma Toc Writtle testing
> This is Two Emma Toc W-r-r-r-ittle testing.
> Hello Ashbridge, Hello Ash ….. Ash Hello
> Are the signals OK?
> Wave if it's all OK.

A handkerchief would be waved through the window. Immediately, there would follow:

> Hullo everybody, Hullo CQ
> This is Two Emma Toc calling
> This is Two Emma Toc calling,
> Hello CQ, Hullo everyone
> Well I think we're ready to begin now.
> And the first thing I've got to introduce
> Is a record entitled …..

Then with scratching and whistling the record would make its debut on 'Two Emma Toc ' (2MT). At this stage, having launched the evening concert, Eckersley would sign off, hand over and go home. But occasionally there would be a little pretence that all was not OK and listeners could enjoy being party to off-air exasperation expressed by Eckersley:

> It's not going out at all?
> Oh dear - well it's your fault. It's what?
> Well for Heavens sake connect it up -
> Oh it is connected up!
> This has all been going out!
> Hello CQ, Hello everyone,
> I'm sorry, there has been a little bit of misunderstanding,
> A little 'technical hitch' - you get them too?
> I know aren't they awful?

(Wander, Tim, *2MT Writtle, The Birth of British Broadcasting*, p72)

The letters CQ, incidentally, were adopted for international communication by the Marconi Company in 1904 and internationally in 1912; they constitute an invitation to everyone to listen in and respond. They are phonetically similar to *sécu(rité)*; thus CQD is a distress signal – *sécurité détresse*.

On 1 April, Burrows received a letter from the music publishers Ascherberg, Hopwood and Crew to say that a singer, Miss Nora Scott, had agreed 'to come down to Writtle on 11 April.' Listeners were once again to enjoy a live concert. Burrows assured the writer, Henry Judd, that a piano would be provided along with a Marconi pianist. A Marconi representative would join Judd and Miss Scott on the 4.58 from Liverpool Street. Mr de Lange of his department would await them just outside the ticket barrier at Chelmsford and take them by car to Writtle. He would be wearing a black velour hat and a navy blue coat. After the concert, de Lange would take them to catch the 8.07 arriving at Liverpool Street at 9.20. The arrangements would have left Miss Scott about half an hour to try over her three songs with the Marconi accompanist and get used to the extraordinary surroundings in which she would find herself. These spartan, hazardous surroundings, not to mention the stench from the nearby sewage works, provided a somewhat deficient ambience for:

'The Sundial in my Garden' (A Emmett Adams)
'Love calling over the Years' (Leslie Elliott)
'Until the End' (Rupert Hazel)

But Miss Scott must have been quite a trouper for she returned to the hut on 23 May to sing once again. On this occasion, Marconi arranged for a photographer to be present. We see a surprisingly tall, hatted lady in a silk dress holding her music. Beside her stands Kirke, microphone in hand. Evening light from the window illuminates her song sheet. To the right, her accompanist sits expectantly at the upright piano; to the far left, a workbench. This (apart from an almost identical one published in *The Star* on 26 August 1936) is the only known photograph to show 'The Studio' portion of the hut in any detail.

In between the two Scott concerts, Melchior came to the hut to sing. The world-famous Danish tenor sang four songs including 'On with the Motley' from 'Pagliacci'; his pretty accompanist, Morwenna Felce, also provided a piano solo. The concert was, however, a disappointment. The 'top' was 'not sharp and bubbly' and Melchior's pauses seemed 'interminable.' Ashbridge later recalled how 'the whole hut shook horribly' to Melchior's powerful voice; and how the engineers felt like country bumpkins in the presence of the great tenor and his charming accompanist (Speeches to BBC Engineering Society on 'The

Reproduced by permission of the Marconi Co. Ltd
Nora Scott with Kirke broadcasting songs for 2MT Writtle, 1922.

Early Days of Broadcasting' given by Eckersley, Ashbridge, and others: 16 February 1960, *BBC Sound Archives*).

Eckersley does seem to have left all responsibility for these 'concerts' to Ashbridge, now the initial routine was established. He was often at Chelmsford or London or anxious to get back to his home in Witham. As he put it: 'I was in the habit of leaving the others to get on with the transmissions' (Eckersley, R., *BBC and All That*, p41). Some of Eckersley's later stories about Nora Scott and Melchior perhaps owe more to invention than to reality, as he was not actually present on these occasions.

On 30 May 1922 the Writtle station underwent significant improvement. First, its wavelength was changed to 400 metres to avoid interference from Leafield. The calibration signals were discarded along with the coupled circuit designed for this purpose. More complicated and expensive apparatus was used in an effort to improve musical quality and cut out all trace of generator hum. The programmes were now scheduled for 8pm British Summer Time (Dowsett, H M, *Wireless Telephony and Broadcasting, vol I*, p59).

Most of the amateurs receiving 2MT would have been equipped with valve sets. A single valve set using a reaction circuit could receive from up to 50 miles away. This meant Writtle could be heard in London and much of the South East including Suffolk, Cambridge, Bedfordshire, Essex, Herts, Kent and much of Surrey. In very exceptional circumstances, 2MT could be heard as far out as Southampton and Birmingham but this usually required two or more valves. Eckersley was not in fact keen on reaction circuits, with their tendency to distort or even oscillate, and advised instead two valves as a minimum, so as to overcome interference, increase volume and prevent the danger of oscillation. Oscillation was a problem throughout the early twenties and Eckersley never lost an opportunity to condemn the excessive use of reaction, an early example being his appeal at the close of the Writtle concert on 7 November 1922 (P P Eckersley, *Wireless World*, 9 September 1922).

The crystal range was mostly limited to the immediate Chelmsford area, although the station could sometimes be picked up over other parts of Essex. Unfortunately, the vast majority of the 10,000 amateurs were crystal users and few of them could pick up 2MT. Two who did were Richard and John Thurlow, sons of the Rector of Widford, the parish being only about a mile from Writtle. The Rector had provided private tuition for the son of Isaacs, Managing Director of Marconi. The boys were therefore *personae gratae* at both Chelmsford and Writtle. They would dash on their bikes over to the hut immediately after the end of the Tuesday evening transmission, arriving while 'the spittle was still wet on the mike.' Richard Thurlow (who died in 1987) later became Secretary of the Radio Society of Great Britain (RSGB), formerly the Wireless Society of London (letter from Richard Thurlow to Marconi, 4 July 1972: *Marconi Archives*).

By August 1922 the basic formula of records, now supplied by Burrows' assistant Stanton Jefferies, must have been beginning to pall. By contrast, London based 2LO, of which we shall shortly learn more, was on air with live programmes, and a new and much more powerful PCGG (the Hague transmitting station) was about to focus on English listeners with programmes produced under the auspices of the *Daily Mail*. At this point Eckersley stepped into the breach reinvigorating 2MT and pretending to offer listeners operatic fare. Amateurs must have been thrilled to hear his voice once again introducing the station:

>Hello CQ, Hello CQ,
>This is Two Emma Toc Wr-r-r-r-ittle calling

> This is Two Emma Toc Wr-r-r-r-ittle calling
>
> Well tonight, we have a most marvellous thing that's going to happen
> We are going to receive Rome.
> That famous Italian tenor …… now what's his name?
> That famous Italian tenor Gridleako is going to sing
> Nonfluatoroma Fortissimo which being translated means …
> Well it is very difficult
> Now we are going to receive it
> There may be some atmospherics (hsssss)
> There may be some jamming (parp, parp, parp, parp,)
> There may be some oscillation (woww wow)
> Hang on CQ, Hang on CQ
> Hang on a minute
> Here it is…..
>
> (Peter Eckersley runs across the room, his voice fading)

Suddenly the old piano bursts into life and a strange strangled voice singing in high pitched mock Italian makes its debut on 2MT (Wander, Tim, *2MT Writtle, The Birth of British Broadcasting*, p70).

From that moment Eckersley 'became in a week the talk of wireless Britain. The Writtle concerts always contained a surprise - a burlesque or something deadly serious or a totally unexpected remark in a transmission of otherwise normal character or the night of grand opera when the whole company of star singers, instrumentalists, scene-shifters and property men consisted of three persons, at least one of whom was engaged in transmitting mock interruptions.' (Burrows, Arthur, *The Story of Broadcasting*, p58). But Ashbridge could never be sure Eckersley would turn up. On one occasion, the engineers were playing the usual Coleridge Taylor record and Wynn had begun to recite Kipling's 'If', when suddenly the door burst open; Eckersley had arrived and transformed the rest of the evening. Yet even he played the records sent by Stanton Jefferies, and on more sober nights, observed the two minutes silence (*Amateur Wireless*, 2 September 1922).

In October, 2MT broadcast the 'Balcony' scene from the play 'Cyrano de Bergerac' by Rostand. Normally acted in semi-darkness by virtually stationary players, this part was particularly suited to radio drama. Eckersley played Cyrano; Agnes Travers, a young actress not long out of RADA, played Roxane and her brother played the part of Christian. There was a family link between Agnes and the famous playwright Ben Travers whose career in the theatre was just emerging. Ben's wife, Violet, was an old school friend of Eckersley's wife Stella.

The fourth person directly involved in the play was Wynn who was in charge of effects and it was in Wynn's digs at 'Deodorea' that the rehearsal was held using scripts typed out by Miss Beeson. These carried instructions such as 'voice raised', 'voice discreet' and 'voice passionate'. On the night of the 17th, amid festoons of wires and benches loaded with apparatus, the three performers read their impassioned lines into a hand-held microphone, the heroine having a tendency to use the microphone as a teacup and Cyrano dangerously gesturing as though on stage.

With negotiations for a national broadcasting service now at an advanced stage, 2MT's days were numbered. 2LO London had been upgraded and was now a powerful 1½-kilowatt station. Under Burrows, 2LO had already acquired respectability in contrast to the Writtle 'spirit' of farce and foolishness. 2LO was allowed to transmit every day, whereas, as Eckersley commented, 'we had plenty of time to listen for things which would give us material for our lampoons and skits.' (Eckersley, R., *BBC and All That*, p44). Burrows even had to break off 2LO's evening programme 'to enable the Writtle Station to carry out its usual Tuesday evening programme without interference' or, as Eckersley put it, 'in order that Writtle should be more clearly heard laughing at them' (Burrows' letter to the *Daily Mail*, 18 December 1922 regarding times of 2LO transmissions).

2MT's programmes usually finished with Tosti's 'Parted' sung by Eckersley in a high tenor voice and accompanied on a piano brought along the lane on a barrow from either the village hall or the 'Cock and Bell.' Rather like the signature tune of 'Much Binding in the Marsh,' new words were devised each time and so a number of different versions have come down to us. One of those probably not yet published went:

> CQ the concert's ended
> Falleth the tottering mast.
> Hark how the engines groaning
> Hell! Will the petrol last?
> Tell us again you heard us
> Your distance and where and how

> Quick for the engine's failing
> Goodbye you old low-brow

The words were apt. Soon 2MT would be gone. By the end of 1922 the British Broadcasting Company was ready for business. Little more than a week later, the BBC made broadcasting history with a transmission direct from Covent Garden Opera House. Eckersley sat for three solid hours, 'rigidly clamped by headphones, completely absorbed, oblivious of discomfort'. It seemed like a revelation. He knew instinctively Writtle's end had come. Within a day or two, he went to Magnet House, London, to see John Reith, the newly appointed BBC General Manager. He entered a room in which the staff, about fifteen people, were feverishly working and at the far end of which the BBC chief was installed in a tiny annexe little bigger than a cupboard. 'I was impressed by the way I was handled and, before I quite realised it, I had promised to shut down Writtle even though I had no right to do so.' (Eckersley, R., *BBC and All That*, p45).

2MT Writtle bowed out on 17 January 1923. The engineers said goodbye to their listeners, drinking their health in a glass of water promoted to champagne by the sound of a popgun. Then it was back to normal routine.

The Writtle engineers had hardly recovered from this first shock of the peremptory close down of their much loved station when Peter Eckersley gave them another. It turned out he had had an interview with Reith on Tuesday 30 January for the post of Chief Engineer, BBC. It was a post that everyone thought had already been filled from Head Office. But it seemed the successful applicant had, at the last minute, turned down the offer, leaving the way open for Eckersley to apply. Ashbridge remembered Eckersley coming into the hut about six o'clock.

> 'He'd been up to London and he said "Well, I've been offered the job of Chief Engineer to the BBC". I responded "You're not going to take it of course" and he replied "I don't know. It's an awful sort of kid's game at the moment but it might become something". I said "Hopeless thing. Look what we're doing here. We're covering aircraft, we're doing army work, we're doing ordinary communication stuff and all you'll be doing will be sending out stock exchange prices and weather reports and gramophone records." Well I was wrong. But he didn't think I was that much wrong.'

By the end of the week, Eckersley had informed Reith he had decided to take the job. Ashbridge's response when Eckersley told him of his decision on the Monday was: 'It's madness; you'll never do any good in a field like that; you're going right out of the main stream of wireless' (Talk by Eckersley to the BBC Engineering Society, 16 February 1960). Eckersley went to see Isaacs who agreed to waive the requirement for a month's notice: 'Get to Magnet House as quickly as you can. There's a great deal to do.' Eckersley thereupon bade 'Goodbye' to his staff. The following day, Tuesday 6 February 1923, he turned up again in the room with the annexe at Magnet House. It was now packed with BBC staff and pandemonium seemed to reign. Within minutes, Reith made clear the 'great deal' there was indeed to do. A greater contrast between the frenetic bustle of the BBC office and the relaxed camaraderie of the Writtle hut would be difficult to imagine. Unfamiliar and strained faces confronted him as he took his place - unfamiliar that is except for one. At another desk in the crowded room sat Burrows, the only man Eckersley knew and just about the only one he had ever failed to get on with.

Soon the process of poaching Writtle's engineers began as the BBC went rapidly from strength to strength. Eckersley offered the job of Assistant Chief Engineer to Wynn. It carried a salary of £350, way above Wynn's Marconi pay of £4 a week. Wynn informed Ashbridge: 'What are you going to do about it?' 'I'll take it.' Ashbridge thereupon likened the BBC to a passing craze like diabolo or roller-skating. 'Anyway', he added, 'if the BBC is serious they'll want a real engineer, not one six months out of university'. Wynn drew back from the brink. But the BBC was not to be a passing craze; by the end of 1926 Kirke, Wynn, MacLarty and even Ashbridge left the Writtle hut for the BBC where all except MacLarty would spend the rest of their working lives.

So it was that Trump, alone of the engineers, carried on at Writtle and at the 'Cock and Bell'. He married Doris, daughter of the landlord and sister of Betty Beeson, Eckersley's former secretary and so put down even deeper roots at Writtle until he retired in 1960.

Miss Beeson never married. She had a sweetheart in the army who survived the Great War only to be a victim of the influenza epidemic that followed a year later. Betty Beeson was eventually buried beside her sweetheart in the Writtle churchyard.

Robert Ellingford (1899/1966), like Trump, stayed on at Writtle, cycling or walking from his house at Oxley Green. He 'had a lot of time' for Eckersley but did not talk much about the others. He often worked nights and his wife listened in to 2LO on headphones.

The hut where Trump and Ellingford worked in the inter war years remained largely unchanged. When little Miss Trump visited her father in the 'thirties she found him in the long isolated hut of 1919. When she again visited him during the Second World War, she was stopped at the gate and her father came to her. Beyond the gate, the scene was transformed with a variety of huts and connecting passageways. Her father was working long hours on radar equipment.

At this time Christopher Cockerell (later Sir Christopher), inventor of the hovercraft, was in charge at the hut and was occupying Eckersley's old office, now enlarged to 12ft long. Other offices of 14ft and 10ft and a laboratory 30ft long made up the 'Mark Two' hut and were approached by a corridor added to the field side of the hut. This connected, at the north end, with another building at right angles to the hut. Here was Trump's experimental laboratory. The old hut was also extended to the north by 20ft and then again extended by a further 30ft or so to provide a Drawing Office. At the south end a window was added to the gable wall and a bulge in the wall contained a safe to house high security documents. These changes explain the hut as it appears in the 1955 photograph and on the wartime plans (Letter from Sir Christopher Cockerell to the author, 26 February 1996. Also from Dudley Shearman, Site Secretary 1945 to 1980.)

Reproduced by permission of the Marconi Co. Ltd

The Writtle hut in 1955

Nevertheless, despite all these changes the hut is made up of First World War boarding and windows from Writtle and conveys the authentic feel and proportions of the original. In one of the two rooms, the scene of the evening broadcast of 23 May 1922 has been vividly recreated. Nora Scott is to be seen in hat and silk dress with her song sheet, beside her stands Kirke holding the microphone uncomfortably close to her mouth, the Marconi accompanist at the piano looks up expectantly. We fully expect this old hut to be filled with music as Nora Scott prepares to sing 'When the Dream is There'.

2LO - The Experimental London Station

For many listeners in the twenties 2LO was the British Broadcasting Company and the British Broadcasting Company was 2LO. The station provided entertainment not only for London but also for crystal and valve set owners in a dozen major cities in Britain. In the latter half of the decade, 2LO's range spread well into the Home Counties and its programmes were fed into the long wave transmitter at Daventry 5XX, serving most of rural England. 2LO had a romantic aura about it, epitomising early wireless, and so 2LO lived on in people's memory long after its actual passing at the close of the decade.

But, as we have seen, 2LO had a still earlier pre-BBC existence as a Marconi experimental station. Throughout 1922 it was in the caring hands of Arthur Burrows. In that year he saw it grow from a small demonstration set to a full blown BBC station with transmission nightly. In this first half of the year, the Postmaster General reined in the station to ensure broadcasting would not commence by default. But once key decisions were reached for a properly organised and funded BBC service, 2LO took off and the next chapter deals more fully with that relationship. Though still deprived of staff and money, programmes became ever more ambitious, many firsts being achieved.

In contrast to 2MT, which remained technically static throughout 1922, 2LO underwent enormous advances, particularly in the later months, and its technical development continued well into its BBC days. Marconi's top engineers, men like Franklin and Round, applied their knowledge and experience to designing the transmitter and aerial and later the microphone and amplifier. Throughout 1922 Burrows' opposite number on the engineering side for operation purposes was R H White.

2LO was situated on the top floor of Marconi House in the Strand, London, its windows built into the upper part of the mansard roof. The building, by the famous architect Norman Shaw, remains externally much as it was but, alas, not the mansard roof. This was sacrificed when, in 1957, the adjoining Gaiety Theatre was redeveloped for offices in a scheme combining the two sites.

Marconi House had originally been built as a restaurant for Edwardian bon viveurs, with a wine bar, a Masonic Temple and apartments. The restaurant was a failure and, in 1912, the whole building was substantially adapted to provide a Head Office for Marconi. Short's Wine Bar, however, continued to occupy part of the Strand frontage.

Reproduced by permission of the Marconi Co. Ltd
Marconi House, The Strand, London; home of 2LO, 1924

In sharp contrast to 2MT's mud track and draughty hut, 2LO's approach was spectacular and impressive. One entered from the Strand into a spacious hall panelled in Honduras mahogany and fitted out with a magnificent fireplace.

A wide stairway with a bronze balustrade led up all seven floors, and was supplemented with a lift. On the top floor a small cinema and projection room enabled trade films to be shown to Marconi customers and visitors. The little cinema was to become the cradle of 2LO.

Key sources refer to the birth of 2LO 'as being in the spring of 1922' (Burrows, Arthur, *The Story of Broadcasting*, p58), with the first broadcast being on 11 May (Briggs, Asa, *History of Broadcasting in the United Kingdom*: Vol I, p75, 1961). This broadcast was arranged at the suggestion of the *Daily Mail* and consisted of a commentary on the prize fight at Olympia between Kid Lewis and George Carpentier. A reporter at Olympia phoned progress of the fight to his opposite number at Marconi House where it was taken down with the microphone switched off. The resulting script was then handed to W R Southney, a Marconi engineer who promptly switched on the microphone and broadcast it. C S Franklin, who had designed the 1.5-kilowatt transmitter, was at the controls along with R H White, the engineer responsible for the transmission. The overwhelming engineering presence arose from the fact that this was the first test of the new transmitter. From the engineers' point of view, the fight more than anything else would attract those with equipment to listen-in and would prompt widespread reports of its effective range (*The Amplion Magazine*, March 1926).

Franklin's transmitter, which was initially installed in his laboratory on the seventh floor, is referred to by Dowsett as 'The Original 2LO Transmitter' (Dowsett, H M, *Wireless Telephony and Broadcasting, vol II*, p95).

But these references overlook a still earlier transmitter. Burrows describes the form this took. It was 'a 100 watt set contained in a small teak cabinet and housed in the cinema theatre on the top floor of Marconi House London'. The transmitter/receiver, being only 3ft wide and 2ft high, fitted into a window recess and so did not get in everyone's way. It provided 'demonstrations to distinguished visitors, principally those from foreign countries.' These visitors presumably also saw the trade films (Burrows, Arthur, *The Story of Broadcasting*, p59: also letter of 8 May 1937 from Burrows to Reith in the *Marconi Archives*).

The licence for this demonstration set replaced the pre-war one of 11 March 1914. It was issued for 2LO on 17 December 1921 and amended on 17 January 1922. The restrictions placed on 2LO at this early stage were muchmore severe than those placed on 2MT. It was lower in power and not

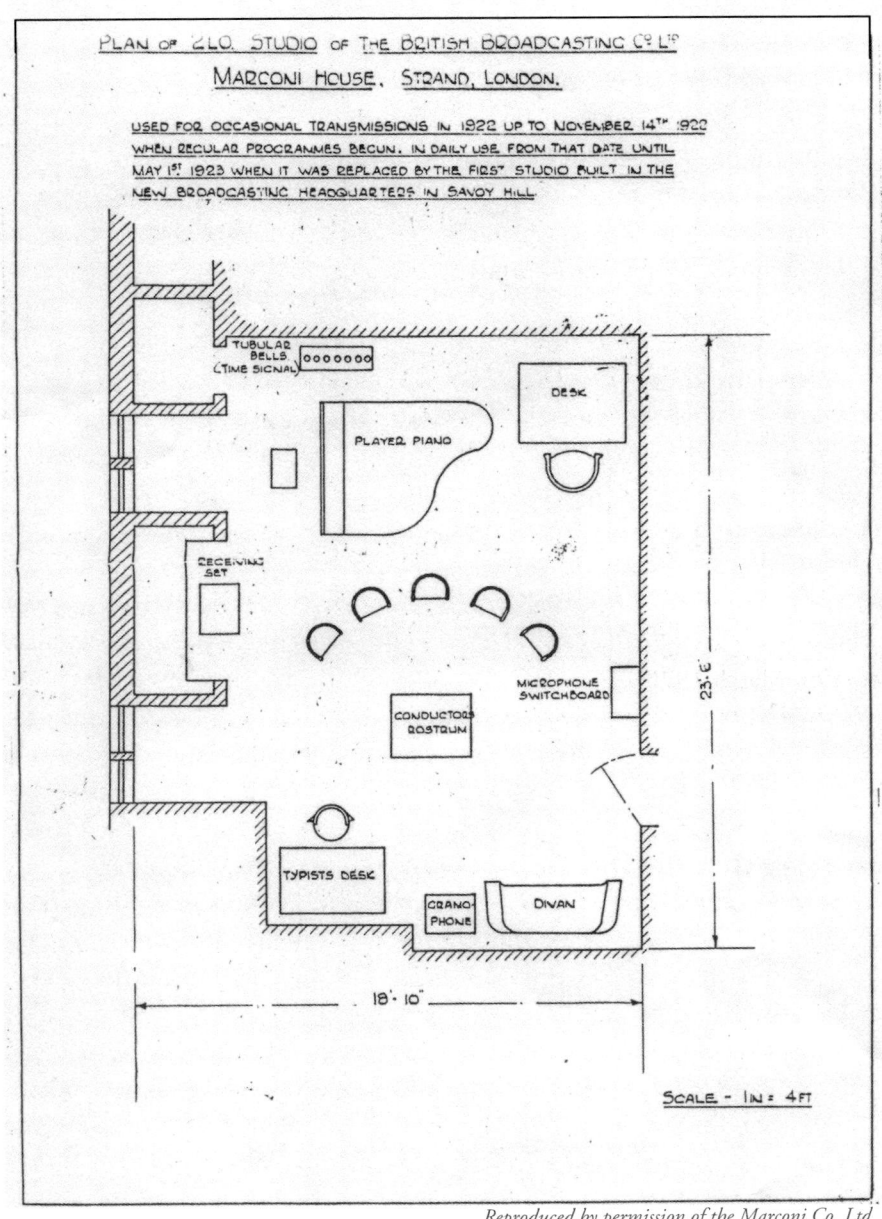

Reproduced by permission of the Marconi Co. Ltd
Marconi **House Studio** Layout, 1922. Plan prepared by Harold Bishop and sent to Sir Donald Banks, Permanent Secretary, Air Ministry, 21 October 1937.

allowed to transmit music:

> transmissions normally to be limited to half an hour and only permitted between 11 am to noon and 2pm to 5pm;
> maximum power 100 watts using a wavelength of 350m;
> intervals of 3 minutes duration following every 7 minutes transmission, a qualified operator to listen for possible messages from the authorities requesting the station to close down due to interference with military, aviation or commercial stations;
> call sign to be 2LO.

With regard to the call sign, '2LO' had already been allocated to Marconi House in advance of the licence of December 1921 (minutes of 22 November 1921 in *Marconi Archives*). The amended licence of 17 January permitted the use of a portable low power transmitter at any location in the London area in connection with lectures. In this situation, the call sign 2SW was to be employed.

2LO's 'demonstration period' provided nothing of interest for the amateur community and could hardly be expected to do so given the restrictions imposed by the Post Office. By May 1922 the Post Office had begun to address the future organisation of broadcasting in Britain and to indicate how this might be handled. To avoid interference with other interests, broadcasting stations would be limited to 1.5 kilowatts and would be established in eight major cities. This changed Government attitude to broadcasting gave the cue to the Marconi engineers. Within a few days the little 100W YB1 teak box transmitter gave way to the substantial three panel transmitter mentioned above as being designed by C S Franklin. A photograph of this improved transmitter fortunately exists in the Marconi Archives and is reproduced here. The modulator panel on the right contains two valves, the smaller being the microphone amplifier and the larger, the modulator. The centre panel contains two rectifying valves on the right and a larger oscillator valve on the left. The high tension panel on the left includes the variometers and, below, a fixed high-voltage (10,000 volt) air capacitor for a anode tuning. The new station broadcast on 360m. (Dowsett, H M, *Wireless Telephony and Broadcasting, vol II*, p95).

The next step involved upgrading the aerial. The solution was to create a 50ft mast on what is now Bush House, which was close by and vacant, a 200ft twin wire aerial bridging the gap between it and Marconi House. By mid 1922

Reproduced by permission of the Marconi Co. Ltd
Franklin's 1.5kW transmitter (Mk1) installed in Marconi House, London, May 1922.

2LO's power had been raised to the full 1.5-kilowatt permitted by the Postmaster General for broadcasting (*Popular Wireless*, 15 and 22 July 1922; *The Broadcaster*, August 1922).

But the station would not be complete without a studio; that is, not merely a room, but one suitably treated and tested for broadcasting, including music. The Post Office finally authorised test transmissions both of speech and music, these to be for special audiences at some institution, hospital, wireless society, private garden party or fête. Each broadcast was subject to individual permit as the general licence still allowed only speech demonstrations, not publicly advertised concerts. According to Burrows, the 'first real concert from 2LO involved three artistes; Miss Beatrice Eveline (cellist), Ethel Walker (pianist) and Charles Knowles (baritone); it took place on 24 June 1922 (Burrows, Arthur, *The Story of Broadcasting*, p60). The concert was sponsored by Sir Trevor and Lady Dawson of Edgwarebury House, Elstree. Special arrangements were made to enable the distinguished guests at the Dawson garden party to listen in. Apparently the cello came over very well; the piano was 'good but variable in strength'; the baritone 'was not good'. The general impression made on listeners was that the concert was taking place in an empty room or in a long corridor with polished walls. In reality, it was taking place in the cinema on the top floor of Marconi House. This had smooth plaster walls and was highly reverberant.

Burrows felt the problem was essentially one of acoustics and took the matter up with one of the managers of Chappell's music firm who had previously been Recording Manager of the Gramophone Company, now EMI. He advised Burrows to drape the room with Kapok Quilting hung from a height of 8 or 9ft so that it just touched the floor. Burrows discovered that quilting would cost about £33 (Burrows minute of 30 June 1922 in *Marconi Archives*; also *Popular Wireless*, 5 August 1922 for the cover picture showing the undraped cinema). In the event, the walls were hung with two layers of butter muslin.

There were limits on how far a broadcaster could go in a room that continued its main function of showing trade films. Indeed the decision to use the cinema as opposed to the schoolroom in the basement was still in the balance as late as 20 June (R H White to Burrows, 20 June 1922, *Marconi Archives*). Stanton Jefferies, who joined Burrows in July, later recalled: 'Occasionally the room was required for its original purpose and then we had to work in the dark or watch a demonstration film that I had seen many times before. By way of retaliation, I would hold one or two auditions. The result was pandemonium' (*Soap Box* by L Stanton Jefferies, *Popular Wireless*, 5 October 1935).

With no budget and limited sponsorship to pay artistes for these crucial early tests, Burrows had to rely on the more prominent artistes offering their services for charity. The real pioneer of this approach to broadcasting had been the remarkable Captain Ian Fraser, Chairman of St Dunstan's, the hostel for blinded soldiers and sailors. Fraser was a young army officer who had been blinded at the Somme. As a schoolboy he had developed a flair for wireless and, after the War, operated his own transmitter, call sign 5SU. He realised the huge potential benefit that wireless broadcasts could provide for the blind and was anxious to promote broadcasting in every way possible.

A very early opportunity to do this occurred in 1921 in connection with a sale of goods in aid of St Dunstan's which was held in the Eagle Hut in the Strand. Here the magic of wireless was revealed to the London public for the first time.

The Eagle Hut had been erected in 1916 as a Canadian servicemen's YMCA. It stood on the site of the old Tivoli Music Hall where Lottie Collins had thrilled audiences back in the 'nineties' with her dazzling rendition of 'Ta-Ra-Ra-Boom-De-Ay.' The theatre had been demolished in 1914 as part of the Strand widening scheme.

Fraser persuaded first the Postmaster General and the military; secondly Marconi, and thirdly the world of the theatre and music hall to take part in this one-off experiment - all without charge, conditions or reservations. It seemed no one could say 'No'. Marconi had a subsidiary, the Marconi Scientific Instrument Company, conveniently situated in St Anne's Court, Dean Street only a few streets away from the hut. The premises were already equipped with a 10-watt transmitter and had a 70ft long twin-wire aerial supported on 70ft masts built on the roof. The Eagle Hut meanwhile was equipped with a powerful valve receiver; this was linked to 28 pairs of headphones.

For a shilling a time the London public could listen in for three minutes to Charles Coburn (remembered now for his rendition of 'The Man who broke the Bank of Monte Carlo'); James Jell (the blind tenor), Doris O'Brien, Raynor Hunt and other entertainers broadcasting from the Marconi premises off Dean Street half a minute away. But the mainstay was a new group - 'The Co-Optimists', led by Davy Burnaby. They were performing nightly at the Royalty Theatre, Dean Street, just round the corner from Marconi. Their show was on Pierrot lines and the group included Stanley Holloway, Melville Gideon, Laddie Cliff, Gilbert Childs, Betty Chester, Phyllis Monkman and Elsa Macfarlane. They crowded round the horned microphone to sing their hit tunes. The Co-Optimists were the supreme concert party of all time. Their show ran throughout the twenties in London and in the provincial theatres, offering perfect escapism. It was a happy show, compounded of Davy Burnaby's geniality as their portly compère, Phyllis Monkman's exuberance, Melville Gideon's music and Stanley Holloway's singing (Baily, Leslie, *BBC Scrapbooks*, vol. 2, 1918-1939, p46). An album issued by 'EMI World Records Limited' in 1976 captures the authentic sound of the Co-Optimists with several recordings made in 1922. The very sounds enjoyed by 4000 visitors to the hut can be

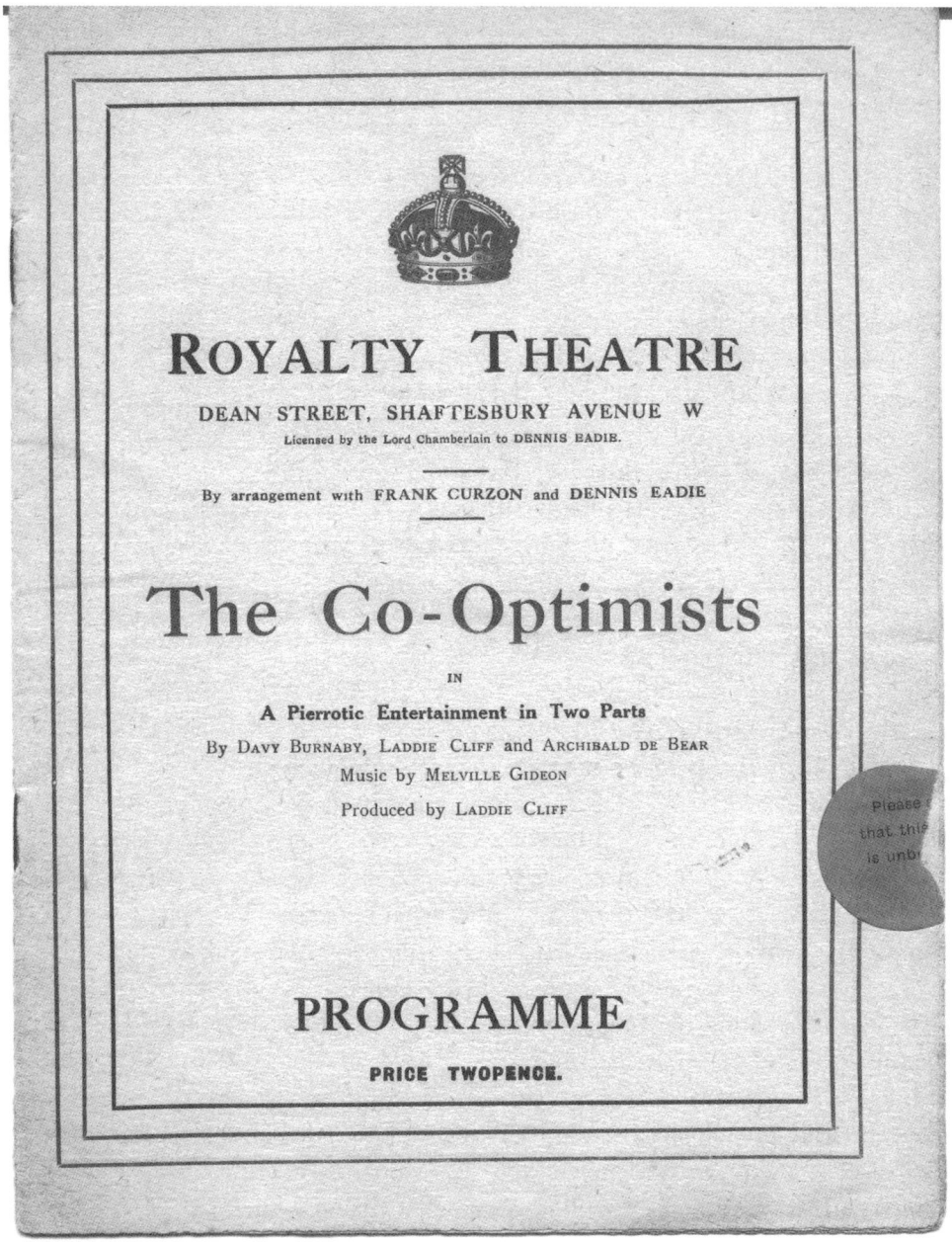

A Co-Optimists theatrical programme. 1921.

Programme.

THE CO-OPTIMISTS

IN

A Pierrotic Entertainment in Two Parts.

By DAVY BURNABY, LADDIE CLIFF and ARCHIBALD DE BEAR.

Music by MELVILLE GIDEON.

Produced by LADDIE CLIFF.

PHYLLIS MONKMAN BETTY CHESTER ELSA MACFARLANE BABS VALERIE
LADDIE CLIFF DAVY BURNABY MELVILLE GIDEON
GILBERT CHILDS STANLEY HOLLOWAY H. B. HEDLEY

PART I.

1. The Co-Optimists Admit Their Own Cleverness.
   ("Bow-Wow!")
2. "She Didn't Know Enough About the Game."
   DAVY BURNABY.
3. "Wind in the Trees."
   STANLEY HOLLOWAY.
4. "The Success of the Dance."
   LADDIE CLIFF.
5. GILBERT CHILDS has a Cut off the Joint.
6. "Sea Fever."
   BETTY CHESTER.
7. Operatic Golf.
   STANLEY HOLLOWAY, DAVY BURNABY, GILBERT CHILDS,
   MELVILLE GIDEON and LADDIE CLIFF.
8. "Amapoo."
   MELVILLE GIDEON.
9. ELSA MACFARLANE will sing.
10. "M'Yes!"
    PHYLLIS MONKMAN and LADDIE CLIFF
11. SEMI-FINALE (with Grand Spectacular Effects).
    BETTY CHESTER and Very Full Royalty Theatre Company

Intermission.

PART II.

1. "Where the Moonbeams Quiver."
   PHYLLIS MONKMAN.
2. Current Puns.
   PHYLLIS MONKMAN, BETTY CHESTER, LADDIE CLIFF,
   DAVY BURNABY, MELVILLE GIDEON, GILBERT CHILDS,
   STANLEY HOLLOWAY.
3. STANLEY HOLLOWAY indulges in the Sincerest Form of Flattery (with apologies to Messrs. Harry Weldon and Jack Hulbert), after singing about "Cloze Props."
4. "The Junior Turf."
   LADDIE CLIFF and GILBERT CHILDS.
5. MELVILLE GIDEON on his own.
6. "On Our Honeymoon."
   PHYLLIS MONKMAN and GILBERT CHILDS.
7. "FOOL-DOG GERALD."
   Ronux STANLEY HOLLOWAY   Phyllis Bending   PHYLLIS MONKMAN
   Razzle .. BABS VALERIE   Dr. Baking-Powder .. GILBERT CHILDS
   Gerald .. LADDIE CLIFF   Snarl Chesterson .. DAVY BURNABY
   Squirms BETTY CHESTER   A Chinese Servant   ELSA MACFARLANE
   Scene 1 ... Gerald's Existing Room.   Scene 2 ... The Tonic So-Fa Room.
   Scene 3 ... The Gt. Central Room.
8. (a) "Coal-Black Mammy."
   (b) "The Old Nigger."   LADDIE CLIFF.
9. "Choosing the Test Team."
10. FINALE.   (And So to Bed).

Costumes and Scenery designed by HUGH WILLOUGHBY (By kind permission of Messrs. Moss' Empires, Ltd.)

Orchestra under the Direction of PHILIP LEWIS.

The grateful acknowledgments of the CO-OPTIMISTS are due to Mr. LESLIE STILES for his collaboration in the burlesque of "Bulldog Drummond."
DAVY BURNABY appears by kind permission of Messrs. GROSSMITH & LAURILLARD.
The music of "Coal-Black Mammy" is composed by Miss IVY ST. HELIER, and of "Sea Fever" by JOHN IRELAND.
The words and music of "Wind in the Trees are by BETTY BOUTELLE', the music of "Cloze Props" by WOSELEY CHARLES, the words of "Roast Beef of Old England" by SAM MAYO and Arthur McCarthy, and the music by SAM MAYO. About the Game," is included by kind permission of Mr. TOM B. DAVIS.
The song, "She Didn't Know Enough About the Game," is included by kind permission of Mr. TOM B. DAVIS.

Copies of the Songs can be obtained from the Attendants.

Pianos by CHAPPELL'S.   Costumes executed by Mme. NEWMAN and MORRIS ANGEL, LTD.

EVERY EVENING at 8.30.   MATS. MON., WED. & SAT. at 2.30
The Box Office (D. A. Whiston) is open from 10 to 10 daily.   Telephone: 3855 Gerrard.

EXTRACTS FROM THE RULES MADE BY THE LORD CHAMBERLAIN.—The name of the actual and responsible Manager of the Theatre must be printed on every play bill. The Public can leave the Theatre at the end of the Performance by all exit and entrance doors, which must open outwards.
Where there is a fireproof screen to the proscenium opening, it must be lowered at least once during every Performance to ensure its being in proper working order. Smoking is not permitted in the auditorium. All gangways, passages and staircases must be kept free from chairs or any other obstructions, whether permanent or temporary.

General Manager ... ... (for THE CO-OPTIMISTS) ... THOMAS MILLER
Stage Director ... ... STANLEY BRIGHTMAN

A Co-Optimists theatrical programme. 1921.

heard today though shorn of the *sotto voce* remarks of engineers in the transmitting room which were sometimes inconveniently audible (*Wireless World*, 20 August and 17 September 1921; *Daily Graphic*, 27 July 1921 and *Daily Sketch* of the same date).

Following the Postmaster General's subsequent authorisation, in mid-1922, of music transmission for special occasions, Fraser returned to the attack. This time a fête had been planned for 7 and 8 July to be held in Regents Park. He suggested Marconi should erect a receiving station in a tent that would seat forty or fifty people. There would be 'concerts' at hourly intervals; each followed by a lecture or demonstration of small sets for the home - sets that would cater later that year for the BBC's first audiences. This time a loudspeaker would be required.

In the event, it was decided to go for 20-minute 'concerts' each followed by a 'popular chat' lasting about twelve minutes, the pattern to be repeated at 40-minute intervals from 5pm onward. 150 to 200 people would be accommodated at a time at a charge of two shillings a head - this to go to St Dunstan's. Marconi even offered to contact possible artistes! The charity broadcast was an immense success. This set in train a whole series of 'Appeals Broadcasts'. St Dunstan's was followed by the South London Hospital on 12 July, Folkestone Hospital on 9 August, and so on. If the fête or garden party was beyond the range of 2LO, the portable transmitter was used as, for example, in the case of the Chichester Red Triangle Club.

On the eve of the first of this series of broadcast concerts, Burrows requested staff to handle the extra work involved. He needed two persons 'of good appearance and manners' and with wireless experience 'to conduct, without supervision, explanatory demonstrations'. Also, a third man of 'sufficient grace and manner to place himself at home with well-known artistes'. This third man did not need to have much wireless experience but had to possess an excellent microphone voice. His job would be to conduct the musical side of the transmission at Marconi House (minute of 23 June 1922 from Burrows to H W Allen, Joint General Manager, *Marconi Archives*).

The appointment of the third man 'was duly approved by the General Manager' (minute from H W Allen to Burrows of 11 July 1922). Stanton Jefferies was the man selected for this role. He became Burrows' right hand man and was soon taking the lead in running 2LO. Trained at the Royal College of Music (RCM), he was well placed to organise small concerts or musical evenings, often falling back on former colleagues from the RCM like Maurice Cole and Miss Cecil Dixon to help. Young and energetic, he possessed the qualities of 'grace and manner' combined with steel-like efficiency and determination to get things done. All this was allied to extraordinary musical versatility and a great sense of fun. Moreover, he was already on the Marconi House staff, a point that went down well with Burrows. Jefferies's own amusing version of how he got the job was published some years later:

> 'I went up one afternoon to the small demonstration cinema at the top of Marconi House where the concerts were held and found to my horror that the fare for the afternoon consisted of half a dozen sopranos, one after the other. Six sopranos taken neat is nobody's idea of entertainment. I suggested it might not be a bad idea to have a musician in charge of such endeavours and my employers agreed. So there I was Musical Director of Marconi in 1922. What good fun those early days were! As far as the concerts were concerned, I was not overworked, as we never transmitted more than two or three in a week. Each was given on behalf of some charity or other. My first concern was to get in touch with artistes to get them interested in the new idea. Unfortunately, artistes were not paid for broadcasting so it was rather like trying to make the proverbial bricks without straw.'
> (*Soap Box*, by L Stanton Jefferies, *Popular Wireless*, 5 October 1935)

Stanton Jefferies' first official assignment in the cinema came on 26 July when he managed the two mini-concerts broadcast in connection with the Hampstead Garden Fête, these going out at 5pm and 6pm respectively and each lasting half an hour. His first challenge was to send out the tuning note for two minutes so that the amateur community could adjust their sets. For this purpose, an organ pipe set in one of the holes of a voicing box was employed. There were bellows underneath this contraption which, being raised, provided a tuning note for one minute, whereupon it had to be raised again. Unfortunately, the air also escaped from the other holes which would not shut properly and the tuning note was liable to end in a 'wail of despair like a dying pig' (*ibid*. 19 October). Jefferies then had both to announce the items and to accompany singers on the piano.

Jefferies' next 'trial' came on 3 August. He started with: '2LO; here are a few words for testing purposes' and then proceeded, Ditcham style, with a count from one to twenty followed by days of the week and months of the year. The concert on this occasion was on behalf of the funds of the Eltham Cottage Hospital. An added complication was that he had to close down and go off air promptly at 7.55pm to avoid overlap with the *Daily Mail* sponsored concert from the Hague transmitting station, PCGG. That was the first such high power PCGG concert and a red-letter day in the diaries of the amateur community. Burrows stationed himself at the Imperial Hotel with a multi-valve set linked to a loudspeaker. Tuning in to 2LO on 360m, he heard Jefferies's opening announcements. They were a great improvement on his previous attempt but rather hurried. Then came a baritone, a violin solo by John Pennington, a contralto - Miss Phyllis Everett, and another song from the baritone. After that, close down. On this occasion, Burrows and Jefferies learned some valuable lessons for the future. First, the need to get the singer and piano in balance - the piano had its own microphone. Secondly, to ensure that the singers were really close to the microphone - about six inches away - and stayed there. And thirdly, the desirability of broadcasting popular, well-known pieces rather than obscure ones chosen by the artistes themselves; his fellow listeners at the Imperial Hotel had clapped 'Annie Laurie' but were not so keen on the contralto's song from 'Carmen.'

Jefferies was soon on his own as Burrows went on leave on 7 August until the 26th. But similar concerts occurred throughout August and, indeed, during the remainder of the year. The Postmaster General still insisted on his three minutes of silence at 10-minute intervals and the presence in the studio of an engineer to listen in on a receiver at such times on the same 360m wavelength. Early in September, a light was installed in the cinema to show when the transmitter was live. This indicated to the engineer when to connect and disconnect his receiver to and from the aerial. It also showed when the announcer could bang the microphones to free up the packed granules.

Another restriction that still seemed to remain was the limiting of transmissions to half an hour. Whilst music was now permitted, concerts were not allowed before 5pm. This led to an evening concert being typically made up of three half-hour sessions starting at 5pm, 6pm and 7pm, before the artistes had to leave for their theatres.

A typical example was that in aid of the Royal Northern and Passmore Edwards Hospitals. The broadcast was associated with a number of fêtes in London at which visitors could listen in to 2LO and enjoy a cup of tea, all for 6d. Their printed programmes informed them in tiny print that the concerts came from Marconi House, London. Normally these concerts could only be announced in advance provided there was no reference to Marconi or Marconi House.

Details of programmes were not provided much in advance. This was due partly to the pressures on Jefferies and Burrows, but also to the fact that the Post Office rarely delivered the licence before the morning of the day in question and sometimes refused permission. However, amateurs were notified of the days and times at which concerts would, all being well, be transmitted the following week. For this purpose the amateurs each sent a stamped (1d) and addressed postcard to Room 35, Marconi House. Here a clerk would apply a rubber stamp on the back and write in the dates and times of transmissions. The cards would then be posted back. A number of such cards from August and September 1922 have survived and are to be found in the Marconi Archives.

The press of course wanted more detailed information. Associated Newspapers, representing the *Daily Mail* and *Evening News*, wrote at the end of July to Isaacs on the matter (letter of 24 July 1922, *Marconi Archives*). Things then began to improve; programmes were issued the previous evening and newspapers sent messenger boys to Marconi House to collect copies. Soon, by a 'superhuman' effort, Jefferies managed to get three days ahead and felt very proud of himself. Marconi even managed to circulate a printed programme, as indicated above, for the concert transmitted on behalf of the Royal Northern and Passmore Edwards Hospitals.

With papers like the *Daily News* and *Daily Mail* now publishing details of programmes, Burrows promptly introduced a 'routine' to be followed when organising concerts for fêtes and appeals:

Apply to PMG for permission to transmit.
Inform Mr Jefferies and officer in charge of transmitter Room 102. Also Director, Associated Newspapers and Mr Tilley, Works Manager, Chelmsford.
Enter in Mr Burrows diary and in diaries of Mr Jefferies and of demonstrating staff in Room 38.
Check facilities for reception at the fête etc. and agree programme hours.
On receipt of licence inform Mr Jefferies, officer in charge of transmitter and 'on site' staff responsible for the demonstrations.
Details of hours of transmission and of the artistes taking part to be notified to:
    a) all who have sent stamped postcards
    b) Director, Associated Newspapers
    c) Editors of principal daily papers

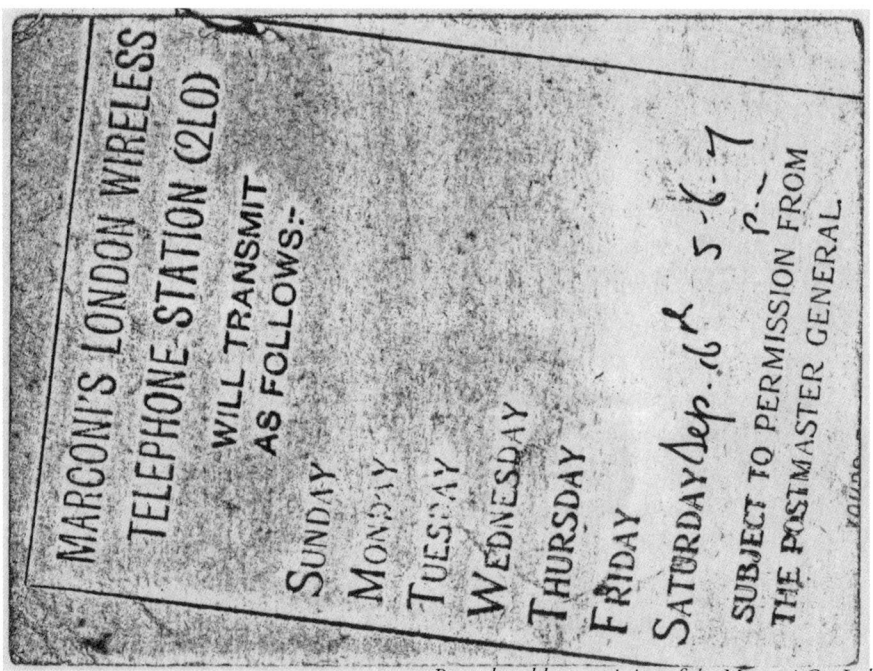

Reproduced by permission of the Marconi Co. Ltd
2LO Broadcast schedule sent to listeners by postcard, 1922.

    d) Editors of the four wireless periodicals
    e) The General Manager of Marconi
    f) The Marconiphone Department

Immediately following a concert, a report to be supplied to Mr Burrows together with the exact expenses entailed in connection with the demonstration.

By 25 September, this routine had expanded to include everyone imaginable; Burrows' thoroughness placed quite a burden on his staff, and indeed on himself (minutes in *Marconi Archives*). As to 'exact expenses', a complete list of concerts and other transmissions exists for the whole of the six-month period July to December with details of fees received to cover the incidental expenses of staff (*Marconi Archives*).

Artistes sometimes performed *gratis* either to aid a particular charity or to advertise their accomplishments. Stars of the theatre often appeared before the microphone to acquaint the public with musicals or plays in which they were appearing. They would appear in the studio before going on to the evening performance at the theatre. Among those who came to Marconi House in those early days of 1922 were Marjorie Gordon (Adelphi), Will Hay (Apollo), Billy Merson (Lyric), Sybil Thorndike (Little), and Huntley Wright and Winnie Collins (Daly's). Sometimes Burrows had to plead: 'I trust you will not find this impertinent but do you think that Sir Titto Ruffo would agree for publicity reasons to sing?' Some artistes were doubtless sponsored by the great houses that laid on charity fêtes with wireless demonstrations, but many artistes were simply paid a standard fee – half a guinea, or later, a guinea - for personal expenses in recognition for their help 'during the transition period' (minute from Burrows to Colonel Simpson, 29 September 1922, *Marconi Archives*). A list exists of these payments by Marconi, the understanding being that the BBC should eventually defray all the costs incurred by Marconi.).

Jefferies's biggest scoop occurred when he rounded up 50 artistes for 27 half-hour concerts all crammed in a single week. Some of these artistes were prepared to perform three or four times for their guinea (list of payments made on 13 October 1922, *Marconi Archives*). Jefferies went to town, printing a programme itemising every artiste and song performed but dutifully avoided any reference to Marconi House. The artistes included not only singers, but ten instrumentalists, four 'humorists' and two comediennes.

This burst of broadcasting activity arose from one of the greatest wireless events of 1922 - the 'First All British Wireless Exhibition and Convention' which opened at the Horticultural Hall, Westminster and ran from 30 September to 7 October 1922. The exhibition (described in the next section) attracted a huge number of people - some 25,000 - and, as they circulated round the stands, they were regaled with music over the loudspeakers broadcast from Marconi House. Each day, concerts were transmitted at 11am, 3pm, 6pm and 8pm. A mainstay of these concerts was Vivienne Chatterton with popular songs like 'Who is Sylvia,', 'Songs my Mother Sang' and 'Dashing away with the Smoothing Iron.' Rex Faithful, another singer, was to become Jefferies' right hand man at Marconi House once the BBC was established and, after four months, took over the running of 2LO so that Jefferies could concentrate on the musical side; his actual name was Rex Palmer (*Programme of Wireless Concerts to be transmitted to the First All-British Wireless Exhibition of Convention*, author's collection).

The culmination of the week's Exhibition transmissions was the broadcast at 7.30pm on 7 October 1922 by the Prince of Wales. His message was delivered from his study in St James's Palace and was intended for the Boy Scouts of Great Britain:

> 'Boy Scouts wherever you may be. I have been received today at the Alexandra Palace by some 40,000 Scouts and 17,000 Wolf Cubs. If the rest of you are like those I have seen, your standard of smartness and efficiency is a high one. But apart from outward signs, I admire more especially the inward spirit of goodwill and patriotism, which makes the whole movement so like a brotherhood. You are all doing splendid work by doing your best to be prepared for making good citizens for your empire. You could do nothing better. Stick to it. I wish you every possible success and good camping.'

For the broadcast, St James's Palace was connected by a Post Office land-line four miles long to the transmitter at Marconi House. Burrows was in charge of the non-technical arrangements and organised a rehearsal the previous evening. One of the key tests was to decide how many inches the microphone should be from the speaker's mouth. Apparently, the Prince had 'a broadcasting voice of really exceptional quality,' and the transmission was a success.

Reports confirming this came in from Scout Troops and individuals over a wide area . Owners of sets did their best to invite Scouts to listen in and of 225

2LO - THE EXPERIMENTAL LONDON STATION

2LO broadcasts from the first All-British Wireless exhibition, 1922.

reports, 73 mention Scouts being invited into the home; one referred to 'as many Scouts as I could cram into my dining room.' The Cardiff Radio Society invited 250 Scouts whilst Mr Tilley, the Marconi Works Manager at Chelmsford invited 100. In addition, there were 50 at the Horticultural Hall Exhibition among the 500 members of the public. Reliance for group listening of this sort was placed on valve sets and this was particularly the case for those outside the London area. The quality of reception appears to have been of a high standard and, well satisfied, Marconi produced a booklet setting out the Prince's speech and the reports subsequently obtained (*Souvenir of a Historic Event*, author's collection).

The Prince of Wales's speech broke new ground both as the first royal broadcast and the first outside broadcast in Britain. The undoubted success of this experiment prompted an even more ambitious outside broadcast less than a month later. This was to involve, in addition to the usual land-line, a long distance Post Office trunk line. Scheduled for 3 November, the evening was planned as follows:

6.00 to 6.45pm
> Lecture by Mr Shaughnessy (of the Post Office Engineering Department) from the Polytechnic, London.

7.00 to 7.05pm
> Sir William Noble at Marconi House to introduce the Lord Mayor of Bristol.

7.10 to 7.20pm
> The Lord Mayor of Bristol to speak from Bristol on behalf of local hospitals (Trunk line used; also a land-line).

7.25 to 7.30pm
> Reply by the Lord Mayor elect of London, speaking from the Guildhall, London (Land-line used).

7.30 to 8.30pm
> Concert from Marconi House.

The Lord Mayor of Bristol's address was telephoned to Paddington by trunk line and thence by land line to Marconi House, London, at the normal audio frequency used in telephony. There the incoming telephone signal modulated the radio frequency at the transmitter and was then broadcast at radio frequency. Ordinary telephone communication between Bristol and London was not affected.

In three London halls, a total of 830 people, each with headphones, heard the experimental broadcast (Briggs, Asa, *History of Broadcasting in the United Kingdom:* Vol I, p89, 1961; also *Western Daily press* and *Bristol Mirror*, 30 January 1945).

In making the technical arrangements, R H White placed Thomas and Petersen on duty at the 2LO transmitter in the 7th floor 'wireless room' with McCullough manning the amplifier on the third floor to which the land-lines were connected. His orders were that: 'In all cases for the above programme the set should be oscillating and connected to the aerial at the time specified and the incoming speech line switch placed in the correct position for speech, either direct from the cinema room or via the amplifier at the time given, those in charge of the cinema room and amplifier being responsible for seeing that the switches are closed and opened when speech commences and is finished.'

It was probably this broadcast that prompted *Popular Wireless* to argue that it would be better to maintain a good musical programme of quality than 'attempting experiments of too ambitious a character which, although of great scientific interest, may not be of universal popularity' (*Popular Wireless*, 25 November 1922). It was another lesson for 2LO.

As to 'universal popularity', Burrows). had already been alerted to this need as he had listened, with others, to the concert of 3 August on his multi-valve set and loudspeaker in the Imperial Hotel. The problem was that, as he was not paying artistes more than a nominal sum, he did not feel in a position to dictate what they should sing - the artistes for their part were unaware that few of their vast audience were habitués of the Albert, Queens and Wigmore Halls and other such places of high class musical entertainment. Only with the commencement of BBC programmes would the position begin to change (Burrows to Jefferies, 29 November 1922, *Marconi Archives*).

Apart from popular songs Burrows was, in September 1922, keen to introduce more instrumental music and, in particular, a small wireless orchestra. Again, he would have to wait until nightly BBC programmes, and the resources this implied, became a reality. There was also a problem with the microphone. Microphone distortion is more marked with the several instruments of an orchestra than with popular songs – a suitable microphone had yet to be invented.

Hope was placed in Dr. McLachlan's extraordinary capacitor microphone, which would be ready at the end of October. This consisted of a large curved and perforated piece of metal several feet across, varnished on its convex face. On this face was stretched some foiled paper which provided a capacity which could be varied by sound waves impinging on the metal concave face. The sound waves, on passing through the metal perforations, tended to lift the paper from the metal. 'This condenser *(i.e. capacitor)* was connected in the modulator grid circuit, a polarising voltage was applied to it and a resistance was connected across the condenser to earth. The effect of sound on the condenser was to cause its capacity to change, and with it the potential applied to the grid of the modulator.' (Dowsett, H M, *Wireless Telephony and Broadcasting, vol II*, p101) The microphone was briefly tested at 2LO but was not a success, so it was back to the Peel Conner carbon microphone.

If he was thwarted on the musical side, Burrows could still branch out in other directions. The first comedy programme written specifically for 2LO was Helena Millais's 'A Cockney Fragment from Life' in which she herself portrayed 'Our Lizzie,' a cockney character. This went out on 20 October. 'Our Lizzie' soon established herself as the station's first comic character. Another initiative was, on one occasion, to let Pett Ridge read one of his 'Little Tales' - short stories which were a regular feature of the *Daily News*. That story, broadcast on 22 September, reflected the 'Bedtime Stories' so popular in America.

An initiative of a different sort was to transmit reports of the progress of the newly instituted 'King's Cup Air Race'. Information about the race was broadcast on Thursday evening, the night before the race. Over the following two days - 8 and 9 September - hourly reports of the progress of the aeroplanes were provided, these being phoned through to Marconi House by the Air Ministry.

Another news event captured by 2LO was the Lord Mayor's Show. The microphone, dangled from the window of the studio, picked up the sounds of passing bands, the marching of the troops and the cheering of the crowd.

Meanwhile, 2LO continued steadfastly with its staple fare - programmes in aid of charities. The Publicity Department under Burrows made the usual applications for licences to broadcast each of these. Burrows' deputy, however, was in for a surprise. On 14 November 1922 the Post Office told him he need no longer apply for licences to broadcast provided the 'Broadcasting Company' agreed the arrangements. The 'Broadcasting Company', of course, hardly existed; it certainly had no address, no head, no staff.

But to suggest that Burrows and his department had no one to consult as the BBC took shape would be wrong. To look ahead to the next chapter (*Electrical Giants Enter the Field*), in the latter months of 1922 Sir William Noble chaired the 'Broadcasting Committee' and this committee was involved in all the key negotiations leading up to the establishment of the British Broadcasting Company. By 14 November substantial agreement had been reached between the various interests - the Government, manufacturers and the press - and the Post Office authorised the start from that date of a nightly BBC service. Throughout the remainder of the year, the Broadcasting Committee took over responsibility for the programmes from the individual companies concerned - Marconi, Metropolitan-Vickers/Radio Communication Company and Western Electric. The Committee undertook the final rounds of negotiations and dealt with the BBC's initial staffing and future accommodation. Meanwhile, for Jefferies, the nightly round of concerts simply meant yet more work in terms of carrying out auditions, finding artistes, planning the concerts and acting as accompanist, night after night, weekends included.

For Burrows, the additional announcing and news reading responsibilities, along with a heavier press and public relations burden, must have weighed heavily, especially as he continued with his normal job as Publicity Officer for Marconi. But, for him, the imminence of the BBC with its own funding opened up prospects for ideas he had long been nurturing: proper payments for artistes; a Wireless Orchestra which would provide real concerts; a news and weather service; a more dignified start to the evening's programme with a replication of Big Ben; and of course, hopefully, a key full-time role for himself and for Jefferies in the new organisation, backed up by suitable staffing. In all this, he would not be disappointed. (Burrows to H W Allen, Joint General Manager, Marconi, 31 January 1922; White to Burrows, 27 September 1922; Burrows to Isaacs, 5 December 1922 *Marconi Archives*.)

Initiating the Public into the Mysteries of Wireless

By September 1922 a national broadcasting service seemed imminent. Even those most intimately concerned with the formation of the BBC fully expected that 2LO's 'concerts' would be announced as 'BBC Concerts' by the end of the month. George Pells, Secretary to the 'Company', drafted a letter at Marconi House on 2 October requesting editors of the various 'Dailies' to state that 'the British Broadcasting Company have arranged for a series of wireless concerts to be radiated from a London transmitting station during the period of the first All-British Wireless Exhibition.' (draft letter, *Marconi Archives*). Whilst Pells was jumping the gun, broadcasting was very much in the air, with 2LO providing almost daily transmissions, 2MT popularising broadcasting with its unique weekly transmissions and the much more powerful Hague transmitting station PCGG focussing its concerts on England now that it had financial support from the *Daily Mail*.

Indeed, the *Daily Mail* was at the forefront in keeping the public in touch with developments. The paper announced that it would promote wireless as it had promoted motoring and flying. 'Watch the *Daily Mail* for the latest developments of Wireless and the latest news of broadcasting' was its exhortation, set out in a half page advertisement in one of the new technical periodicals (*Popular Wireless*, 3 June 1922). In addition to Associated Newspapers (*Daily Mail/Evening News*), the *Daily News, Daily Express, Evening Standard, Westminster Gazette* and the *Provincial Liverpool Courier* all took a special interest in broadcasting and Jefferies was instructed to send complete programmes to their Editors for publication (minute 25, September 1922 *Marconi Archives*). Among the popular magazines, *'TitBits'* published articles on broadcasting in 1922; its Editor, Leonard Crocombe, was to become the first Editor of the *Radio Times* in September 1923.

But was the public ready for the wireless service? Whilst it might keep the public informed, the national and provincial press had to draw the line when it came to initiating readers into the mysteries of wireless. They had to concede that this was a job that only the technical press could perform.

Unfortunately, in the early months of 1922 amateurs and the newly interested public had little more than the publishing house 'Wireless Press', of Henrietta Street, Strand, to fall back on. The Wireless Press had served an earlier generation, before the war, but had, on the whole, simply been soldiering on. It was authoritative and had produced the first textbooks; those by

J C Hawkhead and R D Bangay, 'Old Hawkhead and Bangay', were still being sold after the War. In April 1913 it had also produced the first wireless journal, *Wireless World*, priced 3d and issued monthly. That became a fortnightly periodical in April 1920 to meet increased demand, especially from those men who had been in touch with wireless whilst in the Services and who, returning to civilian life, continued with it as a hobby. But even this did not suffice; from April 1922 *Wireless World* was published weekly at 6d, its title now widened to '*Wireless World* and *Radio Review.*'

But the Wireless Press failed to appreciate the new overwhelming demand from the 'man in the street' for basic information and for guidance on how to build one's own set. Spotting this potential market, several well-known publishing houses launched specialist periodicals in mid 1922. First off the mark was the Amalgamated press with its aptly named *Popular Wireless Weekly*. This made its debut on 3 June 1922 priced at 3d, its yellow cover with blue title and photograph catching the eye, as it lay on the bookstall. It claimed to be 'A New Paper for All' and to be packed with pictures and expert advice. Wireless questions would be answered by post.

Hot on the heels of the Amalgamated press venture came Cassells' *Amateur Wireless and Electrics*. It, too, was a weekly priced at 3d, but its presentation was rather more workmanlike. The first number, issued on 10 June, made no claims and its black and white cover simply listed its contents. It, too, offered to answer the reader's questions individually and to 'bring before him the announcements of the traders in this special industry whose goods he (the reader) will naturally be pleased to hear about'.

Odhams was the next publisher to enter the field at this time with *The Broadcaster: The Radiophone Monthly for Listeners-in*. At 1/- a month, this periodical was decidedly upmarket. Delightful colour covers by Guy Lipscombe depicted happy well-heeled families sitting round multi-valve sets equipped with loudspeaker horns. The periodical gave an overwhelming impression of being newsy but was weak on the technical side. It did not sell well and was soon discontinued.

Though undoubtedly appealing and helpful, none of these periodicals met the real demand, which was for step-by-step substantial yet affordable technical guidance. But the opportunity to fill this yawning gap was not to last. A new publishing phenomenon burst on to the wireless scene in July 1922. This was the Radio Press. From its offices in Devereux Court, just off the Strand, a sequence of affordable books came flowing forth, each hitting the target in terms of the needs and opportunities of the market. The books were planned

The first practical wireless magazine to be published, 3 June 1922.

essentially for those who 'desired to fit up a home wireless set' - as simple as that. Each little volume formed part of a series and took the reader one step further, starting with the assumption that he knew nothing whatever about the technical side or even about elementary electricity. By September 1922 the following series had appeared:

Wireless for All
Simplified Wireless
Construction of Wireless Receiving Apparatus
Wireless Valves simply Explained

Wireless for All sold 20,000 copies in its first week. At 6d, it cost little more than a periodical. Indeed none of the volumes in the series cost more than 2s6d. *Construction of Wireless Receiving Apparatus* cost 1s6d and was already in its third edition within a month or two of initial publication. For the man who was really determined to get to the bottom of it all, there was John Scott-Taggart's *Elementary Textbook on Wireless Vacuum Tubes*. This cost 10s0d but provided the last word on the subject of wireless valves.

On the secondary matter of periodicals, the Radio Press bided its time. When, at the beginning of 1923, it entered the field, the Radio Press had a very clear picture of what was wanted and of what other periodicals were failing to provide. Not surprisingly, its monthly *Modern Wireless* and its ensuing weekly *Wireless Weekly* both met with instantaneous success.

The brain behind the Radio Press was John Scott-Taggart. Still in his mid-twenties, he was acknowledged as the country's foremost expert on valves. Whilst still a teenager, he had built a transmitter and joined the confraternity of three-letter call sign users. During the Great War, he showed both brilliance and bravery, securing a posting to the Army Research Station run by Major Rupert Stanley. There he learnt everything about valve receiving and transmitting sets. He tested these sets under battle conditions, being awarded, when aged 21, the MC at the battle of Lys. At the same time he engaged in research, publishing his results in *Wireless World*.

Scott-Taggart then obtained practical experience with the Edison Co., where he produced the first valves to be available over the counter to the public. He then joined the Radio Communication Company entering, as far as Marconi was concerned, the enemy camp. It was whilst still with the RCC and with their financial backing, that he launched the Radio Press. Having started with a 25% share holding, Scott-Taggart became sole owner in 1923. As he later wrote: 'I

129

became obsessed with the dream of getting people interested in the technicalities of radio as a hobby.' (Scott-Taggart, J, *55 years of Radio*).

The response from those who read Scott-Taggart's books and articles was overwhelming. Ever increasing numbers of informed enthusiasts appeared on the scene and, armed with a clear grasp of how to proceed, resolved to construct their own sets. Having worked out their budgets, their next step was to approach manufacturers for catalogues and dealers for a chat.

Part of the problem in 1922 lay in the embryonic state of the wireless trade. Dealers were few and far between, at least in the sense of specialist retailers, though a few sprang up in the large cities, initially selling surplus war equipment and components to experimenters. Lisle Street, just behind Leicester Square, became a focus for them in London.

The firm of McMichael, later to become central to the wireless trade, began in 1920, with McMichael selling war-surplus equipment from a stall outside his home in West Hampstead. In 1922 his main stock still comprised components and accessories, much of it by then made to his own design specifications by Hesketh of Slough. The two companies then merged and, by the time the 'First All-British Wireless Exhibition' opened, were able to offer complete receivers under the trademark 'MH' (McMichael Hesketh) though still trading as L McMichael Ltd. Their factory, initially only a timber and corrugated iron shed in Wexham Road, Slough, soon expanded (Geddes, K , *Broadcasting in Britain*, p26).

However, McMichaels was still mainly in the business of selling accessories; it claimed to hold the largest stock of ex-government wireless goods in the country, much of it 'going cheap' at one third or half of normal prices. Among this stock were headphones manufactured by S G Brown (of whom we shall shortly hear more), overhauled from ex-government wartime equipment, and Mark 3 short wave crystal receivers 'in un-issued condition'.

But McMichael's traded largely by mail order. Customers could not see the goods they were buying, let alone discuss their merits, unless they made a bus trip to the showroom at Providence Place, Kilburn, London. Birmingham was in a similar position. Goods were also available from a few others, such as 'Turnocks', being 'sent to your nearest Wireless Dealer', often on approval.

The trouble was, manufacturers needed many more dealers. A full-page advertisement in *Popular Wireless, 30 September 1922* by Rogers, Foster and Horrell of Birmingham declared: '5000 Dealers Wanted. Those tradesmen who wish to participate in the approaching boom of wireless should immediately get in touch with RFH Company'. In the same issue Fellows Magneto Co. also advertised for local agents for their products. Manufacturers were presumably looking for something better than dealers to whom wireless would be merely a sideline in unrelated establishments such as newsagents/tobacconists and chemists.

Cycle stores, with their workshops and mechanically minded proprietors were the shops most likely to take up this profitable sideline, their first contact with it often being as battery-charging depots; selling valves, components and receivers was a natural progression, the more so if the wholesaler supplying the shops' cycles also carried wireless.

Two such wholesalers were Lugtons and Brown Brothers. They had begun in bicycles, then they branched out into gramophones and records. Mainly, they supplied the smaller retailers, many of whom had little technical expertise. Lugton and Brown serviced sets for them in large well-equipped departments, which also assessed new models submitted by manufacturers before it was decided whether to stock them (Geddes, K , *Broadcasting in Britain*, pp32, 33).

In the major cities, most large department stores organised a wireless department where the public could hear the sets in action. This doubtless encouraged the sale of complete receivers, both crystal and valve sets. By far the most luxurious and purposeful was Harrods. Here, in the Electrical Department, sets could be purchased ranging from a few pounds to considerable sums, and their respective merits could be discussed at length with helpful and well qualified assistants. Harrods had a 'Wireless Lounge' where, throughout the day, one could hear whatever was 'on the air' - Croydon airport conversing with airline pilots, the Paris time signals, 2LO and so on. It was spartan fare but Harrods livened things up every now and then with sponsored 2LO concerts. For these, guests would be invited to a special reception in the Georgian Restaurant in the building. Harrods' 'Gala Nights' continued intermittently into the opening months of the BBC.

Before the advent of the BBC in December 1922 most of the trade was in components. Many constructors liked to build their own transformers, inductors, capacitors etc, although of necessity they had to buy some complete accessories such as headphones and valves. However, increasing numbers of complete sets were coming on to the market.

Among the first were the Marconiphone 'Crystal A type RB3' and its lower cost sister set, the 'Crystal Junior type RB2'. Both appeared in August 1922 carried the initials 'MWT' (Marconi Wireless Telegraph Co.), and were for headphone use. The 'Crystal-A' retailed at £9 10s 0d including aerial and earth wires. The 'Junior Crystal' cost £5 15s 0d. The 'Rolls Royce' however was the

Marconiphone Model V2. This came out in the summer of 1922 at £25. It used the revolutionary, expensive, but economical to run, Marconi-Osram dull emitters 'LT1' and 'LT3'.

Due to their lower cost, the vast majority of sets, whether purchased complete or home constructed, were crystal sets. They comprised three main elements: first, a tuned circuit connected to an aerial; secondly a very thin metal wire (the 'cats whisker') pressing against a fragment of piezoelectric crystal (forming the 'rectifier') and thirdly, a pair of headphones. The aerial was a length of wire, usually stretched from a chimney to a tree up to 100ft distant. From a point near the chimney, there would be a vertical lead-in through a window frame to the set. The headphones could not be constructed by the amateur and constituted the most expensive component, at £1.5s.0d, though high quality 'phones designed for a wide frequency range could cost double this amount. Cheapest (and worst!) were the ex-government headphones designed for Morse. On social occasions, the poor man's equivalent of a loudspeaker was an earphone at the bottom of a flower vase, which directed the output.

Valve sets were very expensive, not only in terms of initial outlay but also in running costs. A typical bright emitter valve needed a 6-volt accumulator to provide the filament current. The accumulator alone cost £2 10s 0d, and needed recharging at two to three week intervals. In addition, a high-tension battery was needed to supply the valve anode voltage. These cost about £1 and had a life of no more than three or four months. The valve itself had a limited life - about 100 hours - and cost a minimum of 15s 0d

Purchasers knew, even by mid-1922 that in the near future broadcasting stations would be established in several cities. Crystal sets were satisfactory only within about 12 miles of a transmitter; they were subject to hiss and to interference from other stations. Valve receivers were better able to separate stations, gave better quality reception and, being more powerful, could also operate a loudspeaker, allowing the whole family to listen in.

In 1922 loudspeakers were rare and extremely expensive. Examples included the straight-necked cone-like version made by S G Brown and the curve-necked 18 inch horn produced by Western Electric. More advanced was the American 'Magnavox R2B' with its 31 inch swan neck marketed by Sterling Telephone and Electric.

Whether it was complete sets or components, valve or crystal sets, aerials, headphones or batteries, the wireless trade had to feel its way in 1922 guessing what demand broadcasting might generate. Manufacturers were a new breed and had to cater for every eventuality and, with a dearth of specialised retail

INITIATING THE PUBLIC INTO THE MYSTERIES OF WIRELESS

Advertisement for Wireless Receivers. Modern Wireless, May 1923.

outlets, needed a shop-window for their products.

For their part, the set buyers and constructors needed to make direct contact with the manufacturers; catalogues and mail order were poor substitutes. The wider public, their appetite for wireless enhanced by the press, demonstrations at garden fêtes and lectures in the local halls and libraries, longed to get in on the act and to hear the 'magic little boxes' in action. The time was now ripe for a major wireless exhibition.

In September, the 'International Radio Exhibition' opened at Central Hall, Westminster. It was supported by over 40 British and Foreign manufacturers. But it was little more than a warm-up for the major exhibition held at the end of the month. This was the 'All British Wireless Exhibition' held at the Horticultural Hall, Vincent Square, London. The exhibition ran from Saturday 30 September to Saturday 7 October with a special trade day on 2 October. Admission was 1s3d except for 3 October when the more well heeled public paid 5s0d. The doors were open from 10am to 10pm. Fifty-two manufacturers - all British - took stands, as well as the Wireless Press and the Radio Press. The Wireless Society of London (WSL) arranged a series of daily lectures and provided information on local societies and clubs, over eighty of which were affiliated to the WSL - soon to be renamed the Radio Society of Great Britain (RSGB). The exhibition also provided many with their first experience of broadcasting; concerts put out from 2LO at Marconi House, London, were picked up by a powerful valve set equipped with loudspeakers which filled the hall with music. Though organised by Bertram Day, the man who brought it all together was Horace Freeman, WSL's advertisement manager.

It is not difficult to imagine the scene, especially as the Royal Horticultural Hall has changed little in the intervening years. We arrive to find a queue stretching from the entrance steps right round the corner into Elverton Street (*Wireless World*, 21 October 1922). After a tense wait we finally pass up the steps, and gain admission. We buy a catalogue for 6d and pick up a useful leaflet listing all the wireless societies scattered across Britain. The hall is filled with the sound of a bustling crowd, above which can be heard music played by a small orchestra. On all sides are stands with tasteful lettering on their fascias. In the centre is the Trade Demonstration Stand where the public can, during the day, listen in to wireless transmissions on a variety of equipment. In front of this, set in pride of place, is a 12-valve wireless set and frame aerial ready to receive 2LO. All around are various types of visitor to be seen: 'Here is our old friend the catalogue collector; there the men from the country, exhibition catalogue in hand, ticking off each item that nothing be missed; there again is the secretary from a provincial wireless club with his notebook well filled against the night when he shall have to answer innumerable questions as to what he saw at the show' (*Popular Wireless*, 21 October 1922).

Later, in the luncheon room, the talk polarises between light hearted banter and intense discussion. 'We listen to the claims of the crystal merchant and note the indulgent tolerance of the multi-valve friend.' After lunch, one of the lectures seems just the thing. Perhaps it is John Scott-Taggart on his great theme - the Thermionic Valve. Then, back to the stands. Suddenly a new sound dominates the hum in the hall and the shuffle of a thousand feet. It's 2LO broadcasting from Marconi House! 'Mr Rodney Bennett will sing "In Summertime on Bredon", by Peel.' This is followed by another song. Mr Charles Cory then attempts to entertain over the loudspeakers. Miss Olive Sturgess takes up the challenge. Not every visitor is thrilled with 2LO's soprano. Most simply want to wallow in the wireless, to handle the apparatus and to discuss technical niceties with the experts on the stands. Some were anxious to learn, others perhaps to show-off. A few are full of apprehension as they fork out a lot of money on apparatus and components with which they will have to struggle once home, not withstanding detailed printed instructions accompanying each item. Eventually, footsore and weary, and weighed down with apparatus, catalogue, books, umbrella and briefcase, most find the tea room overwhelmingly tempting. It provides welcome refreshment and a last opportunity to check for any stands so far missed or worth a second visit.

All in all the Exhibition provided a unique opportunity to make useful comparisons as to both quality and price. Indeed the poor bemused would-be customers were spoiled for choice. Every other stand seemed to be displaying complete sets - both crystal and valve - that did not exist a month or two earlier. The radio industry had suddenly sprung into life and was determined to impress.

Most exotic and expensive were the cabinet sets, often to period design, which enclosed not only the valves, batteries etc but also a loudspeaker. These were to be seen on at least five stands, including Wales, Elwell, and Telephone Manufacturing - their set retailed at 100 guineas! Two manufacturers offered a 'Radiogram' in which the loudspeaker could serve both the wireless set and an incorporated gramophone deck. No less then twenty-five stands displayed valve sets and five had 'unit' sets, which could be built up incrementally. By comparison only 14 offered crystal sets in their promotional material, one of the cheapest being J B Bower's at £3 15s0d. Even for crystal sets, several manufacturers expected customers to purchase a valve amplifier to increase the output from the crystal.

Telephone Manufacturing broke new ground with a 'permanent crystal detector.' This overcame the troublesome process of randomly prodding the

STATEMENT.

9th November 1922

Marconi's Wireless Telegraph Company, Limited,

To Broadcasting Demonstrations.

To Payments to the following artists:

Mr. John Huntington.	10	6
Miss Eileen King Turner.	1 1	-
Miss Olive Sturgess.	10	6
Mr. Rex Faithfull.	10	6
£	2 12	6

SETTLED.
9 NOV 1922
By Cheque
No. A 6206-7-8-9

Signed Arthur R. Burrows

Reproduced by permission of the Marconi Co. Ltd

Statement of payments to artistes, 2LO London.

cat's whisker on to the crystal for a strong signal as well as adjusting the tuning for the desired station; the operator was, instead, left with just the tuning adjustment. Rogers, Foster and Howell had ideas of portable sets to be taken on walks and drives. They offered a 'knapsack receiver' and experimented with car radio.

Quality headphones and loudspeakers were to be seen on several stands - S G Brown, Alfred Graham, Sterling Telephone and Electrical, and Western Electric. Alfred Graham and Fellows Magneto supplied headphones for ladies, these being carefully designed so as not to mar their clients' coiffure as they listened in.

Some of the nation's biggest electrical companies, dazzled by the success of their American counterparts, decided to get in on the act right on the very eve of broadcasting. Among them, Metropolitan-Vickers displayed 'Cosmos' sets on their stand, General Electric offered 'Gecophones' and the Radio Communication Company offered 'Polar' sets. But they had, with the exception of General Electric, no experience in producing household goods and lacked suitable outlets. Marconi, rather than getting involved with producing domestic products, contracted with Plessey to produce their 'Marconiphone' range.

The question of tuning absorbed the attention of many manufacturers. Normally a variometer (coupled inductors which could be moved in relation to each other) or cylindrical inductor coils with a slider or tappings were employed. For valve receivers a more expensive variable capacitor with semi-circular metal vanes was generally used. For those who wished to pick up stations beyond the normal 'Broadcast Band', interchangeable plug-in tuning coils were available. British Wireless Supply displayed their 'Britware Coils'; Garnbrell showed their high quality coils whilst Harwell displayed their variometer. Igranic Electrical offered their patent honeycomb coils. Nine stands displayed capacitors, Anode Wireless claiming a 'new type' variable capacitor, as did J A Coomes.

With so many valve sets on show, the valve makers made sure they too had stands. Mullard and Cossor were represented, with MC valves. The former company also proudly displayed their 'dull-emitter' valve. Unlike the bright emitter receiver valve, then in universal use, the dull-emitter valve saved a great deal of low voltage current, allowing accumulators to last much longer between charges. But the dull-emitter valve was expensive and still very much the valve of the future.

Accumulator manufacturers were represented by Hart Accumulator who had just inaugurated a re-charging service for the convenience of their customers in outlying areas. For 6d a time, the used accumulator would be collected and swapped for a re-charged one, the customer, of course, having initially to purchase an accumulator from Hart (Hill, Jonathan, *Radio! Radio*, p41). Battery producers were also in evidence at the Exhibition with 'Every Ready' and with Chloride Electrical's 'Exide' batteries.

Accessories and components could be inspected on the stands but hardly had pride of place. Firms such as British Wireless Supply, Gamages, Radio Instruments, Wireless Equipment, Pettigrew and Merrimon, Stanley Prince, Radio Service and, of course, McMichael catered for this kind of demand. Wartime equipment was still being recycled, McMichael's reconditioned headphones and Wireless Equipment's components being cases in point. Wireless Equipment's supplier was a young man of 17. He lived at Southsea, Portsmouth, hard by a whole arsenal of ex-service junk including valves going dirt-cheap. Wireless Equipment offered to take all he could supply. The enterprising young man was L E (Len) Newnham who later became President of the RSGB (Author in telephone conversation with Len Newnham, June 1991).

Part of the joy of the exhibition was that huge quantities of goods could be seen and handled and listened to without any feeling that one's enquiries were expected to lead to a purchase. By the close on 7 October, 25,000 had come to witness the miracle of wireless and to sense the new world it could open up for them right there by their own fireside. The long winter evenings beckoned, as did the imminent prospect of a nightly national broadcasting service. Before the year was out, father and son would be rivalling each other in technical expertise and Christmas would not be got through without the purchase of at least a set of components from which to construct a crystal receiver.

The show closed with the historic event mentioned earlier - the Prince of Wales's message to scouts, many of whom helped pack the hall for this first Royal broadcast. Within a few days the Prince had his own set. Wireless was no longer simply the hobby of a few amateur experimenters. It was a new industry set to capture the home market. As manufacturers jockeyed for position, interest spread like wildfire. The 'All-British' Exhibition had done more than anything else to fan the blaze.

5

Electrical Giants Enter the Field

Electrical Giants form a British Broadcasting Company

In April 1922 the *Wireless World* reported an interview with Godfrey Isaacs, managing director of Marconi, in which Mr Isaacs foresaw wireless sets in every home, allowing 'important announcements to reach all parts of the country along with talks, music, weather, news etc.' He envisaged 'broad-casting' stations (*sic*), for example two or three in different parts of the country, with programmes for different hours of the day. These would go out on particular wavelengths capable of being received only by those who hired suitable receivers. The design of the receivers would vary according to their distance from the transmitting station. Costs would be covered by the hiring charges, which would be a 'modest amount per annum'. Alternatively, sets could be purchased but might quickly become dated. 'I do not think', added Mr Isaacs, 'that anybody realises how big a thing this is going to be'. So far as the Marconi Company was concerned, everything was ready for going ahead both with broadcasting and the supply of sets. 'The moment the necessary authority can be obtained, the project will be put into operation'. Asked whether broadcasting might not lead to competition with the newspapers, he pointed out that the services of the daily press would 'not be interfered with in any way' (*Wireless World*, 29 April 1922).

The interview marked a turning point in British thinking. The very term 'broadcasting' in the radio sense was entirely new to British ears and, even in America where services on the lines described by Isaacs had begun to take off, 'broadcasting' was very much the new buzz word of 1922. Isaac's vision was new in that it was 'entertainment' orientated and 'mass market'. The service was not, he thought, concerned (like Writtle, Chelmsford) to help a limited band of amateurs improve their apparatus; its provision would be universal. As such, it would encourage the development of a whole new industry. In short, Isaacs had outlined the basis for a national broadcasting service.

What was also significant about the interview was the fact that the vision of the future was one which its prophet was himself capable of bringing about. For Isaacs, as Managing Director, could bring the whole resources of Marconi to bear on the new enterprise. Marconi already possessed the expertise and the patents to create the new stations and to manufacture a suitable range of receivers in quantity. Isaacs did not appear to envisage any serious competition from other manufacturers. But in this, he was to be proved wrong.

He also gave the impression that he envisaged that the gaining of approval for the new service would be a straightforward operation. In this too, he was mistaken. It is true that, in the twenties, private enterprise operated in a capitalist world largely free from governmental control, government and industry each operating in separate spheres. But with broadcasting, matters would take on a totally different complexion. Government and industry would be locked together in an unprecedented way, leading ultimately to a new type of a British institution - the Corporation. The procedures leading to gaining government approval were to be lengthy and fraught.

Isaacs also underestimated the cost and complexity of providing the broadcasting service. Hire charges at 'modest costs' might conceivably cover the provision of sets but, in 1922 the needs of the service had not begun to be grasped.

Finally, Isaacs airily dismissed the question of competition with the national press. The press would not treat the matter so lightly. They were to present their case at the end of 1922 when everyone else had thought the matter of the broadcasting service was finally settled. press antagonism against the BBC continued well into 1923 with the government more often than not ready to make concessions to the press barons even though this meant clipping the wings of the BBC.

But if Isaacs did not foresee the difficulties that lay ahead, he had foreseen a national broadcasting service and made it clear that it had the backing of a major - *the major* - manufacturer in the field. He had been to America and witnessed just how profitable the sale of wireless receivers could be. Even as he talked to *Wireless World* reporters, his firm was applying to the Postmaster General for authorisation to launch broadcasting as we know it.

As has been indicated, Marconi was not alone in all this. Other major electrical manufacturers had close ties with America and were conscious of the boom in sales over there. They too sought to establish broadcasting services in Britain. Foremost among these was Metropolitan-Vickers. In 1921 A P M Fleming, head of Metrovick Research, had visited the States hard on the heels of Isaacs. Another visit was made in June 1922. Fleming was able to study the broadcasting stations operated by the American Westinghouse Company and their factories producing radio equipment. In America Westinghouse was in the lead in broadcasting matters and had much experience and information to offer the visiting Briton. Fleming's firm was the successor to British Westinghouse which had been founded by the promoter of the American company of the same name back in 1899. Fleming therefore had privileged entrée to all Westinghouse could show him.

He found broadcasting in America lively but chaotic; practically anybody could set up a station - electrical companies, department stores, universities, public bodies, newspapers. The only constraints appeared to be stipulations as to wavelength - 360 metres was allocated - and power, with a 1.5-kilowatt limit. By June 1922 there were 370 or more stations, these being mainly in the eastern States and on the Pacific slope, all operating with little or no co-ordination. But a US Government conference of interested parties was arranged in Washington in March 1922 and a Bill had been prepared, designed to give wider powers over the control of wireless to the Secretary of the Department of Commerce. Fleming must surely have been comforted with the thought that the Postmaster General would never allow such conditions to develop in Britain.

But this did not mean we had nothing to learn in that area from the States. Among the myriad stations, 25 or so stood out as particularly well organised with regular programmes announced in advance in the press. Among them were three Westinghouse stations - KDKA East Pittsburgh, WJZ Newark and KYW Chicago. Along with these, Fleming visited the stations of the *Detroit News* and the *Detroit Free press*. These two stations co-ordinated their broadcasting and both used Westinghouse equipment. Another station visited was the Federal Electric Company's station at Buffalo.

Typically, programmes would start with a daily menu suggestion for women, followed by the weather at 10am. In the afternoon, talks for women were laid on and in the early evening a bedtime story for children. There would be an evening concert interspersed with a talk and ending with the Arlington time signal at 10pm. It was a formula largely adopted in Britain a year or so later. There had emerged, within a few months, a taste for serious matter, educational and health talks becoming increasingly popular.

Programmes were not limited to the studio. America had already pioneered 'Outside Broadcasts' by linking churches, theatres, and sports stadia to the transmitter by wire. KDKA sent out live commentaries on the Davis Cup tennis matches in 1921 and broadcast on Sundays from the local Episcopal Church. WJZ Newark broadcast live baseball matches and KYW Chicago transmitted from the stage of the Chicago Opera House.

But there were ominous signs, later to be replicated in Britain. Artistes, hitherto prepared to give their services in return for the advertisement afforded, were soon prohibited from so doing by their professional associations. Theatre and gramophone receipts were said to be affected by broadcasting. Even if the broadcasters could get some co-operation, the cost of paid artistes was likely to be high, and would have to be added to that of any resident Wireless Orchestra. A 10-piece orchestra could amount to $25,000 a year (about £5000).

Other important financial lessons for Britain were the cost of establishing and maintaining a station of any importance. The station could cost $50,000 to set up. With a staff of 9 to 15, it could cost $90,000 per annum to operate and maintain. Under a General Manager there would be engineering staff at the transmitter and at the downtown studio; there would also be Outside Broadcast engineers. Programme staff would include announcers working, like the engineers, in shifts; also needed would be staff to devise programmes and attend to press publicity.

On the technical side we had much to learn. American broadcasters had already encountered acoustic problems and were lining studio walls to absorb any undue reverberation. Advances had already been made in microphone design, with carbon button and capacitor microphones that could be distanced from the artiste or orchestra, so making the problem of 'balance' less acute. In this, Westinghouse was in the forefront. Some stations had separate studios for the spoken word and for music, each purpose designed.

Again, on the manufacturing side, America had much to teach Britain. Whilst there existed a vast proliferation of manufacturing companies along with a patent situation that was obscure and complicated, the leading manufacturers had agreed to pool their patents, lodging them with the Radio Corporation of America (RCA) which thereupon acted as their selling agents. In this way, the patent problem was overcome and any British Marconi patent interests were fended off. Prime movers in all this were Westinghouse, General Electric and the US Government. Small manufacturers were not permitted to use patents for which they were not licensed. Much time could have been saved during British negotiations to set up a broadcasting service if the companies concerned had at the outset pooled their patents.

Another lesson for Britain was the seasonal variation in the sale of wireless sets. The main boom period in the US was from December 1921 to April 1922 when demand outstripped the supply. By June, stagnation had set in. A year later, in mid-1923, the same cycle would occur in Britain, affecting sets sold by 'BBC members' and reducing the licences and royalties on which the BBC's financial support depended; no advance planning was done to cater for such an eventuality.

There was, however, a much more crucial lesson, one sadly overlooked by the Post Office in 1922 when devising the otherwise ingenious basis for the future BBC's finance. The British approach stipulated that royalties and public licence charges would only be payable on sets approved by the Postmaster General and produced by BBC member firms. In exchange, those firms would be granted a monopoly on the sale of sets. Yet Fleming had noted that in the US the most striking thing in connection with radio sales was not complete sets so much as the supply of component parts. At first, Westinghouse sold complete sets at a price so high as to give ample margin for the small manufacturer who began to flood the market doing business through hardware stores, opticians, drugs stores, photographic suppliers and even in the '5,10, and 25 cent' stores! From such suppliers it was also possible to secure the component parts for assembling a crystal set, with the sole exception of the headphones. Soon, even Westinghouse was supplying parts for home construction and on such a scale as to account for 40% of the total value of its sales of radio equipment. In Britain, the home constructors, whilst acting fully within the law, would unwittingly be barred from financially supporting the BBC as, not having approved sets, they could not legally apply for licences and so paid no fees.

Few of these considerations however appeared to weigh very much in Fleming's mind when in March 1922 he prepared his case for a Metropolitan-Vickers station in Britain. Like Isaacs, he had seen broadcasting mushroom in the US and saw no reason why it should not do so in Britain. It was mainly a matter of persuading the Postmaster General to give the green light, or so he thought.

Of more immediate concern to Fleming was the need to circumvent the Marconi patent network. Unless this could be done, no Metrovick station could operate even if the Postmaster General did give his blessing. One other leading British company, the Radio Communication Company (RCC), had managed to steer clear of Marconi's patent stranglehold and one of its directors, Captain Hilton, happened to be managing director of Metrovick. Taking a leaf from America's RCA lead, the two British companies arranged to pool their patents and established an agreement as to the sale of receivers. Fleming's opposite number in RCC was Basil Binyon. Together they planned two stations, one to broadcast from the Metrovick works at Trafford Park, Manchester, the other to be constructed at the RCC plant in Slough, 23 miles west of central London.

Having sorted out their own arrangements for co-operation, the next step was to meet F J Brown of the Post Office; there was no time to be lost. As Binyon pointed out 'Several other parties had already made application to the Post Office'. His caution made sense. The meeting was fixed for 30 March at

11.30am. On the preceding day, Fleming and Binyon met to rehearse the line of argument they would put to Brown (Binyon to Fleming, 27 March 1922, BBC Archives).

Their case was presented under innumerable headings and probably contained little that was new to Brown, who not only served as the leading spokesman for the Post Office on broadcasting matters, but was himself familiar with American conditions. He had just returned from the States after attending a conference organised by Herbert Hoover of the US Government, called to sort out the chaotic state of broadcasting in that country. The last thing that Brown was likely to do was to acquiesce in individual company proposals to set up a broadcasting service. The Metrovick/RCC application of 31 March was soon followed by others - five in April, fifteen in May. The reply from the Post Office in each case was that 'the ether is already full'. But even the Post Office realised it could not hold back, Canute-like, the demand for a national broadcasting service and the commercial pressures that lay behind this demand. It would, however, be necessary 'to lay down very drastic regulations' at the outset (Briggs, Asa, *History of Broadcasting in the United Kingdom:* Vol I, p85 and p68, 1961).

The Postmaster General at this time was F G Kellaway. Kellaway lost no time in announcing that the whole question of broadcasting would be referred to the Imperial Communications Committee; in short, the pro-broadcasting lobby would find itself up against the military and those responsible for international communications, both official and commercial. It was going to be a long haul.

In April 1922 the Wireless Sub-Committee of the Imperial Communications Committee set out its initial proposals. These can be summarised as follows:

> Broadcasting to be on 440 metres (later changed to 350-425 metres)
> The power of each station to be limited to 1.5 kilowatts
> An embargo on advertising
> Only news already printed to be broadcast
> Programmes limited to music, entertainment, education and religion
>   (later widened)
> Hours of programmes limited to 5pm to midnight (later changed by
>   the Postmaster General to 11pm)
> Government communiqués to be broadcast if required

The arrangements between the Post Office and manufacturers to be provisional and so subject to adjustment in the light of experience.

It was Colonel Simpson of Marconi who pressed for a wavelength band of 350-425 metres, adding that within this band six to eight broadcasting stations could operate with a view to covering the country. The Sub-Committee went along with these ideas subject to approval by the Post Office of station locations in different parts of Britain. On 4 May 1922 the Postmaster General announced that the Government accepted the proposals of the Wireless Sub-Committee. He decided the new broadcasting stations were to be situated in:

London
Birmingham
Manchester
Newcastle
Cardiff
Glasgow or Edinburgh (Glasgow was later chosen)
Plymouth (Bournemouth was later substituted)
Aberdeen

One or more stations were to be permitted at each location but only British manufacturers of wireless apparatus would be allowed to run these stations. Newspapers, department stores and local authorities were barred from doing so.

In little more than a month, the basis for broadcasting had been set out, a remarkable achievement in Civil Service/Government terms. But it left open the key question as to who was to do the broadcasting in each area. The Post Office did not want one firm to dominate and so create a virtual monopoly. At the same time, it did not want a proliferation of agencies; already over twenty wireless firms had shown interest. Nor did it want to appear to favour particular firms by selecting them from the rest. Kellaway's solution was to ask all the interested wireless firms to meet in the hope that they would begin to sort things out among themselves and come up with an acceptable proposition.

The Post Office made its position clear and fully expected the manufacturers to reach a speedy conclusion as to how the new service would be financed and implemented. It was, after all, in their interest to do so. Three months earlier Brown had noted how, in the US, Westinghouse were selling sets at a rate of 25,000 a month and were unable to meet the demand. But to meet the Post Office stipulations, manufacturers would collectively have to set up one or more broadcasting companies and co-operate among themselves to secure the successful maintenance of the new company or companies. Only in this way could a broadcasting service operate. In short, such a service would be independent of any one manufacturer.

The manufacturers met on 23 May 1922 at the Institution of Electrical Engineers, choosing Frank Gill as their chairman. Gill was President of the Institution and much respected. He, along with his successor, Sir William Noble, seemed to have a clear, non-partisan view of how broadcasting should be organised. He attended the meeting armed with a paper in which he had set out the key issues to be settled. Rather than attempting to reach agreement, the manufacturers appointed a 'Big Six' committee to go into all matters relating to setting up broadcasting stations and running the service.

The 'Big Six' committee was made up of representatives of the six largest electrical firms interested in broadcasting. These were Marconi, General Electric, British Thomson-Houston, Metropolitan-Vickers, Radio Communication Company and Western Electric. So that the smaller manufacturers had a voice, Frank Phillips of Burndept was also asked to join in the 'Big Six' negotiations.

Again, Gill prepared a paper, this time for the 'Big Six' meeting on 25 May. The key matters included:

> Patents applying to broadcasting.
> Organisation of the broadcasting company including its name.
> Holdings in the company by the 'Big Six' and by the smaller firms.
> Directors of the company.
> The revenue needed.

Most notable in all this was Gill's assumption that there would be a single broadcasting company, albeit one financed by radio manufacturers both large and small.

The broadcasting company would therefore not be a monopoly in any commercial sense. In this sense it would simply promote the wireless trade generally and do so efficiently. The 'Big Six' began to put flesh on the bones provided by the Post Office:

> The company would be named the 'British Broadcasting Company' - the BBC.

It would have a capital of £100,000 in cumulative ordinary shares with the 'Big Six' providing £60,000, other member firms providing up to £40,000

Dividends limited to 10 per cent (Reduced by the Postmaster-General to 7.5 per cent).

The Post Office to approve for sale to the public only those receivers made by members of the British Broadcasting Company; such sets would be marked 'BBC'.

The BBC to receive the proceeds of a royalty on the sale of receivers made by its member firms.

The BBC to receive a share of an annual 10-shilling licence fee paid to the Post Office by those possessing receivers (Post Office agreed to a 50% share) (Briggs Asa, *History of Broadcasting in the United Kingdom*. Vol I, pp110/111, 1961).

But all was not sweetness and light. The question arose as to who would build the broadcasting stations. To Gill, this was 'relatively unimportant'. Indeed, it may have seemed so to more than one of the 'Big Six'. Marconi's representative, Isaacs, did not agree; he insisted that only his firm had the technical expertise and patents necessary for the purpose. He could point to the hurriedly constructed London station, 2LO, which had just been tested a fortnight earlier. As though anticipating the Marconi stand, Metropolitan-Vickers under Fleming's direction had built a small 50-watt station at the works at Trafford Park, Manchester. They were determined to show they too had broadcasting capability. Amid considerable publicity, the 50-watt set had been demonstrated on the 17 May 1922 with some readings from newspapers and a few gramophone records. It had been nothing but a gesture, but enough for Metrovick's representative, Archibald McKinstry, to show he need not yield to Isaacs. In this, he had the support of Basil Binyon of the Radio Communication Company and of H M Pease of Western Electric. Gill pleaded for a united front so that the manufacturers could negotiate with the Post Office from a position of strength. But he could not break the deadlock and had to report to the Manufacturers' Committee and to the Post Office that two broadcasting companies might have to be considered.

There was, however, agreement among the 'Big Six' that member firms would only sell sets made in Britain and that these should bear the registered trademark of the broadcasting company (or companies) and be individually approved by the Post Office before manufacture began.

The Post Office went along with the arrangements sought by the 'Big Six' and the Manufacturers' Committee, even to the extent of being prepared to accept two broadcasting companies despite all the problems this would raise in terms of allocating wavelengths and districts and having a duplicate London station. 2LO London had by now begun a whole series of experimental programmes starting with a 'concert' at the end of June. Not to be completely outdone, the Metrovick/RCC/Western Electric consortium appointed a 'Director of Programmes' at £400 per annum with a view, presumably, to initiating its own series of experimental programmes. The man appointed was a Metrovick employee named Cecil Lewis who was later to become one of the BBC's first appointees along with Reith and Burrows. Lewis' role was, however, nipped in the bud, for Isaacs (Marconi) and McKinstry (Metrovick) finally saw sense and agreed to a single broadcasting company. This was, however, subject to Marconi building six of the eight stations and the appointment of a 'neutral' chairman for the new BBC, terms which McKinstry was ready to accept. The two non-Marconi stations were to be Manchester (Metrovick/RCC) and Birmingham (Western Electric). The consortium had only expected to have three stations anyway, the third being in London (Metrovick to Fleming, 12 July 1922).

Thus it was that at their meeting on 8 August, the manufacturers could at last agree to appoint a solicitor to draw up the Memorandum and Articles of Association to establish the British Broadcasting Company. The solicitor, Frank Gaylor, was assisted by George Pells of Marconi who acted as temporary Secretary (Briggs, Asa, *History of Broadcasting in the United Kingdom.* Vol I, p120, 1961).

By now, Sir William Noble had taken over from Gill as chairman of the Manufacturers' Committee. Noble had held high office at the Post Office before taking up a post with the General Electric Company, one of the 'Big Six'. It was Noble who was to watch over the birth of the British Broadcasting Company throughout the remaining months of 1922. With substantial agreement having been reached both among the manufacturers and between them and the Post Office, Noble's committee came to be renamed the 'Broadcasting Committee'. It was actually this committee, rather than the British Broadcasting Company, which launched the first 'BBC' programmes, appointed the first officers of the BBC, and negotiated with the press over the supply of news for broadcasting. In all this, Noble was the driving force and it was Noble who took up the matter of finding a suitable 'neutral' chairman. With this in mind, he wrote to Lord Gainford, assuring him that the duties 'would not be arduous' (Binyon to Fleming, 27 March 1922 and Noble to Gainford, 22 August 1922, *BBC Archives*). Gainford replied with a hand-written letter to say he accepted the 'kind invitation of those interested in the British Broadcasting Company Ltd to become their Chairman'. Gainford was not lacking credentials for the position; he had had a brief spell as Postmaster-General back in 1916 and was a respected public figure.

A notice was sent out on 13 October, under the title 'BROADCASTING', announcing a general meeting of manufacturers of broadcasting apparatus to be held at the Institution of Electrical Engineers on 18 October 1922 when they would receive a report from the Broadcasting Committee. On the same day an advertisement appeared in the newspapers seeking candidates for the first posts in the new BBC. The meeting underpinned the advertisement; Noble told the 200 or so assembled manufacturers that 'complete agreement with the Postmaster-General had been reached'. The manufacturers thereupon welcomed the creation of the new British Broadcasting Company with Lord Gainford as its chairman. They duly ratified the draft Memorandum and Articles of Association prepared by Gaylor. The Company could now be registered (Briggs, Asa, *History of Broadcasting in the United Kingdom*. Vol I, p127, 1961).

The *Daily News* announced 'Full Speed Ahead: Radio Era to open at last'. It reported that the meeting had formally approved a scheme for registering the company. The registration was 'only a week away' and BBC broadcasting would thereupon commence. This would include 'news, information, concerts, lectures, speeches, educational matter, weather reports, theatrical entertainments, etc'. The *Daily Mail*, normally at the forefront of wireless development, referred somewhat archaically to registering 'one Broadcast Wireless Telephone Company'. It forecast the BBC programmes would commence on 1 November. In this, the paper was following a tip-off by Noble (*Daily News/Daily Mail*, 19 October 1922).

The new Broadcast Licence duly went on sale at post offices on 1 November and sets began to appear with the 'BBC' mark from that date. Indeed the ten-shilling Broadcast Licence carried an overprint in red saying APPARATUS USED UNDER THIS LICENCE MUST BE MARKED 'BBC: TYPE APPROVED BY POSTMASTER-GENERAL'. On the back were set out seven conditions, several of which seem to hark back to 1914. 'This licence may be cancelled at any time by means of a General Notice in the London Gazette'; and 'the Licensee shall not divulge any message received by means of the station (i.e. the radio set) other than time signals, musical performances and messages transmitted for general reception'. The licence was valid for up to a year but had to be renewed at the beginning of the quarter in which it was taken out.

Broadcast Licences did not replace the Experimenters' Licences, which had been introduced three years earlier. These too cost 10 shillings and were valid for up to a year. They too carried conditions; these were more stringent with respect to who could take out such a licence but less stringent as to the type of apparatus used and as to whether it was of British origin. To ensure the experimental apparatus would not cause any interference, applicants had, however, to submit details which were checked by officials acting for the Postmaster-General; only then would be a formal licence be issued. From November 1922 the Experimenters' Licence carried an extra stipulation designed to prevent interference with BBC Programmes during broadcasting hours. Up to 31 March 1922 7,690 Experimental Licences had been issued and by 31 October, this number had increased by a further 10,371. In November/December 6,140 Experimental Licences were issued; the comparable figure for broadcast licences was 12,105. In the first quarter of 1923, 11,184 Experimental Licences were issued as against 75,456 Broadcast Licences. Thus, by 31 March 1923 there were some 35,000 experimental and 87,000 Broadcast Licences. The former number would have been 33,000 higher had not the Postmaster-General begun to take a strict line with those applicants merely constructing sets from components in order to listen-in to the BBC (*Figures provided by General Post Office, 19 April 1923*).

On 10 October 1922 the conditions which 'broadcast receivers' had to fulfil were set out. The major concern was to eliminate the possibility of interference with other users. For this purpose manufacturers, who had to be members of the BBC, sent a sample of each type of set to the Post Office along with the relevant wiring diagrams so that it could be checked before being approved. On approval, the set was given a registration number and the manufacturers had to mark all similar sets with this number as well as with the 'BBC: TYPE APPROVED BY POSTMASTER-GENERAL' roundel. The Post Office allocated three digit registration numbers to crystal sets. Four digit numbers starting with 1,000 were allocated to one valve sets; those starting with 2,000 were for two valve sets. The '3,000' series was reserved for low frequency amplifiers. Valves, headphones and loudspeakers, like sets, had to be of British manufacture and made by a member firm of the BBC. They too bore the roundel mark.

THE COMPANIES ACTS, 1908 to 1917.

COMPANY LIMITED BY SHARES.

The British Broadcasting Company
LIMITED.

Memorandum
— AND —
Articles of Association.

Incorporated the 15th day of December, 1922.

Steadman, Van Praagh & Gaylor,
4, Old Burlington Street, W.1.

THE ELECTRIC LAW PRESS LTD., PUBLIC COMPANY PRINTERS, LONDON, W.C.1.

The BBC was incorporated on Friday 15 December 1922.

It was open to any British manufacturer of wireless apparatus to become a member of the BBC and so be able to sell sets to the public. The only stipulations were the deposit of £50 (returnable) and the taking out of at least one share in the BBC. These became available when the BBC prospectus was issued early in 1923. The member had to pay royalties to the BBC for each piece of apparatus sold:

Crystal set	7s.6d.
Crystal set with one valve	£1.7s.6d.
Crystal set with two valves	£2.2s.6d.
One valve set	£1.0s.0d.
Two valve set	£1.15s.0d.
On each additional valve	10s.0d.
Low frequency amplifier: per valve	10s.0d.
Loudspeaker	3s.0d.

Royalties were even paid on headphones and individual valves.

Share certificate No. 11 signed by Noble, Binyon and Anderson, 8 March 1923.

The member firm had to provide a monthly statement to the BBC showing sales during the preceding month along with a remittance for the royalties due; the first statement was, however, to cover November and December 1922. The member had to permit the BBC to use without charge any patents which related to broadcast transmission. The agreement between the BBC and its member firms was to last as long as the BBC's own licence. The licence gave the BBC freedom to broadcast to the end of 1924 and protected the British manufacturers from foreign imports during this period. The small member firms were to be represented on the BBC board; 9 seats were available, of which the Board's chairman and the 'Big Six' occupied seven leaving two for elected representatives of the smaller firms. By May 1923 these numbered over 250 and continued to rise rapidly, the number doubling inside a fortnight. Many would have joined the BBC before share allotments started on 8 March.

The Agreement made between the BBC and its member firms constituted one of the three key elements embodied in the BBC scheme, the others being the 'Memorandum and Articles of Association', establishing the BBC as a registered Company and the Licence granted to the Company by the -General. But before this Licence could be signed and sealed, the Newspaper interests had to be consulted and won round. Without this, there could be no news; and without the news, the BBC's nightly programme service was not, in any meaningful sense, ready to commence. In this respect, the deadline of 1 November failed to be met. For Noble, another round of potentially difficult talks lay ahead.

Broadcasting Commences

With the Broadcasting Committee formed on 18 October 1922 meaningful talks could commence with regard to news broadcasts. A meeting was arranged by the Post Office on 26 October. Apart from the Broadcasting Committee, the international news collecting bodies were represented along with the Newspaper Proprietors Association and the Newspaper Society. These last two organisations looked after the interests of the national and provincial papers respectively.

It immediately became clear that the Broadcasting Committee was in no position to collect news and would have to rely on its being supplied by the major news agencies, a service for which it would have to pay. The details were settled with remarkable speed and an Agreement was ready for signing on 11 November. The parties to the Agreement were Reuters, the press Association, Central News, and Exchange Telegraph on the one hand and the Broadcasting Committee on the other. Noble signed for the Broadcasting Committee. The news agencies would supply, for broadcasting between 6pm and 11pm, a daily summary of world news amounting to 1,200 to 2,400 words. Each news bulletin would commence with the words 'Copyright News from Reuters, press Association, Exchange and Central News'. Payment would be £333.6s.8d. per month on the first 200,000 licences (at that point averaging 5d per annum per licence) with reduced rates thereafter.

The Agreement did not bring the newspapers on board other than to say that the parties entered into it in the 'full spirit and endeavour not to prejudice the newspapers'. But the papers would have more to say on the matter; in particular, on the timing of the news bulletins. However, the Post Office accepted the Agreement as sufficient for them to be able to give the Committee (which became the British Broadcasting Committee from 14 November 1922) permission to commence its nightly service of news, music etc. This was confirmed by Brown in a letter of the 16 November.

The start of 'British Broadcasting Committee' nightly broadcasting was announced by Noble on 13 November:

'Pending the formation (*sic*) of the BBC which will be completed in a few days, the Broadcasting Committee has decided to commence a limited nightly programme from the London station. This will consist of two copyright news bulletins and the official weather reports, broadcast at 6pm and 9pm on a wavelength of 360 metres. The first two bulletins will be broadcast tomorrow, Tuesday evening. Special messages indicating the progress of the General Election will be broadcast as received on Wednesday and Thursday evenings.' (For 'formation' read 'registration'; the (British) Broadcasting Committee had already been formed on 18 October 1922.)

The new nightly service with news bulletins marked the end of experimental broadcasting by Marconi in London and by Metropolitan-Vickers in Manchester. Pending the registration of the British Broadcasting Company, the responsibility now passed to the British Broadcasting Committee. The transitional 'Committee' period actually lasted till the end of the year. But, in so far as the Committee was acting on behalf of the BBC, the BBC service could be said to have commenced on 14 November 1922. Certainly, in all subsequent years, the BBC has chosen that as the date on which to celebrate its birthday.

So it was that on the night of 14 November 1922 daily broadcasting in Britain commenced and has continued ever since. That first occasion of 'BBC' transmissions was however even more sparse in its content than the normal run of experimental broadcasts that 2LO had previously been putting out. There was no 'concert'; just the news, broadcast at 6pm by Burrows and repeated at 9pm - 'in a clear voice'. Burrows commenced with: 'This is 2LO calling, Marconi broadcasting on behalf of the Broadcasting Committee.' The details of the first news broadcasts were given by the *Daily News* the following day:

> 'Mr Bonar Law was announced as having made his final election speech at Glasgow, his policy being 'quietness and stability'. Mr Churchill was said to be none the worse for his rowdy meeting the previous night, and there were to be no police court charges, said the wireless. The skeleton story of a train robbery, the sale of a Shakespearean first folio, and the fog in London were other news items. This first budget of news concluded with the latest billiards scores.'

Also, on that following day, the London 'Dailies' duly reported 'Broadcasting Begun'. The *Daily Mail* referred to 'News messages of about 1,000 words' being broadcast. The *Daily Mail* went on to say the news summary was read by Mr Arthur R Burrows into 'an ordinary telephone receiver connected to a 1.5 kilowatt telephony transmitter'. Before broadcasting the news, 'Mr Burrows explained that he was going to read over the messages twice - once quickly and once slowly.' Burrows asked listeners to let him know whether they preferred this presentation to his reading the news twice fast or just once slowly. It seems normal speed was not an option!

The Times carried a much fuller account referring to the weather reports which had been supplied by the Meteorological Department of the Air Ministry. *The Times* then printed a long statement by Noble in which he made it clear that his Committee was prepared to accede fully to the demands of the press. No programmes would begin before 5pm so as not to interfere with the evening papers and those programmes announcing the election results would stop at 1 am so as not to scoop the morning papers.

On Wednesday, 15 November, the 9pm transmission continued until 1am on Thursday, the first election results coming through at 10pm. For Burrows, it was something of an ordeal, for a 'pea soup' fog hung over London and most of southern England. As he later recalled:

'Sensible people were in their homes, sitting comfortably before their fires, but in two rooms on the top floor of Marconi House in the Strand unusual things were happening. The feature of this particular evening was the broadcasting of the election results'. These results were transmitted only in outline - 'so many Unionists, so many Lloyd George people, so many Liberals, and so on, together with particulars of Mr Bonar Law, Mr Asquith and many of the leaders.'

The results came in from Reuters at fifteen-minute intervals and gramophone records probably helped to fill the intervals and cheer the depressed. Meanwhile the windows of the studio were kept closed to suppress the traffic noises coming up from the Strand (*Reflections at a Milestone, World Radio*, 11 November 1932). Burrows continued with his story of that unusual evening:

'Now the announcing of these results should not have caused me any embarrassment, for I had taken part in a number of experimental broadcasts. But on this night, we had not reckoned with London fog. The studio at Marconi House, was very small. We dared not run the ventilating fan as its noise would have 'gone over' as a background of escaping steam. So we arranged to open the windows during the intervals. In those days we were required by an official ruling to stop broadcasting for three-minutes in each ten. So we then opened the windows. Each time we did this - for we were gasping for air - in came the reddish brown penetrating fog.' (*The First Broadcast,* Arthur Burrows, *Sunday Dispatch*, 15 November 1942)

Wednesday, 15 November 1922 has perhaps a greater claim than the 14th for marking the birth of the BBC for it was on the 15th that something approaching a national service was inaugurated, with British Broadcasting Committee programmes going out from London, Manchester and Birmingham. The news was common to all three, being phoned through by Reuters in advance. In other respects the three stations were largely independent, though conforming to the arrangements agreed by Noble and his committee with the Post Office and the press. 2ZY Manchester was a joint Metrovick/RCC station whilst 5IT Birmingham was a Western Electric station located in the General Electric Company's works at Witton in Birmingham.

How these three stations each came to be built, tested, staffed and operated during the last months of 1922 is explained in the next three sections of this chapter. But a 'snapshot' here of what happened on 15 November in Birmingham and Manchester may be of interest.

In both cities, the installations had hardly been completed before they were 'on the air'. In both, the staff had only 24 hours notice of the requirement to commence official broadcasting. Yet the two stations made their debut by staging a concert with volunteer artistes as well as covering the election results.

At Birmingham, a Western Electric engineer, A E Thompson, had to run the show virtually single-handed; he introduced broadcasting to the Midlands with:

'This is the Birmingham Broadcasting Station, the Western Electric Company. We are transmitting on behalf of the Broadcasting Committee. Tonight and until further notice we will give you, in addition to musical items, copyright news bulletins specially prepared for the British Broadcasting Company by the several English news agencies'.

Like Burrows, Thompson read the news fast and then much more slowly so that listeners could, if they felt so inclined, 'make notes'. The news was repeated at 9pm, again being read twice. For some reason the election results were not received direct from the news agency as anticipated but had to be telephoned through, the source presumably being Marconi House, London. Again, as with 2LO, the transmissions continued to 1am. During this long period, Birmingham's generator became overheated and another Western Electric engineer, A G L Mason, had to spend the whole evening attending to it with a grease gun *(The Manager's Notebook, BBC Written Archives)*.

But that was not the only problem. As with London, a thick fog blanketed the city making it difficult for artistes to reach the Witton works, which were several miles from the city centre. Two of them took a taxi but the driver had such a hectic time getting them there that he parked his car in the Works yard for the night and told his passengers they would have to find their own way home. Arrived at the Works, the artistes had another series of adventures in trying to find which was the studio out of the great block of offices, all empty for the night. To add to their embarrassment, the women found that the way to the studio involved passing through a door marked 'Gents Cloakroom' (Allighan, Garry, *Sir John Reith*, p168).

No less than eight performers found their way to the studio that evening and listeners were treated to excerpts from Il Trovatore and Madame Butterfly, followed by Beatrice Best (contralto) singing 'The Blind Ploughman'. Madge Smith (mezzo) sang two popular songs - 'Annie Laurie' and 'Softly Awakes My Heart', and Arthur Gilbert (tenor) sang 'Take A Pair Of Sparkling Eyes' (This was before the clamp down on the broadcasting of Gilbert and Sullivan, referred to in Ch. 7: *Organising the Programmes*). Florence Winkless (soprano) sang 'Il Bacio', Walter Randall accompanying her on the piano. Interspersed among the songs were contributions from two 'elocutionists' - the contemporary term for those who entertained with short stories and by reciting; Vincent Curran's were entitled 'The Uncle' and 'The Lady and The Tiger'. There was even a children's story read by a lady elocutionist. The other artiste was a flautist - Walter Heard - who, like Randall and Curran, remained on the BBC Books for many years (*The Managers Notebook*, also *Radio Times*, 10 September 1937).

It is probable that the various artistes were provided by Percy Edgar who ran a concert agency in New Street, Birmingham. Edgar later recalled:

'It was here one day in October 1922 that I had a visit from a Mr A E Thompson, of the Western Electric Company. He had come to Birmingham in connection with a broadcasting station which it was proposed to set up in the city, and he asked me if I would supply artistes to take part in the programmes. There was no question of payment to the artistes but I realised the publicity value for the agency and agreed. Within a very short while Thompson offered me the job of Manager.' (*BBC Year Book 1948*, p10).

Edgar's faith in broadcasting was abundantly rewarded. At a time when most thought broadcasting was just a passing craze, he gave up his successful agency and took over from Thompson. His post as Station Director was confirmed by the BBC on 15 January 1923 and Edgar remained in it for the rest of his working life, retiring in 1948 as BBC Midland Regional Director. As he himself later remarked: 'It all started so casually.'

2ZY Manchester was better prepared for broadcasting; experimental programmes had been going out for two or three weeks and had become an almost nightly event. The new features were the news and the election results. Manchester's *Evening Chronicle* set out the programme for the first British Broadcasting Committee evening, describing it as 'based largely on the lines of those in use in America':

6 pm	News
7 pm	A story and music for the children
7.30 pm	Mr X's funny stories
8 pm	Instrumental music and songs
9 pm	Late news followed by popular music
10 pm to 1am	Election results

(*Evening Chronicle*, 15 November 1922)

In contrast to Birmingham, the Manchester Station relied much more on the talent and enterprise of the Metrovick staff. The first 'Auntie' was Miss A Bennie who was still on the staff ten years later when she recalled the night of 15 November:

'On the night that the BBC took over, I did not know till the afternoon that I had to broadcast, and I decided to read a story instead of telling one. I read Oscar Wilde's 'Happy Prince'. I was much too scared to trust my powers as a storyteller before the microphone. After I had done my stint, I hurried home to listen-in on a crystal set.'

Kenneth Wright, another Metrovick employee, was in charge. Wright had much in common with Stanton Jefferies of the London station in that he was at heart a musician and a fine pianist. On the 15th, he rounded off Miss Bennie's performance with some recorded music for children as he did on numerous subsequent nights (Hartley, Ian, *Origin of the Children's Corner*, p14).

Mr X, who came on at 7.30pm, was H G Bell of the Metrovick Research Department. Apart from 'funny stories' he became, with 'Mr Z' (W J Brown), the main source of 'Talks' for 2ZY. Hugh G Bell was not only a broadcaster; his role at 2ZY Manchester was crucial, for he was in charge of the design and operation of the station.

The concert was provided by gramophone records and was concluded by 9.00pm when the second news bulletin was read. Records of dance music followed until the first election results began to come through. The results were phoned through to another room from London. There they were transcribed, the typed sheets then being brought to the studio and handed to the announcer.

A feature of the new British Broadcasting Committee evening programmes broadcast from both Birmingham and Manchester was the hour specially reserved for 'child stories and music'. A Liverpool reporter described how Mr X addressed the children at 6.30pm on Thursday 16 November with stories and music. At 7.30pm, Mr X said 'now children, take those things off and go to bed. Good night; good night.' He was of course referring to their headphones! (*Liverpool Courier*, 18 November 1922).

For Kenneth Wright, the start of nightly broadcasting and of his responsibility for the Manchester programmes opened up a wonderful prospect. 'In the studio of 2ZY on the first night of its regular broadcasting I realised suddenly that it was in my hands to give the world all that I myself had hoped and longed for years without the slightest chance of hearing it'. The BBC's role as the sower of the good seed had begun on 'day one'. Indeed, the very word 'broadcast' commonly referred to 'scattering seed'.

At Marconi House there was initially less air of excitement and improvisation. With a certain formality, Burrows dispatched a memorandum on 17 November to his assistant, Stanton Jefferies, who was responsible for the music side of the programmes:

> 'A R Burrows to L Stanton Jefferies, London Station Director. The British Broadcasting Committee has arranged to transmit the following programme each evening, Saturdays and Sundays included, until further notice, from the London broadcasting station, 2LO: 6pm News Bulletin; 8 to 9 Music; 9 to 9.30 News; 9.30 to 10 Music.'

Burrows later remarked: 'It was the most historic order of the day in the history of broadcasting' (Baily, L and Brewer, C, *The BBC Scrapbooks*, p269).

Like the other two stations, 2LO London broadcast the election results on the evenings of the 15th and 16th November. But its first British Broadcasting Committee concert was transmitted on the 16th. The concert commenced at 7.00pm and finished at 8.00pm. Into the Marconi House studio came six performers - three singers, two instrumentalists and an entertainer. With them, to do the announcing and piano accompaniment, was Stanton Jefferies.

Leonard Hawke (baritone) led off with 'Drake Goes West'. Bruce Mackay followed with two pieces for the flute and Glyn Dowell (tenor) then sang. Billy Beer read two humorous stories and was followed by the first lady artiste, Miss Lily Clare (contralto). Two violin pieces played by Dorothy Chalmers concluded the concert (Programme in *BBC Written Archives*).

The sounds of the concert were re-created and broadcast 14 years later using an early carbon microphone of the type used by 2LO in 1922. This gave a hard quality to the voice and a very poor response to high and low frequencies. Listeners again heard Leonard Hawke with piano singing 'Drake Goes West' on the old microphone. Others taking part in the re-enactment included Jefferies, Burrows, Edgar and Kenneth Wright. Their voices and reminiscences formed part of 'Scrapbook for 1922'. The 'Scrapbooks' - each for an individual year - formed part of a popular long-running series. They were broadcast also on the Empire Service and, due to time variations, they had to be recorded for this purpose. The recording still survives in the BBC Archives (*Scrapbook for 1922* broadcast 21 and 22 January 1937, *BBC Sound Archive*).

The election results were, incidentally, well worth staying up for. They saw the end of Lloyd George's tenure in Downing Street, his party shattered. The Conservatives romped home. The new Prime Minister, Mr Bonar Law, had found a slogan which was the key to the heart of the British people at that period. In one word, it was - 'Stability'.

Curiously, the start of broadcasting caught the technical press completely unaware. The *Wireless World* issue dated 11 November gave no hint of what was about to happen. A week later *Popular Wireless* noted that 'broadcasting in Birmingham is supposed to begin officially on November 15th'. The editor seemed to imply this was just one more promise likely to remain unfulfilled. In its issue dated 25 November, the leader writer admitted that when he heard the news he could hardly believe it. 'Some friendly fellow phoned up the office and warned the editor to prepare for a great shock.'

Broadcasting had indeed begun and, though ostensibly the British Broadcasting Committee, the programmes, like the stations themselves, were still the product of the individual Electrical Companies. If nothing else, the 'Red Flag' rule of three minutes silence every 10 minutes served as a reminder that the curtain had yet to rise on the BBC as a national broadcasting institution.

2LO at Marconi House, London

Looking back to the experimental 2LO days, Burrows declared he was sure no one in this world could have had a happier time than he and Jefferies had during the months in which the station was tuning up for more serious work. 'Our unseen audience, only a few thousand strong, were a typical British sporting community, open handed and highly appreciative of all our efforts' (Burrows, Arthur, *The Story of Broadcasting*, p72). Stanton Jefferies echoed Burrows' sentiments: 'What good fun those early days were. As far as concerts were concerned I was not overworked.' (*Soap Box Days*, *Popular Wireless*, 5 October 1935).

In those relatively tranquil days, listeners loved to hear Burrows opening the programme for the evening with, typically, a verse or two from Longfellow:

> 'As one who, walking in the twilight gloom,
> Hears around him voices as it darkens,
> And seeing not the forms from which they come,
> Pauses from time to time, and turns and hearkens.
> So walking here, in twilight, O my friends!
> I hear your voices, softened by the distance,
> And pause, and turn to listen, as each sends
> His words of friendship, comfort, and assistance.
> Therefore I hope, as no unwelcome guest,
> At your warm fireside, when the lamps are lighted,
> To have my place reserved amongst the rest,
> Nor stand as one unsought and uninvited!'

With November came nightly broadcasting. The tranquil days were over for 2LO. Everything had to move into top gear. The transitional period that was to follow was especially onerous as 'no permanent appointments had been made and the broadcasting duties were carried out for some six weeks in addition to ordinary office routine.' (Burrows, Arthur, *The Story of Broadcasting*, p69). On 3 December, Burrows wrote to Isaacs pointing out that he and his colleagues had worked for between 11 hours and 17 hours a day during the previous few weeks. They were overwhelmed by the magnitude of their commitments. He asked Isaacs about his position in relation to Marconi and the new British Broadcasting Committee. Could he continue to play 'a dual role'?

The sharp contrast between the early days of experimental broadcasting and the nightly 'BBC' service from 2LO was reflected in substantial changes in accommodation and equipment. The Marconi House cinema continued to be used as a studio (room 99 on the plan below) but it was now available on a full time footing and so could be properly furnished for its new role. The adjoining projection room (room 98) was also made available. Mr H A Hankey, who had charge of the cinema, was ordered to remove his equipment from the projection room so that it could serve as an amplifier room. The large office beyond the studio was used, at least part time, as a 'news room' (room 100). Across the corridor was a long, narrow, windowless room with top lighting (room 102). This provided the ideal conditions for housing the new transmitter and was duly made available, along with a nearby room for the batteries (room 115). In short, the whole accommodation around the building's main stairway and lift at the seventh floor level became a broadcasting suite. 2LO, however, lacked a waiting room for artistes; they had to make do with wooden forms provided on either side of the wide passageway at the head of the stairs. Nor was there an office for the station director, Stanton Jefferies, who had to work in the studio, his typist likewise. Later, room 107 was made available; it was half way along the corridor linking the Strand and Aldwych ends of the building.

From Marconi's point of view, the BBC accommodation was seen strictly as a temporary measure. Metropolitan-Vickers were making similar temporary provision at their works for the BBC's Manchester station whilst the General Electric Company likewise accommodated the Birmingham station as an emergency measure. 2LO's occupation was to extend to the end of April 1923 in so far as the studio and its adjoining rooms were concerned; the transmitter and battery rooms at Marconi House were commandeered by the BBC for much longer. As a result, Marconi became more and more restless, if not exasperated, by the situation, complaining, in the words of Adrian Simpson, their deputy managing director, of 'bands of strangers coming in and out'. He claimed that the transmitter was 'by no means a showpiece or as safe as one would like' (West, P E , *BBC Engineering: the First Five Years,* p8). For the BBC, there was no easy solution to the transmitter problem. Their permanent accommodation was to be in the building of the Institution of Electrical Engineers in Savoy Hill but this building had a critical deficiency in that its roof could not support the necessary aerial. So the transmitter remained at Marconi House, a landline connecting it with the Savoy Hill studio and amplifier (see Plans).

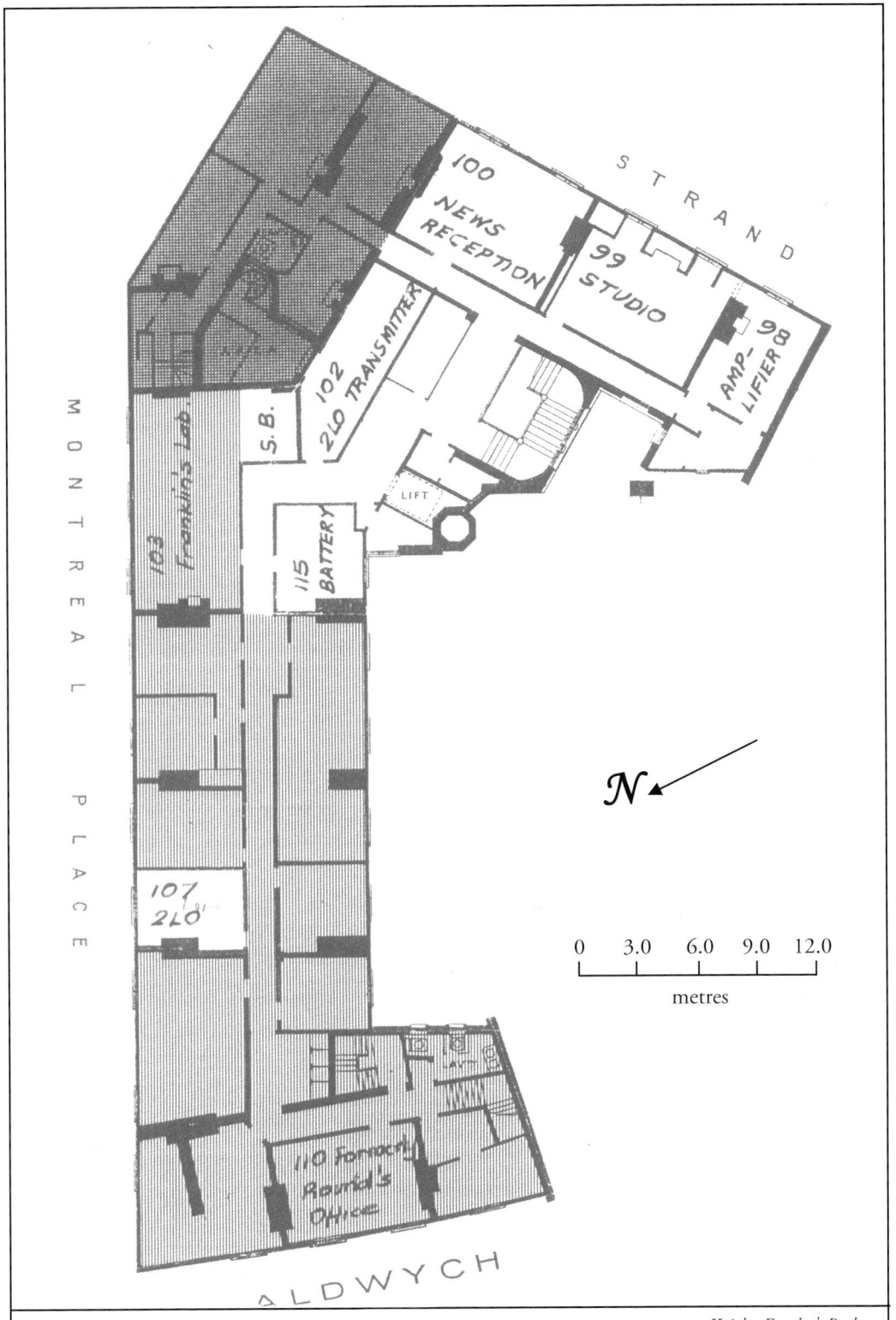

2LO accommodation plan until April 1923; seventh floor, Marconi House, London.

Eventually a suitable replacement transmitter of double the power was constructed along with two towering aerials on the roof of Selfridges's department store in Oxford Street. The new 2LO transmitter station came into service on the 6 April 1925. Meanwhile the old Marconi House transmitter was retained as a stand-by and only removed in October 1929 when the 2LO Station at Selfridges itself closed down in favour of the new London Regional station at Brookmans Park in Hertfordshire. Even then, the 1922 transmitter was not scrapped. It was installed in the studio of the new Brookmans Park station as a primitive museum piece from another era strangely at odds with the cool ordered modernity of its surroundings.

In its day, the 2LO transmitter at Marconi House represented a major breakthrough in design and set the pattern for Marconi 'Q' transmitters both in Britain and abroad. Its designer was the brilliant Marconi engineer H J Round. Like the Chief Engineer Eckersley, Round was, in his bearing and mentality, the very antithesis of a conventional military man, yet both he and Eckersley hung on to their army ranks long after the war was over. Captain Round was 'excessively reticent both about himself and his work'. He was 'often to be seen slouching about with his old felt hat and his greatcoat down to his feet, a cigarette in his mouth and a twinkle in his eye.' (Lewis, Cecil, *Broadcasting from Within,* pp169/170). Stanton Jefferies also remembered him as a 'rather little man with a happy twinkle in his eye'. Many times in late 1922/early 1923 Jefferies had stayed with him while he worked until the small hours of the morning smoking 'innumerable Egyptian cigarettes, lighting the new one from the old, the cigarette eventually to hang from his upper lip in a most haphazard fashion' (*Soap Box Days, Popular Wireless,* 5 October 1935).

The problem facing Round was to design and build a transmitter suitable for broadcasting; one where the quality of modulation was such as to convey excellent reproduction of speech and music. It had to be reliable and it had to have a good range. Range depended on conditions but 'good' implied crystal reception up to at least 10 miles and reception by a two-valve receiver up to at least 100 miles. It was also important that the transmitting wavelength should remain constant. The more sharply tuned the listener's receiver, the more would the intensity and quality of reception vary if the transmitter wavelength altered a fraction of a metre, resulting in listeners having to adjust their sets repeatedly. To use Marconi's contemporary analogy, the transmitter must compare with the ordinary commercial transmitter 'like a Rolls-Royce to a Ford lorry'.

R H White, the engineer in charge of 2LO in 1922 collaborated with Round just as he had done with Franklin and has left the most detailed description of 2LO's equipment and of the subsequent standard Marconi 'Q' transmitter which was developed from it (Wander, Tim, *2MT Writtle, The Birth of British Broadcasting*, pp159/162 based on a paper in *Marconi Archives*).

The Round transmitter underwent a long process of development during the latter months of 1922 trial and error playing a big part in the process. As a result, the transmitter circuits were always changing and 2LO's equipment at Marconi House, though in continual use, never had a very attractive appearance. As progress was made with the 2LO transmitter, Marconi's design experts at Chelmsford were busy producing a smart looking 'Q' version of it for installation in the forthcoming BBC stations at Newcastle, Cardiff and Glasgow. One can imagine the recurrent cussing every time they learned of a major circuit alteration (notes by Petersen in *Marconi Archives*).

The transmitter comprised four units:

the power supply rectifier unit;
the power oscillator unit;
the modulator unit;
the independent drive unit.

In its final form as installed at Newcastle, Glasgow, Cardiff, Aberdeen and Bournemouth, each unit consisted of an open steel welded framework in which were mounted the transformers, inductors, choking coils, capacitors and other component parts. The units were placed side by side but were spaced apart. To prevent accidents, a system of barriers with interlocking switches cut out the supply current when opened.

For the rectifier unit, power at 200-volts d.c. (direct current) was taken from the Electric Supply Company's mains but could be taken from the London theatre supply main should the need arise. It was taken through a switchboard to a 10 horsepower motor coupled to a six-kilowatt single-phase 300 hertz alternator that supplied power at 500 volts alternating current (a.c). The alternator sets were duplicated to allow for possible failure. Arranged on the basement wall above them were two remote control automatic starters operated from the transmitter room on the seventh floor. The alternating current was taken to the top of the building where it was supplied to the primary of a six-kilowatt transformer which was again duplicated. The transformer stepped the supply up to 22,500 volts, centre-tapped to earth. The rectifier unit converted the 22,500-volt a.c. into a 10,000-volt unidirectional or 'direct' current (d.c.). It also smoothed out 'ripple' to prevent 'hum' reaching the carrier wave and being transmitted.

Reproduced by permission of the Marconi Co. Ltd

2LO Mk2 transmitter, 1923.

The power oscillator unit had the job of developing the full power of the (radio frequency) carrier wave and of energising the aerial circuit. The modulator unit's task was to amplify further the audio frequency currents received from the microphone or its amplifier and to impress these on the radio frequency carrier wave by controlling the amplitude of the oscillations generated by the power oscillator.

The independent drive unit was a new concept adding a fourth panel to the three-panel transmitter. Its function was to keep the frequency of the power oscillator constant within carefully defined limits.

The valve filaments were heated by the main battery; the first unit had two MR9 rectifying valves; the second and third each had a single MT2 valve; and the fourth had three (initially four) MT7B and one MT4 modulating valves (Marconi, *The Art and Technique of Broadcasting*, 1924).

The valves, mostly as big as rugby balls, emitted a strange light - not exactly phosphorescent in character although, in Burrows' words, it reminded one 'of the light of a glow worm on a gigantic scale'. There was an otherworldly hum from the transformers. The stillness of the scene, the faint hum and the weird light from the valves combined to create 'a sense of mystical power'. Certainly the extremely high voltages in the railed off portions of the apparatus called for the utmost respect. The boards with 'DANGER' in big red letters were not there for decoration. The enormous brass terminals and flimsy looking bits of wire could, if touched, result in unconsciousness or death. It was nonetheless possible to touch nearly all the components from outside the wooden 'safety' rail and visitors to the transmitting room often used to lean on the rail and extend their arm near the transmitting valve 'just to see how warm it really was', quite failing to realise the possibility of electric shock (Shaw, A C, *World Radio*, 15 November 1935).

The engineer's job was to telephone the studio to ask the studio director if he was ready, pull the switches, and listen to the programmes to check all was well. He also had to act as control engineer, giving advice to the studio, and anticipate extreme variations in sound which might cause 'blasting'. But his biggest challenge was to deal with breakdowns in transmission by diagnosing the problems and correcting them speedily. After that it was a case of 'carry on, quite OK'; the engineer would sit down, light a cigarette, put on his headphones and wait for more trouble.

The Marconi House/Bush House aerial in use from July 1922 had been replaced by the end of the year by one entirely limited to Marconi House. It comprised two cage or sausage type aerials, each of four wires, stretched between two 50ft masts set 100ft apart on the roof. The lead roof, the steel frame of the building and the lightning conductors were bonded together to form a common earth for the system.

The studio measured 23ft by about 19ft but the slope of the mansard roof into which the seventh floor was built reduced the effective width from 19ft to about 15ft. The studio had a faded green carpet and, for acoustic reasons, its walls and ceiling were draped with two layers of a sacking-coloured canvas - 'something more refined than actual sacking but less so than bunting' (Burrows to Reith, 8 May 1937, BBC Archives). In the sooty London air this pale muslin-like material soon became soiled and dingy (Lewis, Cecil, Broadcasting from Within). A plan in the BBC Archives shows how the room was furnished. In the earliest BBC days the studio was referred to as the 'concert room', for by the end of 1922 it was mainly furnished for musical productions. A tiny orchestra of eight players occupied the centre, facing the conductor's rostrum. Behind them and sideways on was a grand piano, the light from one of the two windows falling on the pianist's music score. The conductor had a direct view

Reproduced by permission of the Marconi Co. Ltd

2LO aerial on Marconi House, London, 1924.

of the clock on the far wall, below which was placed a set of tubular bells. These provided the first introduced broadcast time signal, the idea being that the evening programme should be on the hour with a replica of the sound of the Westminster chimes of Big Ben. In the far right-hand corner was a desk for the use of the station director, Stanton Jefferies. A receiving set for the engineer to listen in to any official interval messages ordering 2LO to close down was placed in the alcove between the windows. These messages never came but the three-minute intervals were nonetheless useful for, whilst off air, the microphones usually needed to be shaken to free the carbon granules; the furniture and piano could be moved and last minute instructions given to artistes about to perform. The ventilating fan could be run and the windows opened without having to worry about traffic noise.

    The furnishings in the studio were completed by a worn out leather settee placed against the near wall and, in the corner, a typist's desk. Close to the settee was to be found the tuning note device on the floor. Presumably Jefferies had become more adroit in manipulating this so it no longer sounded like a dying pig as listeners used it to adjust their sets in preparation for the evening's broadcast. At this end of Studio 2 also stood the Cliftophone gramophone hired from the Chappell Piano Company of 50 New Bond Street. Chairs were provided against the long wall and here, alongside the door, was the switchboard controlling the various microphones. Ultimately there were six of these Peel Conner carbon microphones either suspended, or on stands, or, in one instance, buried in the piano. Experiments were carried out on the microphones with a view to accommodating the sound from two or more instrumentalists or perhaps the little wireless orchestra. For this purpose, a hollow truncated pyramid in three-ply cedar wood was clamped in front of the microphone. The one most commonly used was two feet long and 18 inches square at the mouth. A red light over the door showed when the microphone was 'live' and the studio 'on the air' (Jefferies to Reith, 21 May 1937 and Burrows to Reith, 8 May 1937, *BBC Written Archives*).

The studio served during the day for rehearsals and auditions, fifty artistes arriving each day to await their turn for audition. Here too the evening concert had to be planned and arranged. To complicate things further, Round began testing a revolutionary new microphone at the start of 1923. One of Jefferies' colleagues recalled the chaotic conditions resulting - 'two telephones which had a perfect mania for ringing; a typist who clicked away cheerfully morning, noon and night; engineers tapping, whispering and shouting into the microphones, insisting on silence while they did so; artistes arriving and crowding into the room and, amid all this, Mr Jefferies, single-handed, attending to everyone and producing at the end of the day a three hour musical programme' (Lewis, Cecil, *Broadcasting from Within*, pp29/30). To be more precise, the musical programme until the 22 December extended from 8.00pm to 9.00pm and from 9.30pm to as late as 10.30pm, a total of 2 hours. The 9pm News and Weather Report filled the gap between the concerts and the first evening News Bulletin was broadcast at 6pm.

The concerts took off with the formation of the Wireless Orchestra. The first experimental orchestral night occurred on Saturday, 25 November 1922. The diminutive orchestra kicked off bravely with Elgar's 'Pomp and Circumstance (No. 1)'. Other favourites included a selection from 'Peer Gynt' (Grieg), 'The March of the Crusaders' from 'Decameron Nights' (Finck) and a selection from 'Madam Butterfly' (Puccini). The diet was lightened with a foxtrot, a one-step and some amusing stories by two entertainers. A baritone, Mr Topliss Green, sang three songs accompanied by Jefferies at the piano (*Concerts Broadcast, BBC Written Archives*).

In the background was Burrows with clear ideas as to the nature and quality the new 'BBC' service should encompass but wholly lacking resources. The 'caretaker' British Broadcasting Committee proved unable to help with staffing or finance. This had many implications for the transitional period of November/December 1922.

First, there was the matter of the Wireless Orchestra. The London station had been transmitting for months and the perpetual round of vocal and instrumental solos was beginning to pall. On their own initiative Burrows and Jefferies had organised the concert described above with Jefferies rehearsing and conducting the small orchestra of eight. The letters the following day showed 'it had placed an entirely different complexion on broadcasting - one of a most favourable character'. Burrows pointed out that an orchestra working seven days a week would cost about 48 guineas for players, plus the music and Performing Rights fees. He argued it would 'enable us to extend our evening programme and to include dance music for which there is a great demand'. Burrows approached Noble, doubtless showing him the enthusiastic public response to the concert of the 25 November; Noble was sympathetic but unwilling to act off his own bat. In desperation, Burrows then approached Isaacs - would the Marconi Company be 'prepared to bear this expense until such time as the committee will shoulder it?' (Burrows to Isaacs, 5 December 1922).

Then there was the matter of the 'artistes'. They were paid a nominal fee of one guinea a night following their first appearance. At that paltry rate, artistes of any standing couldn't risk throwing in their lot entirely with a broadcasting service run by two men and a committee. On one occasion, Jefferies had prepared the evening's programme only to have four out of five artistes ringing up at the last minute to tell him that their agents had forbidden them to sing (*Soap Box Days*, *Popular Wireless*, 12 October 1935).

Yet still Burrows hoped the standard guinea payments would enable him to call the tune. He sent a memo to Jefferies: 'It has to be brought home to these people that they must adapt their artistry to the limitations of the wireless circuit if they hope to create the most favourable impression upon their vast audience.' Songs had to be free from extremes in 'light and shade'. More particularly, Burrows wanted items 'of a really popular character - not necessarily trashy but items either exceedingly well known' or which would 'go with a swing'. In his view, few post-war songs had sufficient merit, yet too many artistes wanted to sing the latest songs to show how up-to-date they were. In all this, Burrows' dominant purpose was to build up the army of listeners as fast as possible. This would do more than anything else to secure the future of broadcasting and to release the resources upon which a quality service could be instituted. Popular programmes were, he thought, essential 'until we have got the public so interested in wireless that we can lift them above their present standard of musical appreciation'. Like Kenneth Wright, the Manchester station director, Burrows' ultimate goal was educational; he too saw himself as a potential 'sower', broadcasting the good seed and looking forward to a great harvest. The mould for the future BBC was beginning to take shape (Burrows to Jefferies, 29 November 1922, *BBC Archives*).

Financial stringency was not limited to the orchestra and artistes; it affected every detail of the service. The tubular bells were a feature of the new nightly programmes imitating the Westminster chimes and Big Ben with greater or lesser time-keeping accuracy. For the announcer, playing the bells was always a nerve-racking experience. Even Jefferies played them incorrectly at his first attempt and some kind person sent him a book of the various chimes for his edification. On another occasion he hit his finger instead of the bell, which drew the obvious audible reaction. But even the bells had to be hired to save the expense of outright purchase, estimated at between £17 and £20. A more limited set of bells would probably have cost no more than £12 as did those for the Cardiff Station supplied in February 1923 by Charles Hards of Wellington Street just round the corner from Marconi House, London (Invoice in *BBC Archives*).

Noble's caution over taking decisions was not altogether unjustified. He had every expectation that the BBC would be functioning within two or three weeks, making his committee redundant. This time he was not mistaken; the first meeting of the British Broadcasting Company was held on 21 December 1922, the Company having finally been registered on the 15th. Significantly, the orchestra was back before the microphones on 23 December and on a permanent footing. Each instrumentalist received the usual guinea for performing and half a guinea for the rehearsal and the bill for the first week came to £83.13s.10d - rather more than the 48 Guineas estimated by Burrows. Marconi advanced the money as a loan to the BBC, the cheques being signed by Jefferies. The purchase of music came to an additional £25.

It is significant too that the 23 December marked the night of the first General News Bulletin. Under the new arrangements agreed earlier in the month by the Broadcasting Committee and now endorsed by the BBC, the news went out at 7pm with a further Bulletin at 9.30pm. The news avoided any expressions of opinion; sensationalism and unsavoury items were firmly excluded; likewise any news that might relate to betting. The Reuters News Service probably cost as much as the evening concert, the bill for 14 November to the end of the year amounting to £500. Fortunately, Reuters were content to await payment until the end of January 1923 when the BBC settled with an all-encompassing cheque for £833.6s.8d.

The bulletins prepared by the Broadcasting Editor at Reuters were phoned through to Marconi House each evening and recorded on a dictaphone. The Dictaphone Company provided an operator whose job it was to transcribe and type the news. Quiet surroundings were obviously essential for this task and a

Reproduced by permission of the Marconi Co. Ltd
Arthur Burrows playing the tubular bells with Stanton Jefferies, 1922.

room next to the studio was allocated for the purpose by Marconi. The Dictaphone Company charged three guineas a week and Marconi settled the bill up to 24 December. The BBC continued the arrangement until 12 February when it appointed its own operator - Mrs H Esmond. It is probable that Mrs Esmond had acted as operator from before this date for, in a list of staff still serving in 1937, she is shown as the oldest serving member: 'The actual date of Mrs Esmond's appointment is lost in the mists of antiquity but was before the end of 1922!' (*Ariel,* the BBC staff magazine, June 1937).

A private line connected Marconi House to Reuters so that news coming in during the evening concert could be included in the 9.30pm Bulletin.

The Weather Reports for the London area were phoned through to Marconi House from the Air Ministry at Adastral House. There were two reports each day, one at 4.15pm and one at 9pm. Provincial stations at Birmingham, Manchester and Newcastle received their reports in Morse, these being taken down by the engineer who had the job of listening in for possible government messages during the three-minute intervals.

It seems that Burrows more often than not read the news bulletins and announced the items to be played in the first half of the concert. 'The reason for my personal attendance at the evening concert', he explained, 'has been (because) no one's voice yet heard on the wireless has been so well-suited as my own.' He would have to continue announcing 'until such date as the Broadcasting Committee authorise the appointment of one or more deputies'. As a preliminary step, he had seen Professor Acton Bond at the Royal Academy of Music who informed him it all depended on an individual's quality of 'head resonance'. This apparently was pronounced in Burrows' case. In putting these points to Isaacs, he may well have had a sympathetic ear. Isaacs was a member of the Broadcasting Committee and, a week later, the committee duly appointed a deputy - Cecil Lewis - who, by all accounts, excelled as an announcer (Burrows to Isaacs, 5 December 1922, *BBC Archives*).

There can be no doubt but that Burrows followed the transmission of the concerts with a critical ear either in the transmitter room or listening-in at home. He was determined his Marconi station in London 'should be the best of the three'. He felt that a music director was in the best position to judge the quality of the sound broadcast and to ensure suitable musical balance between instruments and between singer and piano. But the job was handled by engineers in the transmitting room, who passed on guidance to the studio, often seconds too late. For this purpose, furthermore, the studio director had to listen for advice using headphones, a practice which was somewhat hazardous: 'Other artistes have a most unfortunate habit of tripping over the phone leads and nearly breaking the (studio director's) neck'. No wonder Burrows preferred to listen in to the receiver in the transmitting room, holding himself ready to rush back to the studio if adjustments needed to be made! (Burrows to White, 18 December 1922 *BBC Archives*).

It seems Burrows took a particular interest in the concert broadcast on 10 December. It was probably the occasion when Burrows suggested 'that a cornet, played at a discreet distance from the microphone might be pleasing to listeners' - the old memorandum of 1922 was discovered years later by Roger Eckersley, older brother of Peter, in a dusty file (Eckersley, R, *BBC and All That,* p65). The cornet he was satisfied with, on the whole, but little else escaped his critical ear. The next day he wrote to Jefferies setting out his impressions of the evening concert:

> 'Your bells were not as good as usual. There was a damping effect, which cut out resonance.
> Kenneth Ellis comes through splendidly but I would suggest that he turn his head just a little bit on one side to avoid jarring the microphone on some of his louder notes.
> Miss Kelmrich has the most beautiful contralto voice but one or two of her notes were almost overpowering.
> The violin and piano were for once well balanced but I think a shade more violin would be an improvement.
> The cornet was good but there seemed to be lacking a fullness of tone.
> The piano as an instrument was passable when played by yourself but when played automatically is horrible. It is a cross between a dulcimer and a banjo and very tinny at that.'

'The blot on the whole evening', Burrows concluded, 'were the long delays between the items. For wireless to succeed everything must go with a bang. There must be no periods of silence.' Apparently, listeners during such 'silent' periods heard Morse signals 'heterodyned by the carrier wave' from other stations.

Part of the problem was one of stage management; but part was clearly technical. A week later he was again complaining that the piano sounded 'tinny', this time whilst being played; yet later in the programme the fault cured itself, the last solos sounding as good as any ever heard over the air (Burrows to White, 18 December 1922 *BBC Archives*). These problems, unlike some, could not be put down to interference but clearly had to do with the Marconi House equipment. Most particularly, Burrows regretted they were no nearer a solution of the problem of 'balancing out the sounds from different parts of the piano'. In short, the Peel Conner carbon microphone, under the lid of the piano, was not up to the job. It could not cope with the full piano range.

There were in the studio no less than six microphones, all controlled from a switchboard by the door. Sometimes, before the studio director returned to the switchboard at the end of an item, the singer had passed a remark on her performance which was heard by those listening in. This could easily be cured, but another problem was that the switching on and off of the relevant microphones was all too audible (Burrows to White, 18 December 1922 *BBC Archives*).

The simple truth of the matter was that the Peel Conner microphones were designed for speech, not for music and for general use, not for broadcasting. They had to be placed very close to the speaker's or singer's lips, or near the individual instruments, otherwise the faint signal was overwhelmed by an objectionable hiss. This made getting the right balance very difficult as it generally called for the use of several microphones at any one time. The carbon granules tended to pack together, reducing the efficiency of the microphone; so, during the frequent intervals, the instruments had to be shaken back into working order. This opportunity ceased to exist when the 'intervals' requirement was lifted on 8 January 1923.

Against this background, Burrows and Jefferies prepared the Christmas programmes. Burrows widened the limited fare of news and concerts with new types of programme. The first 2LO 'Children's Hour'; the first talk; the first appearance on the air of a celebrated star, José Collins, from a current London production. All these went out on 23 December along with the first General News Bulletin and the first regular concert by the 2LO Wireless Orchestra. For his part, Jefferies had now to rehearse the orchestra on a daily basis and plan everything down to the last detail a full week ahead, booking the artistes and checking their repertoire so that he could select the most suitable items to be sung or played.

Details of the Christmas programmes for the 23rd to the 27th December inclusive were supplied to the press in the early afternoon of Friday the 22nd.

The evening broadcast now began at 5pm and ran continuously to 10.15pm or 10.30pm - well over five hours. On Saturday the 23 December, it took the following form:

5.00pm:
: Children's stories followed by Vivienne Chatterton singing 'Simple Simon', 'Hickory Dickory Dock' and 'The Old Woman and the Peddler'. Children's Hour concluded with a Children's Competition.

6.30pm:
: Miss José Collins sang 'The Mirror Song' from 'The Last Waltz' accompanied on the piano by Hubert Bath, Director of the Gaiety Theatre (This was the first of a series of stage celebrity appearances, all of which had to be broadcast by 7.15pm to enable the stars to return to the theatre in time to prepare for the evening performance on stage).

6.45pm:
: The Wireless Orchestra, with Pennington as leader, played Quilter's new 'Children's Overture'.

7pm:
: General News Bulletin and Weather Report.

7.15pm:
: Captain Towse gave a talk on 'Christmas among the Blind' (Captain Ernest Beachcroft Beckwith Towse of the Gordon Highlanders had won the Victoria Cross for gallantry in the second Boer war. He was later knighted for his magnificent work for the blind).

7.30pm:
: Messrs Pitt and Marks entertained with amusing stories under the titles 'Great Election Day' and 'A Fisherman Bold'.

7.42pm:
: The Orchestra struck up with Colonel Bogey (Alford) and played a selection from 'The Mikado' (Sullivan) (before the ban on Gilbert and Sullivan, mentioned earlier, was imposed). The concert included an instrumentalist and another entertainer and ended with dance music including the new One Step - 'Limehouse Blues'.

9.30pm:
: Second News Bulletin and Weather Report

9.45pm to 10.15pm:
: Orchestra - 'Nell Gwyn' Suite (German) and Fred Gibson (Entertainer).

At the piano: L Stanton Jefferies, ARCM.

Christmas Eve followed a similar pattern but broke new ground once again, this time with a play written for children by Mrs Phyllis Twigg - 'The Truth about Father Christmas'. It featured a very up-to-date Father Christmas starting off in his aeroplane with seven tons of toys! The play was performed with Burrows in the role of Father Christmas and was accompanied with appropriate sound effects. Before the play commenced, the Rector of St Mary's, Whitechapel, the Reverend John Mayo, talked to the children. Mayo was back in the studio at 9.15pm to speak, this time, to the adults; it was the first religious address to be broadcast:

> 'I have come from my church in Whitechapel situated amidst all the noise and the turmoil and the dust and the slums - all that Whitechapel connotes; and it is my privilege through the wizardry of Mr Marconi to speak, as I understand, to many thousands of people. Surely, no man has ever proclaimed the Gospel from such an extraordinary pulpit as I am now doing. Having preached, sometimes from cathedrals and sometimes from the kitchen of a doss-house, I notice one great difference. Whether from the cathedral or the doss-house I could at any rate see my audience; here I cannot.' (Recording from *75 Years of the BBC* in the *BBC Radio Collection*.)

Mayo's talk was preceded and followed by Christmas carols and religious music. The concert also included Schubert's 'Unfinished Symphony' played by the little 2LO Orchestra of eight or nine under Jefferies' baton.

Jefferies later recalled that Christmas of 1922: 'Burrows and I held the fort. Broadcasting was a new game and our listeners, sorry that we were working during the festive season, sent us good wishes and Xmas fare. On Boxing Day the studio looked rather like the window of a well set out grocer's store.' (*Soap Box Days, Popular Wireless*, 19 October 1935)

And so, with almost superhuman effort, Burrows and Jefferies created and conducted the first Christmas broadcast, ending on New Year's Eve. As midnight approached, the old year was rung out and the new year rung in on the tubular bells whilst Kenneth Ellis sang 'Auld Lang Syne' into the Peel Conner microphone. Jefferies stood at his side ready to announce 1923, a piper standing by ready to play in not just the new year but the British Broadcasting Company and the reign of Reith, its General Manager. For in the latter part of December 1922 the key steps towards establishing the BBC as working organisation had been taken. Staff had been appointed to fill four of the top five posts in the organisation; temporary accommodation had been put at the BBC's disposal; and a permanent home for the BBC and its 2LO studio had been chosen. The members of the Broadcasting Committee were now serving on the board of the British Broadcasting Company and had held their first meeting.

So, from Monday 1 January 1923 Burrows and Jefferies would no longer be operating 2LO on their own; they would be part of the new institution and working under Reith, a leader of immense vision and ability. Jefferies continued to work in the Marconi House, London, studio where he now acted formally as Director of 2LO. He still had a gruelling stint ahead of him but enjoyed increasing support as the BBC geared up for the task in hand and staff numbers slowly but surely increased.

The coming of the British Broadcasting Company did not mean an end to Marconi development work at 2LO. Round was now actively applying his inventive powers to evolving a sensitive microphone system capable of handling the full range of musical frequencies. Marconi policy was to develop and patent a total broadcasting package that could be employed in BBC stations yet to be built, as well as in those being planned in other countries. 2LO offered the ideal testing ground.

There was no way in which the Peel Conner microphone could be improved; it was a case of starting from scratch. For musical 'balance' one microphone would have to be placed at a substantial distance from the various sources of sound. An amplifier would therefore have to be employed to compensate for the consequent loss of microphone output. To cope with the frequency range, a composite microphone might be needed. With such thoughts in mind, Round turned his attention from the transmitter to the microphones in the Studio. Jefferies, as a result, had to endure all the inconvenience and disturbance of engineers testing in the 'Ditcham' manner - days of the week, months of the year being endlessly recited with an occasional chromatic scale on the piano from the bottom to the top being played by an engineer for frequency testing whilst Round vetted the results in the Transmitter Room - on one occasion, Round going to lunch forgetting to tell the assistant to stop testing.

Round's initial solution had a 'Jurassic Age' character; both the new microphone and its amplifier were of prodigious proportions and a source of immense dread to artistes, to the studio director and to the engineers in attendance. Jefferies remembered his introduction to the new 'Round' moving coil microphone in early January 1923:

'Round brought in a new type of microphone, very heavy in weight but excellent in quality. In his usual casual manner, he had this perched on top of a large box resting on a trolley affair on wheels. The microphone was kept precariously in position by means of straw, though why it didn't fall I don't know, as, apart from the small matter of fixing the microphone itself, the box wasn't fixed to the trolley and had a nasty habit of tilting over. The trolley also took it into its head to take a stroll on its own at the slightest touch. It was a valve box but we christened it the 'Soap Box' and soap box it was.' (*Soap Box Days*, *Popular Wireless*, 5 October 1935)

Apparently it was such an 'ungainly pile' that 'one had to sit on a high stool; if in the excitement of the moment one leant against the box the whole outfit would slowly slide away'. A sketch by Jefferies illustrated the arrangement in its initial form (Jefferies to Reith, 21 May 1937, *BBC Archives*).

The 'Round' microphone worked on the same electrodynamic principle as a telephone ear piece: an electromagnet had an air gap in which a coil of aluminium wire shaped like a disc was lightly mounted. Sound waves impinging on this coil caused it to vibrate in the magnetic field; this movement caused a voltage to be generated in the coil. The moving coil microphone had much less inherent noise (hiss) than the Peel Conner carbon microphone. One could therefore place it further from the source of the sound and make up for the resulting loss in input by using an adjacent amplifier (a 'pre-amplifier'). A pre-amplifier was not a solution for the Peel Conner microphone because of the heavy background electrical noise that the microphone generated, noise that would itself be amplified by any pre-amplifier.

Having achieved a quiet microphone which could pick up sound from anywhere in the room, two root problems remained to be solved; first, frequency response; secondly, amplification. The frequency response of the 'Round' microphone was little better than that of the Peel Conner. Round attempted to get over this by using several microphones in parallel with their diaphragms tuned, by means of knurled screws, to resonate at different frequencies.

By mid-February 1923 all the Peel Conner carbon microphones had gone from 2LO. In their place, the Round moving coil microphone system, a weird Heath Robinson arrangement of four heavy 'shell cases', weighing 20 pounds apiece, was being employed. These were perched upon the pedestal of soap boxes, the whole edifice entwined with wire and string. Eckersley, who, as the new chief engineer to the BBC had encountered the microphone that February, was amused by the screws - four to each of the four 'great iron contraptions'. Packing washers beneath these screws varied 'from bits of yesterday's newspaper rolled in a wad to chunks of fibre collected from the scrap box and, finally, quintessence of neatness, two sixpences shone in undiminished glory on the 'S blaster' as the high note magnetophone was affectionately called'. Within a few days four of these massive instruments were mounted in a wooden box, and set on a four-legged support. The box could be raised or lowered by means of toothed gear wheels and a handle (West, P E , *BBC Engineering: the First Five Years*, p17).

If the microphone was a source of anxiety for the announcer, it struck terror into the performer with its bolts, bars and wires galore. Stanley Lupino, the well-known comedian, described it as 'like a Ford car with the works out and the wheels off'. He had come straight from the Hippodrome where he was taking the part of 'Buttons' in 'Cinderella' and was still in his war paint. He spent several minutes scrutinising the apparatus at a safe distance, and was told it was time to go on. Clearing his throat he commenced: 'Hullo children! Buttons speaking. I wish you could see the thing I'm talking into. Really awful it is, I'm afraid it will go off any minute, so if you hear a bang you'll know what's happened.' (*Popular Wireless*, 31 March 1923)

In reality, the new microphone offered the performer much more freedom. With the Peel Conner, the artiste had to remain in a fixed position. One ragtime singer had found it torture. With her first note her left shoulder and left heel had begun to rise. With a look of terror she suddenly remembered her instructions and then endured the agony of trying to sing without moving a muscle. With the Round microphone the performer simply stood in front of the 'metal mass' and spoke or sang; no more stretching up to reach the hanging poorly adjusted microphones or leaning back when singing high notes. Round proudly announced: 'It will pick up anything in the room'. But he was still far from satisfied. For him, its fond parent, 'every evening's programme was a new experiment - a try out of his day's work. He was single-minded; the output of the microphone had to be constantly improved and that meant making endless adjustments to its amplifier next door.' (Palmer, Rex ,*The Star*, 10 November 1947)

If the microphone struck terror into the performers, the gargantuan amplifier brought many grey hairs to the heads of the engineers attending it. The first stages were especially sensitive and responded to mechanical vibrations even better than to electrical impulses. It was certainly out of the ordinary even for those days. In size it was simply enormous and it literally required a room to

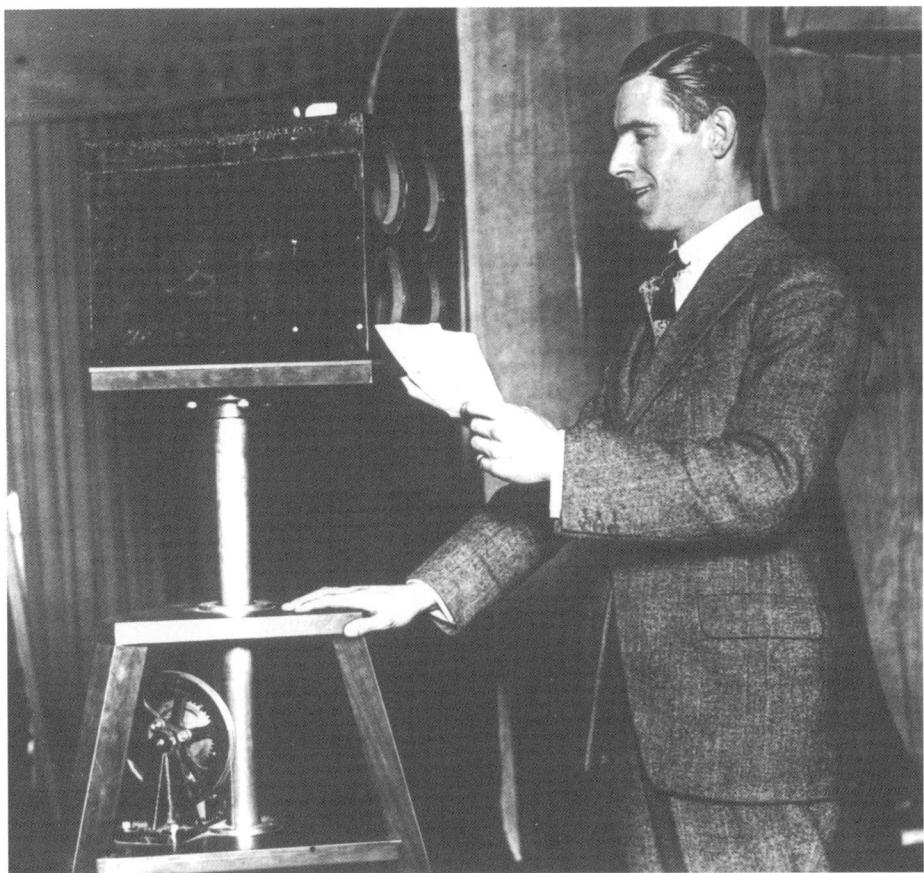

Reproduced by permission of the Marconi Co. Ltd
Stanton Jefferies at Round's moving coil microphone, Feb 1923.

itself, its dimensions being approximately 8ft long, 4.5ft high and about 2ft deep. It was divided into six metal compartments - three above and three below. The former held the valves and various components, while the latter held the L T and H T supplies. There were six stages of amplification, the number of valves used being ten. The last stage consisted of four valves in parallel, these being bright emitters and giving such a strong glare that it was necessary to shield the valves (A C Shaw, *World Radio*, 15 November 1935).

The amplifier had to be close to the studio and was built in the adjoining projection room. All the 'tricks of the trade' were tried to suppress the 'ponging'; for example, valves were suspended in mid-air by means of springs covered in cotton wool; another rather desperate measure was to suspend the valves in the first three stages upside down in beakers of thick oil. Once the equipment was ready for work one dared not move any wires or even approach too near (Harold Bishop, *BBC Yearbook 1948*, p 23).

Completion of the development work on the Round moving coil microphone and amplifier during February 1923 did not see the end to Round's use of the Marconi House studio as his laboratory. The massive composite microphone on its sturdy stand was not a complete success and it had hardly been put into service before Round had begun to work on an moving coil microphone of improved frequency response. By the end of April this latest instrument, though still far from perfect, was ready for service. It was to make its debut in the Savoy Hill studio that opened officially on the 1 May 1923.

Meanwhile, Round had learnt an important lesson. When the performer is at a distance from the microphone, the sound picked up is not wholly direct; a significant proportion is reflected from the four walls, floor and ceiling and muddies the quality of the transmission. Much more absorbent wall and ceiling linings were therefore required than were necessary with the Peel Conner microphones. This too would be a feature of the Savoy Hill studio when it opened for service.

Although the Marconi House studio was in active use for less than a year, and for only half that time was devoted full time to broadcasting , it had not merely a nostalgic appeal in later years but a real historical significance. It saw broadcasting evolve from the first tentative demonstration experiments in 1922 to the beginning of broadcasting under the guiding hand of the British Broadcasting Company in 1923. In terms of programmes, many firsts were achieved even though outside influence and controls limited the scope for what could be broadcast.

In 1937, the suggestion was put to Reith that the historic importance of the building in terms of broadcasting should be formally recognised. The idea came, not from Marconi, but from the BBC's ill-disposed protagonist of former years - the Air Ministry!

This seemingly improbable situation had a perfectly logical explanation. In 1933, the Marconi Company left Marconi House and its 600 staff moved to the new Electra House on the Victoria Embankment. Marconi House, London, was then taken over by the Air Ministry and given a new name - Ariel House. The Permanent Secretary to the Air Ministry in 1936/38 was Sir Donald Banks. He was well known to Reith, having served as Director General of the Post Office in 1934/36. They had got on well. 'With him at the Post Office', Reith had written, 'things will go much more simply with respect to our future constitution' (Reith, J C W., *The Reith Diaries*, 19 January 1934, quoted in

Briggs, Asa, *History of Broadcasting in the United Kingdom*. Vol: II: *The Golden Age of Wireless*, p476).

More to the point, Banks had been Private Secretary to four Postmasters-General in the period 1920 to 1923 when broadcasting from Marconi House was first authorised and when the BBC's future constitution was fashioned. As far as London was concerned, Marconi House was where it all started, the first successful wireless telephony experiments having been undertaken as early as 1913. Not surprisingly, Banks was sensitive to the need for, at the least, a plaque that could perhaps be unveiled with some ceremony (Banks to Reith, 22 April 1937, *BBC Archives*). Reith wanted to go further; he was keen to see the studio reconstituted as an historical exhibit and he wrote to Stanton Jefferies and Burrows for information on the way it was furnished back in 1922/23.

Meanwhile, he visited Marconi House (now Ariel House), perhaps to refresh his own memories of the layout but more likely as an honoured guest of Banks. It was the day that Ariel House became the office of the Department of Civil Aviation and, as such, it was opened by the Duke of Kent. Overhead flew the Empire class flying boat 'Caledonia', piloted by Captain A S Wilcockson of Imperial Airways. The pilot conversed with the Secretary of State for Air, Viscount Swinton, using Marconi transmitting and receiving apparatus installed on the seventh floor of the former Marconi House. It was as though all the threads were being woven together. Though Reith had no inkling at the time, he would himself become Chairman of Imperial Airways just two years later, in 1938, giving up the BBC and much of his life's work.

Assuming Reith and Banks looked around the seventh floor, they would have found the rooms at the Strand end little altered from 1923. The old Marconi cinema/studio may still have retained the 2LO piano. It was certainly there at the close of Marconi's occupation. The narrow corridor had a new door to the old studio but was otherwise unchanged; likewise the transmitter room with its roof lighting, a full 30ft long, 9.5ft wide. It would have been no great problem to bring the old transmitter back home from the studio at Brookmans Park and, fortunately, the BBC engineers still had one of the old Round moving coil microphones of Marconi House days.

On 8 May 1937, Burrows wrote back from Geneva where he occupied the post of Secretary General to the Union Internationale de Radiodiffusion. He was amused to learn that the 'attic' where 'we laid the foundations of British Broadcasting' might become a historic exhibit'. His letter included a sketch showing the studio and newsroom. In a second sketch, Burrows showed the way the studio was furnished. Burrows ended by suggesting Reith should consult Frank Hook, one of the BBC pioneers still on the staff, and Petersen, the Marconi engineer who had the job of constructing the transmitter under Round's guidance. Burrows admitted it had always been a mystery to him how Petersen escaped electrocution (Burrows, Arthur R, *Letter to Reith,* 8 May 1937).

Stanton Jefferies responded to a few days later with a plan of the studio which was almost identical to Burrows' sketch. However it showed the stand by the piano for the old Peel Conner microphone in place of Round's 'Soap Box' microphone which had been shown in Burrow's plan (Interestingly, the Round moving coil microphone appears to be located a full three yards from the orchestra.) Stanton Jefferies also showed the wooden forms in the passage to the stair which thereby acted as a sitting area or waiting room. Another sketch showed the Round experimental microphone of January 1923 perched on its 'soap box' and trolley. Jefferies, like Burrows, suggested Petersen be contacted. Petersen, as it happened, even remembered the room numbers:

> 'The original position (for the transmitter) was room 102 with room 115 as our battery room. We knocked down the partition between 102 and 103. We used 103 as our experimental laboratory.... The studio was in room 98 (just possibly, it was room 99)' (*Marconi Archives*).

Bishop too was ready to help. Using a room plan provided by the Air Ministry, he prepared a detailed plan of the studio based on Burrows' and Jefferies's sketches (Ch. 4: *2LO - The Experimental London Station*). Bishop also provided an original sketch of the transmitter circuit diagram which could be compared with the museum piece at Brookmans Park (Letters from Travis, Air Ministry, to Bishop, 30 August 1937 and Bishop to Sir Donald Banks, Air Ministry, 21 October 1937).

But it was all to no avail. The clouds of war were gathering and the Air Ministry soon had higher priorities.

The very future of the transmitter came under review in May 1939; it seems it was in the way. Bishop fought for its preservation even if this meant handing it over to G R M Garratt of the Science Museum. The Chief Engineer, Sir Noel Ashbridge, was sympathetic; he had saved the transmitter back in 1929 and would do so again.

It was dismantled and moved into a large garden shed and forgotten. Years later John Gilman, an engineer at the Brookmans Park transmitter, discovered it and worked on its assembly as a spare time hobby. It was then returned to its former place and, one night, was tested after close down. It worked perfectly into the station's aerial. The whole affair was kept very quiet. The staff involved were very impressed by the brilliance of the valves. The operation had been carefully planned with components such as chokes and transformers dried out in advance. 'We had a certain sense of awe', Gilman later wrote, 'at seeing it working again after so long' (John Gilman, *Ariel*, the BBC house magazine, 12 September 1981). For a few months in 1992, the veteran transmitter had a place of honour in the entrance hall of Broadcasting House in connection with the BBC's 70th anniversary celebrations.

The 2ZY Station at Trafford Park, Manchester

The name Marconi will always be associated with the establishment of broadcasting in this country. The firm had from the start been the prime mover in wireless communication, its resources being entirely directed to this end. On both the technical and programme sides the organisation had devoted its leading engineers and its most capable officers to the creation of a broadcasting service. They were in a position to do this single-handedly, given government clearance. Indeed Marconi's near monopoly of the relevant patents left little scope for any outside firm to play a part. Marconi's London preserve gave it further advantages when it came to staffing the BBC and accommodating its London station. Not surprisingly, a Marconi background gave applicants for posts an edge over other candidates when it came to working for the BBC and this continued to apply throughout the 'twenties', particularly on the engineering sites.

Other firms, large and small, were naturally keen to grasp the opportunity to expand by producing wireless equipment for the home; the leading electrical firms doubtless expected to corner the market. An investment of £10,000 was a small price to pay for the use of Marconi's long established and most fundamental patents. In all this, only one firm set out from the start to challenge Marconi and it is not altogether clear why they should have chosen to do so. This was Metropolitan-Vickers. It was as though they wanted to play a role equal to Marconi's in building and equipping wireless stations and in creating a national broadcasting organisation. So extreme was their ambition in this regard that they were, as we have seen, prepared to form their own consortium so as to gain approval from the Postmaster General to set up a rival broadcasting company.

The only obvious explanation for such a show of independence is that Metropolitan-Vickers wished to emulate the lead taken in America by Westinghouse, its most closely associated business partner on that side of the Atlantic. The moving spirit to all this was Sir Arthur Fleming, head of research at Metropolitan-Vickers. Fleming never lost any opportunity he had of reminding listeners that broadcasting had been launched by Westinghouse back in 1920 at their station KDKA, Pittsburgh. The inference was that the world did not need to wait for Marconi to show them how it could be done.

Fleming's own roots lay with Westinghouse. In Britain Westinghouse was initially established as an agency for selling and installing the products of the

American firm - gas and steam engines, generators, transformers, switch gear, meters, control gear and arc lamps. The decision was taken in 1899 to manufacture these goods in England and British Westinghouse was set up with works at Trafford Park, Manchester, where good access and an abundant supply of labour was available. The works were quickly constructed on a monumental scale. Behind five storey offices the main shop stretched a full 900ft and comprised five aisles up to 90ft wide and 80ft high. Alternating aisles were fitted with galleries providing a spatial quality not unlike that of Tate Modern, the converted London Power Station. Like the space in which they were housed, the machine tools were themselves gargantuan - the lathe 45ft long and the boring mill 28ft high. Railway tracks penetrated right into the Machine Shop, the wagons looking more diminutive in the great works than they would in any London terminus. On the far side of the access road lay the steel and iron foundries whilst, at the far end of the road, there rose a rather heavily engineered water tower with ample space around it, to allow for further expansion.

Initially, experienced Pittsburgh men took the key positions but future English replacements were hired and given two years training in America. Among them was Arthur (later Sir Arthur) Fleming. In 1908 Fleming took control over the training of apprentices and, in 1917, was also placed in charge of research. Two years later, British Westinghouse was acquired by Vickers who wished to supplement their production of steel, ships, trains and machinery with that of the associated electrical equipment. The name 'Metropolitan-Vickers' reflected the former activity which had its roots in the Metropolitan Carriage, Wagon and Finance Company.

Clearly, the emphasis was on heavy mechanical and electrical plant. Metropolitan-Vickers had no track record in wireless communications; for this they would have to turn to their associated firm, the Radio Communication Company (RCC). However, Fleming was so highly respected and one of the joint Managing Directors - Archibald McKinstry - so keen for Metropolitan-Vickers to make its mark, that its Research Department was given clearance to go ahead on all fronts associated with broadcasting.

The realisation in July 1922 that the Postmaster General might be about to approve two broadcasting companies must have sent a tremor through the high command at Metropolitan-Vickers, for nothing had yet been done in practical terms to cater for such an eventuality. If, on the formal announcement, the press descended on the works, some sign that Metropolitan-Vickers was at least active needed to be demonstrated. At this time, Fleming's research staff was squeezed into a single laboratory and a relatively new office block housed a boardroom, library and similar needs. A 50-watt transmitter of a kind that any wireless ham could have built was hurriedly constructed and the boardroom was taken over as a studio. Following American practice, a marquee like structure some 20ft by 10ft was constructed within the room and a Peel Conner type carbon microphone fitted on a stand. Into the studio went an HMV gramophone and an Aeolian Vocalian machine, borrowed from the maker. A Mignon-Welte reproducing piano became available in August - again on loan. One or two of the staff lent records, and some of the Research engineers agreed to announce them. Others were ready to man listening apparatus at Chorlton. Thus equipped, the Manchester Station, 2ZY, undertook experimental testing on 27 July and 3 August. But within a week, the 'Big Six' had settled for a single broadcasting company and the pressure was off.

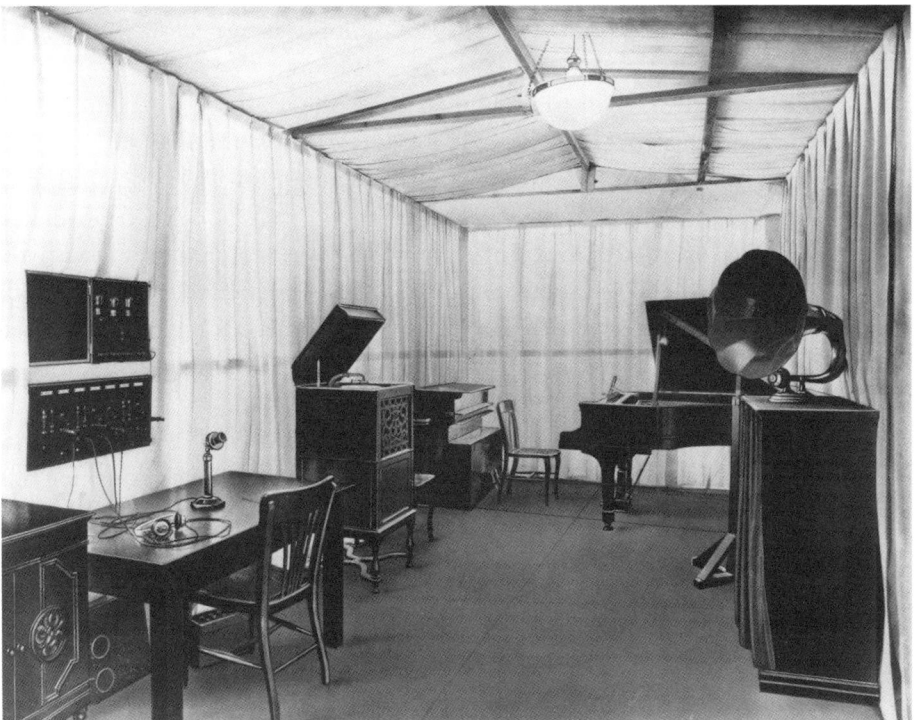

2ZY studio, Metropolitan-Vickers Works, Trafford Park, Manchester.

In October, with the formation of a single, jointly founded Broadcasting Committee, the pressure was on again. This time, it was not to be a question of proving Metropolitan-Vickers could broadcast but one of actually providing a nightly service with live performers broadcasting from a powerful 1.5-kilowatt transmitter.

The full force of what they had committed themselves to became a daunting reality. They had to start virtually from scratch, for at Manchester nothing would have induced them to have Marconi engineers in their own backyard (and *vice versa*), an attitude that persisted throughout the life of the Trafford Park station.

In haste, they turned to their sister organisation, the Radio Communication Company. The RCC were experienced in Marine Communication and would not let them down. Despite a tight timetable of just two weeks, the RCC delivered the essential apparatus. This comprised:

- High tension generators and associated control gear for supplying the valves.
- A 700-watt transmitter.
- Batteries for supplying the filaments of the transmitter valves.
- The aerial.
- A Peel Conner carbon microphone
- A piezophone pick-up (forerunner of the piezoelectric crystal pick-up later to be in common use) and its associated amplifier, for use with the gramophone.

The transmitter employed the choke system of modulation. Two 0/500 Mullard valves were used as oscillator valves and two more as modulators. A smaller 150-watt valve was used in the control circuit.

Norman Lea, RCC's Chief Engineer, installed the apparatus. A small room adjoining the studio became the transmitter room; a boarded off recess contained the batteries. The generators were located in a separate laboratory building about 60ft from the transmitter.

The transmitter was built on a light angle iron framework about 5ft 6in high and 2ft 6in wide. The upper section housed the valves with the aerial tuning inductor on top, transformers and batteries being mounted in the lower part.

The aerial consisted of a single 200ft wire suspended between the roof of a nearby building and the water tower at an average height of 150ft. A wire lead was taken almost vertically downwards from the centre of the aerial to the transmission room. On 2 November, a new cage aerial 80ft long was substituted with a cage type lead-in. The cages comprised six wires supported

ELECTRICAL GIANTS ENTER THE FIELD

on 3ft diameter hoops. On 14 January, this in turn would be replaced by an aerial of similar form but stronger.

It must have been an immense relief to Fleming to have the RCC's equipment installed and tested in time for the start of the regular British Broadcasting Committee service on 14 November. Indeed, it was only on 25 October that the first test of the new transmitter had taken place .

A second challenge was to provide a nightly service of talks and live music to supplement the endless round of records and the reproducing piano. It fell largely on Kenneth Wright, assisted by other staff of the Research Department, to provide the nightly programme; he quickly and quietly slipped into the role of Director of the new station, '2ZY'.

Kenneth Wright had been born in 1899 in a remote Norfolk village. His father possessed an organ and there was music in the family home. The village offered hymns and canticles at church and a village band played at the annual Oddfellows 'do'. Attendance at the City of Norwich school developed his thirst for music but this was not helped when, at the end of the war, he joined the Royal Engineers and encountered poor military bands and canteen pianos. It was his first hearing of the Hallé Orchestra, conducted by Beecham that 'flooded his world like a joyous sunrise'. He became a 'musical snob', to use his own words, spending his post-war government grant on a gramophone and records.

AEI

The original 2ZY transmitter at Metropolitan Vickers Works, Trafford Park, Manchester.

2ZY transmitting aerial supported by a water tower at Metropolitan-Vickers Works, Trafford Park, Manchester.

Meanwhile, he took an engineering degree at Sheffield University, graduating with Honours in Mechanical and Electrical Engineering in 1920, when he joined Metropolitan-Vickers' Research Department.

There can be little doubt that it was Kenneth Wright who prepared the studio for its new broadcasting role. First, a Steinway grand piano with a Welte reproducing attachment was brought into the studio which had to be extended by 4ft to house it. Secondly, various types of gramophone were tested as a result of which a New Edison machine of the latest diamond-disc type arrived to supplement the Aeolian Company's Vocalian Gradvola cabinet gramophone.

The first live concert occurred on 31 October using talent from the works - Douglas Black (violin), Sydney Nightingale (baritone), Miss Louisa Bennie (mezzo-soprano) and Kenneth Wright (piano).

The staff of the Research Department continued to 'do their bit' once broadcasting commenced; Miss A Bennie virtually ran the 'Children's Corner' as the 'Lady of the Magic Carpet', with help from Kenneth Wright (Uncle Humpty Dumpty) and Sydney Nightingale (The Sandman). Captain H G Bell read the news and provided talks as 'Mr X'; W V Brown helped in this as 'Mr Z'. Others stepped in as 'Mr X' whenever Captain Bell was called away. Major Buckley, who had special responsibility for the microphone department, found time to join Arthur Fleming in a double act as 'Rastus and Massa Johnson'.

But the creation of the evening concert stretched Wright's resources to the limit and, not surprisingly, he fell back heavily on the gramophone and the Weltz reproducing player, at least in the initial weeks leading up to Christmas. For this purpose, the Gramophone Company (later part of EMI) was asked to provide records. They agreed, subject to the stipulation that records could only be supplied free of charge provided no other company's records were used and provided that publicity was given to the Gramophone Company.

Burrows, as Director of the Marconi 2LO station was disturbed that Metropolitan-Vickers should embark on such broadcasting on the eve of nightly broadcasting by the British Broadcasting Committee (Burrows to Isaacs, 10 November 1922, *BBC Archives*). Basil Binyon, Managing Director of RCC, also expressed his disapproval. He wrote to McKinstry protesting at 2ZY's excessive reliance on records, noting that most of the live music seemed to be provided by an employee named Black who, with the help of relatives and friends, provided an amateur orchestra. Binyon complained that most of the announcing was done by college apprentices in their blue overalls! (Binyon to McKinstry, 25 November 1922, *BBC Archives*).

In fairness the 'college apprentices' were all, like Wright himself, graduates in mechanical and electrical engineering selected by interview to undertake a two-year 'college apprenticeship' at the works. As such they were the pick of the young talent and went into one of the various Works Departments - manufacturing, design, and research - where they received further training. Fleming's dual role as Head of Research and Education ensured a supply of about 100 college apprentices of high calibre.

The rebuke did not fall on deaf ears, although Wright was acutely conscious of the fact that he could offer no fees, only payment of out of pocket expenses. A case in point is the invitation to Herbert James Harwood to broadcast in early December. Harwood ran a Vaudeville Company. Following the broadcasts Wright wrote to thank him and the others in the group - Miss Ada Lodge, Mr Reid and W J Harwood - 'for the kindly help you gave us' adding 'may I be so bold as to ask if you would be good enough to bring the same party again to broadcast some evening …. If you could bring a violinist also, it would be a very desirable feature, inasmuch as many people's receiving sets distort violin tone less than speech or song.' (Wright to H J Harwood, 8 December 1922, in the possession of his daughter, Mrs Catherine Topham).

Victor Smythe, perhaps the greatest of the 2ZY personalities, had much the same experience when he applied to broadcast. Initially the response was very much to the point,

> 'Dear Sir, With reference to your letter of the 10th inst., I shall be pleased to see you at the above address at 3.00pm on Tuesday next. Yours faithfully K A Wright, Station Director'
> (Wright to Smythe, 14 December 1924).

Little came of this meeting until 1 February when Smythe appeared out of the rain resplendent in 'wide brimmed hat and a long fur-collared coat suggestive of Henry Irving'. He read the news, gave a talk as 'Mr X' and then did several humorous sketches at intervals during the musical evening. One of his comic turns, 'Algy's Priceless Piffle', was so successful it became a regular Saturday night feature (Hartley, Ian, 1932). Despite this, Wright responded to his plea for suitable payment with:

> 'Dear Mr Smythe, I quite appreciate what you say regarding your recent appearance on the air. You will, however, appreciate the enormous publicity value an artiste receives through the radio. I will, however, see what can be done to increase your payments for future engagements.'
> (Wright to Smythe, 8 February 1923)

For singers and instrumentalists the 'publicity value' provided by broadcasting was, to say the least, open to question as long as the Peel Conner carbon microphone had pride of place.

Nevertheless, Smythe was soon working in the studios from 9.30am to midnight as announcer, as Mr X and almost running the place as Wright's number one; but his remuneration varied between 7s 6d and 17s 6d per week, a paltry sum. Unfortunately, it had to come out of Metropolitan-Vicker's coffers as the BBC had determined not to take on provincial staff until they had opened a permanent Manchester station in August 1923.

The engineers looked desperately for an alternative to the Peel Conner carbon microphone that would not prove too expensive and soon realised they would have to develop their own solution. Fleming pinned his hopes on an idea presented back in 1918 by Sir William Bragg and Professor H O Rankine - the photophone.

In the photophone a very small mirror is attached to a diaphragm, vibrated by the impinging sound waves. Light is focussed from a lamp on to the vibrating mirror. The reflected light beams on to a selenium photocell to varying degrees depending on the angle of rotation of the mirror; that converts it into an electric current that, amplified, modulates the transmitter.

Amazingly, it worked, but only after seven stages of amplification had been applied!

Excellent reproduction of music was obtained, especially from the piano once the best position for the latter had been settled by trial and error. Speech, however, was muffled, as it was necessary to use a cone or trumpet as a mouthpiece to concentrate the sound sufficiently to move the mirror. One report called for an improvement 'with regard to the sharpness of articulation of the words occurring in songs .... a slight wooliness (seems) to be present.' (Norman Lea, Chief Engineer RCC, 29 December 1922). Various types of horn were tried ranging from a full blown trumpet to a narrow cone. In general, these simply projected through the studio's draped lining, behind which the photophone was hidden from view.

During the months that followed the photophone's instalment in December, some well known artistes began to visit the studio to perform in the knowledge that the new microphone would do a little more justice to their talent. Photographers were often present on these occasions and their pictures possess a surreal quality as we see artistes like Hamilton, Harris and Isobel Baillie singing or instrumentalists like Isolde Menges playing her violin, facing a great protruding and flared horn.

In some of these photographs, we see Jessie Cormack at the piano. She had become almost the official accompanist at 2ZY by the end of 1922 and as the 'Cloudy Lady' began to play a key part in the 'Kiddies Corner', which was now

THE 2ZY STATION AT TRAFFORD PARK, MANCHESTER

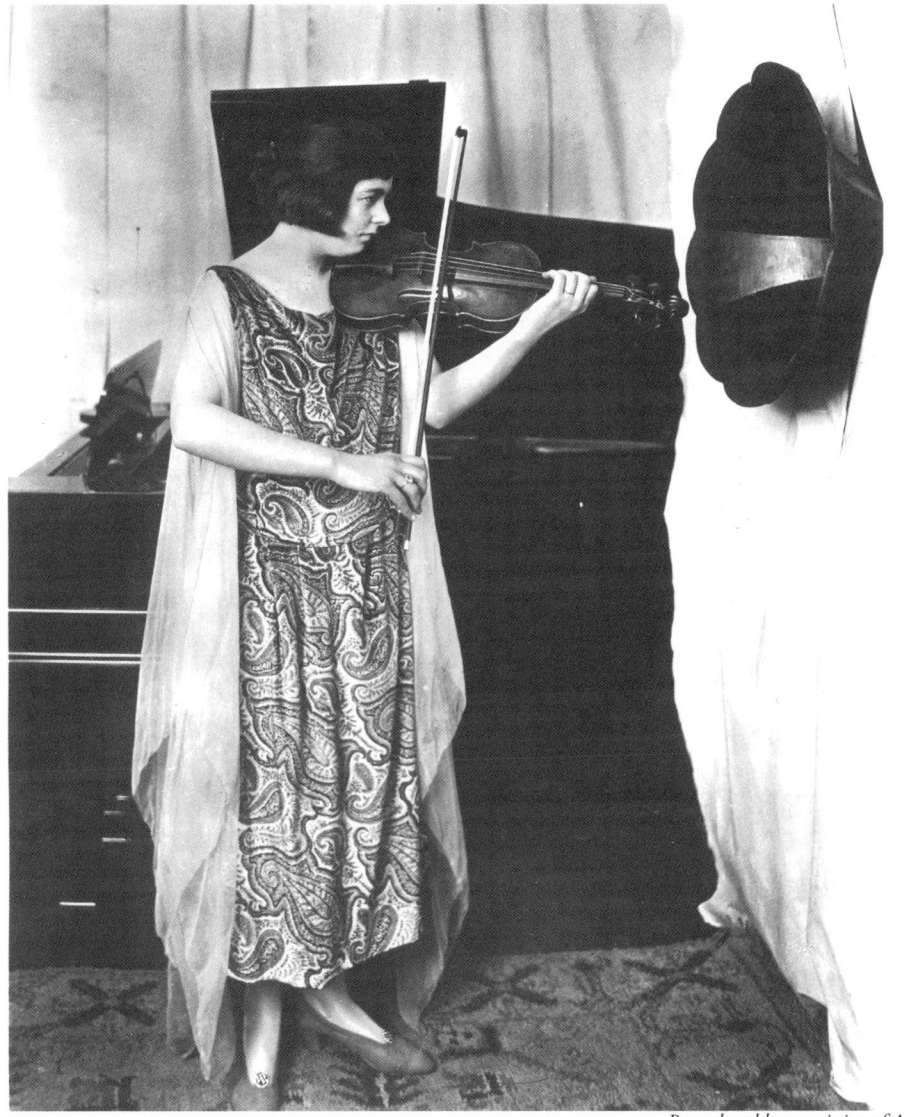

Reproduced by permission of AEI
Isolde Menges with horn microphone in 2ZY studio, Trafford Park, Manchester.

divided into two parts so as to entertain both the younger and the older children. Another photo (not shown) is of the almost resident 'Wireless Trio', comprising Leonard Hirsch (violin) and Sydney Wright (cello) playing into the flared horn with Jessie Cormack at the piano. The picture of Sydney

Nightingale differs from the others in that it shows a slim cone in use in place of the flared horn.

The ingenious photophone was beset with a number of practical problems. It was set on a framework a full 6-ft in length and even this was not as large as the engineers would have liked. Fortunately, there was ample space between the studio lining and the internal wall of the Boardroom in which the studio had been built. A sort of studio annexe 10ft by 4ft was therefore arranged in the gap to house the photophone. Precautions were taken to ensure that the apparatus was not affected by mechanical vibration from, for instance, the nearby piano. The mirror of the photophone also responded to the slightest air movement and many were the cries of 'Keep that b***** door shut'.

Being fixed rigidly in place, the photophone could not be adjusted to the height of the performer who, if necessary, had to stand on a pile of books - one short tenor, standing on volumes of the Encyclopaedia Britannica, stepped back as he reached his crescendo and collapsed ignominiously on to the studio floor!

The photophone demanded an extraordinary level of amplification. The studio already had a three-stage amplifier to cope with the piezophone. This was duly supplemented with a four-stage amplifier. Soon a permanent seven-stage version was built against the opposite wall and the two amplifiers were moved into the Transmitter Room where they were placed on the engineer's desk. This development was in operation by February 1923.

The new arrangement meant, however, that the Transmitter Room could now control modulation. To receive guidance from the Transmitter Room, the Studio Manager had to rely on a panel of lamps each designed to convey a particular message such as 'louder'; 'softer'; 'forward'; 'backward'. At the same time, other lamps on the panel identified the instrument or singer in question. He then acknowledged the instruction by activating a return pilot light in the Transmitter Room and conveyed the necessary adjustment to the artiste performing at the microphone.

The inability of the photophone to cope with speech meant that the studio retained the Peel Conner carbon microphone for announcing and talks. During the evening programme, a good deal of switching from one to the other occurred as speech gave way to music and vice versa. The announcer would press the appropriate switch to alert the transmitter room to a microphone change; there, the operator would re-connect and signal this back by activating the pilot lamp over the appropriate microphone switch on the studio switchboard.

Reproduced by permission of AEI
Sydney Nightingale, with Jessie Cormack, using the conical microphone in the 2ZY studio.

As if all the development work on microphones and amplifiers and switching was not enough to keep them occupied - not to mention their performing roles at the microphone - the engineers turned their attention to the 700-watt transmitter. This operated at only half the authorised power and its four 0/500 valves - two oscillators, two modulators - were under maximum load. The engineers lost no time in upgrading the transmitter, adding an oscillator valve and two modulator valves. By the end of 1922 the set was run at maximum load, the power of the transmitter being doubled - although breakages began to occur at roughly weekly intervals!

It could be argued that 2ZY had achieved the essential requirements for a broadcasting station in terms of power and quality of transmission. But it had not been put on a sustainable footing. The transmitter was at its extreme limit and the microphone was bulky, inflexible, temperamental and insensitive.

The location of the studio at the back end of the massive industrial complex posed one more problem; artistes and speakers must have found it daunting to turn out on cold, dark nights in an attempt to find the little studio in the empty works, especially when they knew that payment would be limited to 'out of pocket' expenses. Fortunately, Isobel Baillie lived close by in Stretford and came escorted by her husband. Moreover, they could enjoy the light refreshments provided from February by Metropolitan-Vickers for the artistes and night staff.

Then again, 2ZY lacked the most essential feature of any broadcasting station - a wireless orchestra. Even if such an orchestra could be funded, fitting it into the diminutive studio and feeding the volume of sound into the photophone mouthpiece would have presented insuperable problems. So it was all down to the engineers, the women employees and even the college apprentices under the direction of the young Station Director Kenneth Wright to provide much of the nightly service - again hardly a suitable arrangement, even to cover the period leading up to hand-over to the BBC. This station was, in any case, not exactly at the top of the BBC's list of priorities; the further north of England and also Scotland and Wales would take precedence. Manchester would just have to struggle on, attending to every problem as it arose.

First, the microphone and amplifier problems were examined. The old RCC three-stage amplifier was brought back into the studio and placed under the photophone; the shorter connecting cable reduced the electrical interference picked up.

The engineers then attempted to develop a new moving coil microphone for use in speech. They decided to use a loudspeaker backwards - by speaking into the diaphragm, obtaining an electrical output at the terminals. Their choice was an Amplion Junior loudspeaker, damped with oil to overcome its tendency to emphasise certain frequencies. The result fell short of the photophone for music and was poor for speech. But it was portable. This meant it could be taken out of the studio and, given a GPO landline, right out of the works. In short, the moving coil microphone could go to the concert hall rather than having the orchestra come to the studio. The Oxford Picture House provided a wonderful opportunity to experiment as it had its own orchestra which played nightly. The moving coil microphone was enclosed in a wooden box with felt packing and fixed on a stand by an adjustable bracket. To achieve balance, two such microphones were positioned at the back of the stage with the piano in between. They pointed outward towards the violins and cellos and away from the piano which would otherwise have dominated everything. After preliminary amplification, the signals were led into the studio for further amplification by either the RCC amplifier or a new screened amplifier on the opposite side of the studio. The nightly programmes from 5 March now included orchestral music starting at 7pm and at little cost to 2ZY!

Finally, on the eve of hand over, 2ZY achieved two remarkable technical breakthroughs; these finally sorted out the problems posed respectively by the transmitter and the microphone. The problem for the former was that its glass valves were limited in practice to 500 watts, since above this power, overheating tended to shatter the glass envelope. The Mullard Company, which had links with RCC, came up trumps with powerful 2.5-kilowatt air-cooled silica valves. One oscillator valve and one modular valve were sufficient to run the station and they were placed either side of the RCC transmitter. The latter was retained as a standby.

More work, directed at making the moving coil microphone a sensitive microphone, had good results. The heavy oil damping formerly applied was replaced by selective Vaseline damping between the pole face and the diaphragm. The horn was discarded and the instrument thus became equally suitable for the transmission of music and speech; microphone switching was no longer necessary. In its little box the microphone could be attached either to a stand or placed in the ceiling of the studio. A pair of microphones was sometimes used, presumably designed to peak at different frequencies like the composite Marconi House 'Soap box' microphone. The new instrument replaced the Peel Conner and the photophone in the studio and also the oil damped moving coil microphone used for Outside Broadcasts. It was patented on 9 June 1923.

Finally a separate control room was created at the other end of the building where monitoring of programmes could take place in a silent room equipped with a suitable receiver. Here the engineers would not have to contend with low frequency sounds coming from the studio nor with the hum of the transmitting valves.

With the completion of a new BBC station in the heart of Manchester at the beginning of August 1923, the BBC abandoned not only the Metrovick temporary station but also all the equipment it contained. At a stroke, a line was drawn through months of exhausting development work. For the BBC it was as though Fleming and his brilliant team had never existed. For Hugh Bell, W J Brown, Major V W Buckley and others the great adventure of setting up 2ZY and amusing an unseen audience with talks, humorous sketches and jokes came to a sudden end. Kenneth Wright was, at last, taken on to the BBC staff but immediately transferred to London; his days as 'Uncle Humpty Dumpty' with a huge following of children was now over. But he always treasured the camaraderie of his 2ZY colleagues in those hectic days. Nothing comparable in London could give him any solace for the loss he felt.

The 2WP/5IT Station at Witton, Birmingham

On the face of it, the Witton broadcasting station, set up in the middle of a great manufacturing works in Birmingham, compared closely with that at Trafford Park, Manchester. Both were ready for the first night of broadcasting and both cities were, to an extent, neglected by the BBC until new permanent stations were built in city centre locations in August 1923. However, for Metropolitan-Vickers at Manchester, broadcasting was a baptism by fire, a great leap in the dark. It had all the doggedness and enthusiasm of Fleming to see it through, allied to McKinstry's determination to block any clean sweep by Marconi across the broadcasting field. In addition, the Radio Communication Company was relied upon to kick-start the operation. The entry of Western Electric into the contest at Birmingham was altogether low key by comparison and certainly a much more natural progression.

Like Marconi, Western Electric was pre-eminent in a major sphere of electrical communication; but whereas Marconi had devoted itself primarily to wireless, Western Electric's whole existence had been bound up with perfecting the telephone as a means of national and international communication. The desk telephone of 1922 hardly differed from its forerunner of 1898 but the way it was connected to all other telephones had, by 1923, been revolutionised.

Landmarks on the path of progress involved the London Toll Exchange, the introduction of automatic telephone exchanges for public use and the development of valve powered 'repeater' stations that amplified speech signals at various points along long distance telephone lines. These repeater stations overcame the degradation normally associated with long transmission lines.

Then there was the development of carrier frequencies by Western Electric, whereby the same telephone line could convey both audio and a number of radio frequencies (each of which could carry an audio frequency) without interference between them, thereby economising in long distance telephone lines. This technique was used when the Mayor of Bristol's speech, described earlier, was relayed to London and broadcast by 2LO on 3 November 1922. Such carrier circuits could be used both for telephony and for telegraphy.

But it was the development of its public address system that directed Western Electric's attention towards broadcasting. The system so magnified the voice that the speaker could address vast crowds. First, a sensitive microphone had to be developed that would eliminate any need to speak close to it, allowing freedom of movement. Secondly, a powerful good quality multi-stage amplifier had to be developed. Finally, loudspeakers were needed to distribute the sound waves uniformly across the space occupied by the audience, whether in a hall or in the open air. Western Electric was well placed to initiate a broadcasting service.

Being London based, with its main works at Woolwich and New Southgate and its offices in Aldwych, Western Electric posed a potential threat to Marconi's 2LO station at a time when, in June 1922, two London stations and two broadcasting companies were a distinct possibility. Marconi may have felt only too glad to reach a deal, whereby there would be one London Station - 2LO - in exchange for Western Electric being allocated the construction of a single provincial station - Birmingham.

Having secured this agreement, Western Electric, like Metropolitan-Vickers, appear to have taken little more action until negotiations on the form of the future BBC had been virtually concluded. It may be that priority was being given to another all-important aspect - the designing, production and marketing of receivers. The period coincided with major exhibitions of wireless equipment in London (see Ch. 4: *Initiating the Public into the Mysteries of Wireless*). Orders for Western Electric crystal sets outstripped supply and had to be dealt with according to the size and date of the order (*Men Of The Day*, Special Illustrated Supplement on the Western Electric Company, September 1923, p705). Valve sets also had to be designed, approved and produced. Perhaps the most striking success lay with the introduction of the Western Electric loudspeaker. It was supplied with a special power amplifier. A feature of Western Electric receivers was the care taken to enclose the circuit components, leaving only the terminals and controls exposed. This made the sets acceptable and part of the furniture in the home. Another advance, one which made for small portable apparatus, was Western Electric's remarkable baby valve - the 'Wecovalve'. This 'peanut' type, only two inches in height, could operate on a filament supply of one dry cell. Yet it functioned just as well as its bigger brothers.

But important though production might be, transmission had become a high priority by October 1922 and whilst RCC raced to complete their 700 watt transmitter, Western Electric, early in October, began to design their own transmitter in a laboratory at Oswaldestre House, Norfolk Street, London - little more than a stone's throw from 2LO. The station was ready for testing by the end of the month.

The station made use of Western Electric's public address 'double button' carbon microphone. This microphone had recently been developed by the Bell Laboratories in America. It had a push-pull arrangement, having carbon granule 'buttons' on both sides of the diaphragm centre, thereby counteracting to some extent the distortion inherent in carbon microphones and extending the useable frequency response.

2LO's Engineer, R H White, anxious to check for possible interference from the Western Electric Station, arranged for both stations to broadcast simultaneously on 5 November from 5 pm to 6pm, 2LO transmitting on 360 metres and 2WP on 425 metres (White to Burrows, 3 November 1922). In the apparent absence of any follow-up, we must assume all was well.

The next step was to take up the offer of the General Electric Company to house the Western Electric station in their works at Witton, Birmingham. The sheer spread of the industrial complex must have looked daunting to the Western Electric engineers as they approached for the first time to install their apparatus. One of them later recalled four of them 'driving up in a taxi to the massive front entrance of the GEC works, greatly wondering, and with something of that feeling which is associated with the dentists' waiting room, we were taken up lifts and along corridors until we arrived in a large sort of store room'. In a corner of this, they had to erect the station. Their instructions were to get it installed in time to broadcast the results of the General Election then in progress. In charge of the operation was A E Thompson assisted by E M Deloraine, A G L Mason and F H Amis. At the London end, the equipment had to be dismantled and packed on to steam lorries on 11 November but, owing to dense fog, it did not arrive at Birmingham until late the following afternoon.

> 'There were just three days in which to clear the floor space, build and furnish the studio, operating and reception rooms, erect the antenna and organise the first programme. Those who took part (were) never likely to forget those hectic days, or the thrill of achievement when, at 5pm on Wednesday 15 November, the Birmingham broadcasting station went on air'
> (Thompson, A E , *The Silver Jubilee of Broadcasting*, Standard News, House Journal of Standard Telephone and Cables; No.3, 1948).

In its history, scale and setting the Witton works had much in common with the Metropolitan-Vickers plant in Manchester. A large area of land on the edge of the city had been acquired in about 1900 on which an engineering works, foundry, drawing office and powerhouse were erected. The Great War saw a huge increase, both in output and range, of work undertaken, the works serving military requirements such as shell production. With the cessation of hostilities, the emphasis was once again on heavy engineering plant such as generators, motors, switch gear and rotary convectors. Administrative offices were built as a centrepiece set back from the road behind a large lawn. The whole complex took on an early 20th century look - one of modern industry - clean, functional and, above all, impersonal. The complex of buildings was not only difficult to reach but was unwelcoming to those intrepid enough to approach it. This was particularly the case after dark when the works were deserted save for those involved with running the little wireless station. One visitor towards the end of 1922 put it in these words:

> 'My visit to the Birmingham Broadcasting Station was after dark. I travelled from the centre of Birmingham by a bumping train route to the very outskirts of the city and, here at Witton after a ten to fifteen minutes walk I at length came to an extensive group of buildings. Here and there in the mass of shadowy buildings there were brilliantly lit windows, whilst the road around them, with crossroads and sectional ways running off in all directions, were illuminated by great arc lamps. A commissionaire led me by way of a double flight of stairs, a long hallway, a narrow hanging bridge, a long winding passage to a door. 'There', he said, pointing. I entered and found myself in a kind of reception room in which there were a dozen persons, some conning music, some talking, yet all waiting. It was obvious I had arrived at my destination' (*Popular Wireless*, 10 March 1923).

Percy Edgar, the first Station Director, had similar recollections of the approach and described the layout of the station in more detail:

> 'Artistes - and it was as an artiste that I first appeared at the station - were transported from the city by taxi each night through that first winter. We entered the main offices of the GEC by a side entrance, climbed a flight of stairs, traversed three quarters of a long corridor, turned left over an iron bridge and found ourselves in three small (adjoining) rooms in the packing warehouse. One contained the gear including the transmitting plant, (one) served the triple purpose of office, waiting room and canteen, (the third being) the studio, a narrow room about 12ft by 20ft hung with heavy grey draperies of coarse material. There was no ventilation. The room contained a

(Weber) player piano, a gramophone (Aeolian) and the microphone, which was placed at the level of the average artiste's mouth and placed on a heavy four-legged wooden stand of the type which, in Victorian houses, commonly supported an aspidistra. Above the roof was the aerial, 110ft long by 80ft high running north and south; 18ft spreaders (supported) four wires spread 6ft apart.'

'Everyone whom I consulted advised me to turn it down. This broadcasting would be just a passing craze. However, I had a strong conviction that for me this was the opportunity which knocks but once at a man's door, and I decided to accept.' (Edgar, Percy, *Radio Times*, 10 September 1937, also *Popular Wireless Weekly* 10 March 1923).

Percy Edgar was already steeped in the world of entertainment when he arrived at Witton. Born in 1884, he had performed on the concert platform during the seven years leading up to the Great War, when he organised camp and military hospital concerts. After the War he continued to organise concerts but clearly still yearned to 'tread the boards' of the theatrical and music hall stage. This meant touring and playing on occasion to rowdy audiences. Edgar's speciality was to present characters from 'Dickens and one second house Saturday night audience 'gave him the bird'. Edgar decided he had had enough and was glad to accept a post in 1921 as director of the Birmingham concert agency. Then came the new calling - broadcasting.

Probably, to check the nature of the task ahead, one of the first things Edgar would have done would have been to consult 'The Manager's Note Book'. This was a book about 8in. by 7in. and an inch thick in which, from the opening night, Thompson recorded the exact content of each night's programme, the names of the artistes performing, their respective roles, the microphone position and the times of the commencement and final close down. Writing in 1937, Edgar referred to the book as 'a precious relic of those early days'. Entries continued, covering the whole period up to 3 March 1923 (*Managers Notebook*, BBC Written Archives).

But the Notebook alone would hardly have prepared Edgar for the exacting duties that lay ahead, duties that would involve working fifteen hours a day. The Station Director had to prepare the nightly programme, book the artistes and arrange their transport. He had to announce the items, read the news, manipulate the gramophone and devise a 'Children's Corner' which would often

AEI
The original studio of 5IT at Witton, Birmingham, 1922.

involve most of the station staff. There was no way Thompson could undertake this on his own nor assume that Edgar would agree to do so if this meant, as it would, giving up his agency and losing his livelihood.

Edgar later wrote how, about a fortnight after his first appearance before the microphone, he was offered the management of the Birmingham Station, and how, shortly after his installation, he had appointed Harold Casey as Assistant Manager. Mr James Sockett joined them as announcer and Amis and Deloraine became the station engineers - in all a staff of five (Edgar, Percy, *Radio Times*, 10 September 1937).

These offers of permanent paid posts must have had the backing of the Broadcasting Committee or at least that of the Committee's Chairman, Sir William Noble. The Committee had in fact taken over formal responsibility for the station on 18 November 1922, changing its call sign from 2WP to 5IT. The Committee's offer came at a time when similar offers of jobs in London were about to be made by them for staffing the future BBC.

Birmingham's desperate need for priority action had been recognised; the Marconi and Metropolitan-Vickers men could afford to wait a few more days. The offer to Edgar in the opening days of December 1922 and the speedy appointment of other staff to 5IT must have constituted the first appointments in Britain to the national broadcasting service. They were confirmed by the BBC early in January 1923, that is, within the first few days of the organisation's existence.

The way was now clear for Thompson to return to London, but not before he had made an enduring contribution to broadcasting history.

> 'Within ten days of the opening of the Birmingham Station the 'Children's Corner' was introduced and 'Uncle Tom' created. For copyright reasons, published literature was forbidden. This was an unforeseen handicap, but one that was soon overcome. In a shop was discovered a grotesque china cat with big, green eyes. Her broad grin suggested the most amusing bedtime stories. She was forthwith adopted as 'Susan' and made her bow in the first 'Children's Corner' along with 'The Dance of the Goblins' and other gramophone records; when imaginary feline adventures became exhausted, a 'cross-talk' partner was acquired. F H Amis was elevated to the status of 'Uncle' and became 'The Fairy Dustman'. Everything was done spontaneously.'
>
> (Thompson, A E , *The Silver Jubilee of Broadcasting*).

Thompson always claimed the 'Children's Hour' as his own idea with himself as the very first 'Wireless Uncle'. The programmes, thrown in as an extra rather than as part of the normal evening 'concert' were not recorded in the 'Manager's Notebook' until 5 December when a note in the 'Remarks' column referred to 'Children's Story 6.30'. A footnote in a different hand referred to the content of the Children's programme. Again it started with the 'Goblin's Dance' (the signature tune?); Edgar - it may have been his first day as Station Director - read a story, 'Spick and Span'; Thompson contributed a trombone solo; Casey as 'Uncle Pat' then rounded things off. From then on, Uncle Thompson and Uncle Edgar become renowned as the joint presenters and a photograph shows them on either side of the microphone talking to the children. Within a few days, 'Uncle Pat' had taken over from Thompson and became very popular as a singer and children's entertainer.

Although steeped in the technical side of broadcasting, Thompson soon learnt that other skills were required when it came to presenting the programmes in the studio.

> 'One of the worst moments was caused by two old ladies giving a pianoforte duet. Signals urging them to begin apparently did not register simultaneously, and as the players continued, blissfully unconscious of the discord, the microphone was switched off. Soon the studio door was cautiously opened and the monitoring engineer hissed into the announcer's ear – "We're off the air!" The announcer whispered back – "You're telling me!". The consternation of the old ladies' friends and the frantic coaxing of their crystal sets when everything went dead can well be imagined.' (Thompson, A E, *The Silver Jubilee of Broadcasting*)

On another occasion, Thompson had persuaded a soubrette from the Aston Hippodrome to come and broadcast. She did - and gave her act as though on stage, 'Prancing from one end of the studio to the other with Thompson panting after her with the microphone and a long, trailing lead. After that he got some old packing cases and made a rough platform on which artistes were required to 'stay put' during their broadcast - if they didn't they just fell off! (Edgar, Percy, *Radio Times*, 10 September 1937).

But the ultimate nightmare for the studio manager was when artistes just did not to turn up. This time, it was Edgar who had to handle the problem. It was Christmas Eve 1922. He did his best to fill in but there was nothing for it but to announce his predicament to listeners. Frederick Warrander, the pianist, happened to be listening and at once collected some music, hailed a taxi and dashed across to Witton where he gave a recital. A Mr Entwistle also arrived with his accompanist to sing. To Edgar's relief the show went on.

Some months later, things began to improve. In March 1923 artistes at last began to be paid and in May, Gladys Colbourn joined the staff as Secretary to Edgar, providing the Birmingham Children's Hour with its first 'Auntie'. A fourth room was acquired to provide a joint office for Edgar, Casey, Miss Colbourn and also for Cecil Lewis on his arrival in June.

Although Western Electric had by then ceased to carry responsibility for the Birmingham Station, the two provincial stations were still having to make their own way independently of London. Although London's 'Head Office' influence became ever greater, there was still scope for the provincial stations to influence

London. For example, the form adopted for the Children's Hour at 5IT with its named uncles and aunts set a pattern for other stations as they came to be opened, not to mention the London Station 2LO, itself. Birmingham also pioneered the 'Radio Circle', a sort of club for children who, for a small subscription, were given a coloured certificate, a badge and had their names read out on the air on their birthdays, sometimes with a greeting from their favourite uncle or aunt. The various Radio Circles did good work for children in hospital, members donating toys or helping in other ways.

The Birmingham Station remained, however, most notable for the quality of its music reproduction, largely as a result of its use of the 'double button' carbon microphone. Despite months of work by Fleming in Manchester and by Round in London, the Western Electric 'double button' microphone outpaced both the photophone and the moving coil microphone and continued to do so throughout 1923, both in the studio and on location. The performer or speaker could be placed one to three feet from the microphone, the loss of strength being compensated for by means of a three-stage 'WE 8A' amplifier. The good natured microphone amplifier posed none of the problems associated with those in Manchester or London.

GEC

Instrument room at 5IT, Witton, Birmingham.

The Western Electric Station, though of high technical quality, lacked the power of its counterparts in London and Manchester, being rated at about 500 watts - a third of the permitted power. The generator comprised three units mounted on a common base-plate. A control panel for the generator stood alongside and a little to the right was the transmitter. This housed two 250-watt oscillators and two 250-watt modulators along with a 50-watt valve for amplifying speech input.

A more serious deficiency than the low power of the transmitter lay in the fact that the studio was so small that it even lacked room for a grand piano and had to make do with an upright. It also lacked ventilation and, with its heavy grey drapes and thick carpet, must have been claustrophobic to work in. 'Edgar later recalled how he managed to squeeze in a brass band - it was the night of 14 May:

> The drummer was the last in, the door then being bolted so he would not fall backwards if someone inadvertently opened it from the outside. Soon, every member of the band had shed everything save under-vest and trousers, their braces now looped over their hips. The conductor, a martyr to the dignity of His Majesty's Grenadier Guards retained his tunic and literally dripped through the performance. The amount of liquid refreshment required to revive them after the experience was prodigious' (Edgar, Percy, *Radio Times*, 10 September 1937, *BBC Handbook 1948*, pp 10-13).

For Edgar, who retired in 1948, reminiscing must have been like looking back into an 'Alice in Wonderland' world of sheer make-believe. 'But tell me, Mr Edgar, what do you do in the daytime?' The SOS for a lost tennis shoe; the request from a listener for the 'Station Master' to broadcast. And then there was the Outside Broadcast of 'Hansel and Gretel', in which a lovely aria was embellished with a North Country accent - 'Eh! For 'eaven's sake stop that ruddy music. I'm trying to get a trunk call through to Leeds.'

THE 2WP/5IT STATION AT WITTON, BIRMINGHAM

Percy Edgar (left) and A E Thompson – Station Director and Chief Engineer respectively – who began Children's Hour, 1923.

6

THE BBC TAKES OVER

The First BBC Appointments

On 13 October 1922 the front page of the *Morning Post* was, as usual, plastered with brief notices and advertisements. The fourth column carried the heading 'APPOINTMENTS (Professional and Commercial)' under which were listed vacancies for an archived clerk, a rep., an apprentice journalist, and for officers to service 'The British Broadcasting Co. (Information)' namely General Manager, Director of Programmes, Chief Engineer, Secretary. 'Only those having first-class qualifications need apply. Applications to be addressed to Sir William Noble, Chairman of the Broadcasting Committee, Magnet House, Kingsway WC2'. Similar advertisements appeared in *The Times,* the *Daily Telegraph,* the *Manchester Guardian* and the *Glasgow Daily Herald*. The *Electrician* and the *Electrical Review* also carried the advertisement with a view to attracting applicants for the Chief Engineer's post. The entertainment journal ERA did likewise in the hope of netting applicants for the post of Director of Programmes.

The advertisement drew from one applicant an immediate and impressive response. It originated from the Cavendish Club, 119 Piccadilly and was signed 'J C W Reith':

> 'Sir,
> With reference to your announcement in today's *Morning Post*, I have the honour to request consideration for the General Managership, believing that I have the qualifications which justify the application.
> I am an Aberdonian, and it is probable that you knew my family. I attach a brief summary of what I have done, together with certain personal particulars. Since relinquishing my last post, I have been abroad, but came to Town last week to make enquiries and arrangements for future work.
> You will observe that I am an engineer by training, but that I have had wide commercial experience and that I have held organising and administrative appointments of considerable responsibility. Might I draw attention to the last paragraph of the attached?
> I should be delighted to give further particulars and would appreciate the favour of an interview when your personal impressions of my character and ability could be formed. I am able to refer you to

outstanding men, whose names I should suggest to you, and who would speak on the two scores mentioned.

The appointment is of the nature and degree which I came to Town hoping to obtain, and I should not apply did I not feel capable of discharging its responsibilities to your satisfaction.'

The letter had been typed in a little used room at the back of the club and placed in the club's post-box. In its original form it carried no reference to Aberdeen. Reith had then looked at the club's copy of 'Who's Who' to find out more about Noble, to whom the letter was addressed. The discovery that he too hailed from Aberdeen provided a potential bargaining counter. Reith persuaded the club porter to retrieve the letter so that he could retype it, inserting the reference to being a member of a well-known Aberdonian family. In later years, he acknowledged that it was this reference that had probably clinched the job for him.

The 'Attachment' explained that he was the son of the Very Rev. Dr George Reith, Moderator of the Church of Scotland. It gave a brief résumé of his education - Glasgow Academy, Gresham's School, Norfolk and the Royal Technical College, Glasgow. This was followed by a five-year apprenticeship with the North British Locomotive Co. and a year with S Pearson and Son in London as Assistant Engineer. The War then interrupted Reith's career; within two months he was at the front and, a year later, wounded.

The gash across his left cheek, created by a bullet, lent his appearance a fiercely rugged character which was to distinguish him for the rest of his life. The wound had other repercussions in that it opened up opportunities for administrative responsibilities of the highest and most pressing nature, starting with his posting to America where he was in charge of contracts for munitions to help Britain prosecute the war. Similar work in Britain followed including winding up contracts at the end of the war. He then spent two years as General Manager, with William Beardmore and Co., Coatbridge, near Glasgow. But Beardmore, like many other substantial businesses, suffered from the nation-wide slump at the end of 1921 and had virtually closed down by May 1922 when Reith resigned.

Reith's 'Attachment' ends at this point in his life. His reference to being 'abroad' was perhaps a euphemism for being 'unemployed' for five months. In the heady days of late 1920, he had purchased a cosy house with a magnificent view towards the hills - Dunardoch in Dunblane. It became the home of Reith and his wife Muriel on their marriage in July 1921 and, after their move to

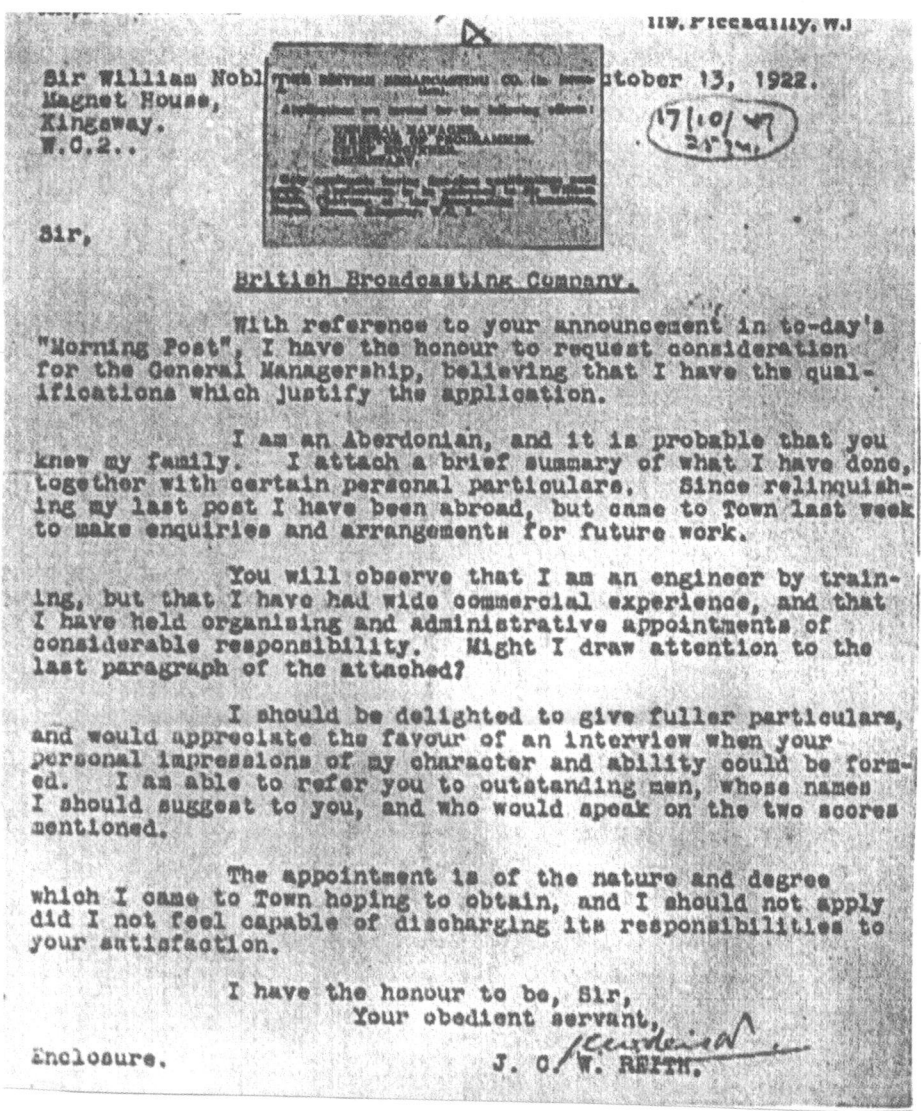

Reith's Letter of Application and CV (following page) to the British Broadcasting Co., 1922

London early in 1923, was still to serve as a second home and residence for his mother until February 1925.

Fortunately for the Reiths, Beardsmores were generous and Reith had resigned with the benefit of six month's salary. But, by September 1922 time and money were running out. In any case, Reith wanted something more fulfilling than running an engineering works. His mind veered towards a

> **Attachment.**
>
> Telegrams - Vendish, Map, London.   Cavendish Club,
> Telephone - Grosvenor 1246 & Mayo.   119, Piccadilly, W.1
>
> Age 33¾. Aberdonian. Son of Vy.Rev.Dr.Geo.Reith, Moderator. Grandson of Geo.Reith, first Gen.Manager, (and Director) Scottish N.E.Railway, and later General Manager of Clyde Navigation Trust.
> 1895-08. Educated at Glasgow Academy, Gresham's School, Norfolk, and at Royal Technical College, Glasgow. Honours certificates in many subjects including electricity theory and practise.
> A.M.Inst.C.E., A.M.I.Mech.E., M.Sc., late Major, R.E..
> 1908-13. Apprenticeship, North British Loco.Co.,Ltd., Glasgow, in all Shops and Drawing Office.
> 1913-14. Assistant Engineer, S.Pearson & Son, London.
> 1914-15. At the Front, Oct.1914 to Oct.1915. Wounded.
> 1915-16. Second in Contract Dept., construction of Gretna Factor
> 1916-17. 20 months in America in charge of contracts for Britai for munitions; 600 assistants and control of 1100 American inspectors.
> 1917-19. Retained in England in charge of various engineering works of urgency, including Admiralty appointment with 2500 men.
> 1919-20. Took over Department of old Ministry of Munitions to settle up all outstanding Ordnance contracts and to bring equipments up to date. 1500 contracts and about £13 million involved. Difficulties increased owing to lack of proper records. Credit was given for settlements effected, for amount of useful material obtained ex-liquidations, and for large sums of money saved.
> 1920-22. General Manager, Wm.Beardmore & Co., Ltd., Coatbridge, two years. Reorganised factory throughout; systems of planning, progress, costing, stores accounting and store keeping installed; physical alterations for new products. Manufacture expedited and cheapened. Variety of engineering products. Badly hit by slump at end of 1921, and virtually closed down in May when I resigned. Letter from Chairman on what had been done and position then
>
> Please note considerable commercial experience in above, in addition to executive work in engineering administration. Negotiation of contracts, purchasing, etc., particularly. On accounting side I took first place of sixty after examinations in a post graduate course of lectures for Chartered Accountants on Industrial Accounting, held last winter in the C.A. Institute, Glasgow.
>
> Reith.

political role.

In September he had given a talk at his old school and afterwards was introduced by the Headmaster to Stephen Bull, son of one of the leading politicians of the day - Sir William Bull. Reith mentioned his interests in undertaking political work and, with the son's encouragement, he had written to Bull on 28 September to ask if Bull would grant him a meeting.

Reith arrived in London and the two met on 3 October. Bull, who headed the London Unionist MP's, must have been impressed for, on 12 October, Reith was offered a position as Secretary to the group. The job would only be temporary, linked as it was to the forthcoming election. This meant Reith would have to scan the papers and keep his ear to the ground if he wanted a permanent job, let alone one to his satisfaction.

But there was something curious in the events that followed. First Reith spotted a suitable permanent post - the one with the BBC - the very next day and applied for it. Secondly, he was content to 'wait in the wings' whilst negotiations leading up to the registration of the British Broadcasting Company proceeded to the point when, two months later, interviews were finally held. Although, before he applied, he had hardly any idea as to what 'broadcasting' meant, he seemed entirely satisfied at the prospect of heading the new company and confident he would be chosen to do so.

Bull had connections with wireless companies and knew Noble. Whilst stopping short of any overt intervention, Bull may well have smoothed the way with Noble; Bull may even have shown the advertisement to Reith and advised him to apply. Whilst there is no known documentary evidence, Andrew Boyle was given information to this effect by Reith's family when writing his biography of Reith (Boyle A, *Only the Wind Will Listen,* 1972). There are certainly signs that Reith took things very much for granted when the call to be interviewed finally came on 7 December; 'most exciting', he noted in his diary, 'it seems an excellent job for me'.

A week later, on 13 December, interviews for the four posts were held at Magnet House in Kingsway, the splendid new Head Office of GEC. Noble took the chair, flanked by the other members of the Broadcasting Committee, with one notable absentee - Godfrey Isaacs of Marconi. Isaacs had, nevertheless, asked to see Reith (among others) before the appointment was finally fixed. Reith described what happened at the interview:

> 'Sir William Noble came out to get me and he was smiling in a confidential sort of way. They didn't ask me many questions and some they did I didn't know the meaning of. I think I had more or less made up their minds that I was the man before they saw me and it was chiefly a matter of confirmation. McKinstry made a remark about the letters of complaint which were coming in. They asked what

salary I wanted and I said £2,000. Noble came to the door with me and almost winked as if to say it was all right'. (*Reith Diaries*)

The following day, Reith waited expectantly at his club. At 3.45 pm Noble phoned to ask if he would come along at once to see him.

'So I took a taxi and went. He received me very nicely, was going to Leamington that night and wanted to see me before he went. The Committee had unanimously recommended that I be offered the General Managership of the British Broadcasting Company. He said he had tried hard to get a salary at £2,000 but some of the others didn't want it to start over £1,500, but that if things went OK I should get a rise soon. Later he recommended me to take £1,750. After a cup of tea and a general talk I departed.'

On Friday 15 December, Reith received a letter from Noble arranging for him to see Isaacs. 'He was very cordial indeed and it seemed most satisfactory. He said he would inform Noble at once that he agreed £1,750. At Noble's request, I telephoned him at Leamington.' Reith must have been gratified to hear that the General Manager 'would within a short time, know everybody worth knowing in the Country.' On that day, the British Broadcasting Company was finally registered. There really was a BBC.

An element of mystery and surprise surrounds the two specialist posts - Director of Programmes and Chief Engineer. In those two instances, 'First rate qualifications' surely implied experience in the broadcasting field. On the programme side (and all this meant in terms of staffing, artistes and costs, and also in the taking of new initiatives and the setting of standards), no one could equal the commanding lead set by Arthur Burrows. He had worked in the field longer than anyone else and his activities extended well beyond those of running a broadcasting station. He was the obvious choice.

But his bid for the post did not go unchallenged. The other contender was one who was totally unknown to Noble and the Marconi camp. But there were others round the table - Binyon, Pease and McKinstry who, fearing a Marconi take over of the BBC, may well have been ready to support the outsider, especially in the absence of Isaacs. In any case, the man in question – Cecil Lewis - had already been interviewed by them, albeit six months earlier when they were selecting a Director of Programmes for their own broadcasting enterprise at Trafford Park, Manchester. Within days of his selection the idea of

Magnet House, Kingsway, London, 1922.

The Architects' Journal

two British broadcasting companies had been scrapped in favour of one, so it had come to nothing. Lewis made no effort to join the Marconi men at 2LO. It seems he was prepared to bide his time until the big opportunity arose, hoping perhaps that McKinstry's support would again stand him in good stead. Like Reith, Lewis' interest in broadcasting appears to have arisen from a chance circumstance.

Lewis was by profession an expert aviator who had distinguished himself in the war, surviving one hazardous encounter after another. It was as though he led a charmed life. After the war was over, he joined the staff of Vickers and was posted to Peking where his task was to train Chinese pilots - it turned out to be an impossible brief, and quite pointless, as the Chinese lacked the infrastructure required for civil aviation and the Vickers Vimy planes for the Peking to Shanghai service could not cover the distance. The contract period had almost terminated when Lewis was indisposed for some weeks and was visited by a colleague named Richards who had gone to Peking to sell trams to the Government; they became quite good friends.

Whilst Lewis and his new Russian wife returned to England by Suez, Richards had gone the other way and came back across the States. Like Reith, Lewis' prospects at this time (mid 1922) were poor. He had no money and no job. But one morning the telephone in his mother's house, where he and his wife had their home, rang. It was the kindly voice of Richards. 'You know Lewis, I think broadcasting's the thing for you'. Again, like Reith, Lewis had no idea what the word meant (Lewis, Cecil, *Never Look Back*, Hutchinson 1974, pp 60/61).

Who then was Richards? There was a William John Richards whom Lewis must have known. He, like Lewis, had served in the RFC and RAF and had subsequently joined Vickers Aviation Department. Again, like Lewis, he was sent to Peking in 1920. His job was to equip Vickers aircraft with Marconi wireless apparatus and to train wireless operators. But despite these close parallels and the link with wireless, W J Richards does not altogether fit the picture. A more likely bet is C S Richards. In 1919 he was employed at senior level in the new Metropolitan-Vickers Export Co., set up under H V Lloyd. A year or so later McKinstry joined Lloyd as Co-Director. In 1922 Richards returned home from the Far East to replace Lloyd and work alongside McKinstry. This would have been at the very time when McKinstry was pushing for a stake in broadcasting. As Lewis later put it: 'They were looking for a likely chap in this absolutely unknown field (of preparing programmes for a broadcasting service). Richards remembered me. I was, he thought, 'artistic' and this was vaguely what was required. So I was interviewed and engaged at £400 pa.'

Quite what Lewis did between mid-1922 and December 1922 is unclear, but his hopes must have risen on seeing the BBC posts advertised in October. When the applications came in, Noble may well have been reminded of the earlier anti-Marconi lobby and this may have been expressed again at the short-listing stage. One way or another, a compromise was reached whereby Burrows would be offered the post of Director of Programmes at £1,000 p.a. with Lewis as Deputy Director at £750. But, apart from this background of internal politics, Lewis would undoubtedly have impressed those interviewing him. It was not only his amazing 'presence', founded by his height and good looks; he combined energy with sensitivity and possessed an excellent microphone voice. Above all, he had the kind of confidence that Reith himself possessed - one founded on high self-esteem and a sense of innate superiority. As for experience in broadcasting, Lewis could claim to have made his debut before the microphone already. On 5 December, he had delivered one of the first talks broadcast by 2ZY Manchester; his subject: 'Flying in China'.

The post of Chief Engineer BBC will always be associated with the name Eckersley. He had established his reputation with the amateur wireless enthusiasts before the BBC had been formed. Soon after, his name more than any other name was the one closely associated in the public mind with broadcasting. With Marconi already committed to building all the remaining five provisional BBC stations, Eckersley's Marconi background added to his range of 'first-class qualifications'. It comes, then, as a surprise to learn that, though he applied for the post, he was not selected to fill it. It was offered to another.

Even BBC historians seem to find it difficult to put a name to the successful applicant for 'Chief Engineer'. The Broadcasting Committee papers do not appear to have survived the Reith regime so we know little about who applied for the various posts. Minutes of the first BBC Board survive and list those appointed; but such appointments could only be made when offers had been accepted. To exchange a good job with Marconi for an uncertain future with the BBC required courage and vision. In later years, those like Burrows and Eckersley who took the step were amply rewarded but felt they had to be discreet about naming the man who baulked at the first hurdle when it came to writing their accounts of the early days. But for the record, he was R H White, Burrows' opposite number at 2LO (*Amplion Magazine*, March 1926).

THE BBC TAKES OVER

For the Committee, it only remained to select the Company Secretary. There would probably have been many applicants for this post as specialised knowledge was not required and the arduous nature of the job was by no means clear at the outset. In the event, Major P F Anderson FISA was chosen to fill the post. Like Reith, he had shouldered organisational responsibility during the war, being one of two or three officers who met in the basement of a house in Grantham to create the Machine Gun Corps. It afterwards became one of the great sections of the Army (*Wireless Weekly*, 18 April 1923).

Firm offers went out to the successful candidates during the week ending Saturday 16 December; letters accepting these had to be in by Thursday 21st, the date of the first BBC Board Meeting. Reith, anxious to press ahead, took instant action on two fronts - staffing and accommodation. Monday and Tuesday were allocated to finding accommodation and Burrows and Lewis were asked to join in the search, along with R H White who joined the group on the second day - and promptly aired his reservations about joining the BBC! As a preliminary, Reith needed to know how many staff and what kind of organisation he would need. Burrows was therefore summoned on the Sunday to throw some light on this. He showed Reith 'a sort of chart' (Reith, J C W., *The Reith Diaries*, 17 December 1922). There would be a Director of Programmes, a Musical Director, a Provincial Programmes Director (responsible for artistes touring the various BBC stations) and a Supervising Engineer. Each would have an Assistant, in addition, the BBC would need a Publicity Chief and an Accountant, working with the Company Secretary. A 'lady assistant' would help to develop programmes of interest to women. The general supporting staff would include six typists, five clerks to take care of filing and Roneo copying, two messengers and two Commissionaires - for the BBC would be active early in the morning and late at night; its doors would be open every day of the week. These would comprise Head Office staff; 2LO staff would be additional.

The subsequent search for accommodation is described in detail in a later section of this chapter; it ended at Savoy Hill where the Institution of Electrical Engineers was located. Preliminary negotiations to lease space in the Institution occurred on Wednesday 20 December, but left some major problems, not least the need for temporary accommodation elsewhere. In writing to Noble to accept the Committee's offer to appoint him General Manager, Reith made the point that he had had substantial talks with Mr Burrows and Mr Lewis, and (had) also had a meeting with Mr Powell, the Secretary of the Institution of Electrical Engineers.

'There need not be any time lost when I am away in the matter of new offices.' (*The Reith Diaries*, 20 December 1922). He now felt free to spend the next week or so with his wife at Dunardoch surrounded by home comforts. Before he left for Scotland, he had an opportunity to be introduced by Noble to the new Chairman of the BBC - Lord Gainford - who was in London to attend the first Board Meeting at Magnet House. But the minutes give no indication that Reith or any other of the newly appointed staff was present at the Board meeting itself.

Held, on the morning of December 21, in the beautifully panelled boardroom over looking Kingsway, the meeting included representatives of all the 'Big Six', with GEC represented by Hugo Hirst. Noble was present as Chairman of the former Broadcasting Committee and was accompanied by George Pells, the Committee Secretary. Frank Gaylor, the BBC solicitor, was also in attendance. The BBC's future bankers, solicitors and auditors, registered office and company secretary were then named and approved, and the Company Secretary's salary was approved at £700. Sir William Noble then reported the appointments made by the Committee - Reith (General Manager), Burrows (Director of Programmes), Lewis (Assistant Director of Programmes). Noble then explained that the offer of the post of Chief Engineer had not been accepted and the Board resolved to defer action on this.

Anderson, the Company Secretary, lost no time in taking the reins from Gaylor and Pells. He had travelled up to London, stayed overnight in a hotel and met Pells for lunch, who told him his appointment had been confirmed by the Board that morning. Anderson then phoned Gaylor to let him know he had taken a house in Harlesden - 2 Craven Road - to which all letters should be addressed. Armed with bulky files from Pells, he then took a taxi home. Next morning official documents came in the post from Gaylor confirming Minutes of the first Board meeting and a memorandum appointing Lord Gainford permanent Chairman of the BBC. Anderson then borrowed a typewriter, hired a temporary typist for one night and dictated some letters and made a note of the various expenses; they totalled £5 4s 9d and were claimed on a BBC petty cash voucher, the first such voucher to be processed. A second voucher for £1 15s 3d again covered his second lunch with Pells, together with a Collins Diary, a Law List and a Wages Book. Arrangements were made with Waterlows to provide a Register of Directors (13s 0d), a Directors Attendance Book (£9s 0d), an Agenda Book (£2 5s 6d), and a Minutes Book (£2 17s 6d). These all survive, the Agenda Book being particularly fine with its indigo boards, maroon spine and brass lock (*BBC Written Archives*). Having set himself up and established with Pells that accommodation would be made available as an interim measure at Magnet House, Anderson left to spend Christmas at his home in Southsea. He had yet to meet his fellow officers - Reith, Burrows and Lewis - and was probably in no great hurry to do so.

There remained the matter of the Chief Engineer. This was to come up again at the Board Meeting on Thursday 18 January and the General Manager, Reith, had been asked, earlier, to submit names for the following meeting. Binyon, Chief Engineer of the Radio Communication Company, entering Marconi House, London, encountered Eckersley just slipping out to buy tobacco, having forgotten to pick some up on the way to work. 'He greeted me as if I were something he needed very badly. "Heavens", he said "of course, you're just the man. I don't say you'll get it, but you certainly should apply and do it at once." I had not the vaguest idea what he meant until he explained.' (Eckersley, R., *BBC and All That,* p46). On Tuesday 30 January, Eckersley and several others were interviewed by Reith. On Sunday 4 February he and a Commander Watson were asked to appear before the BBC Board the next day. That day, he sat on the windowsill of an office in Marconi House very excited. He badly wanted that job. Subsequently, the telephone rang; it was Reith: 'Yes! How soon could I start?' In situations like this, Reith always expected immediate acquiescence, all other considerations to be waived. Eckersley started on Tuesday 6 February.

The only other immediate issue was consideration of the final composition of the BBC Board. This came up at the statutory Meeting of BBC Members held at the Hotel Cecil, Strand at 2.30 pm on 22 March 1923. The room allocated soon filled. The main business was to nominate two more Directors, one of whom would represent the smaller firms. Three eligible names were proposed and seconded so a vote had to be taken; they were Sir William Bull, W N Burnham (Managing Director of Burndept), and Major H S Walker AMICE. The first two were elected; Walker, well known in amateur circles, later joined the BBC Staff where he was in charge of workshops and the drawing office, under Eckersley. Bull became Vice Chairman and, like Gainford, independent of the manufacturer members' direct representation. His nomination owed much to Reith's careful lobbying. Any debt Reith owed to Bull was thus nobly repaid and in a most satisfactory way all round.

These first high level appointments should have completed the framework of the BBC, bearing in mind the organisation had only been granted a two year licence and had an ingeniously engineered financial arrangement on which to build. But even as the BBC took up space in Magnet House at the start of 1923 it had become clear that these financial arrangements were flawed, with the BBC starved of money. Not surprisingly, the BBC raised this state of affairs long before the Postmaster General - or certainly long before the Post Office - were prepared to acknowledge the situation, and still more certainly long before they were prepared to do anything about it. Even then, the Post Office procrastinated by appointing an independent committee. Thus for much of 1923 the BBC fought a battle for survival on the outcome of which depended the whole approach to broadcasting Britain. The responsibility fell squarely on Reith's shoulders. Day to day management had to take second place.

As a result, Reith desperately needed a deputy and confidante. In these respects, the Company Secretary, Anderson, provided little support, seeming to lack any 'BBC Vision' or ability to 'extend' himself. By mid 1923 a new post of Assistant General Manager had been added to the BBC's 'First Division' to fill the gap, Admiral C D Carpendale being appointed. Anderson would give way to Rice - a man of Reith's own choice, though arguably one no more committed or competent than his predecessor.

The story of Reith's epic struggle with the Postmaster General and its outcome is the subject of a later chapter of this book, Ch 8: *Collapse of the BBC's Initial Financial Structure.*

THE BBC TAKES OVER

'Head Office', Magnet House, Kingsway

For Reith, Christmas with his wife and mother at Dunardoch must have afforded a delightful interlude. He had secured a job which appeared to offer infinite opportunities to stretch the exceptional talents which he knew he possessed. He had met the Chairman and Directors and had got on well with both Isaacs and Noble. The gist of their words was - 'We're leaving it all to you.' Lesser men might have been intimidated, but to Reith, their attitude was a source of comfort. For a young man of 33 years, the salary - £1,750 - would, in 1922 have seemed a princely sum, quite enough on which to run both Dunerdoch and a London home. Dunerdoch was especially close to his heart with its garden and a fine view to the hills; here he could enjoy being surrounded by his books and the sense of peaceful, domestic seclusion enlivened by a good roaring fire.

The most urgent matter - accommodation - had already been attended to in principle, with Burrows left to tie up the loose ends. But if Reith imagined he and a dozen or so staff would take up temporary quarters in the building of the Institution of Electrical Engineers whilst partitions were erected around them, he was mistaken. There was even some doubt as to whether the building could provide a home for the all-important London Station. The key questions were, could the roof support two tall aerials. If not, could the Post Office link studios in the IEE building to the existing Marconi House transmitter by landline until a new site for 2LO were to be found? Unfortunately, the one man Reith might have turned to - R H White - had decided not to throw in his lot with the BBC. Behind the scenes, he may have actively been pursuing these problems but it seems there was no direct contact between the two men.

With no immediate solution in sight, Noble stepped into the breech with the offer of a room in Magnet House, Head Office of GEC, as from January. Reith decided to have a quick preview on Saturday, travelling down on the Friday. But, even in this, Reith was thwarted. A telegram from Burrows requested he break his journey at Newcastle to vet the arrangements made to establish the new BBC station in that city (see Ch. 6: *The BBC Reaches Out to the North, Scotland and Wales*). So Reith rose early on the 29th. It was very dark and cold. On the platform at Stirling, he bade his wife farewell. Added to the cold it had now begun to snow. He was going in a train into an unknown future. He arrived at Newcastle at 12.30 pm where he visited the studio and met the acting Station Director, Tom Payne. He caught the 4.28 pm train to

London arriving at 10.10 pm and finally retired to bed at midnight. It had been a long day.

Next morning he set off for Magnet House arriving at 9 am. Reith's appearance there was premature, unannounced and unexpected. But someone had put up a notice in the entrance hall - 'BRITISH BROADCASTING COMPANY SECOND FLOOR'. Reith:

> 'An enquiry was made regarding my business. 'BBC', I said, deliberately. 'Nobody there, yet Sir' replied the Commissionaire, 'but we're expecting them on Monday for the first time.' Who is them?' I asked. 'The new Company' he replied. 'So I told him I was it, or part of it; one quarter, approximately. As he bore me upward in the lift, I detected a scornful curiosity in his veiled scrutiny. He was very polite. He conducted me to the door already labelled BBC which he opened for me with some ceremony. I entered ... I heard his footsteps echoing along the corridor. A wild thought came to me that I would hail him and bid him loose me again, but I heard the clang of the iron gate; it was too late.
>
> 'A survey of the premises revealed a chamber some 30ft by 15ft furnished only with long tables and a few chairs. A door at the far end invited examination. It gave on to a sort of powder closet 6ft square. 'This,' I said 'is the General Manager's office.' A telephone suggested communication with the outer world. Hat, coat and umbrella went on to the window ledge.'

Reith lifted the telephone and was relieved to hear a female voice answer. He desperately tried to think of an excuse for phoning and asked whether she had had any instructions.

> 'It was about 9.30 when the outer door opened and a gentleman appeared with some manifestation of authority - an air of being where he had a right to be; a silk hat, two attaché cases and several legal-looking books under his arm. 'The Secretary', I thought, The 'General Manager' he thought. Somewhat like Livingstone and Stanley we each 'presumed' and that was that.'

THE BBC TAKES OVER

Conversation was not brisk and had already flagged when the door opened again and a cheery individual entered and introduced himself as 'Gamage, Secretary to the GEC, you know.'

> 'Now Mr Gamage's welcome to me that sombre morning, his kindly offers of help - 'anything you want' - his general determination to bring us what comfort, not to say consolation and assistance he could, remain very clearly with me. Further, when he spoke, things got done with astonishing celerity and success.
>
> 'We were in that temporary office about ten weeks. We must have been an appalling nuisance to them, for in an incredibly short space of time, ten telephones and twenty staff were operating in that single room. We made persistent offers to pay for our room, for our lunch, our tea, for our telephone calls, but all were as persistently declined by Mr Gamage and his Chairman, Hugo Hirst.' (Allighan, Garry, *Sir John Reith*)

The reference to 'twenty staff' is a sure sign of the explosive growth that occurred in that tight space in the first few weeks of the BBC. The first day saw Reith installed in his little annexe at a 4ft 6in secondhand pedestal desk acquired for £10. Burrows and Lewis shared a desk and telephone on one side of the room while the Secretary and his assistant (R M Page, or possibly a M V Gorridon) occupied a desk on the other side. If there was one member of the tiny staff about whom Reith felt uneasy, it was the Secretary, Anderson. Reith discovered he thought he was to be independent of the General Manager, having been appointed directly by the BBC on the 21 December (the BBC's first appointment) and not by the Broadcasting Committee. Reith adjusted Anderson's thinking 'satisfactorily and quickly'; the relationship between the two men remained strained from then on.

Reith lost no time in appointing his own Secretary - Miss Shields. The choice resulted from help given him by Miss F I Stevenson, CBE, Lloyd George's Secretary, and so came with high level political support. She was a young graduate of Newnham College, Cambridge. Reith took her on following a good talk explaining 'exactly what (he) wanted'. She remained with him right through until the time of her marriage in 1928. It was always 'Mr Reith' and 'Miss Shields'. She began officially on 8 January 1923 and soon found herself working far into the evenings - so much so that neither she nor, for that matter, her boss even had any opportunity to slip across to 2LO at Marconi House and witness broadcasting in action. The one time Reith did make the attempt he arrived on his own and unannounced. It was an important evening for 2LO, as a celebrity speaker had agreed to broadcast and the press was present in force. Burrows was announcing and Stanton Jefferies cleared the studio, getting the reporters to sit on two long, but very hard, wooden forms outside. He asked them which journals they represented and was about to return to the studio when someone else arrived - a tall stranger. Jefferies sat him down and enquired as to which paper he belonged. 'Oh, don't worry about me,' came the reply, 'my name is Reith'. Jefferies, shocked at meeting his boss in this way, realised he had refused him admission to his own studios (*Soap Box Days*, by L Stanton Jefferies, *Popular Wireless*, 12 October 1935).

For Burrows and Lewis, liaison with 2LO was quite another matter. No matter how hard pressed they were, as 5pm approached, everything was dropped and, putting on hat and coat, they sprinted out of the office and down Kingsway to join Stanton Jefferies in the Marconi House studio for the children's programme. This procedure began on day one and as Uncles Arthur, Jeff and Caractacus, they immediately caught the imagination and rapt attention of their audience (Lewis had liked the thought of being 'Uncle Cecil'; however, he had been to a West End play in which one of the characters was named 'Caractacus' and decided to adopt that name). A large proportion of the mail that soon weighed down the long table at Magnet House came from their 'nephews and nieces'. But the antics of Burrows and Lewis did not end with the Children's Corner. One or the other stayed on as a matter of course to help Jefferies conduct the evening programme; the two younger men - Jefferies and Lewis - 'hit it off' immediately.

One of the earliest accounts of conditions at Magnet House stems from Eckersley's visit in early or mid January. Reith commented later; 'He intimated his desire to call. I was quite intrigued.' If it was a sort of interview, one wonders who was being interviewed (Eckersley may already have got wind of names being put forward for the post of Chief Engineer). He 'found the BBC's Chief Executive installed in what was little more than a cupboard opening off an office in which the rest of the staff, about fifteen people, were feverishly working.' Soon he was back, this time for formal interview.

February saw a continued growth of staff. On the Tuesday the sixth, Eckersley arrived to find his desk piled high with unanswered letters. Within minutes he was ushered into the closet by Reith who - as he had done with Anderson and Miss Shields - launched into a long monologue in which he explained exactly what was required:

First, Eckersley must recruit new staff, in particular to man the new Marconi-built stations at Newcastle, Cardiff and Glasgow.

He must ensure that the stations were properly installed.

A new site for the 2LO transmitter was a matter of urgency.

He would be expected to liaise with contractors in the matter of new offices and studios in the IEE building at Savoy Hill.

He would have to dissuade amateurs from using the broadcast wavelengths.

Technical journals were asking for articles on the BBC.

There were some parting shots: was it necessary for Eckersley to live in Essex? Perhaps a better suit of clothes might help. And would he dine with Reith and his wife in their flat in Queen Anne's Mansions when 'we can talk things over more fully?' (Eckersley, P P, *The Power behind the Microphone*, p62).

Shortly after Eckersley's arrival, Walter C Smith, an old friend from Reith's Coatbridge days with Beardmore and Co., received an invitation to become Publicity Officer. Smith correctly interpreted this as a 'summons' and purchased a 'single' ticket to London, having packed a small case. The starting salary amounted to £300 pa, this being increased on 1 December 1923 to £500. He was to report direct to Reith and, of course, to start work immediately.

Another key appointment was made on 19 February when W H B Harley became Accountant. With four provincial stations now in operation it had been decided that all payments be made direct from Head Office. The stations were to send advance details of expenses along with fees payable to artistes. But the Accountant's work included the Head Office scene as well. Once again Reith took the initiative. Harley was to adopt 'a conventional manual system appropriate to a limited liability company - with ledger, cash book, journal, salaries and wages books, and day books.' (Briggs, Asa, *History of Broadcasting in the United Kingdom*. Vol I, p203, 1961). The cashier's work would continue to be handled by Miss Mallinson as it had been from the start of the year. At the Board meeting on 8 March, Reith was able to claim that all accounts had been brought up-to-date and an abstract of income and expenditure was tabled. This presumably reflected the work of R M Page, who was already in post handling the registration of BBC Members and the payment by them to the BBC of royalties raised on the sale of sets.

The next significant step forward was the appointment of Caroline Banks to take charge of typing and filing services - what later became known as the

'General Office'. She was interviewed by Reith, Anderson and Eckersley and took responsibility for all the women clerical staff, of whom where were about a dozen - mostly, if not all, at Magnet House. She was 26 and was living with other career girls in Russell Square where the girls were provided with meals, laundry and other domestic services. The atmosphere was 'Bloomsbury' - they were bright, confident young women of the 'twenties. Under Caroline Banks, the smooth running of the BBC's vital clerical services was assured throughout years of explosive growth at Savoy Hill. With two breaks, she finally retired 33 years later, in 1956, having returned in 1951 to her original job as Supervisor of the General Office, Central Services (letter to the author from Mrs Hilary Vincent, daughter of Caroline Banks, 1995).

That one room in Magnet House had to take the brunt of all this physical growth and functional diversification. Hard-pressed senior staff were forced to work and to make important telephone calls amid the cacophony of the typewriters and duplicating machines. The room imposed limitations on staff which, in turn, meant long working hours and a slowing down in the ability of Head Office to influence and service the provincial stations. Within the room itself, conditions bordered on theatrical farce. Burrows later recalled how 'Throughout the day we worked like lunatics in a pandemonium such as I hope will never fall to anyone else's experience.' Lewis wrote of the avalanche of mail dumped daily on the large table in the centre of the room with about ten people trying desperately to sort it. 'Dotted about in every corner were typists' desks, filing cabinets, duplicating machines' all check-by-jowl with the desks of the senior staff. 'The room was crowded to overflowing, it was physically impossible to get any more people into it.'

As if this were not bad enough, positively encouraged by the sign on the door 'BBC: WALK IN', a flood of visitors descended on the distracted staff and 'a queue of manufacturers, retailers and others' soon became a commonplace sight, queries being raised on every side.

> 'From morning to night the office was bombarded by the press, the public, the wireless manufacturers, people of every kind and class who, for some reason or another, were interested in broadcasting. There was no time for lunch; a cup of coffee and a few sandwiches would be swallowed at intervals, between dealing with correspondence and seeing countless people.' (Lewis, Cecil, *Broadcasting from Within*, pp26/28; Burrows, Arthur, *The Story of Broadcasting*, pp78; *BBC Year Book 1930*, p186).

THE BBC TAKES OVER

The end came on Friday, 16 March 1923 when Reith, 28 staff, and an office boy named Pell, left Magnet House for Savoy Hill, taking with them the historic little sign 'BBC: WALK IN'. Long hours of work, changes in organisation, explosive growth and new challenges from outside were long to be hallmarks of the BBC, but nothing could quite equal Magnet House. Reith summed up the Magnet House era with the brief comment: 'I do not suppose that any who shared those early days will be likely to forget them.'

With so much at stake for the 'Big Six' and BBC members generally, one has to ask why additional space was not made available at Magnet House for BBC use. One answer may be that no one in December anticipated such a rapid take-off. Another could be that the occupation of space at Savoy Hill was not expected to take the best part of three months. It must also be remembered that Noble, of GEC, was no longer in the driving seat vis-à-vis the BBC and neither Gainford nor Reith felt at ease in accepting even such hospitality as had been extended to them. Magnet House was a prestigious Head office; to have people 'of every class' and background coming in at all times and treading their way up to the top-management/Board Room floor already amounted to a major intrusion.

It was not as though Magnet House was a normal office block. Its space had to serve a complex and inter-related variety of functions. Half the building served as a warehouse; goods were brought by lorry from the various GEC factories, lifted on the runways leading into the building and checked in. The whole of the fourth and fifth floors comprised stockrooms, whilst on the third floor was the dispatch department with its packing benches and bins. Cranes lowered the goods via runways into waiting lorries in the van dock at the ground level. The ground floor had a splendid entrance hall beyond which a sales area included a counter 140ft long. From here stairs led down to showrooms crammed with light fittings and other products, each room reflecting a particular period style. The first floor comprised a spacious 'Counting House'. At the second floor level were to be found the Board Room and offices for the top management - all panelled. Here too was a catalogue and information bureau. The rest of the space used moveable partitions with glazed tops to form the offices for the departmental managers and a large general office. This, in practical terms, was the only area where space could be set aside for the BBC, as the top (sixth) floor accommodated the drawing office, staff canteen and a large lecture room for 350 people. Space for offices was, therefore, very limited, in what otherwise appeared to be an impressively large, if complex, building (*The Architects' Journal*, 4 January 1922).

That one room then, 30ft by 15ft, with its lamps burning far into the night, had to serve as the launch pad for the BBC.

John Reith

The BBC Makes its Debut

As far as the outside world was concerned, the BBC made its debut in the voice of 2LO, the London Station. 2LO had already made its mark with the Christmas programmes but within a week or so of the BBC's first working day, listeners began to be treated to broadcasts such as they had never heard before or even dreamt of. For the BBC had burst out of the confines of the little top floor studio in Marconi House, London, to join the opera buffs and theatre-goers and those celebrating 'Burns Night' and other events in the heart of London. If anything could be said to mark the debut of the BBC, pride of place has surely to be given to the opera broadcast from Covent Garden on the night of Monday 8 January 1923. In place of the customary muffled sounds of the seven strong 2LO Wireless Orchestra, listeners found themselves transported to the great auditorium itself. Even the BBC staff was unprepared for what they were about to witness. Lewis:

> 'We all assembled in a little room on the top floor of Marconi House where a loudspeaker stood on the table. Suddenly, with a loud click, it was thrown into circuit, and a confused babble of noise was let loose. At first indistinguishable, it soon became apparent that we were hearing the talk and rustling of programmes in the auditorium. Finally there was a burst of clapping, which died down to dead silence, and was followed by two sharp raps; a second later the huge orchestra had leapt into its stride, swelled up to a great crash of brass and cymbals, which could be heard all down the corridor at Marconi House. Our excitement was immense. The broadcasting of opera was an assured success. The sound of the great orchestra contrasted so forcibly with our little band of seven in the studio, that it came as a revelation of what the future of broadcasting might be. It carried us forward to the days when we should have great conductors and orchestras in our own studio.' (Lewis, Cecil, *Broadcasting from Within*, p33)

On that first night of opera transmission the little group in room 107 would have included Stanton Jefferies and his newly appointed Deputy, Rex Palmer. Round probably broke off from his work on the studio microphone to witness the new phenomenon. Reith would doubtless have been otherwise pre-occupied at Magnet House. Sadly, Burrows, on whose initiative the whole enterprise was launched, had left that very day to check the situation prevailing at the Birmingham and Manchester Stations. He was to miss all that week's opera transmissions.

The suggestion had come from W J Crampton, a consulting engineer whose responsibilities extended to Covent Garden Opera House. He and Burrows lunched together at the Metropole at the beginning of January. Follow up action was immediately taken. There was no time to be lost; the opera season was drawing to its close. Reith's backing had to be obtained along with the support of the British National Opera Company and the Opera House. Western Electric took on the installation of the microphones and amplifiers, the former comprising two double button microphones set among the footlights and linked to a three valve amplifier placed under the stage. From this point, the Post Office took over and within 36 hours, under the direction of Mr Rumaine, installed a lead-sheathed cable a quarter of a mile long to Marconi House. Noble, who until 1922 was Chief Engineer to the Post Office, pulled the necessary strings. The final touch was a telephone line enabling Richard and Wright, the Western Electric engineers under the stage to keep in touch with Marconi's engineers in the transmitter room.

So it was that, at 8 pm on Monday 8 January 1923 Mozart's 'Magic Flute' was, for the first time ever, transmitted live into thousands of homes across London and beyond. The following morning brought in a flood of letters and postcards. That evening the experiment was repeated - this time with 'Hansel and Gretel'. It was 'Writtle' (Chelmsford) night and Eckersley had taken his place in the 2MT hut down the boggy Essex lane. Forewarned, he put on the phones and tuned into London at 8 o'clock. There followed the revelation referred to in Ch. 6: *The First BBC Appointments*, 'I have never forgotten the thrill with which I suddenly sensed the feeling of a large auditorium and was translated from the prosaic interior of the hut into the front row of the stalls at Covent Garden. When the music itself came on, I sat absolutely amazed for three-quarters of an hour' (Eckersley, P P, *My Radio Career,* Popular Wireless). The incongruity of the contrast in quality and content between 2LO and 2MT struck Eckersley's ears like a thunderclap - 2MT was finished. He also knew that broadcasting had a future and a high purpose. Even if the top engineer post had eluded him, he would immediately seek his fortune with Reith. 'Pagliacci' followed on Wednesday - a late transmission of the last Act lasting from 9.15 to 11.00pm. Lewis held the fort at Marconi House before taking a taxi home to

THE BBC TAKES OVER

Cheyne Row, Chelsea. 'Siegfried', Acts 1 to 3, followed on Thursday starting at 7.15.

The press was now sitting up and following not only the opera itself but also its transmission. The Times music critic was ill and unable to attend. Nothing daunted, a friend set up a receiver with a horn; an aerial was fixed to a third floor window and led down to first floor level where the set had been placed on a table. An earth line was connected to a cold water tap to make all ready. Through the horn came the sound of distant music, slightly tinny, but the real thing - Siegfried.

Before the start of each act the operator, manager or high priest of the Broadcasting Company would give a very succinct account of the story of that act. Time was needed to prepare these synopses. Moreover, only a BBC presence on stage could ensure smooth transmission from studio to opera house and back at the most appropriate moment. Finally, silent events on stage had to be conveyed to listeners by interpolation. Sometimes this had to be superimposed on the music. It was agreed that Stanton Jefferies, equipped with score, telephone and microphone, should occupy the prompter's box at the side of the stage. Lewis:

> 'The day's work over and the children's hour also, we would snatch up our hats and make for a tavern nearby to discuss the evening's work while munching meringues and cream - for that was our favourite dish! .... You might have seen us there, pencil and paper in hand, Mr Jefferies with the score of the opera making up the story by reading through the music, while I entitled it and wrote it down. He would then repair to Covent Garden and I to the studio to deliver the story before the opera began. Having told the public what was going to happen I would repair to the Transmitting Room where there was a direct telephone line to Mr Jefferies at Covent Garden. I would call him up on the telephone with the switch connecting the Opera House to the transmitter in my hand. When the (key) moment came, he would say 'Are you ready? .... Stand by.... Shoot!' In went the switch, out went the opera. 'She's up' I would call back and then, immensely pleased with ourselves, we would regale each other with the gossip of the moment - how the soprano looked when she came off stage, and what the conductor said when the chorus miscued the last Act. Great days! Already I look back on them with a certain wistfulness and regret.' (Lewis, Cecil, Broadcasting from Within, p34-36)

The scene in the tavern strikes an amusing insight into the BBC at work during the first two or three weeks of its operational life. We see two confident young men keen to stretch their legs after being cooped up all day, both anxious to get away from the noise and bustle of the Strand and into the quieter precincts of Covent Garden. The first suitable venue would have been the appropriately named Opera Tavern in Catherine Street. Only yards from Marconi House, its location would have enabled Lewis to begin his synopsis ahead of Jefferies settling into the prompter's box at the Covent Garden Opera House. Upstairs, away from the crush at the bar, the two could sit in a room warmed by a glowing fire. Other customers must have been both intrigued and impressed to see the score of the night's performance spread across the table: Few would have imagined they were witnessing the high priests of broadcasting at work; still less when the two men emerged from the ornate Victorian tavern into the gas-lit street. For here, the two would go their separate ways. The taller of the two, glancing at his watch, heads for Aldwych only to vanish seconds later into the dark interior of Marconi House. His colleague, a man of infinite mystery to the performers, meanwhile headed for Covent Garden and took up his position in the wings of the stage, festooned with the wires of his telephone and microphone. He was soon to be heard in thousands of homes, the music momentarily taking second place to pronouncements 'furnished by his ghostly voice interjecting such remarks as 'Mephistopheles has come into the garden', or 'Siegfried enters with his horse'. 'The value of such aids (was) disputable ... too often they lead to laughter in the wrong place' (*Daily Telegraph*, 22 January 1923). 'Disputable' hardly does justice to the vehement feelings aroused in some quarters; Burrows remembered a letter arriving one morning threatening death by shooting if any such interpolations were made during Valkyrie - broadcast on Thursday 18 January.

Meanwhile the opera broadcasts continued with The Marriage of Figaro (Friday), Faust (Saturday), and Madame Butterfly (the following Tuesday), reaching a crescendo on 17 January with Melba starring in La Bohème. Harrods opened its doors that evening, so enabling the public to enjoy the event in the Store's Georgian Restaurant.

On the last night of the season, La Bohème was repeated, Acts 3 and 4 being broadcast. Once again, the great diva, Dame Nellie Melba, held the audience enthralled. Listeners heard the roars of cheering and clapping that greeted her as she came on stage. In a speech from the stage which closed the Season, Pagot Bowman referred to the microphones among the footlights and to the invisible audience who enjoyed hearing Melba in their own drawing room.

He hoped they would take the opportunity to enjoy the actual performances when the opportunity next arose. Telegrams received that night were read out and listeners presented Melba with a remarkable floral tribute - two thousand roses, portraying a house with an aerial and two doves representing the flight of song through space.

The public received the open broadcasts with great enthusiasm. Over 600 letters and postcards arrived each day. The sale of apparatus shot up, advertisements and catalogues carrying alluring references to opera from Covent Garden. More significantly, the press began to take broadcasting seriously.

With the conclusion of the opera transmissions, the BBC took its place in the theatre - in particular, seeking out musical comedies, musical plays and pantomime, all of which lent themselves to the wireless medium. First came 'Cinderella' (Hippodrome) in two excerpts - 12 February and 13 March; 'The Last Waltz' (Gaiety) in four acts - 24 February, 8 March, 9 April and 18 April; 'The Lady of the Rose' (Dalys) 1st Act only - 16 March; 'The Battling Butler' (Adelphi) 1st Act - 21 March; and an excerpt from 'Marriage by Instalments' (Ambassador) on 29 March.

Listeners were transported to the Princes Restaurant on 'Burns Night' - 25 January - and heard the welcome to guests delivered by the Chairman of the London Burns Club, followed a little later by G K Chesterton's toast to 'The Immortal Memory'. The next day - Australia Day - listeners found themselves in Australia House for a talk by the High Commissioner and a special concert. The technical arrangements were placed in the care of A E Thompson - Uncle Tom - the Western Electric Engineer who set up the Birmingham Station. Another Outside Broadcast was of a debate held at the Kingsway Hall on Communism..

Technically, the Outside Broadcasts represented a major breakthrough. The portable nature of the equipment and the ability of the Post Office to create a network of land lines gave mobility and flexibility to broadcasting, increasing both its variety and quality. The Western Electric double button microphone was particularly suited to stage work, as it could collect sound both from the stage behind and the orchestra in front. The audio-frequency three-stage amplifier operated without undue distortion; The operators were equipped with receivers enabling them to monitor the volume of speech and music fed into the cable. At the transmitter, further control was, of course, exercised.

For 2LO, the pre-Savoy Hill's Outside Broadcasts were more than a technical breakthrough; they provided a lifeline. They gave the Station flagship status at a critical time, a time when it had no more, and perhaps less, to offer than its provincial counterparts. The staple fare of Children's Hour, News and evening concert had been acceptable in 1922 but the public expected more of the much-heralded BBC. They were not to know that royalties and funds from the broadcasting Licence had hardly begun to flow into the BBC coffers. Nor were they to realise that the staffing position remained just as fraught and the accommodation just as limited as it had been at the end of 1922.

The conditions under which Stanton Jefferies laboured in the early months of 1923 have already been described (see Ch. 5: 2LO at Marconi House, London). The studio had to serve as an office, an audition room and a laboratory for Round's development work on the new moving coil microphone. The daytime duties of running the Station rested squarely with Jefferies, though for the evening presentation he could look to Burrows and Lewis. The Broadcasting Committee papers have long since vanished but presumably included a reference to Jefferies's appointment as 2LO Station Director. Lewis, writing in 1923 refers to the appointment in the same breath as those for other top posts (Lewis, Cecil, Broadcasting from Within, p26). The BBC minutes carry no reference to the appointment of Jefferies nor, for that matter, to the appointment of Rex Palmer as his Deputy.

Palmer was no stranger to broadcasting, albeit solely as a performer. As 'Rex Faithful' he had taken part in the concerts relayed to the 'All British' wireless exhibition back in September 1922 and had sung before the microphone on a number of occasions in the intervening months. He had kept in touch with Burrows and lost no time in seeking an interview with Reith, - in Reith's first week at Magnet House! He found the interview 'something of an ordeal', especially waiting to go into the mysterious cubicle beforehand. But Palmer's wishes were amply fulfilled; it was probably another example of 'when can you start - Monday?' For, by Monday 8 January, the first open night, he had joined Jefferies at 2LO and was quickly initiated into the Children's Hour as an uncle - Uncle Rex. Palmer had graduated in engineering at London and spent most of the war years with the Royal Engineers, transferring later to the RFC and training to be a pilot. After the war, he joined a firm of advertising consultants and developed a keen interest in music, taking up singing as a hobby. On starting with 2LO, he had to share the studio space with 'Jeff' (*The Star* 10 November 1947).

Palmer's secretary, Miss Lillian Taylor, came across to Marconi House after a short spell at Magnet House. She later recalled how she had been seen by Major Anderson who asked a few questions and then said: 'You'll do, can you start now?' The urgency soon became apparent. Following her appointment on

THE BBC TAKES OVER

12 February, she immediately found the staff worked all hours and then took more work home (BBC staff Magazine *Ariel*, April 1937). By March, L B Page had also joined Jefferies and Palmer though his role at this time is not clear.

Jefferies needed more help with the evening transmissions than Burrows or Lewis could ever provide. A fellow student from Royal College of Music days - Miss Cecil Dixon - came to the rescue as official piano accompanist. Like Palmer, she was already familiar with studio work as a performer. From the beginning of January, she was taken on by the BBC, joining the uncles at five o'clock as the first and only 2LO auntie - 'Aunt Sophie'. Like Palmer, she possessed an excellent signing voice; like Jefferies, she was a brilliant pianist, progressing at the RCM directly from student to professor. From that first beginning, Aunt Sophie's professional life became bound up with broadcasting.

2LO's 'resident' Wireless Orchestra had to be regularly supplied with music. From 22 March the orchestra's pianist, Frank Hook, was taken on full-time to build up a BBC Music Library. In later years, he remembered the first excursion with his assistant (Miss Wright?) to buy music in Charing Cross Road. The music was brought back and stored close to the studio over a kitchen range! To make fullest use of the scores, the music was packed into baskets and sent from one BBC Station to another, its condition deteriorating steadily with every move. Apparently, the baskets resembled a laundry basket and one distracted provincial Station Director found himself in receipt of somebody's laundry on the eve of a concert instead of the scores he had requested! Leather trunks were soon substituted.

Incidents of this kind seemed to characterise the early days. Palmer remembered the player-piano that ran amok when left unattended. It was an instrument fitted with a 'Duo-Art' mechanism and equipped with a goodly supply of perforated rolls. One merely inserted the appropriate roll and started up the mechanism. This, the (unnamed) announcer duly did and went down in the lift at Marconi House, out into the Strand and turned left (into Shorts) for a quick half pint. On his return, he found that 2LO was no longer on air! The machine had gone berserk and festoons of perforated paper littered the studio floor in all directions. An agitated engineer was in the process of starting the gramophone (letters from Rex Palmer, *Daily Telegraph*, 26 July 1966).

Then there was the day the studio caught fire. An eminent baritone was having his photograph taken by 'flash'. As the smoke was subsiding, Jefferies was horrified to see the roof of butter muslin was alight. It so happened that only the day before he had been given one of those large conical-shaped red fire extinguishers - 'In case, Sir'. Jefferies rushed for the extinguisher and hit its nose on the floor. It exuded a nasty vicious liquid that eventually reached the roof and sides putting out the fire.

> 'The wretched thing still continued to operate so I stuck it out of the window, its nose resting in a gutter. It was, however, full of further evil intentions, as it still continued to pour its contents on the passers-by. I think it cost Marconi quite a pretty sum in compensation for my enthusiasm in fire extinguishing.' ('Soap Box Days', *Popular Wireless*, 19 October 1935).

Similar mayhem attended the Harrods' Gala Night when a piano got jammed in the studio door - one of the items apparently required two pianos. The problem was resolved but the atmosphere of hilarity and farce continued that evening, the studio being used as though it were a stage with David Burnaby and Laddie Cliff of 'Co-Optimist' fame doing a one step and proceeding round the room using the microphone edifice as a pivot. The fun waxed fast and furious until the 'Co-Ops' finally retreated down the corridor singing 'Bow-Wow,' the hit song of 1923. The strains of 'Bow-Wow' could still be heard as Cecil Lewis read the weather forecast and news.

Within a week of the 'Gala Night' the Marconi House studio was abandoned, the 2LO staff joining their colleagues in Savoy Hill. Within six months, Lewis would be looking back on the Marconi House era as 'The Great Days'. They were days of frantic activity and high stress, yet the Children's Hour conveyed none of this to its young audience - only of three or four jolly uncles and an auntie laughing and singing and telling the most improbable stories or engaging in impromptu banter. The same voices were often to be heard at the close of the evening's programme bidding 'Good-night' to the faithful band of listeners spread across London and beyond. The atmosphere created by the announcers, being one of peaceful contentment and friendly cheer, belied the reality.

Burrows:
> 'The night shall be filled with music,
> And the cares that infest the day
> Shall fold their tents like the Arabs
> And as silently steal away.'
>
> *Longfellow*

Jefferies, though less poetic, made an excellent impression. 'How many times' wrote 'Ariel' of *Popular Wireless*, 'have we heard him say, "We hope you have enjoyed our concert"; and how many times have our friends involuntarily cried out "Yes, we have", as 2LO regretfully announced "we are now closing down"'.

Lewis:

'When the 'Good-nights' have been said, the switch pulled out and the lights turned off, down we used to go in the lift and out into the busy Strand, teaming with people just out of the theatres and brightly lit with electric signs. Leaping on a bus amongst one's fellow passengers, one would think of the thousand things that there was no time to do that day.'

As he walked home after jumping off the bus, Lewis noted the aerial posts like spears against the sky. Beneath one of them perhaps, a lighted window where a family linger over the fire before turning in - a family to whom he had been talking earlier in the evening. And on he would go to his own house 'meditating on the strangeness of it all.' (Lewis, Cecil, *Broadcasting from Within*, p38).

No. 2 Savoy Hill

For plans of Savoy Hill premises see Plans.

The Institution of Electrical Engineers (IEE), Savoy Hill, provided the first permanent home of the BBC. Occupation occurred in two stages: first, Head Office staff moved on Monday 19 March 1923 vacating Magnet House. Secondly, 2LO moved officially on Tuesday 1 May, its staff moving across from Marconi House (see Plans). But, as so often happened with the BBC stations, the contrasting requirements of the studios and transmitters meant that these often had to be housed in buildings separated from each other by up to two miles. Savoy Hill could accommodate the studio suite and amplifier but the transmitter and aerial remained, as a stop gap measure, at Marconi House until suitable premises were eventually found elsewhere.

Although Savoy Hill (plan 1) served the BBC right through its first decade, the closest association between the two occurred during the 'Company' years - 1923 to 1926. By the end of this period Savoy Hill had become fully occupied, with 400 staff, seven studios, a control room and workshops all serving a variety of needs and all packed into the one building group. From 1927 on, the BBC - now the British Broadcasting Corporation - simply erupted like a volcano, scattering fragments of its departments month by month into any available space within half a mile radius. The Engineering Division became a major detached element with its own premises in the Brixton area.

The term 'Savoy Hill' covers two phases of growth; the second phase is associated with the years 1925/26 and with what was then known as Savoy Hill Mansions. The Mansions were later named 'Savoy Hill House'.

For our purposes it is the first phase of growth in 1923/24 that is of more immediate concern. This period is essentially linked with the BBC's occupation of space within the building of the Institution of Electrical Engineers. The IEE building still survives, basically in its original form, set back from the Thames Embankment and backing on to the Mansions. The building is mainly one of brick with stone dressings, comprising ground, first and second floors rising to about 60ft. The third floor, about 11ft in height, was top-lit and originally concealed behind an elaborate cornice. The front and side wings were all built to this pattern leaving a hollow court in which was constructed a splendid semi-circular lecture hall. Over part of the lecture theatre, two floors of offices 11ft high were fitted in, the lower corresponding with the second floor of the main building (plan 1). The premises were designed by Stephen Salter and opened for

The original control room at Savoy Hill, 1924.

Reproduced by permission of the BBC

Enlarged control room at 2LO, Savoy Hill, 1927

Reproduced by permission of the BBC

medical use in 1889.

The Institution of Electrical Engineers commenced occupation in 1909 but much of the space was surplus to requirements and was let to 'allied' companies and organisations with electrical interests. Even so, part remained in some kind of medical use during the Great War, the space being leased from the IEE by the London County Council. This LCC space was mainly in the west wing and comprised two large rooms on each of the first, second and third floors with an access stairway between them leading out at street level on to Savoy Hill, the doorway being 'No.2' of that short street. Through that humble doorway, with its little steps and railings, would soon pass a flow of politicians, eminent churchmen and scientists and outstanding artistes from the worlds of the theatre and concert hall, for this would become the entrance to the studios and offices of the BBC.

Today, the great mass of the western flank of the Savoy Hotel overshadows the little street giving it an air of dreary seclusion. And so it was back in 1922, when Reith and his colleagues first ventured into it. We may find it difficult to

THE BBC TAKES OVER

Radio Press

The Institution of Electrical Engineers, 1923.

imagine that Savoy Hill once had its day of glory when, in the eighteen nineties, it provided access to the main entrance of the Savoy Hotel. Cabs and carriages drove up and off it into a large courtyard in the middle of which a Della Robbia fountain played, palms providing an exotic effect in the background. In later years, the hotel's ballroom was built on the site of the old courtyard. From here, the Savoy Orpheans, under Debroy Somers and the Savoy Havana Band under Bert Railton broadcast almost nightly, starting in 1923.

But all this still leaves us with the question - how did the BBC come to be associated with Savoy Hill in the first place?

It seems Sir William Noble, of the GEC, took the first step back in August 1922 when he took over from Gill and set up the 'Big Six' Broadcasting Committee. He made tentative enquiries as to whether the IEE had any rooms that might serve as offices of the Broadcasting Company. The Institution responded by sending plans, after consulting the London County Council as to their future needs. Noble thereupon wrote to Isaacs suggesting he should visit the IEE to see which rooms might be most suitable (Noble to Isaacs, 14 August

1922). Binyon and Isaacs met Gill who was President of the IEE, and Rowell, the IEE Secretary. Having sketched some accommodation needs, literally on the back of an envelope, they belatedly concluded that space on the second floor overlooking the Thames should be taken. This included the South Room in the West Wing and the adjoining South Wing, plan 5b. The combined rent would be £1,400 p.a.

In the meantime, the initiative had passed to Burrows, Director of Programmes, who had a much clearer grasp of the staffing needs on which the office accommodation requirement would be based. In addition, Burrows' opposite number on the engineering side - R H White - could advise on the area of search, for the IEE was not the only building to be inspected; others would need to be looked at provided they were within a mile of the Marconi House transmitter. Other factors were cost, the absence of street noise and other noise generated within the building itself (for example, by machinery in the basement) and the existence of a room large enough to house an orchestra of, say, twenty instrumentalists after being adapted to meet acoustic requirements (Burrows to Colonel Simpson of Marconi, one of the 'Big Six', October or November 1922).

In his minute to Simpson, Burrows made it clear that the IEE building came closer than any other to meeting these requirements. With sure judgement, Burrows identified the room which would become the BBC's first studio:

> 'There is vacant a large room, 44ft by 27ft, which by re-arrangement would make an excellent concert room and the necessary retiring room for artistes. This is on the third floor and adjacent to it on the same floor are three rooms 20ft by 12ft, one room 12ft by 12ft and one ante-room 12ft by 7ft. On the second floor below these smaller rooms, is another set of rooms of similar floor space. The combined rental, including rates, for the ten rooms and the top-lit room for studio use would be £850 p.a.' (plan 3, plan 2).

Although Burrows had set out his ideas on staffing in this minute, the space he suggested fell short of what was required to house the staff. The problem lay in the lack of any guidance as to the financial resources likely to be available to pay these staff, to cover the rent for any accommodation, and the capital costs of adapting and furnishing the studio and offices. A further complication was the degree to which Head Office would be expected to service the provincial stations. With so many unanswered questions, neither Noble nor the

Broadcasting Committee, let alone Burrows, felt in a position to make any firm decisions. The matter was put off pending the registration of the British Broadcasting Company and the appointment of the Company's senior staff. After all, it was they who would be here to occupy and use the accommodation and the BBC that would bear the costs.

Once the appointments had been made, Noble took immediate action. On Monday, 18 December, he led the search for accommodation (internal minute, Reith to R H Eckersley, 22 January 1923). It was a historic day - the first time the BBC staff had met, although only three of the four appointed by Noble's committee were actually present. The search party met on the pavement at the bottom of Kingsway opposite Bush House. One of the men, Lewis, stood 6ft 4in but another was even taller and had 'a sort of lofty detachment surrounding him'. There was no mistaking this man - John Reith, the new General Manger of the British Broadcasting Company. The impression made on Lewis on this first encounter remained with him forever more. 'The gash on his cheek from a war wound added a certain severity to his mien. He had a pronounced Scottish accent, a neatly rolled umbrella and very fine hands.' (Lewis, Cecil, *Never Look Back*, p 64)

And so the party set off, its leader for practical purposes being Burrows who had been collecting together, over the previous weeks, a list of addresses to visit. Typically, the list was punctiliously prepared; it even included a gold 'flatting' mill, lying in Hop Gardens just east of St. Martin's Lane in the heart of theatre land and 550 metres west of Marconi House. In this mill, gold rolling and beating had been undertaken and, on the conclusion of operations, every piece of flooring had been torn up and burnt with the object of recovering the precious metal. The result was that the building resembled one that had been gutted by fire. It is difficult to imagine such a building becoming the BBC's Head Office but it was included in the tour all the same (Burrows, Arthur, *The Story of Broadcasting*, p77).

Not surprisingly, the exercise continued the following day, this time with the four members of 'staff' - Reith, Burrows, Lewis and White - forming the search party (In actuality, Reith had still to accept his job offer and White likewise; indeed, this was probably the occasion when White indicated to Reith his misgivings about switching over from Marconi). It turned out to be a long day and, to Reith, each site visited seemed worse than the last. Reith:

'Finally, as dusk was falling, we came to Savoy Hill. First, we had to locate and interview the caretaker of the Institution of Electrical

Engineers. Yes, the Institution had large premises vacant in their block with separate entries and so on. Being instructed by him to present ourselves at another door, the game, so to speak, began. Having circumambulated the block, we composed ourselves before one gloomy portal to attend till such time as, by devious underground channels, the caretaker might reasonably be expected to arrive at the same entrance, but on the other side of it. This, in due course, he in fact did, but it was apparently not the intended rendezvous, for no entrance was obtained. It is difficult to receive geographical directions from behind a solid door, and in this case it was quite unsatisfactory. There were many other doors. Finally, however, the two parties succeeded in arriving simultaneously at opposite sides of the same openable door, and we were admitted.' (Allighan, Garry, *Sir John Reith*)

Reith's account is reminiscent of the humour of Gerald Hoffnung. He goes on to describe the scene that met his eyes once inside the building:

'What a depressing place it was. It had been used for some mysterious LCC medical activities, vacated some months earlier, and much dirt and depression had accumulated since then. It was difficult to see any convenient arrangement for offices (but), if ever the windows at the end of one vast chamber could be made transparent, a fine river panorama would be obtainable.'

The 'vast chamber' was the south room of the west wing, second floor (plan 5b). It was 60ft long, 21ft wide and 18ft high and its division into 'convenient offices' certainly posed a problem. Nevertheless, it was a problem which, in due course, was overcome and the windows were indeed made transparent, becoming those of Reith's room and affording 'one of the finest views in town'.

However depressing Savoy Hill appeared internally, it had a whole range of advantages that would have found favour with those in the search party. Its location, especially in the IEE's west wing, had a precinctal character, the Savoy Hotel and other buildings masking the roar of Strand traffic with all the hooters and grinding of brakes which normally accompanied this. The almost windowless top floor would be ideal from White's point of view for the studio, workshops and transmitter. If the transmitter could not be transferred owing to inability of the IEE roof to support the aerials, the building's proximity to

Marconi House, 240 metres, made a linking land line a perfectly acceptable solution, at least from the technical standpoint. Indeed, this kind of solution would become commonplace for BBC stations.

Reith's perspective on Savoy Hill was altogether more visionary but no less practical. He had a prophetic sense of the BBC's destiny and of the part he would play in fulfilling this. This was abundantly apparent from the very day when, back in October, he applied for the job. His view of the BBC was an exalted one and had little to do with its commercial roots. An institutional home would reflect the status to which the BBC sought to aspire. The Institution of Electrical Engineers provided 'neutral' ground and its Secretary was clearly sympathetic to the needs of the fledging BBC. In particular, he could, and, Reith hoped, would, meet the BBC's most important requirement - space for massive growth - even if this had to occur stage by stage to economise.

This ability to grow incrementally would also have been a key consideration in Burrows' eyes, uncertain as he was as to the financial situation that lay ahead. The calls on the BBC's purse were going to affect his ability to pay artistes. At all events, Savoy Hill's proximity to Fleet Street and the theatrical and music agents were points in Savoy Hill's favour for Burrows and Lewis, responsible as they were for news, talks, music and entertainment. Already the stars of London's theatrical world had been making their way to the Marconi House studio; it was important that any new premises should be equally accessible, enabling stars to get back to their theatres for the evening performance. With eminent scientists, churchmen and artistes arriving to broadcast, an independent entrance, stair, lift and corridors, all supervised by the BBC's own Commissionaires, were matters of the utmost importance. By the same token, with an avalanche of mail arriving day by day, most of it relating to programmes, the BBC had to have its own unique address; '2 Savoy Hill' fulfilled this need.

His mind fully made up, at least in principle, Reith met Rowell, the IEE Secretary, the following day. The BBC would take the second floor of the west wing with its two vast chambers; also the adjoining north wing with its five rooms (plan 2). Finally, the northern chamber of the west wing on the third floor was to be included for studio use (plan 3). Rent was agreed at £1,200 p.a., this to include rates and heating. It would be paid from the date of occupation, that is, only after all the modifications and redecoration had been completed.

As though it was a 'done deal' Rowell informed the IEE Council in a single sentence that 'seven rooms' on the second floor had been let to the British Broadcasting Company, along with one on the third, all on a two years agreement. However, as the IEE was itself a tenant of the Duchy of Lancaster, the Duchy being owners of the huge Savoy Estate from medieval times, their permission also had to be obtained. This did not come through until 7 March; hence the lease was not ready for signing till 15 March, four days before the BBC moved in (Appleyard, R, *History of the Institution of Electrical Engineers*, p257 and letter from Duchy of Lancaster to IEE, 7 March 1923).

As though aware that the studio would not be ready for occupation, the lease only made provision for space needed to move Head Office staff from Magnet House; 2LO staff at Marconi House were excluded from Reith's thinking in planning this first stage. Plans in the IEE Archives show the space at Reith's disposal. The stair at No.2 included a small antiquated lift operated by an IEE lift attendant during normal working hours, plan 2. From here, at second floor level, one could turn right into one chamber (the one with the view) or left into the other, northern, one. Traversing the latter, the far door opened on to the stair at No.4 Savoy Hill where lavatory accommodation existed. Turning right, a passageway led along the north wing, off which five offices with angled fireplaces looked out into the courtyard over the IEE's lecture hall.

There were, therefore, three components to play with: the long, high south room; the north room - equally lofty but shorter and wider; and the office suite. A sketch by Reith in the BBC Written Archives and dated July 1923 shows the layout and allocation of space adopted. The south room was to have what were termed the 'best offices' - Reith's domain. They were approached through a glazed swing door leading into a short corridor off which were, on the right, the Board Room, an office for the Company Secretary (Anderson), an office for Reith's personal assistant Miss Shields and, at the far end, Reith's own room, wider and longer than the others as befitted the office of the General Manager. The 'Management' offices were thickly carpeted, the walls papered and hung with pictures, pendant bowl lamps were supplemented by bronze standard lamps with green and white opal reflectors. The Company Secretary's room was equipped with a safe.

The north room of the west wing became the General Office - Caroline Banks's domain. Alongside, a new corridor provided access to the north-west stair and the corridor, glazed sprung doors led into the General Office. Here there were signs of economy. The floor was covered in lino and a large but old table had been renovated and covered in baize. Two rows of plain, pendant lamps with 'Aladdin' shades served for artificial lighting. A hat/coat rail was supplemented by a stand with a zinc tray placed outside in the corridor for

THE BBC TAKES OVER

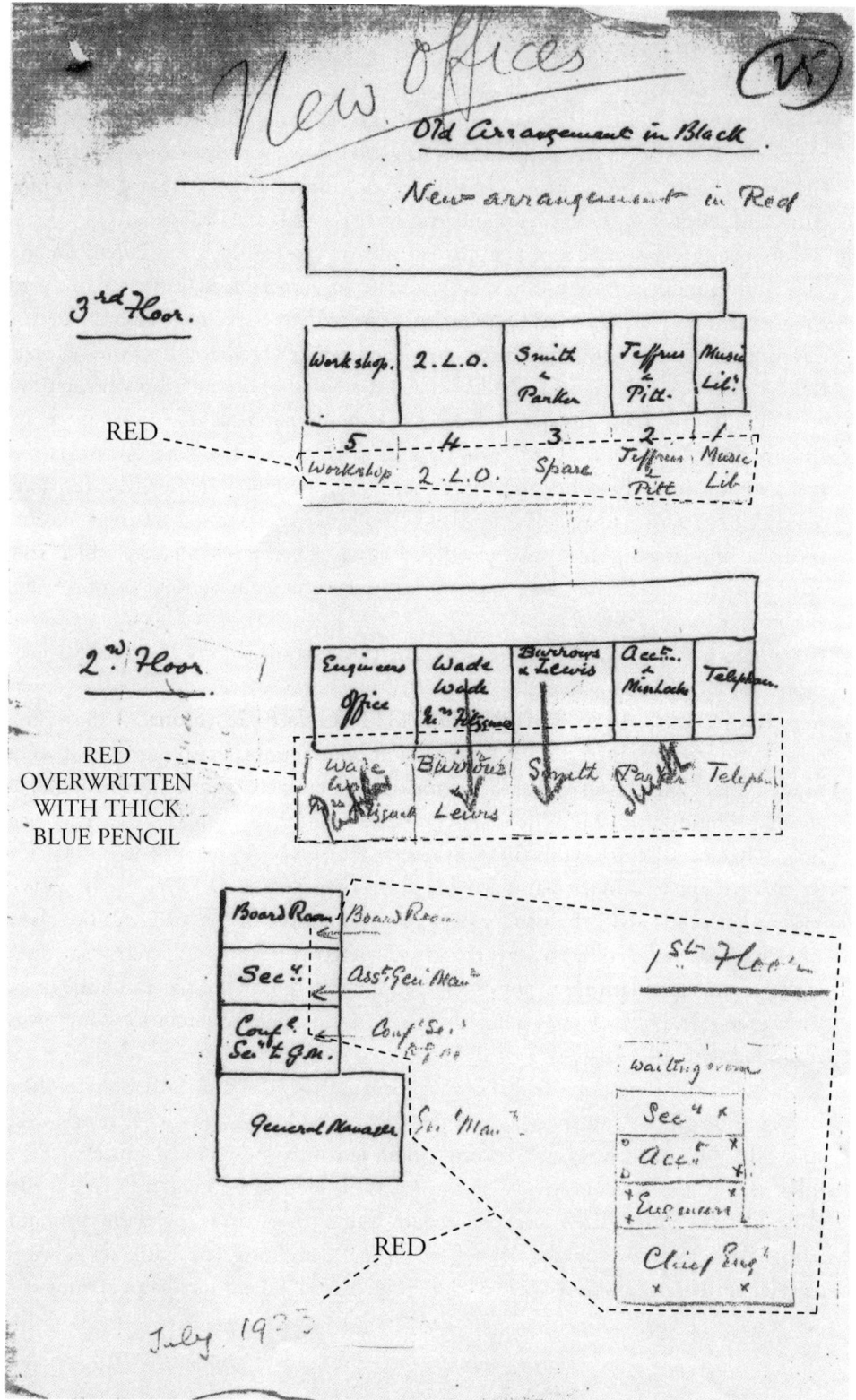

Proposed BBC Room Allocation, IEE, Savoy Hill, July 1923

umbrellas and wet clothing. A cupboard beyond the General Office was fitted out as a tea-point.

Turning into the north wing (plan 2) the corridor led to rooms allocated to the Engineers, Publicity, Programmers and the Accountant (Harley). The stoves in these rooms were re-enamelled and the chief officers - Eckersley, Smith, Burrows, Lewis - had pleasing carpets, opal bowl lamps and pictures on the walls. At the end of the corridor, in a little 7ft wide room, was fitted a telephone switchboard with a reflector light over. This was under the supervision of Miss May who had previously worked in Magnet House for GEC, transferring on the day of the move to the BBC (Details of furnishing taken from invoices in the *BBC Archives*). Other staff would doubtless have shared these offices, Miss Mallinson, the BBC cashier, sharing with Harley and Miss Huntington, Burrows' secretary sharing with Burrows and Lewis. R M Page, the Registrar, had to work in the General Office 'amid the continual roar of typewriters' (Reith to Binyon, 20 July 1923 *BBC Archives*).

All the windows were made to work smoothly and were filled with sprung Holland blinds. At the main entrance a newly appointed Commissionaire - Plater - took up his position on moving-in day. His first act was to fix a piece of card to the right of the entrance door bearing the words:

BRITISH WIRELESS BROADCASTING CO   2nd. Floor

The name was suitably embellished with electric flashes. When the brass nameplate finally arrived some months later, Plater was loathe to remove his handiwork but was, in the end, prevailed upon by Reith to do so.

And so it was that the BBC began its occupation of Savoy Hill, Reith leading 28 staff, the office boy, commissionaire and cleaner into the building, unlocking its door on Monday, 19 March 1923. In typically English fashion, a cup of tea was the top priority once inside; but, having been cosseted by the GEC, the BBC's tea-point was not ready for action. Urgent calls to 'The Initial Tea Cabinet' in Goswell Road saved the day and the BBC could begin its serious work!

THE BBC TAKES OVER

No. 2, Savoy Hill: the West Entrance of the Institution of Electrical Engineers.

The Savoy Hill Studio

Once work on the second floor was completed, the contractors were able to make a start on the third floor studio (plan 3). This was to be built in the North Room of the west wing, a space 44ft x 27ft. Only 11ft 3in high, the central portion along the length of the room had been raised to form a glazed lantern or room light with exposed steelwork.

The first step was to get rid of unwanted fittings and to make good. A wall of breeze block was then built the whole length of the room reducing its width by about a third. A second wall reduced the length of the main space leaving a studio 37ft by 18ft with a door to the 'Operating Room' beyond. A new ceiling was then formed by joists spanning from the long partition and across to the West wall these being covered by boarding on top and lath and plaster underneath, hiding the roof lantern. From the stairway there was access to a small anteroom with a door on the left into the studio and a door ahead into the Green Room. Directly ahead, a glazed partition with its own door led into the studio. These three little rooms had natural lighting, a window in each looking into the internal courtyard of the IEE building (Specification prepared by G E Wallis and Sons dated March 1923 with amendments in red dated 5 April, *BBC Written Archives*; also sketch plan in *IEE Archives*).

The studio would be a room like no other. Its treatment marked the beginning of seemingly endless experiments by the BBC to achieve optimum acoustic conditions for the new moving coil microphone then being developed by H J Round, Marconi's chief engineer. The Marconi House studio had signally failed in this respect, its butter muslin drapes doing little to prevent sound echoing around the walls and entering the microphone. Round recognised this complication; his ideal was for the microphone to take all its sound directly from the performer and from no other source. Any sound reaching the walls, ceiling or floor had to be absorbed by them. The walls of people's homes would themselves provide adequate reverberation, thereby producing a natural effect from the loudspeaker output just as from a person's voice.

To approach this ideal, the walls were lined with no less than five layers of canvas stretched on wooden frames to create 1in. gaps between each layer. A sixth layer consisted of yellow net curtains. The floor had a thick wall to wall carpet. The treatment was effective, bringing the reverberation time down to a quarter of a second creating conditions which even speakers found disconcerting and singers found themselves fighting against. It was like performing in the open air.

Illustrated London News Picture Library

Layout of Studio suite, May 1923.

Having no windows, the studio had to rely on artificial illumination and ventilation. Grills in the ceiling hid two electric fans but these were noisy and could not be used during transmissions. From these grills, two bowl lamps were suspended on oxidised silver chains. Supplementary lighting took the form of two silver lamp brackets with shades, fitted to the pilasters; these broke up the length of the two long walls of the studios. These pilasters were painted deep blue, picking up the colour of the carpet. The general furnishings were completed by armchairs and a settee covered by gold and blue striped fabric, several circular tables and a number of unpolished chairs soon to be confined to the Board Room and replaced by black wax-polished versions.

The adjoining Artistes' Waiting Room (the 'Green Room') was equipped with a similar settee and was thoughtfully provided with a circular mirror, a hat and coat stand and a writing desk. The floor was covered in grey hair cord, the wall being painted blue up to about door height. Artificial illumination, both here and in the adjoining ante-room, was by Italian alabaster bowl lamps. Painted over the door were the words 'DO NOT TALK LOUDLY.' The door at the end of the waiting room led into the Band Room. The Band Room was used by the Wireless Orchestra and sometimes served for auditions – the southern end of the third floor, west wing, had not yet been acquired. The

Reproduced by permission of the Marconi Co. Ltd
Waiting in the artistes' reception room, 2LO, late 1923.

room housed a dozen chairs, two Windsor armchairs, an upright piano and a couple of tables as well as being fitted with a window seat.

The studio suite was completed by the Listening Room (inaccurately named in Wallis's specification 'Operating Room'). This was linked to the studio by a small soundproof window through which the engineer could signal instructions to the studio manager. The engineer could hear the quality of the transmission on his receiver and fulfilled a vital role in ensuring, both at rehearsals and during the actual performance, the best placing of artistes and instrumentalists relative to the microphone and to each other. This 'Quality' engineer kept in touch with other engineers in the Amplifier Room and also with those in charge of the transmitter in Marconi House.

The most astonishing feature of the studio suite lay, not with its advanced acoustic linings and quality control, but with its microphone. The old Marconi House stand now supported a mysterious box or 'meat-safe', precariously balanced on a wad of newspaper. Gone was the massive four-cylinder moving coil microphone described in Ch.5: *2LO at Marconi House, London*; in its place, the new Round-Sykes moving coil microphone. This microphone, subject to much development, would, in due course, become known alternatively as the Marconi-Sykes moving coil microphone (or magnetophone) and be the standard type for BBC studios and even for Outside Broadcasts; in fact, it symbolised broadcasting in the company years. Known as 'the meat-safe', it was normally covered with fabric on a wooden frame that carried the pot-like microphone in a sling of sorbo rubber. The front of the frame was covered in copper gauze to prevent damage from careless handling or by air currents set up by the studio's ventilating fans.

Like its predecessor, the new moving coil microphone required an amplifier in close proximity. To fulfil this need the Marconi House amplifier was transferred to Savoy Hill and placed in the first room in the North Wing, as this was the one closest to the studio and big enough to take it (plan 3).

The opening of the new studio called for celebration and provided a wonderful opportunity for the BBC to address its listeners and the wider world of government, the press and the entertainment industry. It was not without its lighter moments. The main addresses were given by Lord Gainford, Sir William Bull and Lord Birkenhead, those being interspersed by music played in the new studio by the Band of the Grenadier Guards and two entertaining interludes provided by one of the stars of early wireless - Norman Long. All the BBC Directors and most of the senior staff were present so Reith 'splashed out', getting Lyons (the caterers) to provide a buffet in one of the rooms. Major

Reproduced by permission of the Marconi Co. Ltd
Marconi-Sykes magnetophone (i.e. moving coil microphone), 1923.

Anderson laid on a supply of beer and whisky for the guardsmen, to see them through the three-hour session; he had the drinks put in his own room.

Unfortunately, the good news spread, the Directors with one accord resorting to the Secretary's room. Many were the good natured jests at the expense of Reith and his tea party, one of the noisiest jokes being cracked just as Reith appeared in the doorway. The incident did nothing to heal the rift that had developed between the two men (Allighan, Garry, *Sir John Reith*, p181/2).

Lord Gainford, though somewhat 'old school' in his manner, had an excellent microphone voice and came across well. He used the occasion to justify the BBC's existence and refute suggestions that it operated as a monopoly. He outlined the deficiencies that had emerged in the arrangements under which the BBC had been set up, leading to inadequate funding and an uncertain future for the British Broadcasting Company. He then touched on the opposition the BBC was beginning to undergo from theatrical and concert hall interests, assuring listeners that the BBC would not be discouraged but would find other ways of giving the very best possible service.

Sir William Bull echoed some of these points in more colloquial terms. He saw a time when a man could hear a summary of the day's news whilst shaving. The irresistible march of invention would see to this. Further great strides forward would be made even in the coming year (Opening of Savoy Hill Studio, *BBC Written Archives*).

Lord Birkenhead caused some consternation by failing to appear at the appropriate time. Telephone calls to his home, however, revealed he was not far away but lingering over dinner at the Savoy Hotel next door. Lewis and another official were sent post-haste to kidnap the worthy Earl and bring him, by force if necessary, round to the studio. Birkenhead, on being found, offered no resistance but rose, impatiently brushing aside a helping arm. So the party proceeded into the street, the escorts carrying his Lordships' hat and cigar for him. Any relief Reith may have felt on seeing Birkenhead was quickly dispelled when Lewis whispered 'He's as high as a kite'.

> 'Reith showed little sign of being troubled; he calmly stood in front of the microphone and, on the dot of ten o'clock, introduced Lord Birkenhead to the listening public. Though rocking unsteadily on his feet, his Lordship delivered his speech without so much as glancing at his script. Reith then made the concluding announcement and, as the Guards Band struck up, conducted Birkenhead away, giving Lewis a ghost of a smile'
> (Lewis, Cecil, *Never Look Back*, p70).

The acquisition of the studio, much larger than the Marconi studio, had repercussions. There was a demand for ample writing space for the artistes and proper offices for those responsible for running the station. In addition, the Head Office programme side had embarked on a process of growth and specialisation.

On the 'spoken word side' Ralph Wade was appointed on 2 April to take charge of Talks; Ella Fitzgerald was appointed on 7 April to initiate and run the Women's Hour. She also had the task of putting the Children's Hour on a more organised footing; under the 'Uncle's', too much reliance had been placed on extemporisation.

A new Music Department was created under Stanton Jefferies, supported, from 1 May, on a part-time basis, by Percy Pitt, of whom more is said in a later section. Frank Hook's music Library was transferred from 2LO to the new department. At the same time, Palmer replaced Jefferies as Station Director.

To cope with these new demands for accommodation, a revised transfer lease was signed on 25 March 1923 that added the two large south rooms in the West Wing's first and third floors, along with five offices in the north wing of the third floor. The new rent would be £2,050 pa. The agreement included use of the lavatories on the west and northwest stairs and joint use of the lavatories on the northeast stair and of the little lavatory adjoining the south room, third floor. The lift at No.2 Savoy Hill would be for exclusive BBC use. At the last minute, however, economy measures were introduced; in particular, the first floor room was excluded, as a temporary measure, bringing the rent down to £1,600 p.a., payable quarterly in arrears and commencing at the end of June. The third floor south room of the west wing was taken, but without any attempt to sub-divide it or to hide the roof lantern. As for the joint use of lavatory accommodation, Reith took pains to ensure BBC staff were not responsible for breakages or blockages, condemning in no uncertain terms the rubbish found deposited in urinals and wash-basins such as small pieces of paper, orange peel and cigarette butts.

With the studio now having to serve both morning and afternoon transmissions, separate space for auditions had to be found. By May, an average of 250 artistes a week were being given auditions at Savoy Hill by Jefferies. The long bleak third floor chamber provided for these, serving in the evenings as an overflow reception area for artistes who could not be accommodated in the Studio's Green Room. At the far end, engineers could be seen at work, for the chamber had, in addition, to serve as a workshop where new techniques such as 'Simultaneous Broadcasting' could be developed. This troubled Reith and may have been the occasion for his instruction to engineers not to 'show their braces whilst working if there are visitors around.' (*Popular Wireless*, 26 May 1923, also Reith to Binyon, 20 July 1923, *BBC Archives*).

The third floor north corridor was reached from the Listening Room by descending a short flight of steps (plan 3). The first room was made available to house the huge amplifier, on its transfer from Marconi House. A contemporary description paints a science fiction description of 'silent men wearing head phones standing before a multitude of switches, dials and glowing bulbs!' (Alexander, E, *Broadcast Listeners' Year Book*, 1924). The next room was allocated as an office for Palmer, his secretary, Lillian Taylor and assistants. Into the third room moved Smith, the Publicity Head, and his new assistant, Parker. Beyond this was the new Music Department with an office for Pitt and Jefferies and an annexe for Hook's Music Library. Smith's old room on the second floor was now re-allocated to accommodate Wade and Ella Fitzgerald (sketch by Reith dated July 1923 in *BBC Written Archives*).

With the BBC, overcrowding seemed to be endemic, but this has to be seen against the background of an ever changing and rapidly growing organisation. At all events, the opening of the Savoy Hill studio brought the London staff together under one roof. Savoy Hill's long ascent to becoming the powerhouse for British broadcasting could now commence.

The BBC Reaches Out to the North, Scotland and Wales

The existing stations in London, Birmingham and Manchester all demonstrated serious deficiencies. London's aerial needed constant modification before the engineers found a compromise solution made possible by the fact that Marconi House was a steel framed building. At Birmingham and Manchester, the problem lay with the distance from the city centres and the general ambience of industrial sites, neither of which were conducive to attracting artistes on dark, winter evenings. In planning the new provincial BBC stations at Newcastle, Cardiff and Glasgow, Marconi went for a radically new approach. The stations would be located in the city centre, preferably close to the main railway station and hotel, and well within reach of contract agencies. The aerial would make use of a powerhouse or other tall chimney at an altogether separate site but within a mile or so of the studio. The aerial, transmitter and generators would be linked to the studios by a special land line.

5NO Newcastle

The first station to adopt this principle was 5NO Newcastle. The studio was in premises rented for £250 p.a. at 24 Eldon Square, space on the first floor being taken for this purpose and serving also as an artistes' waiting room. Further accommodation on the second floor provided an office for the Station Director along with another office and two attic offices for the Station's staff. Peel Conner carbon microphones were installed; it must be remembered that 2LO London was still using these despite their limitations, until replaced by the Round moving coil microphone in January 1923.

The transmitter was located a mile from the studios in the Co-operative Wholesale Society premises in West Blandford Street. Here the Co-op had a stable yard, the transmitter being housed in one of the stables. A factory chimney supported the far end of the aerial at a height of 140ft. The near-end of the four-wire cage aerial, 80ft high, had (like the far end) a termination of 'cage' design.

The transmitter was the first of the Marconi 'Q' types developed by Round in prototype form at 2LO (Ch. 5: *The 2LO Station at Marconi House, London)*. It was to become the standard 1½ kilowatt BBC main station transmitter and its four panel design would be a feature of Cardiff and Glasgow and, indeed, of later stations.

Planning began on 10 December with the 23 December 1922 as the promised date of opening, a special programme being organised by Tom Payne, the Station Director. Difficulties arose with connecting the studio to the transmitter and drastic measures had to be taken so as not to let listeners down. E O P Thomas, the Engineer in charge, had several empty horse drays wheeled into the stable yard; chairs were placed on them and microphones connected to the nearby transmitter. Tom Payne made the opening announcement, not knowing whether anyone could hear him. He then gave a violin recital; Miss May Osborne sang and Mr Griffiths played a cello solo. Thus, under the most adverse conditions, the inaugural programme of 5NO Newcastle was punctually carried out (Baily, L and Brewer, C, *The BBC Scrapbooks*, p272).

The following day, 24 December, the studio/transmitter link-up was ready for service; this is officially considered to be the opening date of 5NO. Listeners would receive their Christmas programmes. A howling dog, kennelled nearby, frequently interrupted these, but by far the worst feature was the habit adopted by Payne of incessantly repeating the call-sign - 'This is 5NO calling... This is 5NO calling,' (*40 years of Television,* BBC gramophone record*).*

Burrows may have sensed that Payne, though popular in many quarters, would fail to live up to full BBC expectations; that could explain why he had cabled Reith asking him to break his journey south at Newcastle so that he could meet Payne and vet the arrangements made for the BBC's first provincial station (see Ch. 6: *'Head Office', Magnet House, Kingsway*). Though he had many other matters on his mind, Reith fell in with Burrows' wishes and met the new Station Director. Learning that Payne already had detailed plans for programmes some weeks ahead, Reith concluded that he should carry on as Station Director 'at least for the time being'. That inspection, carried out on 29 December, constituted Reith's first BBC engagement as General Manager. In fairness to Payne, it has to be remembered that he worked in isolation and with little in the way of precedent ground rules. Unlike Jefferies, he had no support staff of any calibre; unlike Wright, there were no engineers to whom he could turn for providing regular talks. For artistes, even for pianists, he looked to W P Crosse's Concert Agency. Another agency received and transcribed the news phoned through from Reuters.

At the end of January, Lewis arrived at Newcastle, hot foot from London, ostensibly with ideas for talks. He was back again in March to replace Tom Payne who 'had tendered his resignation' (*Popular Wireless*, 7 April 1923). On this occasion, Lewis' main task was 'to initiate Bertram Fryer into the mysteries of running a broadcasting station'. Fryer had excellent qualifications for the job with years of experience as an actor, producer, and manger of theatrical entertainment. He also excelled as a showman and soon became very popular with listeners, though his time with 5NO was limited to a mere six months before he found himself transferred to start up the Bournemouth Station (Lewis, Cecil, *Broadcasting from Within*, p163).

As 'Uncle Jack', Fryer not only adopted the best features of other stations such as Birmingham's Radio Circle, but encouraged young children to develop a real love of animals and plants (with the Fairy Flower League) and tried to widen the outlook of adolescents. In all this, he had the support of Mr Simpson (Uncle Will), who joined the station staff in March, and Colonel Millican (Uncle Nick), who provided a link with the world of education in organising a scholars' half-hour every week. The idea pioneered by Manchester of broadcasting cinema orchestras was also taken up. 5NO reciprocated by setting up receivers with loudspeakers in the cinema so the audience could listen-in to a 5NO programme as they watched a silent film on wireless communication. Sound and vision had come together! (*Wireless Weekly*, 20 June 1923).

5WA Cardiff

5NO Newcastle set the pattern for 5WA Cardiff where a nightly service commenced on 13 February 1923. When the search for a studio site began in January every inch of office space within reasonable distance of the station and hotels appeared to be occupied. The BBC was compelled to accept a cramped but convenient site over the cinema opposite the castle. The studio, 19ft by 17ft had windows facing the road and no amount of shuttering proved sufficient to cut out the rumbling noises of trams passing below. The studio used Peel Conner microphones, the Round microphone still being under development (Burrows, Arthur, *The Story of Broadcasting*, p156).

The Marconi 'Q' transmitter was positioned in an electricity sub-station in Ninian Park Road, Cardiff. A land line connected it to the studio at 2 Castle Street, a mile away. A four-wire cage aerial extended up at a steep angle to a height of 150ft where it was attached to a nearby chimney.

That station's opening was attended by Noble, Gainford and Reith but, as with Newcastle, without a suitable Station Director. Rex Palmer was duly despatched from 2LO London to run the station for a couple of weeks. It provided a good training ground and it was Palmer's business-like efficiency, that stood out so clearly, that resulted in his selection as Station director of 2LO in April.

Meanwhile the BBC, determined to learn from its Newcastle experience, decided only the most exceptional man would do for Cardiff. Author, composer, playwright, barrister-at-law and public speaker, Corbett Smith brought many talents to his role when he took over in March as Station Director. Lewis, who had relieved Palmer at Cardiff, remembered meeting Corbett Smith for the first time:

> 'He arrived at the Cardiff Station one evening during the progress of a concert; I was sitting in the studio, while the orchestra was playing, when he entered, a short well-knit figure with a very straight forehead and something vigorous and rather aggressive in face and carriage. He became at once interested in what was taking place, listened to the balance of the orchestra, and as soon as the concert was over, engaged the first violin in eager conversation as to procuring music, arranging for larger orchestras etc.' (Lewis, Cecil, *Broadcasting from Within*, p162).

The Children's Hour was mainly in the hands of Mr Settle (Uncle Norman), Mr Page (Uncle Leslie) and Miss Grimwood (Auntie Betty). L B Page had been one of the Marconi House pioneers and was transferred to Cardiff as Announcer in June or thereabouts (Burrows, Arthur, *The Story of Broadcasting*, p157).

5SC Glasgow

5SC Glasgow was technically an advance of Newcastle and Cardiff for it combined a Marconi 'Q' transmitter with a Western Electric double button carbon microphone and amplifier. Not for Glasgow the primitive Peel Conner carbon microphone of an earlier age. The Marconi engineers had the help of A E Thompson, the man who set up the Birmingham station back in 1922. But the accommodation, situated at 202 Bath Street, was inadequate for the studio, control room and staff. Matters became worse when space had to be found, not only for the Station Director, but also, eventually, for his supervisor who had overall responsibility for Stations in Scotland and Northern Ireland.

The transmitter was housed at the top of the tower that formed part of the magnificent Port Dundas power station, situated a mile from the studio. Below lay the glass roof of the power station while above rose two chimneys between which was slung the four-wire cage aerial 100ft long and 160ft high and a lead-in to the transmitter.

A skirl of bagpipes heralded the opening by Reith on the evening of 6 March 1923. Reith then introduced Gainford who was followed by the Lord Provost of Glasgow. The Principal of Glasgow University gave a short address and Noble wound up the proceedings.

H A Carruthers, a fine organist and conductor, took over as Station Director, assisted by M M Dewar (Uncle Mungo) and A H E Paterson (Uncle Alex). Kathleen Garscadden (Auntie Cyclone) took charge of Women's and Children's Hours.

The completion of three Marconi stations in less than three months must, by any standard, be regarded as a major achievement. The BBC had, in effect, established itself as a national service. Work by Head Office would increasingly consolidate this service as specialists came to be appointed in the ensuing summer months and a major technical breakthrough would enable stations to share each other's programmes, so enabling news and important national events to be heard across the nation.

This point would be reached in September 1923. Meanwhile something had to be done about 2ZY Manchester and 5 IT Birmingham, which still languished in their old 'company' premises at Trafford Park, Manchester and Witton, Birmingham, miles from their respective city centres.

2ZY Manchester

It happened that the Manchester Corporation Power Station occupied a central site and could support the aerial. Space on the fifth floor of an adjoining warehouse was taken for the studio and transmitter room. The usual land line could therefore be dispensed with.

An excellent description of the new Manchester Station has been provided by R H Wood who took up his post with the BBC on Monday 23 July, to help create the station as deputy to the Engineer-in-charge:

'I came out of the railway station at Manchester that July morning to seek my fortune at 57 Dickenson Street. It was easy to find because it was the site of a giant power station whose tall chimneys would soon support the BBC transmitter aerial. I discovered that number 57 was the home of Calico Printers, a large industrial concern. The BBC had taken the top floor. I walked into the gloom of the warehouse and a porter directed me to a contraption in the corner; it was a hydraulic hoist, built to take a terrific weight and used to haul the bales of calico to the upper floors. I stepped in rather nervously and stood well back since the thing had no doors at the front. The porter tugged on a cable to start it off.

'We came to a halt on the top floor, which was quite bare, but crowded with unopened packing cases. A man introduced himself as Mr V C Cameron, the BBC's representative. With him was Major Binyon, chief engineer of the Radio Communication Company, the firm supplying the transmitter, and one of his senior engineers.' (Wood, Robert H, *A World in your Ear*, pp34/35)

The first step was to decide which room should be the studio and which the transmitter room. Into the latter was fitted the Western Electric amplifier on its frame. That room also served as a control room and a window was knocked out to provide a view of the studio, which was hung in the usual way with drapery. Even so, the studio suffered acoustic defects, sounds travelling all too easily through the sand filled partition between it and the transmitter room. Matters were not helped by the limited size of the studio, which had, on occasion, to be extended into the adjoining artistes' waiting room whenever a larger orchestra had to be accommodated.

All the hard work of Fleming and his team in developing new microphones such as the photophone and the moving coil microphone were dispensed with. Eckersley would have no truck with these. He was convinced that, pending the development of a practical version of Round's moving coil microphone and amplifier, the only reliable microphone for broadcasting was the Western Electric 'double button' and the amplifier already in use at Birmingham and Glasgow. This was to be used at Manchester's new station from its opening on 3 August 1923. The same month saw the 'double button' installed at 5WA Cardiff and 5NO Newcastle, replacing the antiquated Peel Conner carbon microphones.

The decision to go for a combined site was not the only departure from what was fast becoming standard BBC practice. In place of the proven Marconi 'Q' set, the station used one designed by the Radio Communication Company. In this, the BBC was honouring the 1922 commitment to allow two of the eight stations to be provided by the Metrovick/RCC/Western Electric consortium. The RCC model was actually a converted ship's transmitter and could occasionally prove very temperamental. It consisted of three main panels set in a continuous unit structure 9ft 2in long and 6ft 2in high. To cope with the high operating temperature, the main power valve was of clear fused silica as were two of the modulating valves (Dowsett, H M, *Wireless Telephony and Broadcasting*, vol II, p103).

The prominent chimney stacks of the power station enabled a sloping aerial to be erected but electrical interference from the power station itself was a continuous problem and eventually, on 28 January 1924, a huge new aerial was slung from the power station roof to one of the chimneys. It comprised a 'T' aerial with an upright 200ft high and a cross piece of 85ft. Robert Wood, who designed the aerial and supervised its erection, described later how 'early morning shoppers in Oxford Street got a crick in the neck watching the sky where a team of dizzy engineers manhandled the aerial, trying very hard not to look down from the roof whilst professional steeplejacks fitted the other end to the chimney. Work began on dismantling the old aerial as soon as broadcasting had finished.' (Wood, Robert H, *A World in your Ear*, pp38/39)

The move to Dickenson Street robbed the station of some of its best programme support staff, unofficial though these were. Worse still, Kenneth Wright was called to Head Office to help form the new Music Department. Not only was continuity sacrificed but the BBC made the fatal mistake of confusing two disparate roles - those of Station Director and Musical Director. Wright's replacement, Dan Godfrey, fell squarely into the latter category. However, in Manchester, at this time, it was organisational experience and energy that mattered more than musical prowess. As a result, a wholly disproportionate burden was thrust on the shoulders of Victor Smythe, his newly appointed, but rather more experienced, deputy.

Lewis, writing a few months after the opening of the permanent Manchester Station, came closer to the truth than many of his readers perhaps realised when he described Dan Godfrey's regime as Station Director:

> 'He is easy-going in manner and seems to carry his responsibilities lightly. In these days of high-pressure work, nothing is perhaps more irritating than to see the Manchester Station Director steadily putting on weight while others get thinner and thinner every day!' (Lewis, Cecil, *Broadcasting from Within*, p165).

But Dan Godfrey's achievements as de facto Music Director became abundantly apparent as he built up the Station orchestra and chorus. Years later Wood recalled the 'amazing orchestral pieces he conducted in the tiny studio. Dan was a strapping man who played rugby every Saturday, and he used to conduct these concerts dressed in his striped rugby shirt, standing in the scrum of musicians, gesticulating and encouraging in a studio that grew steadily hotter and hotter' (Wood, Robert H, *A World in your Ear*, p39)

Victor Smythe's name will always be associated with the Manchester Station, where he guided its output in terms of light entertainment and variety over three decades. Smythe had already acquired experience in films, concert parties and the legitimate theatre before turning to broadcasting. Ebullient, entrepreneurial and ever-smoking, he became the mainstay at Dickinson Street, working all hours. Sidney Honey (Uncle George) took responsibility for the Children's Hour and his talks to children became a very popular feature. He was assisted by Rosalind Rhodes (Auntie Rosalind).

5IT Birmingham

It fell to Western Electric to provide the last station, Birmingham, in the series of six. This made sense as it provided a replacement for the Western Electric station, 2WP, housed in the GEC plant at Witton, Birmingham. As with 5WA Cardiff, it proved difficult to find a suitable site until space was found on the second floor of a large building at 105 New Street. Again, like Cardiff, the studio was over a cinema and approached by long flights of stairs. The accommodation included not only a studio 24ft square but also an entrance hall, reception room, band room, control room and two offices - one for the Studio Director (Edgar), and the other for his deputy (Casey) and Musical Director (Joseph Lewis). The station opened on 11 August 1923 just a week after 2ZY Manchester.

The studio used thick felt on the walls and a ceiling covered in mauve and dove-grey hangings. Four centre lights and four double bracket lamps provided illumination; windows could be opened between turns to allow for ventilation, these being supplemented by fans. The studio was equipped with an Aeolian grand piano and an orchestral organ. The microphone generally employed was the 'double button' carbon microphone that, as at other stations, required a three-valve amplifier set up in an adjoining Control Room. The Control Room also contained a signalling panel to guide artistes, a master clock, a three-valve receiver and a crystal set with loudspeaker. To a large extent, it replicated the Witton Station.

The transmitter made use of the Corporation's power station at Summer Lane about half a mile away, where a two-roomed building housed the generator and transmitter respectively. The transmitter, with its adjoining power panel, had simply been moved from Witton. A 'T' cage aerial over 200ft high spanned the gap between two chimney stacks. The Western Electric broadcasting equipment, transmitting about 500 watts, was doubtless satisfactory for American Stations but failed to meet the usual BBC standard of 3000 watts. This deficiency remained a feature of the Birmingham Station until September 1925.

Another unique feature was the frequent use of the capacitor microphone, in which Western Electric were at the forefront of design. A thin steel diaphragm, stretched to give it a high natural frequency, provided one plate of the microphone, while the other comprised a rigid disc, separated by an air gap of one-thousandth of an inch in thickness. The absence of the substantial electrical noise associated with the carbon granule microphone meant that an excellent signal to noise ratio could be achieved, enabling sounds to be picked up from over 30ft away without undue background noise. Distortion was also much lower than even the 'double button' carbon microphone. However, the extremely small voltage produced meant that an amplifier was needed in the studio itself. This was mounted in a polished mahogany cabinet harmonising with the rest of the studio furniture. The filament and anode batteries were contained in metal trays in the lower compartment, which had access doors. An output cable connected the studio amplifier to the standard W.E. No.8A amplifier in the adjoining Control Room.

The high quality capacitor microphone did, however, have a weak point; any moisture in the air gap caused an alarming 'frying' noise. This was particularly apt to occur when an orchestra was playing in a badly ventilated studio. The engineer had then to fall back on the 'double button' carbon microphone. To reduce this problem, the capacitor microphone was taken out of the studio when not in use and stored in a cupboard containing a saucer of calcium chloride to keep it dry. For the time being, 5IT Birmingham persevered with the capacitor microphone but it did not find its way into any other studios - at least, not until much later (Dowsett, H M, *Wireless Telephony and Broadcasting, vol II,* p104; Pawley, E, *BBC Engineering, 1922 to 1972,* p 41).

One of the most pressing needs - and there were many - facing Eckersley on his appointment in February 1923 was to take over the provincial stations from the companies. Already, Marconi had completed the new station at Newcastle and Cardiff and Glasgow's opening was only days away. Marconi men were still operating 2LO London. Marconi, at the BBC's request, invited staff at these stations to transfer to the BBC, the senior man at each to be paid £250 pa and his deputy £200. There were also openings for area maintenance engineers at

£300 pa. In addition, each station would have two assistant engineers, giving an overall four engineers at each station to man the transmitter and studio centres.

The post of Southern Area Maintenance Engineer went to Harold Bishop on his appointment on 10 May, with V M A Cameron taking the northern post.

These and other appointments represented an important step in the founding of the BBC's Engineering Division and were echoed at Head Office by the establishment of departmental posts concerned with engineering research and development. The most far-reaching and rewarding outcome here lay with the emergence of Simultaneous Broadcasting.

Simultaneous Broadcasting Creates 'One Nation' Broadcasting

With six stations operating by April 1923, a large portion of the British population was able to enjoy BBC nightly programmes. But all it amounted to was local radio with only the most powerful valve receivers being able to pick up some distant stations. However, before the year was out, the Station Directors, kings in their own castles, would be would be able to select and broadcast the pick of talks, drama, music and feature programmes put out by other stations; London voices would read the news. In short, two or more transmitters would be able to 'simultaneously broadcast' the same programme. This would be achieved by making use of Post Office telephone trunk lines. Simultaneous Broadcasting represented a major breakthrough for the BBC.

In 1923, however, the trunk line circuits were themselves still limited and unreliable. The more traditional comprised heavy gauge copper wires carried overhead on poles. They were subject to the vagaries of the weather as well as cross talk (mutual interference) between adjacent lines. The newer lines used underground cable; although these had higher attenuation this was compensated for by telephone repeaters (amplifiers) at intervals.

The first attempt to use a Post Office trunk line for broadcasting had occurred back in November 1922 when the Lord Mayor of Bristol's speech was fed into the 2LO transmitter. The experiment had gone off well, but this still left doubts as to whether music could be successfully conveyed from one part of the country to another. The opera broadcasts had of course shown that use of a Post Office open line or cable for music presented no problem over short distances but countrywide was quite another matter. So the BBC decided to hire two lines between London and Birmingham for the night of 20 March 1923, one for control of the experiment and the other for the actual transmission itself. The originating station was Birmingham where an orchestra in the studio used the Western Electric double button microphone linked to an amplifier in the adjoining Control Room. The amplifier was connected to the Post Office trunk line to London where a Western Electric power amplifier and loudspeaker were installed in Marconi House and connected to the incoming line. Neither station needed to broadcast on this occasion, though the test was in fact transmitted - at least by 2LO. The transmission included a string orchestra, a cello solo, a piccolo solo, a piano solo, a piano accompanying a man singing, a woman singing and speech. The results exceeded all expectation, even though some high note distortion occurred.

On 16 April, the same tests were made from Glasgow, again using Western Electric equipment and Post Office trunk lines; this time, heavier open-air lines with less transmission loss were available. Reception proved better despite the greater distance involved.

A major problem lay with the strength of the signal required to operate all the distant transmitters simultaneously. In 90% of cases, 2LO would be the originating station and, even when it was not, London would act as the re-distribution point for any other station. To allow for loss of strength whilst in transit from London, the Simultaneous Broadcasting centre would, it was anticipated, need to provide input of 7½ watts for each receiving station. With up to five provincial stations simultaneously broadcasting a London programme, the input into the trunk system would be of the order of 40 watts. This implied not only very heavy loading of Post Office lines but huge amplification at the London end.

It was decided to obtain the necessary power by employing an amplifier normally used in the Western Electric public address system. This was installed in a small room in Marconi House with links to the various Post Office lines. The 'double button' carbon microphone was placed in an adjoining room. Control and transmission lines were then made available by the Post Office for sole BBC use on the afternoon of 13 May 1923, these going out to each of the five provincial stations. Thus all was set for the first Simultaneous Broadcasting attempt that afternoon.

The Post Office engineers monitored the test and soon became agitated. With such high power input, cross talk on the trunk lines resulted in making normal telephone use impossible. A lower power was therefore substituted but the problem remained. In a third attempt, a bank of six Western Electric loudspeaker amplifiers was made up, the output of each being connected to a different trunk line. It must have been a bitter blow to the engineers to find that cross talk stubbornly continued to be a problem. At the microphone, an exasperated Cecil Lewis cried out, 'What the devil do I do next?' As it happened, he was in an undraped room and his words were almost unintelligible due to reverberation.

With the whole future of Simultaneous Broadcasting in the balance, a further test was conducted on 17 May. The Savoy Hill studio was used with the microphone connected to a bank of loudspeaker amplifiers, but bypassing the Control Room amplifier. The input to each of the five telephone lines was reduced to 1mW to each line - one six thousandth of the 40 watts originally estimated, but still twenty times the power normally arriving at a telephone ear piece; to compensate for the reduced input, amplifiers were placed in the provincial stations. But Post Office engineers were still not satisfied by these enormous concessions; there was still too much cross talk.

The next idea was to balance the lines. This was effected by splitting the output from each amplifier into two equal and opposite phases (or halves) before feeding it into the line, so that the interference from one half roughly balanced out that from the other half. The day was saved (Sandeman, E K, *Wireless World*, 21/28 May 1924).

With the successful elimination of cross talk, developmental work on Simultaneous Broadcasting at Marconi House had reached the end of its first stage. Engineers like Locke of the Post Office and Petersen of Marconi were ready to hand over to the BBC engineers, the first step now being to transfer the Simultaneous Broadcasting equipment to Savoy Hill where it was fitted into a cul-de-sac well away from the amplifier room (Shaw, A C, *World Radio*, 15 November 1935). This 'cul-de-sac' comprised the far end of the long third floor room used for auditions and doubled as a laboratory for Development Engineers working under the newly appointed Captain A G D West (plans 3, 4).

The Simultaneous Broadcasting equipment represented a marriage of two remarkable examples of 'twenties technology - trunk line telephony and wireless telephony. But, in appearance, it was far from impressive. In a railed off corner of the laboratory/audition room at Savoy Hill was placed a kitchen table covered with American cloth, to which a vertical wooden framework had been added. On this, a sheet of plywood was screwed to take the electrical gear. This consisted of a row of six Western Electric loudspeaker amplifiers in small boxes, each serving a different station with London on the left followed by Cardiff, Birmingham, Newcastle, Glasgow and Manchester. Each amplifier was provided with a centre-tapped transformer to achieve a balanced output and impedance matching the Post Office lines.

The same amplifier served both outgoing and incoming lines. Furthermore, the earlier idea of hiring two lines soon gave way to a more economic solution, whereby a single line served for both control and transmission. Communication between engineers at provincial stations and London had, therefore, to take place before and after, but not during transmission. Telephones on the Simultaneous Broadcasting table were provided for this purpose.

The justification behind the creation of Simultaneous Broadcasting was explained by the BBC at the outset. It was to enable special programmes of

THE BBC TAKES OVER

Reproduced by permission of the Marconi Co. Ltd
The first Simultaneous Broadcasting 'room', Savoy Hill, 1923.

wide appeal to be heard and enjoyed by a wider audience. There was no suggestion of creating a single national programme, though something on these lines did in fact begin to emerge as low-power relay stations came into service in 1924. Simultaneous Broadcasting, therefore, offered economies of a kind not even thought of back in 1923 (Frost, Capt.C C U, *Wireless World*, 30 June 1923).

The first 'special programme' to benefit from Simultaneous Broadcasting was the talk by Sir Ernest Rutherford on the nature of the atom, delivered to the British Association on 12 September 1923. But more important than any single event was the fact that Simultaneous Broadcasting enabled the news to be broadcast to all stations from a single source - the 2LO studio. And so it pulled down the curtain on all the phoning, transcribing, and typing that had been a nightly ritual at each of the provincial stations. The first Simultaneous Broadcasting of news was read by John Reith on 29 August 1923. From then on, the nightly news from London helped to carve the initial 'BBC' ever deeper on the public consciousness, providing a single, all-encompassing and instantly recognisable service.

Growth and Change at Savoy Hill; 1923

The move into Savoy Hill was completed at the beginning of May 1923. Yet within three months, Reith had a serious problem on his hands; the BBC work became hampered as it outgrew the space available. It was not just a matter of overall staff members but the seniority of the appointments made at this time and the need to accommodate personal assistants with their bosses. But, quite apart from their spatial implications, the new appointments are of major interest in unfolding the way the BBC emerged as a working organisation during this crucial period.

Most importantly, Reith himself needed help. His role as General Manager of the Company had become overshadowed by the need to serve on the Sykes Committee; this had been charged by the Postmaster General with examining every aspect of the Company's existence and future survival. It was as though the negotiations of 1922 had still not been concluded. 'The Committee is a dreadful struggle', he wrote in his diary; 'I have to watch everything that is said and read every word of evidence afterwards' (Reith, J C W., *The Reith Diaries*, 10 June 1923).

The case for having an Assistant General Manager must have been evident to all concerned and was agreed in principle on 10 May. F J Brown of the Post Office suggested Vice Admiral C D Carpendale for the job. On 14 June Reith interviewed Carpendale who, when he took up the invitation to see Reith, had not realised it was for the number two position. Apparently the Carpendale 'was amazed at the grilling he got' - the interview took up two hours. Carpendale wrote on 19 June expressing his wish to go ahead and on 5 July Reith offered him the job, subject to the agreement of Gainford, whom Carpendale met the following day (Briggs, Asa, *History of Broadcasting in the United Kingdom*, Vol I, pp198/199, 1961).

Carpendale's relaxed manner provided a sort of calm to Reith's more up tight character, softening Reith's missionary zeal and his chronic inability to suffer fools gladly. At the same time, Carpendale posed no threat to Reith's domination of the BBC or to his aspirations for his future. It was the perfect partnership and would prove a lasting one. Carpendale was in his element at the BBC. As to accommodation, a two-week stint touring the provincial stations meant that Carpendale's duties at Savoy Hill did not commence before August, when he took over Anderson's room in the exclusive Managers' corridor.

THE BBC TAKES OVER

Having neatly sewn up Carpendale's appointment, Reith could immediately proceed with his long cherished dream of removing Anderson, the Company Secretary. He had prepared the ground well, convincing Gainford that Anderson 'was quite inadequate and should never have been appointed'. On 11 July Anderson duly handed in his notice - three months was the stipulated requirement. The BBC Board resolved to accept this 'with regret', adding that the secretary should 'be released at an earlier date if a successor (was) chosen'. By the beginning of August, Anderson was gone. The press reported that 'Major Anderson (had) resigned to take up business on his own account,' and that he had had an extremely arduous task, as he was almost the first official of the company to be appointed. 'Major Anderson's health (had) not been very good of late and he (was) anxious to be relieved from the very heavy burden of office' (*Wireless Weekly*, 1 August 1923 and 15 August 1923).

The Reith/Carpendale regime was exercised in a way that appeared far from sympathetic to the cultural ideals that underpinned BBC policy. Neither man lay any claim to ever having had any time for either higher education or culture; this was clearly expressed, at least within the organisation, by their demeanour. Unlike Reith, the Admiral had the social airs and graces but rarely expressed deep convictions on any matter. Reith certainly had convictions but seemed most animated when confronting and defending these against those who undervalued broadcasting or stood in the path of its progress. He rarely became aggressive in front of such an adversary but had a knack of looking almost worried. His expressive eyebrows would go to different levels; he would gesticulate a little with his hands and his voice seemed to become a bit sad as he sought to get his view across. This done, a smile would light up his whole being. But neither man could make good the cultural shortcomings except through calling in outside help.

The loss to broadcasting was most notable on the music front where young Station Directors with inadequate wireless orchestras and studios, struggled to raise standards. At Head Office, the position was no better. Neither the Director of Programmes, Burrows, nor his Deputy, Lewis, had a musical background and the head of 2LO lacked any formal training. Musical interests outside were, almost without exception, antagonistic to broadcasting; the one exception was the British National Opera Company (BNOC). This had, as its Musical Director, a man steeped in every aspect of music - Percy Pitt. He was known and admired across the continent for his knowledge and experience. Obtaining the services of Pitt, even on a limited part-time basis, would do much to place the BBC's musical output in experienced hands and on a respectable footing. So it was that Reith sought to get Pitt 'on board' and, needless to say, his almost mesmeric powers of persuasion prevailed.

Percy Pitt's duties included responsibility for:

> an operatic night once a fortnight;
> a male voice quartet twice weekly;
> a string quartet weekly;
> the musical side of Sunday programmes;
> groups of singers/players who would 'tour'.

His remuneration was to be £250 a quarter and his title 'Controller of Music', starting 1 May 1923. What the contract omitted to say was that he would have to share a small room with Jefferies, Director of Music - a young man still in his mid-twenties.

By comparison with Jefferies, Pitt belonged to a bygone pre-war era. He had collaborated with Henry Wood in staging some of the earliest Queen's Hall promenade concerts, having studied at the best schools of music - all continental - and learning to speak fluent French, German and Italian. In 1906 he had become Musical Director of Covent Garden and was soon known and loved throughout the world of opera and, indeed, of music generally.

The war drew down the curtain. Efforts to revive opera following the war by setting up the BNOC in May 1922 were dogged by economic uncertainty. Broadcasting could hardly begin to reflect the magical world of Covent Garden; but the BNOC was consistently co-operative, lending out its singers in 1922, co-operating in the first outside broadcasts in January 1923 and agreeing to Pitt's part-time involvement in May. For Pitt himself, the 'opportunity to bring a great flood of music to the ears of his countrymen was one not to be missed. Over this flood, he was to reign supreme, a river god, at the source.' (Chamier, J Daniel, *Percy Pitt of Covent Garden and the BBC,* p212).

A major Head Office breakthrough was also needed on the second broad front - that of the 'spoken word'. Little could be done to extend the news coverage or ways in which this could be presented. But the arrangement of talks placed a heavy burden on Station Directors and a Head Office Department was required, analogous to that under Jefferies, which 'toured' artistes and circulated music. The officer appointed would be supervised by Lewis, the Deputy Director of Programmes, but on day-to-day matters would report to Palmer, the London Station Director. Ralph Wade, the man selected (and in later years one of the 'pillars' of the BBC), described the Reithian nature of his appointment;

THE BBC TAKES OVER

'On the Thursday (before Easter 1923), I was working in the Ministry of Pensions, having previously been in the Ministry of Munitions under Mr Reith. I received a telegram which merely said 'Please ring Regent 6727.' I rang and spoke to a man, R M Page, whom I had known in the Ministry of Munitions, who told me that Mr Reith would like to see me. I arranged to go that evening to No. 2 Savoy Hill, Reith asked if I would care to join his staff. I would go round the provincial stations and tell them what was wrong with their programmes!'

Evidently Wade agreed and was pressured by Reith to persuade his employers to waive the normal 'notice' and start the following Tuesday, 3 April. As usual, Reith got his way:

'My first job was to sit down with a copy of 'Who's Who' in front of me and write to anyone who sounded as if they had done something colourful in their lives. I offered them no expenses but freedom of the ether. There was only one censor and that was myself!' (Wade, Ralph, *Early Life in the BBC*, p3).

Wade had to provide 21 talks a week, including religious and charitable appeals. His superiors, Burrows and Lewis, occupied the next room and Wade recalled how Burrows would arrive immaculate in morning coat and bowler hat and throw the desk papers into the air saying 'Look what I have to do today!' As most of the papers related to listeners reactions to programmes and Burrows was working a 14 hour day, bringing his dress clothes in a kit bag, it was a clear cry for help. Before he knew it, Wade was responsible for 'Programme Correspondence' much to the relief no doubt of both Burrows and his P.A., Dorothy Huntingdon - another Reith import from the Ministry of Munitions, a Magnet House pioneer who had made the switch to the BBC on 21 February 1923.

The other aspect of the 'Spoken Word' needing overhaul was the Children's Hour. Burrows, in an unguarded moment referred to this as a 'Wireless romp'. Impromptu backchat between the uncles and a tendency to lump children of different ages together as 'kiddies' did not auger well for what should have been one of the most creative and fruitful areas in broadcasting. As mentioned earlier, Mrs Ella Fitzgerald (a relative of Reith), took on the task of bringing some order to bear and also initiating 'Women's Hour' although Lewis regarded both as central to his own sphere of responsibility.

Wade's brother, Charles, arrived on 11 June to help out with 'Special features' and specialised programmes; meanwhile Phyllis Thomas was taken on to help with 'Women's Hour'. Both joined their seniors in the room next to Burrows/Lewis.

Of equal if not greater significance to the BBC at this time was the evolution of the Engineering Division at Head Office. A broad distinction between operational and development work emerged with the appointments of Harold Bishop and J M A Cameron to cover the former and of A G D West the latter. Bishop, appointed on 10 May, shared a room with Eckersley and was responsible for the London, Birmingham and Cardiff Stations; Cameron took up quarters at the Glasgow Station and looked after Manchester, Newcastle and Glasgow Stations. They were known respectively as Southern and Northern Area Maintenance Engineers. Bishop went on to enjoy an outstanding career rising to Chief Engineer, BBC.

In June, A G D West arrived to take control of research. He had worked at the Cavendish Laboratory under Rutherford. He joined Eckersley and Bishop in the Engineers' Room. With more engineering posts in the pipeline, the accommodation deficiency was now clearly acute.

Under the lease of 25 March, the long south room on the first floor had been included for BBC use but, at that time, money was tight and the idea was dropped. The subsequent appointment of the Sykes Committee opened up a rosier prospect, particularly with regard to BBC funding. The time had come for reviving the earlier proposal. In making his case Reith pointed out that the Company Secretary had lost his accommodation to the Assistant General Manager; that the Engineers Room was overcrowded with five people; that Page, the Registrar, had to work in the General Office amid the continual roar of typewriters; that the Music Section - Pitt, Jefferies and their assistant - were squeezed into one room; and that the Accountant and his two assistants (Miss Mallinson and Miss Lock) also had to make do with one small room. 'We propose', he wrote, 'to divide the large room that is underneath my office into five separate offices' (Reith to Binyon, 20 July 1923, *BBC Archives*; also plan 4).

Enclosed with the letter was a sketch plan showing the existing uses of the Savoy Hill accommodation in black and the proposed uses in red. The first floor would be allocated (starting from the prestigious southern end) as follows:

Eckersley/West/ Secretary   (ENGINEERING)
Bishop/Litt/Carter   (ENGINEERING)
Harley/Miss Mallinson/Miss Lock   (ACCOUNTANT)
Rice   (COMPANY SECRETARY)
Waiting Room

T G Carter had been appointed as Personal Assistant to Eckersley at about this time and H W Litt took over as Head of Development in August. According to Pawley, Captain W (Jack) Frost was appointed to take charge of Equipment and Stores including Engineering Buying (Pawley, E., *BBC Engineering, 1922 to 1972*, p73).

It is probable that Carpendale filled the gap between the sudden departure of Anderson and the arrival of Rice as Company Secretary. Wade remembered Guy Rice as 'a charming, tubby, little round-faced man who never appeared to take anything seriously. Everyone liked him but (Wade) had (his) own personal doubts whether he ever did much work.' (Wade, *Early life in the BBC*).

Smith and Parker had previously shared a room sandwiched between Palmer and Jefferies/Pitt. Smith now transferred to the former Accountant's Room and Parker to the former Engineers' Room (Reith's plan as amended in blue: see Ch. 6: *No.2 Savoy Hill*). Parker had been taken on to prepare the launch of the '*Radio Times*'. This launch was held up by the Sykes Committee, but finally went ahead in September. Wade described Parker as 'an odd fish, not well adapted to the teetotal outlook of the General Manager'. His assistant was Emily Bryant 'a middle aged person with an astounding sense of humour'. She was responsible for most of the earlier issues according to Wade, but, in fact, had only been appointed on the eve of the magazine's publication and was probably concerned with practical matters.

All this time Simultaneous Broadcasting was creeping up on the BBC but the implications had not been recognised in Reith's July sketches. Lewis took on responsibility for the advance planning that Simultaneous Broadcasting entailed and for feeding the information over to Parker for inclusion in the *Radio Times* programme pages. Simultaneous Broadcasting implied close liaison with the Station Directors. Lewis had become 'Organiser of Programmes' and needed an office for himself and his Simultaneous Broadcasting staff. Mrs Fitzgerald and Miss Thomas joined Parker and Miss Bryant so as to leave room for Lewis to move in (plan 4, 2nd. floor).

Gerald Beadle was duly appointed in early October 1923 as Simultaneous Broadcasting Assistant and a large board was fixed to the wall of Lewis room.

This was divided into days with hours along the top and the stations listed down the side. All was now ready for the 'game' to commence.

> 'It is a sort of glorified "Happy Families" where everyone is asking everyone else what they have got or what they want. "Can you give me the Savoy Orphaeans at nine forty five? Thank you very much, Goodbye." As events are offered to the Stations, their acceptance is (shown) on the chart.' (Lewis, Cecil, *Broadcasting from Within*, p66)

Beadle remembered Lewis as 'a tall fair haired, good looking young man with a very beautiful Russian wife; a colourful personality who lived in a perpetual state of rush and did most of the talking' (Beadle, G, p17, 1963). Ralph Wade had stayed on when Lewis, Beadle and Miss Minns arrived to play 'Happy Families'. He remembered Lewis' long conversations with his wife - no doubt conducted in a mixture of languages. Everything was to be going well for Lewis; though still in his mid twenties he enjoyed a very high salary; a high level post at the heart of broadcasting, the respect of his colleagues, the confidence of his seniors, opportunities to explore new ideas, a beautiful wife, a baby boy of six months and a home in a fashionable quarter of Chelsea (The author had the pleasure of meeting Lewis' first wife in later years - still in Chelsea and retaining memories of the early days and of her Tsarist Russian background).

The re-organisation to accommodate the Simultaneous Broadcasting programming work did not impede the remainder of Reith's plan (which he showed in red on his sketch) from being realised (Ch. 6: *No.2 Savoy Hill*). The departure of Smith and Parker from the top floor of the North Wing meant their room could now be made available to either Palmer (2LO) or to Jefferies (Music) or possibly both, for they occupied the adjoining rooms. The London Station had no Musical Director and K A Wright was transferred from Manchester to help Palmer. Wright sorely missed the camaraderie of Trafford Park and always felt Fleming's pioneering work had gone unrecognised (Ch. 5: *The 2ZY Station at Trafford Park, Manchester*).

All these changes of course depended on securing the first floor space for BBC use. A new lease was drawn up on 22 August 1923 and formal occupation began on 7 September when the new higher rental commenced.

The second part of Reith's plans concerned the long south room of the west wing on the third floor. There was 'nowhere for the better class of artiste to wait and no proper workshop for the Development Section.' He proposed 'to divide up the room into Waiting Room, Audition Room and Workshop'. Surviving invoices show that two bays were set aside for the Reception Room, two for Auditions and the far one for the Development Workshop (plan 4, 3rd floor).

On completion in September 1923, the Reception Room and its approach from the lift were relatively luxurious. A new ceiling was provided to hide the roof trusses and lantern light. Both the new ceiling and walls were panelled and edged with a cornice. The floor was covered in best quality grey Axminster carpet and settees and armchairs similar to those in the studio were provided, but covered in grey. The dark mahogany chairs had matching grey cloth seats and a circular mahogany table was placed in the centre of the room with small square tables near the walls. A piano was provided for an artiste wishing to rehearse and a receiver with a loudspeaker horn enabled those in the room to listen to the performance under way in the studio.

A community door led into the Audition Room. This too had a false ceiling but was more sparingly furnished. Plain brown lino covered the floor and a long wall seat and twelve chairs were provided together with a circular deal table.

The end bay was equipped with a workbench and shelving, with a railed off section on the right to house the Simultaneous Broadcasting Board (see Ch. 6: *Simultaneous Broadcasting Creates 'One Nation' Broadcasting*).

At this time, May 1923, the arrangements for general circulation were simple. Everybody used the one entrance at No.2 Savoy Hill, with its new brass nameplate. A few outside steps led up between railings to the door, beyond which appeared a small bleak hall with a stone stair leading upward (plan 4, ground floor). However, a sign pointed to the lift tucked behind an opening on the right. This lift was small, slow and antiquated. Visitors with appointments to see officers of the company would take the lift to the first or second floor and emerge into a lofty, well-lit passage where an attendant would enquire their business and show them into the adjoining Waiting Room, whilst he phoned the officer concerned. All being well, the visitor would be invited to 'step this way please' to one of the four suites of offices, each of which carried a polished name-board.

Artistes and those arriving for audition would be taken up to the third floor and shown into either the Reception Room or the Auditions Room (plan 3). Artistes would proceed to the studio suite at the appropriate time, perhaps spending a few minutes in the Green Room. Here, the cool breeze from the river wafted the scent from a vase of flowers and the muffled strains of a singer's voice would be heard coming through the closed door of the adjoining ante-room. The artiste would then be called upon to enter the studio proper and find himself or herself facing the 'meat-safe' with the microphone lurking, firmly visible, the whole contraption supported on a four-legged trestle.

After the performance, the Commissionaire, stationed in the ante-room, would open the stair door with a few brief words of encouragement and direction. 'It came over very well, sir. There's the steps, sir; don't wait for the lift' (Alexander E., *Broadcast Listeners' Year Book, 1924*).

Holborn Photographic Co.
Staff on the steps of Savoy Hill, 1922.
Left to right: Top row: D Godfrey, H A Carruthers, Arthur Burrows, Percy Edgar, Cecil Lewis
Lower row: B Fryer, Corbett Smith, Rex Palmer, Stanton Jefferies, Percy Pitt

7

Programmes

Organising the Programmes

The end of April 1923 marked a turning-point in the BBC's early programmes. Up to that time reliance had to be placed on informal arrangements with artistes and their readiness to perform for nominal fees. Against all the odds the BBC had, in effect, operated local radio with a remarkable diversity of music and talks along with an almost impromptu nightly Children's Hour. Station Directors shouldered the main burden, not only in organising the programmes but also in putting them over in the evenings. They and their staff became uncles and aunts in the Children's Hour. They read the news and gave talks on many subjects - often of a humorous or topical nature. Men like Jefferies and Carruthers conducted the evening concerts or acted as studio director. The success of the opera broadcasts led the BBC to tap into the world of theatre and there occurred a mushrooming of Outside Broadcasts, particularly in London. With six stations up and running, the BBC was now able to offer a national service and the economies of scale favoured a more centralised programme making organisation.

As tariff payments began to flow into BBC coffers, the financial squeeze became less acute and, at its board meeting on 22 April 1923, the General Manager was authorised to make more generous payments to artistes; contracts could now be prepared eliminating the stress caused so often by last minute cancellations. One such contract was with the British National Opera Company, which was to broadcast for £40 a night 'as and when needed'.

Public support was also running high, spurred on by events like the Daily Mail Ideal Home Exhibition at the New Hall, Olympia, that included 42 stands in the gallery with the 2LO broadcasts relayed three times a day over big loudspeakers. In the same month - March 1923 - the All British Wireless Exhibition was staged in Manchester. Harrods felt that the time was ripe to hold one of their 'gala concerts'. It would include the ebullient 'Co-Optimists', who did more than any other group to brighten the post-war London of the early 'twenties. Their antics in the old Marconi House (London) studio have already been described (Ch. 6: *The Savoy Hill Studio*). There would also be George Robey and Billy Merson - stars of the theatre and musical. Norman Edwards, editor of *Popular Wireless*, determined not to miss the fun and games, headed for the studio, to find, to his surprise, that Robey had already arrived but was sitting in the corridor and looking a picture of misery despite his serge suit and natty brown boots. Edwards:

'"Hello", I said, "what's up?" Robey looked up with a wan smile. "Hush", he said, "it's no good; they won't let me." And George told me a pathetic tale about the Theatrical Manager's Association who had turned the screw on at the last minute and so prevented him from participating in the Harrods' gala concert. Along the corridor came a young man. A very immaculate young man who stopped and spoke consoling words to the unhappy George. It was Mr L Stanton Jefferies.'

Quite suddenly, the clouds had gathered and the BBC found that it was on its own, at least as far as the entertainment industry was concerned. Some of broadcasting's greatest opportunities had already been lost due to the intransigence of the press; more would now be sacrificed due to an excessively negative attitude on the part of the entertainment tycoons. The industry had lost much of its pre-war self confidence and felt threatened. The music hall's best days were over and theatrical managers like C B Cochran felt broadcasting would tend to keep their traditional audiences at home in the evening. Theatrical agents took a similar line. In vain did the BBC point to the advertisement value of broadcasting excerpts from the plays, musical comedies and reviews; such excerpts were much more effective than posters plastered on the sides of buses.

The same negative attitudes were instantly adopted by those responsible for the Capital's music, whether it was concert givers like Enoch and Sons, Cramer and Co., Lionel Powell, or performers' agents like Ibbs and Tillett, Daniel Mayer, L G Sharpe or E L Robinson. The Directors of the major halls, especially William Boosey, virtual owner of the Queens Hall, the home of the Promenade Concerts, took a similar line and cemented the forces lined up against the BBC.

The main impact was to reduce Outside Broadcasts to a nominal level and to make the BBC all the more determined to create its own concerts and drama, a process which required not only innovative flair but also technical development of a high order. The effect on the programmes is examined in the following sections; in this section we explore a more fundamental revolution - the passing of responsibility for organising the programmes from individual Station Directors to Head Office. Broadcasting was becoming more and more a centralised and unified function with every day that passed. The output was fed to the 2LO station and thence to an increasingly large proportion of the BBC's provincial audiences. By the end of 1924 broadcasting had become closely identified in the public mind with 2LO and 2LO with Savoy Hill.

Leaving aside the morning trade demonstration programmes, 2LO came on air every day of the week. An early issue of *Radio Times* shows what listeners could expect to hear in October 1923. On weekdays, the station did not transmit before 5 pm. A half hour women's programme then commenced followed by a three quarter hour children's programme. The station then closed down until 7 pm when the first bulletin of national news was broadcast and transmitted by Simultaneous Broadcasting to all stations. A weather report and local news then followed. The period 7.15 to 7.30 provided a slot for a talk in which the BBC's literary, music, theatre or film critics frequently took part, these also being relayed to all stations by Simultaneous Broadcasting. The evening concert then commenced, provided by the studio orchestra but including outside singers and instrumentalists. Other entertainers would often be given a slot. A second talk was given before the second news bulletin was read at 9.30. The concert might then resume but, perhaps, with dance music until close-down at 10.30. As a special treat this would be transmitted from the ballroom of the Savoy Hotel where the Savoy Orphaeans played under the baton of Debroy Somers.

On Sundays, there was an afternoon programme between 3.00pm and 5.00pm - perhaps an organ recital from an outside source. Evening transmissions did not start until 8.30pm so as to avoid clashing with Sunday church services. In place of a talk, a religious address would be given - often by a well-known preacher and accompanied by a hymn, music perhaps being provided by a military band, thus completing the week's transmissions.

In all, 2LO's output amounted to about 33 hours a week with half this time devoted to music and half to the spoken word (This breakdown is based on the main occupations of the programmes). The 'spoken word' element includes Women's and Children's hours which account for 44% of the 'spoken word' time.

Perhaps the most remarkable feature, however, is the prominence given to Simultaneous Broadcasting, especially as a permanent rig had only recently been put into service; Simultaneous Broadcasting to all stations accounted for over a third of 2LO's output. All the national news bulletins now came direct from London. The more distinguished speakers, including the BBC arts' critics, were invariably put out over Simultaneous Broadcasting; likewise the Savoy Orphaeans' melodious syncopation was transmitted to all stations and the Savoy Havana Bands encouraged listeners to clear the floor and dance the night way. . .

Another way in which London fed the provinces was by 'touring'. 'Touring' round the stations were artistes, speakers and even objects like scripts and sheet music. Artistes were usually sent out in pairs having signed contracts for a given number of performances. Sheet music still circulated in big leather trunks as it had from very early days, any necessary repairs being made on its return. The sorting and packing of music and checking of railway timetables all formed part of the work of organising the programmes. Like Simultaneous Broadcasting, it called for close liaison between London and the provinces. Moreover, all the details had to be settled at least a month in advance of transmission so that the programme details could be handed over to those responsible for compiling the *Radio Times*.

A year later, in October 1924, the embargo by the theatrical and concert interests still held firm but the BBC had begun to take a variety of initiatives to fill the vacuum. Pitt had shown that the BBC could itself cover the cost of providing the occasional full scale concert. New departments were created for handling talks/education and for drama; an Artistic Director was appointed to explore the possibility of new types of feature programme; and the first wireless stars had become household names. Few of these latter had been heard of before, their unique ability being to project their personality over the air with no reliance on audience reaction. In this, they differed from the stars of the stage and music hall and formed part of a wider circle of broadcasting 'naturals' like A V Alan, the consummate story teller, or Sir Walford Davies, the eminent musician who brought Schools Broadcasting into its own.

The programmes put out by 2LO in October 1924 followed much the same pattern as those of 1923 with Children's Hour and the two news bulletins as fixed points around which everything else was arranged. Women's Hour had fallen by the wayside in favour of talks to schools.

Broadcasting hours had now risen to about 45 hours but the balance between music and the spoken word remained roughly equal, as in 1923. Talks now accounted for the biggest 'spoken word' element - 40% compared with 20% in 1923.

Entertainment was still in the doldrums with an old wartime group, 'The Roosters', holding the fort; but there were a few newcomers, including John Henry who had appeared on the scene as one of the first and longest lived radio stars. Radio drama had yet to take off as an art form and does not feature in the week chosen for analysis (*Radio Times*, 31 October 1924). However, the week did include one of the first feature programmes. Devised by Corbett Smith, the Artistic Director, it looked back nostalgically at the works of the Music Hall.

ORGANISING THE PROGRAMMES

Nor was Simultaneous Broadcasting a one-way operation. 2LO not only transmitted material to, but also received material from, other stations. In the week in question the Birmingham Station provided a concert by the City of Birmingham Symphony Orchestra conducted by Landon Ronald, a friend of Pitt's and a supporter of the BBC's efforts to improve musical standards and public taste. London repaid with a comic opera - 'La Cygale' - produced in the studio, and with a Music Hall show. It was these 'star' programmes that required the greatest amount of forward planning as they needed to fit into the varying schedules of a number of stations and, unlike the news or the Savoy Orphaeans, could not be organised with ease.

The same 'star' programmes were also liable to have financial and technical implications involving officers in the administrative and engineering divisions. To cope with this, a Control Board met weekly on which the Divisional Heads were represented. But, of course, the bulk of the organisational work fell within the ambit of the programme staff. Even so, co-ordination pointed to the need for a Programme Board at which the departmental heads sat along with the Organiser of Programmes - Cecil Lewis - who provided a link with the Station Directors. The officer responsible for each 'star' programme was then nominated by the Board and expected to work up the programme in detail at least six weeks ahead of performance. At the same time, Lewis notified Station Directors who had two weeks to complete their own schedules. In the fourth week before performance these schedules were forwarded to Head Office and thence to the Editor of the *Radio Times*, final proofs being sent to press some three weeks before the performance. This last step all too often involved a last minute dash by one of Lewis' assistants - Beadle or Douglas Clarke - to Fleet Street with some last minute adjustment to the proofs.

The decrease in the proportion of programmes produced locally as a result of Simultaneous Broadcasting still left a heavy burden on Station Directors. They all had musical directors, at least two programme assistants, an announcer and someone responsible for the Children's Hour. Preliminary work included booking the performers, auditioning for new talent, copyright clearance, fees and rehearsals. There were experts like Dick Howgill in Head Office who were often called upon to help with checking the ownership of performing rights and the kind of fees payable. Fortunately, the BBC rarely encountered difficulties and had, from 1923 onward, built up good relationships with organisations like the Performing Rights Society and the Music Publishers Association. Embargoes were placed, however, on the broadcasting of Gilbert and Sullivan and on Kipling.

PROGRAMMES

Simultaneous Broadcasting programme board, October 1926.

But apart from all this preliminary work, Station Directors shouldered the task of putting it all across on the night. 2LO London, which originated most of the 'star' programmes, now had the inestimable advantage of possessing two studios. One was ideal for music, being high and spacious. Unlike the original studio of 1923, it needed only light draping as its reverberation enriched the sound rather than confused it. By contrast, the older studio, with its shorter reverberation time, proved more satisfactory for transmitting speech. Burrows has provided a contemporary description of a night in the studio (Burrows, Arthur, *The Story of Broadcasting*, pp91/101). He sets the scene in the 'music' studio, where the electric fans had been running at full tilt and the seats and music stands had been positioned to a pre-arranged plan. On the wall at the south end hung a chronometer and six feet away stood the microphone on its four-legged trestle with rubber tyred wheels. Close by, on the western wall, hung a pair of headphones and an electric bell-push. Over double-folding doors at each end of the room electric lamps with red bulbs indicated when the studio was on air.

Burrows:

'It is five minutes to seven. The announcer, with a packet of documents in his hand containing the first news bulletin, runs down the stairs from his office above, checks everything is ready and arranges his papers on the piano. He looks at the clock, which approaches half a minute to seven and, stepping across the room, picks up the headphones. He hears the conclusion of the shrill buzzing sound which is radiated for two minutes to enable valve users to adjust their sets to the most sensitive positions.

'Suddenly the chimes of Westminster break upon his ears followed by the deep, sonorous and slightly harsh notes of Big Ben. He looks towards the entrance door where the red light flickers, an indication from the engineers that all is clear for transmission. A double press on the bell push indicates (the studio) is also ready and they respond by switching on the red light permanently. Red lights also come on outside and in the space above the studio to ensure silence prevails.

'The announcer seats himself in front of the microphone and starts off with the well-known formula: 'London calling the British Isles. This is the first news bulletin, copyright from Reuter, press Association, Exchange Telegraph Company and Central News'. Midway through the news, the studio door opens; it is the news stenographer (Mrs Esmond), who receives the bulletin from Reuter and distributes the local news to the relevant stations by private wire. She also brings the SOS or distress messages from their various sources. At the end of the bulletin this SOS is read slowly.

'A speaker is now introduced for the first time to the microphone. He is informed as to where to stand and the need to avoid rustling his papers (He may already have read similar instructions in the waiting room). He is announced and left to his own devices, his script having already been checked by the Company. After the twelve minute talk there is a three minute interval.

'The double doors are thrown open and the orchestra files in. Normally it is about 23 strong but is augmented on this occasion. They take the seats allotted at rehearsal earlier in the day. At the other end of the studio the chorus and principals file in rapidly and go to their allotted places. The conductor mounts the rostrum and, with a few final words to principals and players, indicates he is ready. The engineers put the studio on air switching on the red lights and the performance is put under way.

'Meanwhile, preparations have been pushed forward in the upper studio for a short drama depending for its effects on various noises (The equipment for creating these sound effects was stored in the adjoining Band Room as this was now little used for its original purpose). The concert beneath is just finished. The announcer, breathless after his race up the several long flights of stairs, rushes in, gives a brief description on the now live microphone of what is about to happen and leaves the studio to the players.

'It is approaching 9.30. Our play has come to an end. For some few minutes the announcer has been anxiously watching the clock lest the play should overlap the time set apart for the second news bulletin. The engineers switch into circuit first the chimes from Westminster and then the time from Greenwich observatory. The melodious bells are immediately followed by six crisp pips, the last giving the half-hour.

'With the second bulletin finished a return is made to the musical programme'.

This continued until close down.

Any description of the procedure for the day-to-day production of programmes, however interesting, cannot begin to do justice to the pioneering work of men like Pitt who started in very inauspicious circumstances to create the BBC as an independent and powerful musical institution. Before the end of 1924, his achievement had become recognised. R E Jeffrey, responsible for drama, faced a more severe challenge; in part this was technical; but in the main it arose from the need to evolve a completely new type of drama, one suited to the broadcast medium. It would take longer than two years to evolve radio drama. In other directions progress was blocked altogether by the press who barred eye-witness accounts of national events and running commentaries on sports and racing fixtures. As will be apparent from the following sections, progress in 1923/24 was not equal across the board but was nonetheless impressive, laying the foundations for all that was to come in the remaining years of the decade.

Music

It is difficult to imagine any programming challenge facing the BBC greater than the dissemination of music. First the broadcasters had, from the outset, set themselves a new revolutionary goal - that of bringing good music into the home and raising public taste. It must be remembered that few of its listeners frequented the great concert halls. Most had gramophones but self selection governed their record collections; the educational element hardly featured. Secondly, the very organisations which, with the BBC, had at last the opportunity to bring good music into the public domain, refused to collaborate with the BBC. Yet this was a task in which neither party could do without the other. Finally, wireless transmission, quite apart from listeners' own apparatus, always reduced the sound quality, particularly if trunk telephone lines were employed in the process.

May 1923 marked the end of the primitive phase of BBC music, a phase caricatured by Peter Eckersley as one in which 2LO's Wireless Orchestra of 'about three instrumentalists plugged bravely on from morning to night, looked after by Stanton Jefferies who was always cheerful and bumptiously reliable.' (Eckersley, P, p56, 1941). Certainly Jefferies was always auditioning during the day, performing as a jolly and versatile Uncle in the Children's Hour, conducting the diminutive Wireless Orchestra - actually about seven or eight in number - in the evening, whilst contriving to act as guide for those new to the terrors of the microphone. May 1923, however, saw a number of important developments, particularly in London.

First of these was the new purpose built studio decked out in blue and gold on the first floor of the IEE building. This was not only much larger than the Marconi House studio but possessed a prototype of what was to become the standard BBC microphone of the mid-twenties - the Marconi-Sykes moving coil microphone. Gone was the dreaded 'Soap Box' contraption that had served as a microphone at Marconi House.

The larger studio and the sensitive microphone that could pick up from any part of the room, allowed the Wireless Orchestra to grow. A cornet, trombone and piano céleste were added, the latter being used to simulate woodwind effects until it was replaced by a single woodwind, two horns and a contra-bassoon. Next the strings were augmented and then the woodwind. This gave a nucleus of eighteen, but under Pitt's dynamic direction the orchestra was sometimes expanded to 37 for special occasions.

The second important development comprised the creation at Head Office of a Music Department. Responsibility for 2LO passed to Rex Palmer. Stanton Jefferies, relieved of the Station Director burden, continued to be heavily involved in most of his earlier musical commitments. He acted, in effect, as 2LO's music director, the first official music director not being appointed until May 1924 when Dan Godfrey transferred from Manchester. The new Music Department included Frank Hook's Music Library located next to Jefferies's office. In his work of purchasing, storing and packing music for touring, he was assisted by Miss A Wright.

At about the end of 1923 the Music Department was reinforced by the appointment of Warwick Braithwaite as deputy to Jefferies and Dorothy Wood as P.A. In March, the gifted young Stanford Robinson arrived. Both he and Dorothy Wood were to have long and distinguished careers with the BBC. R U F (Dick) Howgill took over copyright work. He too enjoyed a long and outstanding career in the Music Department.

Hulton Deutsch Collection Ltd
Crowded into Studio 3: the BBC Wireless Orchestra conducted by Stanford Robinson, December 1923.

The most significant music event of May 1923 was not the new studio, nor was it the establishment of a Music Department in the BBC. It was the appointment of Percy Pitt as Controller of Music. Pitt's appointment, referred to in Chapter 6, was a stroke of genius although one not entirely surprising for, though he did not belong to the professional ring of academics who dominated English post-war music, he belonged to the British National Opera Company - the one organisation which supported broadcasting. Pitt was in no way intimidated by the attitudes of the establishment order. If he had to go it alone, so be it.

All the same, for one steeped in the world of opera and all this implied - star performers and Covent Garden with its magnificent interior and its first nights - the BBC must have come as a shock. His BBC staff comprised one man, with whom he had to share a room that was not only small but looked out on a dismal courtyard. The facilities at Savoy Hill at that time were limited to one claustrophobic studio with a diminutive Green Room, a Band Room and a long chamber which served as a performers' overflow room in the evenings.

Yet this was the setting in which Pitt laid on and conducted the first broadcast symphony concert on 21 June 1923. On 26 November 1923 he staged an ambitious all-Wagner programme with forty players in the orchestra. A greater triumph was to follow. After much suspicion and caution, the Trustees of the Central Hall, Westminster, agreed to let the hall to the BBC for a series of concerts commencing 22 February 1924. Conductors included Landon Ronald (Birmingham symphony), Hamilton Harty (Hallé), Eugene Goossens and Elgar - a close friend of Pitt's (Kenyon N, *BBC Symphony Orchestra, 1930 - 1980* p7). The concerts were well patronised but the acoustics were unsuited for broadcasting. By the end of the year Pitt had thrown in his lot full time with the BBC at £1,500 a year.

Although the subsequent second studio was acoustically superior for music transmissions, it still fell short of what engineers and musicians desired. Furthermore, not only did listeners' own sets limit further the quality of broadcasts, but Simultaneous Broadcasting had to use trunk lines that were designed for speech. In some educated circles wireless was seen as a mechanical music maker - little more than a toy.

Pitt could not solve such problems but he was determined to improve the quality of what the BBC transmitted as far as this lay within his power. The biggest obstacle here lay within the music profession itself. Although the best musicians had constant calls on their services, none of the opera houses, theatres or other ensembles could afford properly constituted orchestras and so had to rely on ad hoc personnel. In the economic conditions of post-war London, players could not expect full-time posts. If a musician was asked to play in a concert and then received a more lucrative offer he simply sent someone else without reference to the concert manager. This was even more likely to apply to rehearsals, when deputising was rife. With players arriving unrehearsed and relying on their previous familiarity with the music, only the more popular pieces could be selected for the programmes.

Despite the difficulties inherent in the 'deputy system', Pitt managed to arrange contracts with those selected to play in the 2LO orchestra under Dan Godfrey's baton (Kenyon N, *BBC Symphony Orchestra, 1930 - 1980*, p8). Proper rehearsals could now be arranged and more difficult and demanding works could be attempted.

Another welcome development at 2LO was the formation of the London Chorus. A small outside choir used to sing at Savoy Hill from the beginning of 1924, but in September a permanent chorus was established by Stanford Robinson, thereby extending the repertoire of 2LO's output. Thousands were auditioned for the chorus in the next few months.

It would be wrong to assume from all of this that the BBC's musical output was primarily 'serious' in character. Half was 'popular' and if music of universal appeal is included the proportion rises to two thirds. Only a quarter could be described as 'classical' and the remainder comprised dance music. Kenyon indicates that music in 1925, in particular popular music, had occupied a larger proportion of overall programme time than in 1923 and 1924. The BBC could not afford to ignore popular demand (Analysis based on October 1925 figures) (Briggs, Asa, *History of Broadcasting in the United Kingdom*. Vol I, p390, 1961; also Kenyon N, *BBC Symphony Orchestra, 1930 - 1980*, p7)).

Chamber music, dance music and even military band music all lay within the capacity of the 2LO orchestra but the BBC recognised that it had to look outside for the real thing. Only the best would do for its listeners.

In the field of light music this involved persuading De Groot to broadcast from the Grill Room of the Piccadilly Hotel. De Groot was a pioneer of restaurant music in this country back in the days preceding the Great War. For him, excellence held top priority; jazz was anathema. He first broadcast on Sunday, 27 April 1924, a year before Albert Sandler's Palm Court Orchestra broadcast from the Grand Hotel, Eastbourne. In a typical 1924 programme from the Piccadilly Hotel we find:

> Strauss: 'Valse de Concert',
> Elgar: 'Salut d'Amour',
> Wagner: 'Fantasia' from 'Die Meister-Singer',
> Verdi: a song from 'Traviata'
> Bishop: 'Lo! Hear the Gentle Lark'
>
> (*Radio Times*, 31 October 1924).

Earlier the same evening, listeners could have heard an address given by John Mayo, Rector of Whitechapel, the original wireless 'padre'. The address was sandwiched between two hymns, the whole being introduced by a Bach anthem.

Earlier still, a substantial programme of military band music had started the Sunday broadcast from 2LO. Military Bands supplied about 10% of all music transmitted and many extraordinary accounts survive of such bands being squeezed into tiny studios with instrumentalists packed on and even underneath the piano whilst temperature and humidity rose to unbearable levels. The Guards bands bore the brunt of this activity. Reference has already been made to H.M. Irish Guards who performed at the opening of the first Savoy Hill studio on 1 May 1923, when listeners adjusted their sets frantically and fruitlessly whilst Lord Birkenhead swayed unsteadily from side to side instead of delivering his words into the microphone (see Ch. 6: *The Savoy Hill Studio*).

Most welcome for the average listener, however, were the dance bands, especially the Savoy Orphaeans conducted by Debroy Somers. They first broadcast in the studio on 13 April 1923, but from 3 October 1923 the 'Orphaeans', along with the Savoy Havana Band, broadcast direct from the ballroom of the Savoy Hotel. Old Columbia recordings, under Bert Ralton, recreate something of the magic of their syncopated orchestration. Debroy Somers could play most of the instruments of his band and had studied musical composition. A tall and distinguished figure in his white tie and tails, he brought a degree of class to the ballroom and broadcasting meant a wider public could enjoy the fruits of his work. To ensure dancing couples were not tempted to put across a message or greeting to their friends, the microphones were suspended high up near the ceiling. Stuart Hibberd, who had by the end of 1924 become an announcer at 2LO, later recalled the procedure adopted for the Savoy broadcasts:

> 'We announcers used to enjoy going over to the Savoy. We could dance if we wanted to, but most of us were content to change after closing down in the studio at 10.30 and get to the Savoy just before

11.00 in time to announce back-stage the numbers which had been played. An excellent supper was provided by M. de Mornys, the Savoy entertainments manager, in a private room upstairs. We came down again to announce the changeover from the Orphaeans to the Savoy Havana Band and finally made the closing down announcement just before Big Ben at midnight.'

(Hibberd, Stuart, *This - is London*, p5)

Listeners were witnessing the beginning of the great dance band era which would extend into the forties with their conductors' names and distinctive band styles and orchestration becoming familiar throughout the land as a result of radio and gramophone records.

The provincial stations received their military bands and dance music direct from London by Simultaneous Broadcasting but often proved more capable than London of putting out serious music whether from Outdoor Broadcasts or from the studio. The embargo that so affected 2LO's opportunities seems to have held little sway in the provinces. 5IT Birmingham had a good relationship with the City of Birmingham Symphony Orchestra whilst 2ZY Manchester could count on the support of Hamilton Harty and the Hallé. The same applied to 5SC Glasgow. 2LO London benefited from such broadcasts as a receiver rather than as a source of Simultaneous Broadcasting.

Studio based music varied in quality according to the size of the orchestras that could be accommodated. In the primitive days of Marconi House (London), Trafford Park (Manchester) and Witton (Birmingham), only the smallest wireless orchestras were possible. Conditions at Newcastle, Cardiff and Glasgow still left much to be desired, as did the 'permanent' Manchester station in the Dickenson Street warehouse where the studio was 33ft by 14ft, irregular in shape and substantially occupied by a huge grand piano. 'Ariel' of *Popular Wireless* visited 2ZY Manchester in December 1923 when he found a symphony orchestra of 45 instrumentalists assembled in a room normally intended for a maximum of 25. Dan Godfrey arrived to conduct in his rugger shirt. He had formed a chorus drawn from the Beecham and Hallé choruses, which had to sing in the adjoining artistes' waiting room when the orchestra filled the studio, inter-connecting doors and curtains being pulled back. The station also had the Don Hyden Quartet and a Radio Military Band under Harry Mortimer. Dance music was supplied by the Garner Schofield Band which first broadcast on 6 February 1923.

Manchester's space problems were finally sorted out by transferring the studio, control room and offices from Dickenson Street to a new site - Orme Buildings, The Parsonage, being selected. The move took place in December 1924 and two studios were fitted out in the basement, one for music and a smaller one, more heavily damped, for talks and drama. The building's close proximity to the polluted River Irwell made it far from pleasant as a working environment.

Cardiff's cramped and noisy environment led to a move from Castle Street to 39 Park Place in May 1924, whilst Glasgow moved from its inadequate accommodation in Bath Street to 21 Blythswood Square in November. Newcastle set up in more spacious accommodation in New Bridge Street in 1925. A few weeks later Birmingham left New Street and took up new quarters in Broad Street; this despite the ample size of the New Street studio, which had broadcast the first studio opera -'Il Trovatore' (Verdi) on 11 October 1923.

With the bigger and more versatile orchestras came a need for Musical Directors and by October 1924, Musical Directors were to be found at most stations. With their music directors, their new, larger studios and bigger station orchestras the Regions were now well placed to provide a wide range of musical programmes, both instrumental and choral. Music became part and parcel of specialised talks, Sunday addresses, schools broadcasting, feature programme and Children's Hour, blurring the boundaries between the spoken work and music in the BBC overall.

Talks

It is true that the withdrawal of support by the theatre managers and booking agencies amounted to a set back, but it may have proved to be a blessing in disguise. Theatrical presentations were inherently unsuited to microphone and studio work as artistes on the stage relied on their audience for feedback, and their humour often depended on what was seen more than on what was heard. The theatrical Outdoor Broadcast's world may ultimately have stifled radio drama and the emergence of the 'Radio Star'.

Transmission quality, though important, was usually a less critical consideration with the spoken word than with music. News and talks could be absorbing even on poor quality receivers; few of the 'home constructors' of the early days showed any sign of being unduly fastidious on this score.

According to Cecil Lewis, Reith 'paid no attention' to programming. 'He didn't bother about programmes at all, never'. But there was one exception about which he bothered a great deal and over which he was locked in battle with the press. He was determined that the BBC should have access to great national events such as the Cenotaph Service and major sports fixtures like the Cup Final, the Derby and the Boat Race. The lengthy, unrelenting, negotiations that ensued finally convinced the Post Office that the BBC had a case. But it was all to no avail. The press were not inclined to give up any of the ground they had already won back in 1922 when Noble, not Reith, represented the BBC. In consequence, the News followed a pattern that in Company years hardly changed, the two Bulletins, weather forecasts and local news, amounting to three and a quarter hours each week (Briggs, Asa, *History of Broadcasting in the United Kingdom*. Vol I, pp262/267, 1961).

The 'News Typist' from the beginning was Mrs Esmond, the prototype of the News Department of later years. The second nightly bulletin included an update of the first. For example, late items included the trial of Russian priests for refusing to hand over to the Soviet the treasures of the Orthodox Church, a brief report on the condition of Lenin, a railway dispute, a 'sensational' billiards match, and a meeting of the West End Theatre managers at which a resolution was passed declaring that broadcasting from theatres was prejudicial to the interests of the profession and suggesting that facilities be withheld. All these items of news were phoned through to Mrs Esmond from Reuters during the evening of 6 April 1923. She also had to take down an updated weather forecast from the Air Ministry:

> 'A shallow depression persists over Northern France, while another depression west of Ireland is spreading east slowly. Weather will continue cloudy and unsettled with a risk of rain at times and moderate or rather low temperature.'
> (*BBC written Archives*)

Wade, Head of Talks in 1923, remembered Mrs Esmond as 'stately and middle aged. She always appeared to be about Savoy Hill at almost any hour of the day or night. She had to be at hand to take down verbatim the news which came through from Reuters by phone.'

Wade was perhaps a little out of his depth among the programmers, where the staff tended to have artistic flair and theatrical experience. They included Cecil Lewis, Percy Edgar, Corbett Smith, Victor Smythe, R E Jeffrey and Bertram Fryer. Wade's background lay with insurance and the Civil Service; he had been hand picked by Reith who knew little of programme creation and appeared to care even less. He found himself in a situation which was delightfully haphazard. There were

> 'no planned programmes, no announcers, producers or musical specialists.' (It appears he was not very much involved with Marconi House!) 'I was entrusted with getting people to talk.'
> (Wade, R, Early life in the BBC).

He got the impression that listeners were not at all interested in talks, preferring light music. After finding suitable and willing speakers, Wade would write asking them to prepare their script and submit it for approval. He would then duly mark it with a circular rubber stamp 'Censored by' R Wade. The script would then be given to whoever was studio director on the night. He, in turn, handed it to the speaker at the appointed time to be read to the impersonal microphone. No fees were paid.

Wade's assignment was to provide 21 talks a week, including religious addresses. An analysis of talks on 2LO prior to his appointment shows that they began, effectively, on 27 January, they continued intermittently throughout February and March, averaging 3½ talks a week and numbering no more than 33 altogether. With Wade's appointment at the start of April, a talks service immediately took effect, the number in April and the first half of May averaging 9½ a week. Talks given on Women's and Children's Hours are not included in these statistics. In general, talks were limited to 1500 words - the equivalent of a little under 15 minutes delivery time. It was felt listeners' attention would begin to wander if they lasted any longer.

Religious addresses increased this figure further. These were Sunday and Holy Day talks by popular preachers, continuing the pattern already in existence when Wade arrived. True, there was a 'Sunday Committee' but it provided little practical assistance. Transmission of a complete service had to wait until 1924 and religious initiatives remained with Reith despite his efforts to interest Davidson, Archbishop of Canterbury, in the spring of 1923.

In these various talks of 27 January to 15 May 1923, wireless was a favourite topic; other topics included:

    home, garden and motoring;
    sport, recreation and health;
    music, art and literature;
    nature and astronomy;
    international;
    stories and humour.

On 27 March there commenced a series of 12 talks on music by a Major Bavin. Among the first to broadcast were three eminent men of science and pioneers of wireless:

    Admiral of the Fleet Sir Henry Jackson (23 January);
    Professor J A Fleming, inventor of the thermionic valve (16 February);
    Sir Oliver Lodge, FRS, pioneer of wireless telegraphy (20 February).

All had to face the primitive moving coil microphone in the Marconi House studio. Soon it was the turn of other notables, culminating with the arrival at the new Savoy Hill studio, on 2 May 1923, of Princess Alice, Duchess of Athlone.

Some of the most appealing talks were those illustrated with songs and records, one of the first being given by Percy Scholes on 'How to enjoy music' (9 February 1923). Scholes became the BBC's 'Music Critic' in the summer of 1923 and his weekly talks were among the first to benefit from Simultaneous Broadcasting in the autumn of that year. The idea of giving a series of talks by one speaker had already been tried out in March when Major Bavin spoke on 'Some things we find in music'.

Not all the talks were serious; humour and fantasy leavened the diet served up on the air. Talks had begun, effectively, on 27 January 1923 with Major Christie's 'How to Catch a Tiger.' It made a lasting impression and Major Christie was soon back again with 'The Gentle Art of Snaring Unicorns'. Heath Robinson caricatured difficulties of erecting an aerial and F W Thomas spoke on 'The Incomplete Angler', parodying Isaac Walton's classic book. Gilbert Frankau broke new ground with a story (9 March) and read excerpts from his book 'Men, Maids and Mustard Pots', newly published by Hutchinson.

Talks aimed at women were given by women. The first was 'The trend of Fashion', by Florence Roberts (3 March), followed by 'Latest Variations of the Foxtrot', by Edith Baird. When a special 5pm slot was provided for a programme to be known as 'Women's Hour' its content was wisely put in the hands of Mrs Ella Fitzgerald who also bore responsibility for Children's Hour. Wade would have been completely out of his depth devising a daily Women's programme!

To complement Women's Hour, Lewis devised a 'Men's Hour'. The only trouble was that, unlike the other two 'Hours', there was no appropriate time for the men's programme. The 'Men's Hour' had either to be split and sandwiched into the evening concert or tagged on at the end of the evening. Either way, it could last no more than 15 minutes without upsetting either the concert or domestic routines or both. The themes were decidedly masculine - business, recreation, motoring, racing tips and the like. Politics were, of course, banned. The businessman was advised on how to keep fit (3 May), Hubert Winter talked on lawn tennis, J A Wood on camping and Major Christie on 'The Best Trout Fishing in Europe'. Captain Twelvetrees became a regular broadcaster on motoring, and 'Titus Oates' on racing form.

But the 'Men's Hour' was doomed from the start. Few speakers were prepared to turn out on cold winter nights to make their way to Savoy Hill to broadcast at 10pm for a purely nominal fee (Wade, R, Early life in the BBC).

In a rather different category were the religious talks delivered on Sundays and important days in the church calendar. Reith's first order to Burrows was to arrange for Dr Fleming of St Columba's, Pont Street, to give the Sunday address on 31 December 1922. Soon a steady procession of popular preachers was finding its way to the little attic studio in the Strand:

Evangelist 'Gypsy' Smith on 21 January 1923.
Revd. 'Tubby' Clayton, founder of Toc H on 28 January.

Revd. J A Mayo, Rector of St Mary's, Whitechapel on 14 February (making a return visit).

Revd. G Studdart Kennedy MC, of St Marylebone's, otherwise "Woodbine Willie", chaplain of the First World War, on 25 March.

The talks were slotted into the evening concert and, to help blend them in, were introduced and concluded with a hymn.

The pattern continued into the Savoy Hill days with Ralph Wade making the arrangements and even censoring their talks! (Wade, R, Early life in the BBC) This may seem absurd, but churchmen were not necessarily aware of the constraints under which the BBC laboured, especially those relating to anything of a potentially controversial nature. Indeed, the actual broadcasting of services was itself controversial. In an attempt to widen religious involvement and to spread responsibility, Reith and Davidson, the Archbishop of Canterbury, initiated negotiations to set up a Central Religious Advisory Committee. This met for the first time on 18 May 1923 and was the first of many Advisory Councils covering various aspects of the BBC's work. The new Committee, however, made slow progress; the churches' attitude remained poised between disinterest and suspicion.

In mid 1923, as though aware of its setback on the concert and theatrical fronts, the Programmes Division decided to provide listeners with weekly resumés of informed comment on what was happening in the world of music, theatre, literature and films. The radio critics were respectively Percy Scholes, Archibald Haddon, John Strachey and G H Atkinson. Their talks were later broadcast by all stations through Simultaneous Broadcasting once this became available.

Another development was the appointment of Ralph Wade's elder brother, Charles Reginald Wade, on 11 June 1923. His role encompassed 'special features, series, talks, research etc' (Briggs, Asa, *History of Broadcasting in the United Kingdom.* Vol I, 1961). He shared a room with his brother and Mrs Fitzgerald and presumably assisted in finding speakers, especially those prepared to give weekly talks.

The need to handle programme correspondence, however, acted as a brake on Wade's 'Talks' output. By October 1923 the 'Spoken Word' mainly comprised Women's and Children's Hour (44%) while News, Talks, and Drama/Entertainment each accounted for 19%.

The most far-reaching development in 1924 was schools broadcasting. This had commenced on 4 April with a transmission by Sir Walford Davies from the new 2LO studio where he conducted choirboys of the Temple Church. Schools broadcasting extended BBC transmissions into a new field and into a new time zone - afternoons, Monday to Friday. The Board of Education - the Government Ministry responsible for schools - took a deep interest in the new concept and met in the Minister's room to listen in to Walford Davies's inaugural broadcast. Present were Reith and a member of the Schools Inspectorate, J C Stobart. Reith now saw an opportunity to raise the level of public understanding. Just as he had appointed Percy Pitt to improve taste in the sphere of music, he now appointed Stobart to educate the public by means of the 'spoken word'. He was, in any case, dissatisfied with Burrows' handling of Talks output and Wade appeared to be giving too much priority to programme correspondence; talks were making little progress. Church attitudes remained generally negative; religion had won a breakthrough in the broadcasting of a complete service but that was due to one man - the Revd. H R L Sheppard of St Martins-in-the-Fields.

Reith decided to form a new 'Spoken Word' department under Stobart. It was to be responsible for these neglected areas and it was to be independent of the Programme Division. Both the quantity and the quality of output would be improved. Stobart bore the title 'Director of Education' - a clear expression of BBC intent. By August 1924 Stobart and his staff were established in their Savoy Hill Mansions offices overlooking the churchyard of the Savoy Chapel (see Plans). Ralph Wade was now given the single role of Programme Correspondence, having set up that section on 19 May. He therefore remained in the IEE building.

By October 1924, Talks were forming 30% of 'spoken word' output and Schools Broadcasts brought this figure up to 40%. Stobart should have been well satisfied, but he was always conscious of his educational background and he placed education before entertainment. In short, the delicate balance the BBC had to tread eluded him and his relative isolation in his ivory tower did not help - the programmers' experience could not be tapped. His quarterly reports make sad reading; in October he noted that 'there are listeners who resent anything but Music Hall items'. By July 1925 he seemed to be near despair: 'This Department must remain on target for criticism, in so much as it has to perform the least popular function of the BBC.' (Briggs, Asa, *History of Broadcasting in the United Kingdom*. Vol I, p257, 1961) But Stobart did not give up; education found a firm and lasting foothold in British broadcasting, albeit after a long process of trial and error.

Children's Hour

From the start the BBC's 'Children's Hour' had a split personality. In the first few months the hour relied almost exclusively on the talents of the station's staff and this meant top staff like Burrows, (strictly, Head Office), Palmer, Stanton Jefferies, Percy Edgar and Kenneth Wright. They in turn roped in their assistants, secretaries and commissionaires; not even the station engineers were exempt. Absolute improvisation followed in an impromptu 'nightly romp' in which one uncle would be full of outrageous fun whilst another tried to keep him in order so he could lead the songs. The children loved to hear the adults 'letting their hair down' like the jolliest of uncles and aunties and were easy to please - this was, after all, 1923! The uncles were surprised and flattered at the fan mail they received. They felt they had a special relationship with their tiny listeners and decided this was something to be cultivated.

Aunt and Uncles in the 2LO studio.
L to R: Miss Cecil Dixon (Aunt Sophie), Stanton Jeffries (Uncle Jeff), Rex Palmer (Uncle Rex), Arthur Burrows (Uncle Arthur) and Cecil Lewis (Uncle Caractacus).

'Uncle-ing' became something of a cult. Those who took part adopted names and their numbers and their fame increased by the day, encouraged by the popular wireless press. This 'primitive' phase had to be given some clear direction and planning. The 'Children's Hour' had started without any official order but was now recognised as a key part of the BBC's work and its content was too valuable and influential to leave to chance. Accordingly Ella Fitzgerald was appointed to co-ordinate the Children's Hour across the stations and to eliminate its worst 'uncle-ing' excesses; so the Children's Hour took on a new personality. An example of Mrs Fitzgerald's work is her report on a visit to 5IT Birmingham in July 1924 where Miss Bancroft was in charge of the Hour. She found things not to her liking - 'sheer jollity throughout with no less than five uncles and five aunts producing programmes appealing only to children from four to eight'. Only two short stories were read and these struck Mrs Fitzgerald as 'feeble' and 'pretty-pretty.' But apparently the programme did end with a 'Teenagers Corner' during which a talk on science or travel would be given.

Mrs Fitzgerald's reforms were clearly taking a long time to encompass the provinces. Here the establishment of 'Radio Circles' had strengthened the influence of the aunties and uncles, bringing them even closer to their nephews and nieces. The 'Radio Circle' had originated in Birmingham back in 1923 and had spread to most of the other stations with an astonishing rapidity (Ch. 5: *The 2WP/5IT Station at Witton, Birmingham*). Kathleen Garsadden of the Glasgow station had one of the most exotic titles - 'Auntie Cyclone' - and enjoyed reminiscing about the earliest days:

> 'For our first picnic we chartered a train and took a whole bunch of children to the head of Loch Lomond. We walked in a long procession and ran races in the field. And then we had parties every Christmas, sometimes for children who weren't very well off. Well-known entertainers in the Glasgow pantomimes came and sang and played with the children. It was all such fun. It was just a lovely party (being on the 'Children's Hour'); people would stand outside every night, waiting to have a look at us.'
>
> (*Radio Times*, 12 to 18 February 1983).

In Manchester, Sidney George Honey (Uncle George) was in charge of the Children's Hour, helped by Rosalind Rhodes, Cousin Edward, Uncle Victor (Smythe), Uncle Willie (Cochrane) and Nephew Eric (Fogg) and his talks to children set the right tone - bright and purely informative. Unfortunately, Honey fell out with Head Office in 1924 and resigned.

The first children's wireless annuals - 'Hullo Boys!' and 'Hullo Girls!' - appeared at the end of 1924, their contents made up of stories by the radio uncles and aunts. They provide a first-hand record of the kind of talks and

Hullo Girls! annual, 1924.

stories included in the Hour; like the Radio Circles, the annuals helped the uncles and aunties to relate to their youthful audiences.

Back in London, Ella Fitzgerald made no attempt to ingratiate herself with the children. She had no nieces or nephews. She was, under Lewis, an organiser and her responsibilities extended beyond just Children's Hour. She found a Children's Hour which varied from station to station and in which local staff had entrenched positions. In October 1923 the 'Hour' varied in length from 30 minutes in Glasgow to 45 minutes in the other five stations. Commencement was generally at 5.30 pm but Birmingham started at 6 pm and Newcastle at 5.15 pm. The programme titles also varied:

Children's Stories	(London/Cardiff)
Kiddies Corner	(Birmingham)
Children's Corner	(Glasgow)
Children's Hour	(Manchester)
Children's Transmission	(Newcastle)

By October 1924 the title had been standardised to 'Children's Corner' but its length and time of commencement still varied.

If the influence of Head Office was now manifest, the uncles and aunties were by no means in retreat. Their numbers were always on the increase with cousins now swelling the ranks. Many were new recruits and had little chance to learn from past mistakes. The most worrying aspect was the fake relationship between the performers in the studio and the children in their homes, for there was no child in the studio to provide reaction; the uncles and aunties cultivated make-believe 'little dears' who, in their younger years, grew up amidst fairies and were charmed by the minuets and mazurkas tinkled on the piano. Uncles and aunties always maintained a certain dignity; they could be full of jollyness and jests but there were unwritten rules - boundaries not to be crossed. 'Back-chat' was hardly ever robust. Being complimentary to each other was the 'Number One' rule -'I am sorry that is over; can't you do it again?'. The slap-stick of the pantomime and of Stanley Lupino, Will Evans and Billy Merson had no place in 'Children's Hour' - nor the music hall songs of the day. In reality older children of the 'Just William' mould were not taken in by the uncles and aunties any more than by any other 'grown-ups', although they doubtless chortled when a howl from Uncle Jeff's dog interrupted the proceedings (*Radio Times*, 30 January 1925).

'Women's Hour' evolved from 'Children's Hour' and always preceded it. After all, women had to learn how to switch on the receiver and to get the best signal as few fathers would be home by five thirty; adjusting a valve set was quite an elaborate operation, whilst handling a cat's whisker crystal set required endless patience. Children would be an additional distraction if all was not ready in time for their favourite programme and for their beloved uncle or auntie's greeting.

What did women hear in those earliest Women's Hour sessions? Well, mostly chats of direct relevance to their lives:

Fashions	(Lady Duff Gordon)
Beauty Culture	(Miss Muriel Alexander)
Child Welfare	
Household Hints	
Tennis Chats	(Eileen Heaton-Smith)
Dancing Lessons	(Edith Baird)
Gardening Notes	
Kitchen Conversations	
Milk and Health	(Colonel Blackman)

Mrs Fitzgerald herself contributed two talks a week. She would use her lunch times to gather material for an 'In and Out of the Shops' feature, first broadcast on 15 May 1923 and was astounded on one occasion to find the entire board of Directors of a London store awaiting her arrival; they wanted to know what the charge would be for a broadcast about their new departments!

It seems Mrs Fitzgerald's former Fleet Street connections stood her in good stead. With virtually no money - her weekly BBC allocation amounted to £10 - she exploited old colleagues shamelessly. Several would come once or twice without fees just for the novel experience. At other times she would get permission to use published material, telephoning the Secretary of the Author's society, often at the last minute when the programme was about to go on air. She would cautiously open the studio door to give a nod of assent to the reader who was waiting with script or book in hand. On one occasion a talk was given by London's first women publisher, who insisted on bringing her dog to the studio. She fastened it on a short lead to a chair-back. As she finished she stepped back away from the microphone. Instantly the dog made to follow her, causing the chair to tilt over and biff it in the rear. It thereupon raced around yapping for deliverance. Mrs Fitzgerald, as she reached smartly for the microphone switch, wondered just what her listeners would make of it all.

The half hour devoted every day to Women's Hour amounted to 3 hours a week or approaching a fifth of all the time devoted to the 'Spoken Word'. Each station organised its own Women's and Children's Hours. For instance, in Birmingham, travel and careers were favourite topics and a good deal of music was featured. The provinces made no attempt to look to London; in fact, the London programme had little to offer, sticking to the same formula month after month and finally fading from the air in 1924. The London 'Women's Hour' did, however, produce some excellent contributors including women like C S Peel whose 'Domestic Conversations' were well received and Marion Cram who became something of a radio star with her 'Gardening Chats'.

Drama, Features

With the embargo on Outdoor Broadcasts from the theatres, broadcast drama had to retreat into the studio. Its very existence was still dependent on outside professional producers and actors as the BBC had no specialist staff. Everything depended on one man's enthusiasm and foresight - that of Cecil Lewis whose programming role already extended right across talks, Children's Hour, entertainment and Simultaneous Broadcasting. Fortunately, a handful of outside professionals came to the rescue and tried their hand with the new medium.

The earliest serious effort in this direction comprised scenes from a number of Shakespeare plays performed by members of the British Empire Shakespeare Society under the direction of Professor Acton Bond. Later in the year a few of Shakespeare's plays were broadcast with the help of Kathleen Nesbitt - Twelfth Night (May 1923), Romeo and Juliet (July 1923), A Midsummer Night's Dream (July 1923), Macbeth (October 1923).

Then Milton Rosmer produced Gertrude Jenning's farce, 'Five Birds in a Cage', which was based on a breakdown in a tube lift. Nigel Playfair followed with three short plays. A few weeks later Lewis Casson, the husband of Sybil Thorndike, produced Maeterlincks's 'Death of Tintagiles' (Burrows, Arthur, *The Story of Broadcasting*, pp 81-82). These plays were invariably short and in the theatrical tradition with music played between the acts. None had been fully successful because they did not take advantage of the opportunities that wireless afforded. In the first place, actors no longer needed to fill the auditorium with their voices. For radio drama, voices had to be modulated, so as better to express feeling, the delicacy of tone and colour corresponding with every shade of mood. Secondly, the broadcast play needed to develop quickly, each voice character being sharply contrasted and the number of characters being strictly limited so as not to confuse the listener. Thirdly, in the absence of visual aids, a narrator would sometimes be needed to set the scene (Lewis, Cecil, *Broadcasting from Within*, pp119-120).

A major consideration which the pioneers of radio drama had to face was the immense time, money and energy that had to be spent on rehearsal for even a single performance, particularly if music or sound effects were to be employed. The wireless play, once performed, has finished its run. In contrast, the traditional theatre could expect to recoup its costs by repeated performances.

PROGRAMMES

Quite apart from the tasks of familiarising producers and actors with the new medium, means had to be found for substituting visual effects with their sound equivalents. These sounds had to be carefully adjusted in intensity and had to occur at the right psychological moment. Some of these noises were genuine - thus the sound representing splashing water was actually obtained by the use of a lead tank of water about 8ft long and 5ft wide. Other sounds were made by a collection of devices in an ante-room which remind one of an old-time marine store. Rotating cylinders, gripped by bands of canvas, created the effect of violent winds; large shallow drums, covered with coarse buckshot, when tilted, reproduced the breaking of waves and their backwash on a beach; another rotating drum, against which is pressed a pair of roller skates, was used to create the impression of a railway carriage bumping over the joints in the rails as the train travelled along at high speed. Stout sheets of metal helped, when shaken, to build up the storm scene, and hollow pipes with chains and percussion instruments helped depict appropriate noises at a distance (Burrows, Arthur, *The Story of Broadcasting*, pp98-99). The Properties Store was formerly the Band Room, the latter being no longer required following the opening of the first floor music studio in January 1924. The variation in intensity of these various sounds was obtained by opening and shutting the doors between the studio and the property-room where the sounds were made!

It is generally accepted that the first play written entirely for broadcasting was 'Danger' by Richard Hughes and produced in January 1924 by R E Jeffrey. This brief but effective tragedy was set in a coal-mine. Shortly after, a comedy, 'Light and Shade', again used the new techniques of wireless drama. It was the first of many radio plays to be written by L du Garde Peach. However the first full-length radio play, 'The White Château' by Reginald Berkeley, was not produced until November 1925 as costs and other difficulties inherent in the new medium were just too great.

In July 1924 the BBC finally decided to establish a new drama department, under the direction of R E Jeffrey. Jeffrey was accommodated in Savoy Hill Mansions where he had ample room for rehearsals. Perhaps this was just as well as one of his first experiments with sound effects involved firing a shotgun over the banisters into the well of the staircase. He did not succeed; the noise sounded like flat champagne. A few months later Jeffrey was allowed to spend £50 for experimental purposes in connection with sound effects, and in November 1924 A Whiteman joined Jeffrey's staff as 'Effects Man' (Briggs, Asa, *History of Broadcasting in the United Kingdom*. Vol I, p201, 1961).

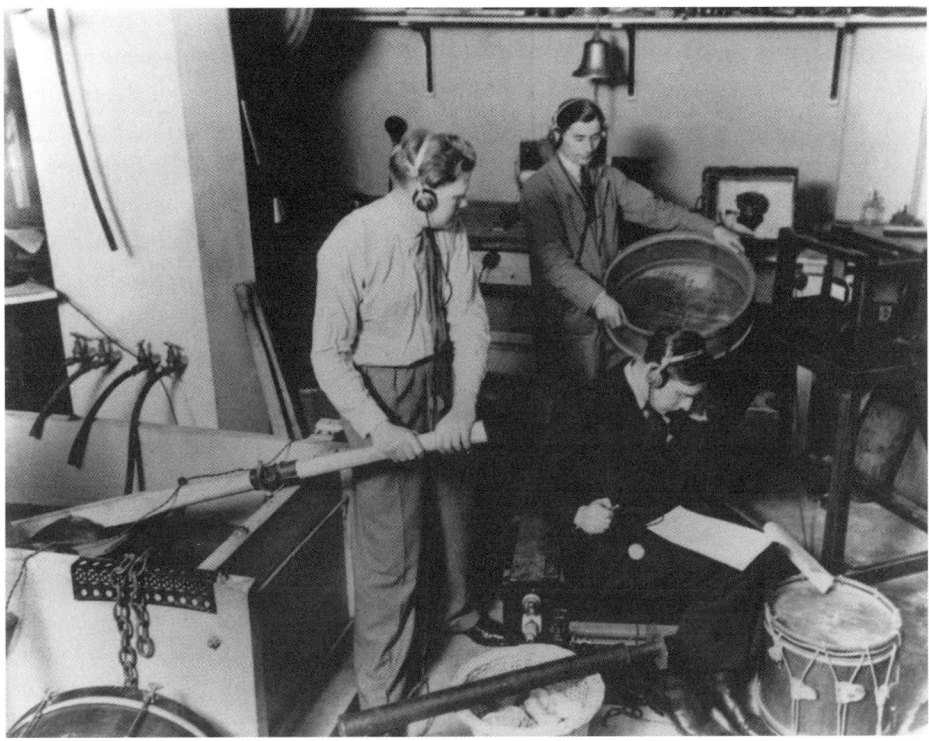
Reproduced by permission of the BBC

Sound effects room, basement of Savoy Hill Mansion.

Despite the rather colourful nature of his job, Jeffrey was regarded by his successor, Val Gielgud, as lacking a real grasp of the enormous potential which radio drama possessed. Gielgud remembered him as conventional, with his spats, pipe and smoothly brushed hair.

The regime of Jeffrey and Val Gielgud depended very largely on the support they received from the producer, Howard Rose, whose work at Savoy Hill became ever more prolific. On being invited to join the staff, Rose had responded with 'Oh all right - just until you get started.' He joined at the end of 1924 on a part-time footing, became full-time from July 1925 and went on to complete two decades of outstanding work with the BBC.

A new and equally exciting art form and one closely related to wireless drama was the Feature Programme. Whereas the radio play dealt with fiction, the Feature Programme dealt with fact. It consisted of a descriptive narrative with dialogues and episodes, sound effects and music, taking the listener through historic events and strange lands with extraordinary realism. The

Feature Programme employed the techniques of radio drama and so needed the services of a producer and actors. Like the radio play it took time to emerge; the first Feature Programme fully worthy of the name was broadcast in the autumn of 1925, the subject being 'Episodes in the Histories of British Regiments'.

To attribute the concept behind Feature Programmes to R E Jeffrey or indeed to anyone else on the drama side would probably be a mistake. It is more likely that Features developed in the fertile mind of Corbett Smith who had transferred from his post as Station Director, Cardiff, to London in March 1924 to become 'Artistic Director'. He was given a great deal of autonomy, bypassing not only Jeffrey but also Lewis and Burrows. Feature programmes became his major preoccupation and actually preceded developments in drama. But, unlike Jeffrey, Corbett Smith had no corps of outside professionals to whom he could turn and train in the new medium, nor did he benefit from writers keen to extend the range of their work. Within the organisation itself he ploughed a lonely furrow with no staff to help and no specialist accommodation. Fortunately he possessed a prodigious range of accomplishments with several opera and other compositions to his credit. He was a barrister by training and a fellow of the Royal Geographical Society while being very much a man of the world, having served in the army as a major and as the Editor of 'The Journal of State Medicine'. Always seeking new horizons, his time at Savoy Hill amounted to little more than a year. But it was enough to enable Corbett Smith to launch several embryonic Feature Programmes.

The first was set in an English country house of fine sporting traditions. Sir Theodore Cook, Editor of *The Field*, played the part of Sir Lumley Basing who had invited a dozen or so famous sportsmen to celebrate his birthday. The nuts and port are going round and with them a flow of stories, memories and song. After drinking the host's health the conversation turns to the 'Varsity Boat Race; then in turn to the Grand National, England v Australia at Lords, a Cup Tie and The Derby. In each case a picture in sound paints the scene; for example, we hear the noise of the crowd at the Derby with a barrel-organ playing in the distance.

A month later, on 3 November 1924, Corbett Smith took his listeners back in time to one of London's old Music Halls. The year is 1870 and the auditorium is lit by tiers of opal globe gas lamps. The atmosphere is laden with tobacco smoke. We hear the murmur of voices and clinking of glasses. On his Olympian throne, immediately in front of the orchestra and with his back to the stage, sits the Master of Ceremonies who, with his hammer and his tremendous voice, announces each item and encore. On both floors are capacious refreshment bars, to which patrons resort when not interested in the turn occupying the stage. In this re-enactment, Willie Rouse acts as Chairman, and the supporting cast, aided by the orchestra, provide impressions of Vesta Tilley, Marie Lloyd, Dan Leno, Eugene Stratton and other legendary figures. Corbett Smith persuaded the ageing Charles Coburn to round off the show with some reminiscences of old Music Hall days and to sing 'by special desire' his most famous numbers, 'The Man who Broke the Bank of Monte Carlo' and 'Two Lovely Black Eyes.'

PROGRAMMES

First Stars Of Radio

'Radio Stars' can best be thought of as those who caught the imagination of listeners on the wireless. As such they became household names and they owed this distinction to the new medium rather than to any eminence in another field. The 'stars' had hardly begun to emerge before 1925, but they included a small elite group which extended the science of radio or the art of broadcasting in new fruitful directions. To these rare talents can be added, in many cases, a special ability to project their personalities in the unnatural circumstances to be found in the studio. Here, they found themselves in rooms that swallowed up the human voice, rooms which lacked both natural light and ventilation and which were virtually cut off from the outside world. In place of an appreciative audience they faced a heavy microphone and trailing wires. Yet these stars of broadcasting appeared to be entirely at their ease as though they were speaking directly to people in their own homes, listening in attentively and, where appropriate, with amusement and laughter.

Without doubt one man stands head and shoulders above all others as a Radio Star. That man was Peter Pendleton Eckersley. Long before broadcasting was even thought of Eckersley was active in developing radio for aerial navigation. With the cessation of hostilities in 1918 he joined the Marconi Company and became head of the team developing wireless telephony for civil aviation. Although the team was isolated from Head Office and worked in the austere setting of an old army hut, Eckersley maintained their spirits by the informality and buffoonery which he encouraged. The team could turn their hands to any problem that might come their way, so the request from Head Office to provide an evening service of wireless telephony was one they just took in their stride. It was not long before the weekly telephony service developed into half an hour of sheer entertainment in which Eckersley erupted into non-stop, unscripted, hilarity (Ch. 4: *2MT Writtle*).

Quite apart from his work for Marconi, Eckersley was a prolific contributor to technical periodicals designed to help wireless amateurs to whom he became a sort of father figure. On the wider front he was a man of great vision and one of the few who saw a future for broadcasting. It was this vision, allied to his exceptional competence, which led to his appointment as Chief Engineer of the BBC shortly after its formation. Initially the BBC relied on engineers from Marconi, like H J Round, to develop suitable transmitting apparatus. However, following his appointment, Eckersley acquired not only responsibility for the day-to-day running of the service, but also responsibility for extending its range and improving its quality.

With the astronomic growth in the number of licence holders, his audience grew larger; but the same comic voice of the 'Wizard of Wireless' could still be heard on the air, his humour conveying, more often than not, an important message. In particular, he pleaded with his listeners to ensure their sets did not cause interference with other sets in the immediate neighbourhood. The guilty ones were told to 'stop howling!'

Meanwhile, his BBC role as Chief Engineer continued to expand as he attended to such matters as Simultaneous Broadcasting, provincial relay stations, control room lay-out and studio acoustics. On the wider front he sought to co-ordinate wavelength allocation in Europe, working closely with Braillard. From this emerged the 'Regional Scheme' under which the BBC was to build a smaller number of much more powerful transmitting stations. Some of this lies outside the ambit of this book, but demonstrates the unique contribution Eckersley made to broadcasting at every point in its early evolution.

Another star performer at the microphone, who has been referred to in Ch. 7: *Talks*, was Sir Oliver Lodge - 'the wisest and friendliest of all broadcasters'. He knew how to speak simply and directly about the most difficult scientific subjects, establishing confidence between expert and layman. He persuaded rather than lectured, sharing secrets rather than just imparting information. He paused frequently, seeming to be searching for the perfect word and he projected his personality as well as his ideas (Briggs, Asa, *History of Broadcasting in the United Kingdom*. Vol I, p285, 1961). Stuart Hibberd remembered the way he would clear his throat immediately after he had been announced and before he began to speak. So regularly was this sound produced that it used to be called his signature tune (Hibberd, Stuart, *This - is London*, p26).

Oliver Lodge already occupied a prime place in the history of wireless long before telephony, let alone broadcasting, was conceived. As early as 1897 he had introduced 'the tuned circuit', the means used in the transmitter for the generation and amplification of a particular wavelength for transmission, and at the receiver end to tune into and amplify the particular station wanted. Lodge took out a master patent and this was subsequently acquired by the Marconi Company. Throughout the following quarter of a century he maintained his eminence in wireless, possessing an appearance of great authority and learning.

The third Radio Star could hardly be a greater contrast to the two whom we have already described, but that he was a star is uncontroversial. Whenever he was due to broadcast 'people rushed to get their accumulators charged' (Lazell, D, 1989, pp64/67). He was 'Dick' Sheppard, Vicar of St-Martin-in-the-Fields, Charing Cross. He had come into prominence during the Great War, opening his church to provide rest and refreshment for soldiers in transit across London. The same welcome was extended in the years following the war to those needing either physical or spiritual help. Unlike his fellow clerics Dick Sheppard sought to encourage religious broadcasting, including religious services. He himself conducted the first such broadcast in January 1924, the services being broadcast at monthly intervals from 23 April as Outside Broadcasts. Dick Sheppard provided a sure and lasting foundation for religious broadcasting and years later his name was still fresh in the public mind. The periodical *Radio Pictorial* (November 1937) summed up the secret of his popularity:

> 'It was his qualities of simplicity, honesty and sincerity which shone through that friendly voice of his. It was his gift of happiness which made him love telling humorous anecdotes, even in his sermons. And it was his great sympathy for his fellow men.'

Another area of broadcasting from which one would hardly expect radio stars to emerge was that of education. Throughout the 'twenties the BBC's goal with respect to education grew slowly but surely. The start was made with schools broadcasts in 1924, when Sir Walford Davies introduced the service with a talk on music.

> 'He soon proved himself to be the greatest popular evangelist of the gospel of music. Knowledgeable but never opinionated, he had that sense of intimacy which, broadly speaking, is the prerequisite of successful broadcasting. He was far more widely known than any of the individual pieces of music he introduced or played.'
> (Briggs, Asa, *History of Broadcasting in the United Kingdom.* Vol I, p284, 1961; Hibberd S, *This – is London,* p27)

Whilst men like Dick Sheppard and Sir Walford Davies took the art of broadcasting into new and unchartered waters by virtue of their consummate skill at the microphone, others who were far from being national figures led broadcasting into the world of popular entertainment as comedians, singers and storytellers. Many had emerged from relative obscurity as local and seasonal entertainers whose previous experience had been in entertaining the troops during the Great War, touring popular seaside resorts or working the provincial music halls. The first wartime concert party to gain a firm foothold in broadcasting was 'The Roosters' who first appeared before the microphone on 20 October 1923. Individual comedians with a special gift for studio work included Norman Long, Willie Rouse and John Henry.

Norman Long had the advantage of being almost an older brother to the British Broadcasting Company, having made his debut on 28 November 1922, before the latter had commenced its operations. He was adept at maintaining a flow of non-stop patter, but liked to fall back on his skills as singer and pianist to vary his repertoire - so he was well equipped to deal with the biggest danger of all - that of 'drying up'.

Willie Rouse - 'Wireless Willie' - lacked this versatility, but would enliven his humour with spur of the moment gags which usually found inspiration in the orchestra, the announcer and in one of the BBC 'Aunties' who was normally present as an accompanist. He first broadcast on 24 January 1924 and later in that year introduced to radio Bertha Wilmot, who did much to popularise the old music hall songs.

John Henry was, rather surprisingly, a civil servant by training. He had tried to make a go of it in the theatre but this had come to nothing. Still yearning to perform before the public he fell back on broadcasting. John Henry began to make a name for himself quite early on, first broadcasting on 31 May 1923 at the Savoy Hotel. He specialised in a Yorkshire accent, relating a series of adventures which he shared with his wife 'Blossom' and his dog 'Erbert'. His dry intonation and droll delivery was quite unique and, in its way, extremely funny.

Two of the most successful radio comedians of all time saw themselves in an entirely different light when they first thought of the BBC as an outlet for their talents. The first, Tommy Handley, had emerged in the post war years as a singer who could use his voice with humorous effect, as he was capable of singing in low registers. 'He discovered the merriment to be exploited in quasi-solemn recitations of earnest monologues when dropping from normal pitch to basso profundo. He could imitate old gramophones, birds, animals and military goings-on.' (Lazell, David, p104, 1989).

The BBC had hit upon the idea of creating their own concert party and were recruiting suitable members. It would be known as the 'Radio Radiance Concert Party'. James Lester acted as Producer and, with the help of John Sharman, undertook the necessary auditions. They suggested Handley should sing a humorous song of some kind. He was well rehearsed and had nothing to fear. The producers told him they would be departing to an audition room at the other end of the building in order to listen-in. Just before they went, Lester said: 'By the way, when you've finished the song, you might just say something funny.' Tommy learned later that they merely wanted to hear his ordinary speaking voice - the Fat Stock Prices would have suited him just as well. Handley takes up the story:

> 'I thought that my powers as a comedian were to be tested and the idea terrified me. As the last bars of the accompaniment died away, I stood literally gibbering with terror, my mind a complete blank. Then something seemed to snap in my brain, 'Thirty days,' I announced proudly, 'hath September, April, June and November; all the rest hath thirty - all the thirty - all the March.' My voice trailed away into a horrible silence. A few seconds later the producers were back in the studio, both of them convulsed with laughter. They shook me warmly by the hand and assured me that I should never say anything half so funny again in my life.'
>
> (Kavanagh, T, pp68/69, 1949).

The second comedian had even less to qualify her for being a radio star than did Tommy Handley; she was Mabel Constanduros, an actress and an amateur one at that. The one thing that distinguished her from a thousand other actresses was her ability to write monologues, a few of them of a mildly amusing nature. As for broadcasting, she had never listened-in and regarded the wireless simply as a new craze. But someone mentioned her to one of the staff of the BBC and she was invited to attend for an audition as an actress. It was a day of warm drizzle in February 1925:

> 'At half-past nine in the morning I was walking up and down the gardens on the Thames Embankment in a nervous agony of indecision. Nobody at home knew I was coming here; nobody would know that I had lost courage and gone away without trying my luck. But when Big Ben boomed out 10 o'clock I directed my shaking footsteps to the door in Savoy Hill and walked in.
>
> 'I was ushered into an ante-room outside the top studio at 2LO. There were several other people there. I had prepared a few bits of lyric verse, a Scottish ballad, some Shakespeare and a speech or two

from modern plays. My name was called. I jumped to my feet, dropped my umbrella, picked it up again and tottered to the door. An efficient secretary ushered me into a vast seemingly unfurnished room. She waved her hand with a macabre brightness. "Now begin." She shut the door and left me alone.

'But now a dreadful thing befell me. I forgot everything I had prepared. In despair, I plunged into one of the monologues I had written. I had begun another when the efficient secretary opened the door to release me.'

(Constanduros, pp5/6 and pp38/39.)

Miss Constanduros was acutely aware that her nerves had got the better of her, denying her the opportunity to show her talents. She was amazed when the secretary phoned to offer her a job in the new BBC Repertory Company, which had only about nine members. Apparently the BBC were particularly interested in her ability at writing monologues - perhaps because these were inexpensive to produce. Mabel Constanduros was, however, aware that one voice can become tiresome on the air if it goes on a long time, so she invented her cockney family - Mrs Buggins, the good-natured, much tried housewife; grandma (an old tartar if ever there was one); and two children. Occasionally she added neighbours, and Aunt Maria who came from the north. The new sketches were not only entertaining but remained economic as Mabel herself played all the parts - as many as seven occurred in one epic broadcast (Constanduros, p43).

Chance circumstances dealt the BBC another broadcasting 'ace' with the discovery of A J Alan. It wasn't so much that Alan was a minor figure in the entertainment world who had simply forgotten his lines. Alan's credentials were, it seems, totally non-existent; he was merely part of the great BBC audience who had been listening to Sir William Bull complaining of the decay of story telling. The next day Alan called on Rex Palmer, Head of 2LO, to say he had some ideas for radio stories and would like an audition. Palmer was so impressed by his visitor that he signed him on at once (Briggs, Asa, *History of Broadcasting in the United Kingdom.* Vol I, p285, 1961).

It was probably on this occasion that the BBC learned all it ever knew - or needed to know - about its new story-teller. He was a civil servant, Leslie Harrison Lambert. The rest was wrapped in mystery. The mystery was deepened by the selection of the name A J Alan, plucked by Palmer from a telephone directory (Lillian Taylor writing in *Ariel*, the BBC staff magazine).

What nobody even guessed was that Leslie Lambert was working for the 'Government Code Cipher School', an innocuous sounding name that provided cover for British Cryptography and Code-Breaking at Queen Anne's Gate in London. This fact only emerged years after Lambert's death, when Admiral Sir William James published 'The Eye of the Navy' in 1955. To the outside world the Lambert who walked into the Savoy Hotel was a forty year old elegant military-looking man with a BBC accent. The first of his stories, 'My Adventure in Jermyn Street', had all the hall marks of those which were to follow throughout the next two decades. For example, they were punctuated with difficult hesitations, artfully contrived to give the illusion of spontaneity. The stories themselves 'were a masterly combination of the matter-of-fact with the unexpected, the ordinary with the bizarre'. He projected a slightly raffish, ex-public school, ex-officer ethos with connections to Scotland Yard and the secret world.

His photograph was never published, but some fascinating details of his early life were traced by a BBC engineer, Norman Duret (*The Listener*, 25 August 1977). Duret discovered that Lambert had been a professional entertainer, visiting Edwardian country houses and offering his services as a 'prestidigitateur,' (sleight of hand). He performed on several occasions for royalty. He had developed an extraordinary skill, through incessant practice over six years, and became Vice-President of the Magic Circle (*Radio Bygones*, June/July 1991 issue).

The same incessant rehearsal characterised his work in the studio. Nothing was left to chance. On arrival he would remove from his brief case his 'tools of the trade' - some sheets of cardboard, a steel tape measure, a stop-watch and a hip flask. The pieces of cardboard were to put the script on so that the paper wouldn't rustle. The tape measure was to ensure that he was exactly 18 in from the microphone; the stop-watch was to time himself. As for the hip-flask, he always gave himself a little swig before transmission. Thus equipped, Alan gave his first broadcast in January 1924.

In a 1925 broadcast, he commenced a story: 'To begin with I ought perhaps to confess that for the last sixteen years I have been rather deeply involved in the science of wireless telegraphy.' If closer to fact than fiction, this would date his wireless career as starting in 1909. He was involved in the secret world of intelligence during the Great War and for the remainder of his working life so he could not afford the glare of publicity which any other radio star would have revelled in. Apparently, on one occasion, having completed his broadcast, he was about to leave when the commissionaire at the Savoy Hotel came to the door and said 'I think you ought to know, Mr Alan, that there are some people outside waiting to take your photograph':

> 'So we peeped through the window curtains and there they were, four or five of them, and they'd got a blooming great camera on a tripod and flashlight apparatus and goodness knows what. So I went out by quite another door and wandered down and joined the group, and after a bit I saw them take an excellent photograph of the announcer when he came out.'
> (Baily, Leslie, *BBC Scrapbooks*, vol. 2, 1918-1939, p82).

To sum up, the seed of broadcasting entertainment had been sown by men like Norman Long, Wireless Willie (Willie Rouse), and John Henry; but for deep and lasting roots we have to look to those who appeared to have least to offer - Tommy Handley, Mabel Constanduros and A J Alan. The broadcasting art form they introduced extended BBC entertainment in new directions and probably did more than anything else to forge a close and lasting rapport between programme providers and their listening public.

PROGRAMMES

Outside Broadcasts

The celebrated broadcast from Covent Garden on 8 January 1923 referred to in Ch. 6: *The BBC makes its Debut*, heralded the BBC's cutting of the apron strings that bound it to the studio. Programmes could now advance physically into the great wide world that lay beyond. Technically, the great national events, exciting sports fixtures and the joy, laughter and pathos of the stage could be brought into everybody's home. But, as has been explained, embargoes, operating to protect the press and the entertainment industry, put much of this outside world beyond bounds, limiting Outside Broadcasts to a mixed bag in which the 'plums' were the evening dance bands broadcast from the Savoy Hotel.

All these London Outside Broadcasts and many of the provincial ones used Western Electric equipment, the double button microphone and a suitable Western Electric amplifier, linked to a nearby Post Office trunk line. In most cases a two-valve Western Electric loudspeaker amplifier was employed. To make it easier to transport the Outside Broadcast equipment, the amplifier would be housed in a large teak box within which it was held in place by springs. High and low tension batteries also went into the box along with the microphone, telephone and headphones. Once on a location, the microphone was removed and fixed in an appropriate position.

Of the provincial stations, Birmingham and Glasgow employed Western Electric equipment from the outset. Cardiff acquired its Western Electric set in September 1923 and from then on could adopt a similar practice to the other two stations. Since, there, the studio was sited directly over the Capitol Cinema and the latter had its own orchestra, it was an easy matter for the Cardiff Station to transmit on a daily basis directly from the cinema. The Control Room engineer merely had to go down to the cinema where he would switch on the amplifier, switch on the microphone and announce the programme (Pawley, E., *BBC Engineering, 1922 to 1972*, p58).

Cardiff was not the only station to make regular use of a cinema orchestra. Early in 1923 Manchester was connected by land line to the Oxford Street Picture House which was located close by. The whole set up was typically experimental. At the cinema an moving coil microphone using a large loudspeaker base and damped with Vaseline constituted the microphone. No adjacent amplifier was needed and therefore no engineer. The Studio Control Room simply phoned the cinema manager to request him to switch on the microphone at the appropriate time. The assorted experimental apparatus developed by Fleming was discarded in August 1923 when the Manchester Station was relocated and Western Electric equipment installed.

Much of the Western Electric apparatus was itself superseded by Marconi sets in 1924, not only in the studio but also for Outside Broadcast assignments. By the beginning of 1924 the Marconi-Sykes moving coil microphone had been developed into a remarkably reliable microphone. Possibly its first Outside Broadcast use was for broadcasting the chimes of Big Ben, which transmitted on a daily basis from 9 March 1924. The microphone was enclosed in a biscuit tin filled with cotton-wool and placed on a roof of a building directly opposite Big Ben. Soon, however, it was transferred to the tower itself. The amplifier was the prototype of the Marconi 'A' amplifier which later became standard in most studios, being placed near the microphone as a 'pre-amplifier' and followed by a more remote 'B' main amplifier.

On some occasions the Post Office land-lines could not handle the Outside Broadcast and communication was by radio link to base - this is discussed in chapter 8: *Technical Development*. For example, the broadcast on 23 November 1923 of opera from The Old Vic was by radio link to an aerial erected for the purpose on the roof of the Savoy Hotel. A radio relay was again used, on 3 October 1924, for an Outside Broadcast from the London Zoo. In this instance the Outside Broadcast transmitter was mounted on a trolley with a couple of bamboo poles to support the aerial.

These brilliant technical Outside Broadcast developments and the excitement they brought into the homes of the listeners were completely eclipsed by the voice of the King himself when he opened the British Empire Exhibition at Wembley. This historic event occurred on 23 April 1924. As can be well imagined, nothing was left to chance.

What nobody could possibly have anticipated - neither the King, nor his subjects, nor indeed any of those associated with the BBC - was that a month later - no more - a broadcasting legend would burst through the airwaves. The programme then in progress was silenced as though for an important Government announcement. But what listeners heard was the song of the nightingale.

It is difficult to unfold this story without seeing romance, suspense and humour at every turn. First, we need to know a little of the lady who had by sheer chance experienced a remarkable event and who sought to share it with others. She was Beatrice Harrison, Britain's leading cellist.

Beatrice had three exceptionally gifted sisters - May, Monica and Margaret. They performed at the centre of British musical life during the inter-war years, attracting the especial friendship of men like Elgar and Delius. Finding themselves in need of a new home they decided to look for a house in the country. Their search ended at a cottage named Foyle Riding, located close to Oxted in Surrey. In the following months the tiny cottage was extended and water laid on. The garden began to take shape in the hands of their head gardener, blue flowers predominating. The following spring (1923) was glorious, the wood being filled with bluebells and primroses. Beatrice was filled with a longing to play her cello in the wood as night fell and the moon shone through the branches. Beatrice Harrison:

'I began to play very lazily all the melodies I loved best. After some time I stopped. Suddenly a glorious note echoed the notes of the cello. I then trilled up and down the instrument, up to the top and down again; the voice of the bird followed me in thirds! The sound did not appear to come from the high treetops but from nearer the ground; I could not see, I just played on and on!'

The following spring Beatrice Harrison made repeated efforts to attract the nightingale. One memorable night she took part in a broadcast of Elgar's Concerto, he himself conducting. She spoke to Rex Palmer, head of 2LO and announcer on this occasion, suggesting that Outside Broadcast equipment should be set up in the wood at Foyle Riding in the hope of transmitting the nightingale's song and its cello accompaniment. She had a hard tussle as the BBC thought it would be a waste of time to come down to Surrey but at last it was agreed and on 19 May 1924 the engineers, led by A G D West, arrived with their equipment. This comprised a Marconi-Sykes moving coil microphone that they placed on a stool at the edge of the wood and the new GA1 (or 'A') amplifier which they placed in the front porch of Foyle Riding. This, in turn, was linked to the Post Office trunk line to London.

At about 9 o'clock Beatrice Harrison crept up with her cello to a ditch, placed her chair half in and half out of it and commenced playing. Curious noises did take place, such as the buzzing of flies attracted to the microphone by the heating up of the magnetising coil and, more worrying, rabbits nibbling at the wires. Time passed, their pet donkey started to bray loudly; still the nightingale failed to sing.

Barratt's Photo press
Outdoor broadcast equipment, 1925: Capturing the song of the nightingale.

'Suddenly at about quarter to eleven the nightingale burst into song as I continued to play. I shall never forget his trills, nor the way he followed the cello so blissfully. My greatest wish was accomplished.'
(Beatrice Harrison edited by Patricia Cleveland-Peck, p132, 1985)

Back in London the dance music had been taken off the air without any explanation. The Outside Broadcast experiment was repeated, even more successfully, the following week.

In the spring of 1925 two microphones were employed in different positions in the hope of picking up a dialogue between a pair of nightingales. This necessitated the use of two GA1s which were placed by the engineers in the porch of Foyle Riding.

Fortunately, HMV made a gramophone record of the former event so that we can still catch today the thrill of that magic moment in broadcasting history.

PROGRAMMES

Wireless World

Outdoor broadcast equipment, 1925: Broadcasting the song of the nightingale.

The Radio Times

From its inception in September 1923 the *Radio Times* fired the imagination of listeners. A quarter of a million copies of its first issue were printed and by the end of 1923 sales stood at 130,000. But circulation then leapt to 600,000 (Briggs, Asa, *History of Broadcasting in the United Kingdom.* Vol I, p297, 1961).

Briggs does not explain why this phenomenal growth occurred, but he suggests that it was due to Reith's understanding and confidence with respect to broadcasting. If so, this confidence had not been shared by those outside radio circles. Reith had found it difficult to interest publishers in the new enterprise, placing the whole venture in grave jeopardy. It was time for persuasion.

A publishing house, George Newnes, had among its editors one who had taken a particular interest in broadcasting from the earliest days - Leonard Crocombe. He had initiated a long series of articles in the periodical *TitBits* in April 1922. The series was later continued by Arthur Burrows early in 1923. About this time, Crocombe gave his first radio talk despite the misgivings of the Post Office who imagined that the editors would use these opportunities to advertise Newnes publications.

One summer morning in 1923 Crocombe received a phone call from Burrows inviting him to lunch with a view to discussing a new project - the *Radio Times*. The inference was that, once negotiations were complete, Crocombe would be invited to serve as editor, collaborating with Herbert Parker of the BBC publicity department who would feed him with programme pages. With this understanding, Crocombe agreed to take on the job, given a suitable cut on the profits and full editorial control. Newnes saw nothing special about the Radio Times. It would be simply one more addition to their portfolio of magazines. Crocombe went to Belgium on holiday for a month, expecting Newnes to contact him as and when required.

It is not possible to exaggerate the shock he received on his return. Apparently the negotiations between the BBC and the publisher had been completed in his absence and he was ordered to produce the first number of the *Radio Times* within seven days. Charles Tristram was appointed to assist in this breakneck task. Using information provided by Parker and his assistant, Emily Bryant, Crocombe spent days and nights in hectic improvisation. Copy had to be written and sub-edited, type set, illustrations obtained, blocks made and the first proofs read and measured. Mr Bausor, Newnes's Master Printer, was soon on the phone asking for some copy and 'make-up' along with guidance on type faces. There was no time to design the magazine so it followed the format of another Newnes publication - *John O'london's Weekly*. press day was followed by the night when the new paper had finally to be 'put to bed'. Crocombe and Tristram took up their position at Newnes printing works, checking the proofs page by page until nearly midnight, when the last page proof was passed and the machines 'began their wondrous work of printing the finished copies' (*Radio Times* 25 September 1953).

Back in Savoy Hill, preparing the programme pages and obtaining copy from station directors became an increasing burden throughout 1924 as the number of stations increased and programme sharing became more and more common. Soon, much of the work devolved on Lewis' young staff - Beadle and Douglas Clarke, who were already responsible for Simultaneous Broadcast work.

Crocombe found himself less and less involved with Parker and more and more with the keen young men of Lewis' Programme Department. Unfortunately they not only sent too much copy but insisted that not one line be omitted. In the weeks ahead Reith would often be phoned from the printing works around midnight with the news that programme copy would have to be cut.

So what was it about the Radio Times that made it different? In terms of practical value it helped people to know what was on the air so they could look ahead and plan their listening. For the small minority who could select distant stations, it revealed what programmes could be picked up from them. But the magazine's appeal went well beyond its practical value. It brought every aspect of the modern world to the listener's notice, opening up new worlds, both popular and educational. Above all, it catered for the whole family, highlighting programmes for women and for children. The *Radio Times* complemented the spoken word with the written word and it did this with flair and humour.

An early issue reveals the editorial content. First, there was gossip about people who featured in the programmes. Secondly, selected talks were reproduced in full. Reith was induced to write the leading article, enabling listeners to appreciate all that the BBC was trying to do. By contrast, a page of listener's letters showed what they expected the BBC to do. For the children, a piece of cheerful chat was provided by Uncle Caractacus aimed at cementing relationships built up between the Uncles and Aunts and their nephews and nieces. Finally, listeners would be introduced to BBC personalities in an informal way. For example, Eckersley was depicted 'by one who knows him' (Miss Shields, Reith's Secretary) as 'slouching down the passage, shoulders well up, hair on end, pipe in mouth, hands in pockets and looking like a road

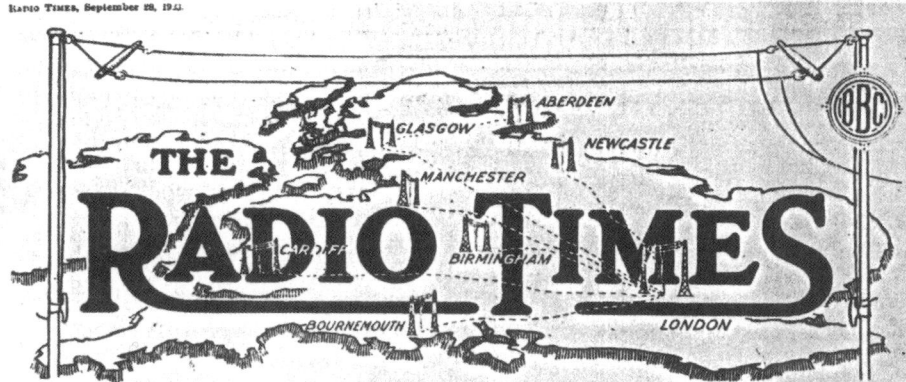

First issue of the Radio Times, Volume 1 No. 1, 28th September 1923.

mender with Bolshevistic tendencies. He sported a tie like yellow fever with measles'.

The magazine usually included humorous cartoons, but otherwise lacked illustrations apart from miniscule photographs of artistes and, of course, advertisements showing products for sale. This format, established in 1923, had hardly changed a year or more later. The only concession was the Christmas number when the *Radio Times* presented a cover that was a blaze of colour.

With sales at 750,000 by the end of 1924, the *Radio Times* offered fertile ground for sowing the BBC philosophy. There was then raised the question of the balance to be struck between those who placed stress on entertainment and those who sought to raise public taste. For example, John Stowbart, who was appointed BBC Director of Education in August 1924, favoured a magazine with a much more academic character while Pitt of the Music Department pressed for a supplementary periodical with the title 'Radio Music'.

These views completely ignored the fact that the *Radio Times* had already adopted a manifestly successful formula. It had achieved widespread popularity without failing to attract contributions from men of culture and of the highest intellectual calibre. Fortunately, those who had been at the helm from the beginning understood this and accepted the point of view that changes could do more harm than good. The *Radio Times* was already a success.

8

BBC Triumphs

Against Adversity

Collapse of the BBC's Initial Financial Structure

The creation of the BBC was the outcome of a series of checks and balances that would have done credit to a complex clockwork mechanism. This was true right from the very start.

In the first place Britain could field manufacturers capable of establishing a whole new wireless industry. They had worked on the wider front of creating the new electrical age. Certainly the engineers had very limited experience of wireless, apart from the outstanding exception of the Marconi engineers, but some had contacts with sister companies in America where wireless manufacturing was more advanced, whilst others were prepared to learn on the job. One way or another they were determined to push ahead.

It was at this juncture that the first of the checks came into play. Britain was unique in that wireless communication had, from the start, been subject to government control with responsibility placed in the hands of the Postmaster-General. It was his task to attend to the potentially conflicting demands for wireless communication. These emerged from a whole variety of sources - military, mercantile marine, shipping, aircraft, international financial dealings, inter-governmental/Empire communication and the trans-oceanic telegram traffic known as 'marconigrams'. Not surprisingly, the Postmaster General showed some initial reluctance to extend this list further.

Matters were not helped by the fact that broadcasting struck him as a possibly short-lived craze. Leaving the manufacturers to one side, the main supporters of wireless telephony appeared to consist of those who regarded the whole thing as a scientific hobby in which the content was a side street. Their interest centred on exploring the limits of what could be achieved, in particular what lay within the scope of their own apparatus. They were all required to take out an annual licence, but broadcasting for its own sake had little appeal for them when it finally arrived; their licences were 'experimental' and had nothing to do either with the manufacture of sets or the provision of programmes.

In these circumstances the Postmaster General of the day, while honouring the position of experimenters, might well have been forgiven for turning his back on broadcasting. But he could not bow out quite so easily. The country's economic position left much to be desired and the opportunity to encourage the marketing of wireless sets was one not to be missed. He decided, therefore, to introduce counterweights. The first was to protect the embryonic British industry from foreign imports. The second was to minimise expenditure on programmes by avoiding wasteful duplication. This was the 'spring' that brought the British Broadcasting Company into existence. Leaving the experimenters aside, a royalty would be paid on each approved set sold and the owner of the set would be required to take out an annual 10 shilling Broadcasting Licence without delay. The Licence fee was to be paid over Post Office counters and so into the hands of the Postmaster General. He in turn passed half to the BBC, thereby helping to meet annual costs. Licences would only be sold where wireless sets were of British manufacture. The BBC, therefore, had two sources of income - licence fees and royalties.

At the time - 1922 - the thinking appeared to be well-conceived, if complex. For a while, it operated like clockwork. But by the beginning of 1923 the first signs of trouble ahead were evident. People had begun to build low-cost sets from component parts for which no single manufacturer was responsible. As a result, no royalties were paid and, as their sets did not meet the requirements laid down by the Postmaster General, they were unable to qualify for a broadcast licence. So the BBC was deprived of licence fees as well as royalties. Owners were not necessarily dishonest and many sought to regularise their position by taking out a ten shilling experimenters licence, but without success.

Broadcasting was catching on. Radio was no longer a rich man's toy for by April 1923 demand was coming from the less affluent. To have extended the original requirements regarding 'BBC Approved Sets' would have acted against the interests of the less well-off who made their own sets. For the new Postmaster General - Neville Chamberlain - it had become something of a hot potato and his successor, W Joynson-Hicks, was equally nervous of its ramifications. Joynson-Hicks procrastinated and week by week the BBC's financial prospects looked ever more bleak as the market for expensive ready-made sets dried up.

Somehow Reith managed to keep the show on the road and the outside world was not aware of the strain that this involved, but behind the scenes, the approaching demise of the BBC was becoming all too evident to its employees. A veteran of those troublesome days was Mungo Dewar, Assistant Station Director at Glasgow. Dewar:

> 'About ten thirty one dark night, the inquiry bell rang in the attic office above the ground floor studio. I went down the rickety wooden stairs. There stood the tallest man I'd ever seen. He introduced himself as John Reith, general manager, and then said "Who are you?". I replied, "Mungo Dewar". He humphed a bit, asked me into

the studio and invited me to join him on a small settee which I expected to collapse at any moment. "What do you think of the licence question?" he demanded. I promptly said "not much". Reith rose swiftly from the settee, stood up to his full height, and roared down at me: "Why?" I replied: "Simply because I have not received any wages for several weeks. I have to spend all my own money on stamps and items of petty cash". Reith melted at once and became contrite, almost gentle. By the next week I got all my back pay and a refund of what I'd paid out of my own pocket.'

(Boyle, Andrew, p148, 1972)

The BBC staff were probably unaware of their manager's skilful swordplay behind the scenes. Reith employed all the advocacy he could muster to press the Postmaster General for a new deal. For his part, the Postmaster-General was probably unaware of the desperate conditions with which the BBC had to cope and under which it laboured. The deadlock called for radical rethinking - starting again from scratch. There was only one answer - to appoint a committee.

Meanwhile, Reith was determined to maintain and indeed to improve the quality of programmes and, confident of ultimate success on the finance front, staff were invited to increase payments to artistes!

The Postmaster General was also aware that the BBC faced problems that went beyond funding - problems such as censorship, conflict with the press over advance publication and the importance of protecting British manufacturers. He therefore decided to widen the terms of reference of the committee well beyond the immediate concern of securing adequate funding for the BBC.

The committee was duly appointed on 24 April 1923 under the chairmanship of Major General Sir Frederick Sykes. But its wide remit did nothing to help the BBC financially. It simply meant that a lot of time was spent addressing less essential issues with the result that the Committee's report did not become available until August 1923 and probably did not satisfy everyone when it did finally emerge. It certainly did not satisfy Reith, to whom it seemed unduly concerned to protect British manufacturers from foreign competition, even at the cost of delaying improvements to the BBC's funding.

Reith's lone stand on this meant that a report which met with the agreement of the Post Office, the BBC and the British wireless industry was not finally published until 1 October 1923. The final report did, however, mark a turning point in the BBC's fortunes. The BBC could settle the huge debts it had so far incurred with Marconi and other companies while investing in new stations and in improving the accommodation at Savoy Hill.

Clearly the matter of licences lay at the core of what needed to be addressed by the Sykes Committee. Yet, curiously, the solution adopted was one hammered out not by the committee but by Reith's negotiations with the Postmaster General in the final few days.

Leaving aside experimenter's licences, which, once granted, were totally unrelated to BBC funding, the nature of the solution was as follows:

> Introduction of a new type of broadcasting licence shorn of conditions and therefore applicable to all wireless sets used for receiving BBC programmes. This would allow simplification of procedures.
>
> Post Office to retain 2s6d to cover the cost of collecting, 7s 6d going to the BBC. At a stroke the BBC's income from licences would be greatly increased.
>
> The new broadcasting licence would be introduced only after a 'protection period' during which the problems currently facing British manufacturers had been resolved. During this period the 'BBC' sets would continue to pay royalties, but at a reduced rate.
>
> Any new sets made from parts would require a constructor's licence. The main parts would have to be of British manufacture, and marked accordingly. To compensate for the loss of royalties, constructor's licences would be sold over Post Office counters at 15s0d, of which the Post Office would retain 2s6d.

All parties had to accept that too many low-cost sets had already been constructed for there to be any going back. There was no point in attempting to differentiate between past constructors and genuine experimenters, but where owners had no licence they were required to pay for what were to be known as 'Interim Licences'. The Interim Licence would have much in common with the Constructors Licence, but it would apply to sets already in existence and legalise possession. No conditions as to British manufacture would apply and the licence would be retrospective, but owners had to apply without delay. In practice, this meant 14 October 1923, a fortnight after publication of the Sykes report.

Protection until the end of 1924 had been specified but to simplify administration, the standard broadcasting licence was made available from 1 July 1924 with just a single condition, namely, that until the end of the year any new parts should be British. Thus, from mid 1924 all complications such as royalty collection on 'BBC Broadcast Licences' came to an end. The umbilical cord linking the BBC's financial support to the trade was severed. With the new standard licence available from July, the sale of constructors licences ceased; licences purchased by those who had built their own sets were therefore renewed by the taking out of a new standard broadcasting licence.

Perhaps the most striking feature of this whole process was the number of those who had already built their own sets without the benefit of a licence and were now prepared to put their house in order. In the first part of October 1923, 200,000 Interim Licences were purchased. The effect on licence numbers at the end of 1923 is evident when seen in the light of overall growth:

31 December 1922	35,774
31 March 1923	112,155
30 June 1923	163,433
30 September 1923	179,616

1-14 October 1923: interim licence for existing unlicenced sets.

31 December 1923	597,239
31 March 1924	721,002
30 June 1924	821,303

1 July 1924: Standard licence available; royalties cease.

30 September 1924	998,288
31 December 1924	1,130,264

(*Report of the Broadcasting Committee*, 1925, HMSO, 1926)

The figures shown above appear to include Experimenters' Licences. These rose to about 35,000 in the early months of 1923 but flattened out once the Sykes Committee was in progress.

Reference has already been made to the debts incurred by the BBC and a graphic illustration of the difficulties under which the BBC staff laboured has been given above. A meaningful breakdown of expenditure does not appear to be available, but some interesting figures as to capital costs have been published and these appear to relate to the period ending in December 1923:

Premises £7,940
Furniture and fittings £9,944
Plant £50,130
Music/other Programme Libraries £2,479

Running costs had to cover staff which rose in numbers throughout the period, ending with 177. Administrative expenses totalled £30,044. Expenditure on programmes and associated engineering amounted to £167,518 (Allighan, Garry, *Sir John Reith*, p195).

From October 1923 costs such as these could be looked upon with equanimity by Reith and a host of new horizons was opened up. The BBC's board of directors were entirely happy to see the Broadcasting Company shed the close relationship with the trade which had formerly seemed so important. Indeed, they wholeheartedly endorsed the proposal that Reith's status should be raised from that of General Manager to Managing Director with a seat on the Board. Reith's salary was increased to £2,500, with an additional £200 applicable to all board members. A degree of permanence could now be enjoyed as the life of the British Broadcasting Company was guaranteed to the end of December 1926.

Growth and Change at Savoy Hill: 1924

The BBC's accommodation had been confined to the west and north wings of the Institution building. Towards the end of 1924 the take up of space in the west wing was completed and had afforded the opportunity to build a second studio. But this did nothing to meet the need for office space.

The solution lay with the renting of a magnificent room with a fine river view. This room was situated on the second floor of the south wing and cost the BBC £1,000 a year in rent. It was a full 100ft long, 30ft wide and 18ft high (plan 8, 2nd floor, to which Reith's sketch also refers) It would obviously need sub-division, but would provide a splendid General Office with the typing pool under Miss Bank's supervision occupying the eastern flank. The middle position served as a general office with a filing area and post room. The western flank was subdivided to provide a boardroom, the office for the Secretary - G V Rice, and an adjoining office for the registrar - R M Page. The Managing-Director had direct access to the boardroom. Across the corridor two more offices facing on to the internal courtyard were created for the accountant - Harley - with the second office for the cashier - Miss Mallinson and Harley's assistant, Miss Lock. A new passageway led to the stairs and ensured that typists and other staff did not need to use the access within the Managing Director's suite (plan 5b).

The last room in the west wing to be occupied was situated on the first floor directly over the Institution's Council Chamber (plan 5a). It provided a poorly lit space 44ft long, 26ft wide and 18ft high and could accommodate the Wireless Orchestra. This included 23 instrumentalists with space to spare for an augmented orchestra, together with chorus and principals. The letter approving the use of the space for the studio still survives. The only stipulation insisted on was that broadcasting and rehearsals should not occur whilst IEE council meetings were in progress (*IEE Archives*).

The interior was much less claustrophobic than the original studio on the third floor. In the first place, the longer reverberation time needed for music (compared with talk) could be achieved with hessian solely behind the drapes. Secondly, a delightful interior in cool colours was devised, the walls being hung with grey drapes. To provide relief, the two long walls were fitted with full-length 'windows', adorned with curtains of a beautiful emerald shade. The four pseudo-windows themselves afforded no view for they were covered in silver foil finished with an orange coloured net. Concealed lighting gave an effect of cold sunlight entering the room. Unfortunately they were rarely switched on as they generated too much heat.

Like the earlier studios, red lights were positioned over the doors at each end. To achieve sound proofing, duplicate sets of doors were provided, the outer ones likewise being equipped with red lights. Similar lights were even

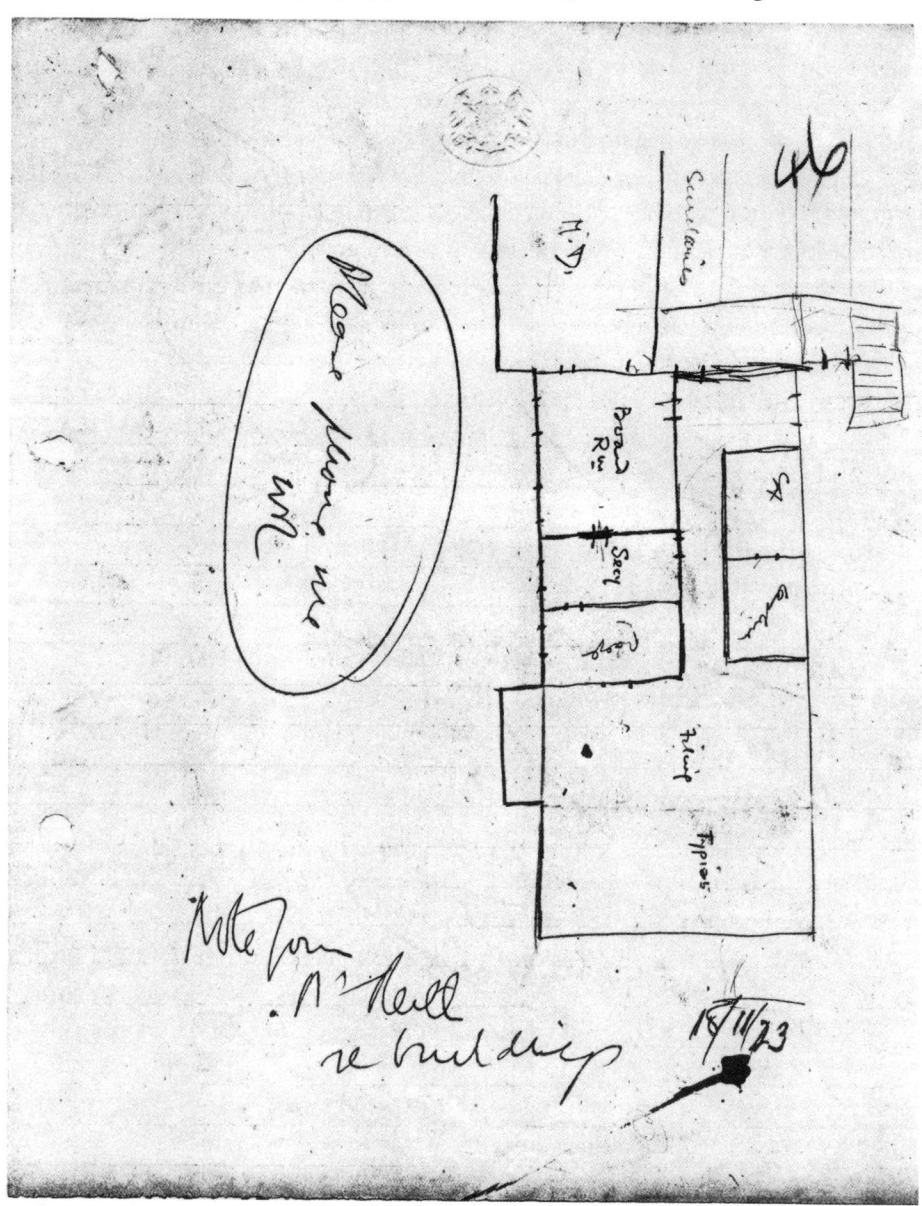

Reith's sketch for accommodation on floor 2, south wing, IEE building, November 1923.

fitted on the approach to the room above to warn their occupants to be careful not to thump on the floor when broadcasting from the studio was in progress (Burrows, Arthur, *The Story of Broadcasting*, p91). The old pair of doors to the north end of the second floor corridor still bears the original plaque with its invocation: 'Please walk quietly when red light is on'.

Brian Hennessy

The original plaque still on the pair of doors leading to the studios: 'Notice Please walk quietly when red light is on.'

It was the availability of two studios that enabled specialisation to be possible, with the old studio handling the spoken word and the newer one being reserved for music, the acoustics of each room being designed for the individual needs of speech and music respectively. A result of having these dedicated studios was that elsewhere every inch of space was needed and there was no question of carving out space for an artistes' 'green room' in which they could await their turn. The positioning of artistes and instrumentalists in relation to the microphone was undertaken during rehearsals by the producer. A Band Room was still needed for housing instruments and this made use of space on the far side of the main stairs leading down to the entrance at No.2. .

By this time (the end of 1924) Round had completed work on the 'A' pre-amplifier which needed to be installed near the microphone; for the new music studio, it was set behind a glazed door built into the north wall. It was wall mounted and needed no attention.

Round had also completed work on the 'B' amplifier, located in the control room. The control room represented a major advance in broadcasting technology and will be described in the section *Technical Development 1924*, below.

With regard to office space, perhaps the biggest remaining question was the future use of the old General Office. A minute of January 1924, stamped with the Reith's authoritative style, discusses this question. Reith pointed out that top staff like Burrows, Lewis and Smith needed sound proof offices and also that the old General Office, with its 18ft high ceiling, was more suited to division with 11ft partitions. Staff were later described as being 'packed into loose boxes' (Snagge, John and Barsley, Michael, *Those Vintage Years of Radio*, p3).

As much of the space had already been reorganised and as the north wing, second floor, housed senior staff, Reith turned his attention to the north wing, third floor, *plan 7a*. Here the music department and 2LO competed for space. Following sub-division, it was decided that 2LO staff should have accommodation in the old General Office. One room there was reserved for the Station Director - Palmer. The second office was for 2LO staff, which comprised musicians such as Wright and Godfrey, and announcing staff - Dodgson and Broadbent (who by the end of 1924 had been replaced by Stuart Hibberd). In the third room were housed the 2LO engineers - Shaw and Thompson. Into the fourth room went the Radio Times staff - Parker and Miss Bryant.

At the end of March the third floor of the north wing became available in its entirety to the music department (plan 7b). The removal of the redundant amplifier meant that the room closest to the old studio could be used for auditions and also by artistes. The next room housed the music directors - Pitt/Jefferies. Beyond this were housed the music department's staff -

Braithwaite/Robinson/Howgill. The end room served as the music library with storage in an adjoining annexe.

The remaining portion of the office space requiring attention comprised the second floor of the north wing (plan 7a). In the first room the departure of Parker enabled Ralph Wade to move in and establish a new Correspondence Department. With him were those responsible for Women's and Children's hours. In charge of Children's Hour generally was Miss E Elliott who was appointed at the end of 1923. Mrs E Fitzgerald continued to oversee the Women's Hour. In the adjoining room, Lewis remained in overall control with the title Organizer of Programmes. Burrows, too, was left undisturbed in the third room along the corridor; likewise Smith, the Head of Publicity, who occupied the 4th room. In April 1924, Corbett Smith was brought from Cardiff to act as Artistic Director and was given the tiny end room for his office. This had been the location of the telephone switchboard and its two operators, but the telephone lines were heavily overloaded, so the BBC needed a new switchboard and more space. This space was created by filling in a staircase in the 2nd. floor south wing, adjoining the filing room (plan 5b). A new ten line switchboard with a single telephone number was installed. The switchboard became, in effect, part of the new General Office.

Filling in the staircase was a desperate and expensive effort to squeeze the last inch of space out of the IEE building as staff expanded. It left no room above ground level for further extension. Other major electrical organisations were already renting the eastern wing and much of the central part of the building provided space for the Institution itself.

However, the IEE building formed only part of the street block for, backing on to it on the north side, rose Savoy Hill Mansions (plan 1), overlooking the ancient Savoy Chapel.

'The Mansions' was a symmetrically designed Victorian building with a central section flanked by matching portions at each end (plan 1). The latter contained the main entrances to the building. The whole of the western end, together with its entrance, had, however, been damaged in a Zeppelin raid in 1917, and this put paid to providing a direct access between the Mansions and the IEE building.

Once again the stamp of Reith's vision is evident. With the BBC's official existence extending no further than to the end of 1926, Reith anticipated the future and resolved to take over the whole of Savoy Hill Mansions and undertake the rebuilding needed - a complete change in scale of both office and studio accommodation. The amount of space available for BBC offices would

Reproduced by permission of the BBC

Savoy Hill Mansions, October 1926.

be more than doubled and there would also be room for additional studios. An initial lease covering the bombed portion was signed on 29 August 1924, but it would involve many months of reconstruction work. A further lease was taken in May 1925 for occupation of the undamaged portion of the Mansions. Work on the corner block and on the 3rd, 4th and 5th floors of the main building were completed by December 1925 (plans 13 to 17).

As a temporary measure, space was found in the surviving part of the Mansions and offices were created for two new departments, one for drama, headed by R E Jeffrey, and the other for talks and education, under Stowbart. With Jeffrey worked Howard Ross as producer from January 1925; also Whitman, who handled dramatic effects. The accommodation included a rehearsal room. Stowbart's appointment in August 1924 coincided with Jeffrey's. Initially, both new departments shared space on the first floor but by the end of the year further room became available on the second floor. Inevitably the new temporary space was almost wholly isolated from the rest of the BBC staff and management. Entry to their offices could only be effected by going out of the front door at No. 2 Savoy Hill and walking right round to the eastern entrance to the Mansions. Here, after braving the caretaker's dog, and getting rather a fright from the head of a bison hung on the wall in a dark passage, one found the dramatists and educationalists aloof in their secluded quarters (*BBC Yearbook 1930*, p171).

New Main and Relay Stations

By September 1923 permanent BBC stations had been established in each of five provincial cities - Birmingham, Cardiff, Glasgow, Manchester and Newcastle – and, under Eckersley's influence, Western Electric double button microphones with Western Electric amplifiers were provided in them. But the period when Western Electric equipment in the studio centre appeared to reign supreme was in fact very brief. Manchester soon joined Newcastle, Cardiff and Glasgow in being fitted with a 'Q' type Marconi transmitter, and its Studio Centre adopted the (Round) -Marconi-Sykes moving coil microphone, as did the other stations. Only Birmingham retained its Western Electric equipment. Not surprisingly, when the last of the main stations was built in October 1923, at Aberdeen and Bournemouth, they employed Marconi equipment.

2BD Aberdeen opened on 10 October 1923. The transmitter was housed in the Aberdeen Steam Laundry at 40 Claremont Street. The aerial was supported on masts rather than on the more usual power station chimneys. The studio centre was at 17 Belmont Street, a mile away.

6BM Bournemouth was the only main station to be purpose-built. It was opened on 17 October 1923. The transmitter was located in North Cemetery, Bushey Road, and had 110ft masts. The studio centre was built 1.5 miles away at Holdenhurst Road. The studio itself was equipped with the microphone amplifier and was adjacent to a 4.5ft wide control room in which an additional amplifier could be located along with the necessary batteries and charger.

The building of the Aberdeen and Bournemouth stations completed the commitment undertaken with the Postmaster General to establish eight stations in agreed locations, and fulfilled the Marconi Company's stipulation that it should be responsible for the construction of six of these, including at least one in London.

The power of these main stations was such that there would have been mutual interference had their number been increased. However, only about half the population could be served from them. To this extent broadcasting had reached a stopping point. It had reached the maximum number of high-power stations yet half the population could not receive programmes.

The first attempt to fill the gaps was made in August 1923 in Sheffield with the help of the local university. The moving spirit behind this attempt was F Lloyd, president of the local Wireless Society. A low power transmitter was installed in his garage and the studio used a room in his house. Initially, the

NEW MAIN AND RELAY STATIONS

Studio at 6BM, Bournmouth Station, 1925

Reproduced by permission of the Marconi Co. Ltd

station put out its own programmes; this could have been an expensive operation if applied across the country. The solution lay in using Simultaneous Broadcasting to take programmes from the main stations - initially Manchester, but later London too.

Sheffield had introduced a new concept; that of a low power 'relay' station principally designed to use Simultaneous Broadcasting to relay programmes from the main stations. It was cheaper to build, cheaper to run, caused little interference and served a sizeable urban population. As such, it was the first of a whole series of relay stations. The Sheffield relay station proper opened on 16 November 1923; both its transmitter and studio centre were located in the Union Grinding Wheel Company building in Corporation Street. Power was initially limited to 100 watts and the aerial was anchored to a nearby chimney. The next relay station, after Sheffield, was at Plymouth. The 100-watt transmitter was located at the Sugar Refinery, Mill Street and the studio at Athenaeum Lane.

Early in 1924, H S Walker, a well-known radio amateur who had joined the BBC, designed a standard relay station. Like all the others that would follow, it was rated at 200 watts. It used the Marconi-Sykes moving coil microphone. The control room was alongside and housed the amplifier.

The Edinburgh relay station was opened on the 1 May 1924 with Walker's new standard transmitter. Both the transmitter and the studio were located in the university buildings in Teviot Place. Plymouth was upgraded to 200 watts at the same time.

Liverpool was the next to open - on 11 June 1924 - and was followed by Leeds/Bradford on 8 July, where the studio was housed at Basinghall Street, Leeds; the transmitter, initially at Claypit Lane, Leeds, was replaced four months later by one at the Corporation 'Destructor' in Stanley Road, Burmantofts, Leeds. A further five stations were subsequently opened. The advent of these relay stations in 1924 increased the population served from 22 million to 29 million.

The standardisation of relay station design meant that valuable space at Savoy Hill did not need to be taken up. The stations were virtually prefabricated at Hendon in London and assembled on site. Hendon's staff were able to enjoy a degree of hospitality from the furniture producing firm in which they worked, a hospitality beyond anything they might have expected at Savoy Hill.

There remained one unresolved problem, that of finding BBC premises for the 2LO transmitter. The BBC had long since exhausted the hospitality they could expect from Marconi. In reality the Marconi claims that the transmitter and its aerial were 'by no means a showpiece or as safe as one would like' sound a little hollow as do their complaints about 'bands of strangers coming in and out'. But the station needed upgrading anyway, and in the end the BBC were glad to accept the use of the roof of Selfridges Department Store in Oxford Street for their new transmitter and aerial. Here a large hut housed a 'double Q' transmitter. Not only did this replace the prototype transmitter of 1922, its augmented power was more in tune with the vast extent of the built-up area of London. The aerial was supported by two steel pylons 125ft high and the fortunate engineers, like their brethren at Hendon, enjoyed first-class hospitality from their hosts.

The station opened on 6 April 1925. Meanwhile, the Marconi House transmitter was retained as a standby and by a series of fortunate circumstances, described in chapter 5, *2LO at Marconi House, London,* has survived to this day as what is probably the most precious artefact in broadcasting history.

Technical Development: 1924

By 1924 the Marconi broadcasting system had a reliable microphone and transmitter. If it lagged behind its Western Electric equivalent this was due to its lack of a suitable amplifier in the control room. The amplifier in use at Savoy Hill was the same one that had been developed at Marconi House at the beginning of 1923 and was highly temperamental. Perhaps too much was expected of it, for at this point a new method of control was introduced which revolutionised transmission technique. First, a small 'A' amplifier was positioned close to the microphone. This needed little attention. Secondly, a 'B' amplifier was introduced. This required constant attention but could be positioned at a 'control position' some distance from the studio.

The 'B' amplifier was adaptable. It was mounted on a bench and was flanked on one side by an input board for selecting the programme source and on the other side by the output board for programme destination routing. The programme source could be one or other of the station's studios, the time signal or an outside broadcast point. The destination could include lines to the Simultaneous Broadcasting amplifiers.

It was immediately evident that a special control room would be needed. In the first place, at least two amplifier benches or 'control positions' would be required along with a check receiver and apparatus for receiving the time signals from Greenwich and Big Ben. The number of other outdoor broadcast lines was also increasing and had reached over a hundred. But most notable of all was the dramatic extension of the Simultaneous Broadcasting panels. These were still using Western Electric loudspeaker amplifiers, but these would now have to serve not only the main stations but a whole string of relay stations.

It was decided that the southern room on the third floor of the west wing should be devoted to engineering requirements. As a first step, the auditions room would become the new control room, with amplifier benches set against two of the walls and a Simultaneous Broadcasting board erected against a third. Creation of the control room involved a massive rewiring task, encompassing practically all the broadcasting circuits at Savoy Hill, and had to be completed without any break in programme transmission (plan 7c).

This was not by any means the only consideration. A whole sequence of rooms for research, control and development were required (Pawley, E., *BBC Engineering, 1922 to 1972*, pp54/55). The last bay continued to serve for Development, although without the Simultaneous Broadcasting board. The beautiful reception room, only seven months in use, had to be given up for research. The only compensation was the opportunity to move the original amplifier to this location where it served for a short time as a standby. As a result, the room in the north wing close to the original studio could now be cleared for use as a waiting room and for auditions (plan 7b).

Research and development also benefited from the provision of a workshop in the basement of the west wing (plan 8a). Access was by lift, although the workshop could also be approached through the archway at No. 4 Savoy Hill and down the slope of the little carriageway. The southern portion of the basement accommodation served as the engineers' storeroom (plan 6).

The Marconi system was described in a promotional company booklet issued in 1924. A description of the Round-Sykes microphone and its 'A' and 'B' amplifiers was given by H J Round in *Wireless World*, 26 November 1924, but neither of these sources referred to the use of Marconi equipment for outside broadcasts. Yet, as we have seen, Marconi amplifiers had been used for this purpose at Foyle Riding in May 1924 when the first transmission of the nightingale had delighted the world.

The use of Post Office land-lines for outdoor broadcast work was normal practice and meant that an outside broadcasting transmitter was not normally needed. Occasionally, however, the Post Office system was either poor in quality or not available at all. Such occasions occurred where the source of the Outside Broadcast was itself a mobile one; it could also be a problem in situations where Post Office lines involved several Exchanges, involving multiple switching. In these circumstances radio relays from the Outside Broadcast location provided a solution. For example, due to complex routing, the broadcast on 23 November 1923 of opera from The Old Vic used a 30 watt transmitter, the signal being received on a special aerial erected on the roof of the IEE building. This signal was then amplified and broadcast in the usual way.

A similar problem occurred when it was decided to broadcast from the London Zoo. The difficulty here was that the microphone had to be mobile in order to collect sounds from the various animal houses. H L Kirke therefore designed a mobile transmitter installed in a unit like a tea trolley. This was called the 'pram' and was trundled around the zoo to get live outdoor broadcasts for the Children's Hour programme. The ten watt transmitter used several LS5 valves, and a couple of bamboo poles were used to support the aerial.

There was hardly any aspect of broadcasting in 1924 which was not undergoing quantitative change. Thus Control desks had to output to an increasing number of provincial stations with Simultaneous Broadcasting becoming more common. At the input end of the Control desks the number of permanent outdoor broadcast points would, before the year was out, double to 200.

2LO had reached the point where it was providing about half the programme material broadcast across the nation and this gave rise to an increase in the number of studios and the allocation of these to particular needs. Already, the original input studio, Studio 3, catered for the spoken word and Studio 1 catered for music. Plans for rebuilding the corner block would provide three more studios - one devoted to talks and the news, a second for drama and a third for reviews of a kind that mixed music and speech. The new studios took time to build; Studio 5 (Talks) went into service on the 1st. floor on 7 November 1925; Studio 4 (Variety), also on the 1st. floor, was the next to be opened; finally Studio 2 (Drama), which included an Effects Room with a sophisticated approach to acoustic effects, was opened on the 2nd. Floor (plan 14).

Clearly the art of studio design, particularly with regard to acoustics, was worth pursuing and was the subject of much thought in 1924. Reverberation was a major factor. Having regard to the additional reverberation that takes place in the home, the appropriate reverberation time in the studio for speech was considered to be 0.75 second, for an octet 1.5 seconds and for a large orchestra, between 2 and 4 seconds. There was, therefore, no reason for reducing any studio's reverberation time to below 0.7 seconds.

Studio 1 (music) was designed on this principle. It had only a single layer of hessian lining behind its grey drapes. But all was not well. Reverberation time was found to vary across the frequency range, giving prominence to low frequencies at the expense of high ones. The low ones enjoyed a full second, whilst the higher frequencies had only 0.5 second reverberation. There was, therefore, a lack of 'brilliance' in the musical output of Studio 1, but at least it was a great improvement over Studio 3 where higher frequencies were well-nigh eliminated. The studios planned in 1924 learned the lesson presented by their two predecessors.

Good acoustic practice when designing studios for music was to make these as large as possible. This understanding was brought home to development engineers when they conducted outdoor broadcasts from dance halls and concert halls, most of which were much larger than any studio and which gave excellent results.

Another idea for improving studio production was put forward in 1924 and initially rejected. The idea was to build, for the announcer, a wooden kiosk or part. A special lamp would show which microphone was in use - the one in the studio or the one in the silence cabinet. In putting the idea forward, Lewis pointed out its advantages. First, announcers could continue their work in front of an orchestra that was moving out of the studio. Secondly, the kiosk would shut out from the announcer's microphone rustling of music, people coughing and so on. Thirdly, comments could be made about a famous conductor or artiste without fear of causing embarrassment. Finally, time would be saved as announcements could be made while the musicians were getting into their places and tuning up.

In his memo to Eckersley, Lewis recalled how his otherwise good idea was held up on technical grounds, because it was not possible to transfer from one microphone to another without 'clicking'. Clicking was a feature of the knife switches and meant that every attempt to connect and disconnect a circuit was heard all too clearly by listeners. But the introduction of two control desks in April 1924 produced an important advance in switching. The programme

BBC

Master clock, synchronised to the Greenwich time signal, and the tuning note apparatus, May 1927.

previously on air could be faded out at one desk and another, for example dance music, could be phased in from another desk. Knife switches no longer needed to be employed and Lewis' proposal for silence cabinets could now go ahead (memo from P P Eckersley, incorporating an earlier memo from Lewis to Eckersley - *BBC Archives*, end 1925. *See also* Burrows, Arthur, pp96/97, 1924).

With the construction of the new purpose-built studio suite at Savoy Hill, the BBC endeavoured to ensure its announcers improved the accuracy of their timekeeping. As a first step, a Hope-Jones 'Synchronome' was put into service at the beginning of 1923. This worked on the 'master 'silence cabinet' in the studio, about 6ft by 4ft and glazed round the upper clock/slave clock' principle, using electric impulses, thereby ensuring that all the clocks in the studio suite agreed with each other and with the master, installed in Studio 1 (plan 8b).

The announcer was to take up his position one minute before the hour and observe the studio clock. Thirty seconds before the hour he was to start counting from 30 to 59 guided by the swing of the clocks pendulum. On the sixtieth second the old tubular bells would be struck a number of times, corresponding to the hour. The counting routine was not a nightly performance but was given on every third day. The Hope-Jones clock was checked for accuracy every morning against the time signal put out from the Eiffel Tower in Paris.

Synchronomes were also employed in the Cardiff, Newcastle and Glasgow stations. A similar arrangement, known as the Pulsynetic system and manufactured by Gents was installed at Birmingham, Bournemouth, Aberdeen and in Dickenson St, Manchester.

Despite all these precautions, it was quite usual for the 'Westminster Chimes' to be played by the announcer several seconds outside Greenwich Mean Time, though by the end of 1923 an accuracy of about one second was achieved. The ultimate answer was to connect Greenwich directly with Savoy Hill. Using two highly accurate Victorian Dent chronometers installed at the observatory, pips were broadcast at one-second intervals, starting five seconds to the hour and ending on the hour at the suggestion of Hope-Jones. Hope-Jones pips became a feature of broadcasting from 5 February 1924, the apparatus being placed in the London control room.

But the old idea of introducing the evening programme with the sound of Westminster chimes had not been forgotten; a Marconi-Sykes microphone was installed in the tower of Big Ben and activated by remote control from Savoy Hill. From March 1924 listeners heard the sound of the Westminster chimes ringing across the nation.

Studio 4: Variety Studio with Silence Cabinet, 13 April 1929

Illustrated London News

9

Foundation for the Future

Reorganisation at Head Office

The expansion into Savoy Hill Mansions brought an additional 10,000 square feet of office space into use - enough to accommodate an additional 150 members of staff. Small corridors and stairways allowed them access back into the IEE building (plan 13a). Reith and his divisional heads now had the opportunity to house their staff into division sections - floor by floor and building by building.

But by far the most innovative development at this time (December 1925) was the creation of a whole suite of studios in the rebuilt section of the Mansions building. At second-floor level, a drama studio, studio 2, was constructed (plan 14); this heralded a new phase in studio acoustics, for it included an echo room which could be opened off the main studio and had its own microphone, thereby enabling the effective reverberation time to be varied. In addition, the studio possessed an effects room, again equipped with its own microphone. The three microphones were controlled from a desk in the silence cabinet from which the producer could select the combination to be used at any time.

On the first floor, immediately below this room, was a studio for Variety, studio 4 (plan 14). To create the right ambience for artistes it allowed space for a small audience to look at a stage, lit with amber spotlights. It, too, had a silence cabinet. Across the corridor from here a tiny Talks studio, studio 5, was built, later to become the News studio.

At the same first floor level, but in that part of the main building that had not been bombed, a double-height studio was formed, studio 7 (plan 16); this was not unlike some of the ballrooms used for outside broadcasts. Across the corridor from here a further studio was built, suitable for talks and small concerts, studio 6. Alongside, a large room was set aside as a music library. Located on the first floor, it could serve not only several of the studios in the Mansions but also Studio 1 on the first floor of the IEE building (plans 8b, 13a).

At third floor level, space in the Mansions was wholly devoted to Programmes (plan 12); This included Stobart's responsibilities for talks and education, Pitt's for music and Cecil Lewis' for Children's Hour. Programmes involving outside broadcasts were organised here, as was the enormous range of work now handled by the London station, 2LO.

The conversion of the fourth level of the Mansions to office use in June 1925 created an opportunity to form a new division with the title "Information" (plan 12). This dealt with every aspect of the BBC's involvement with publications, in particular the *Radio Times* and *World Radio*. The division handled all matters relating to the press. A specialist broadcasting library was set up and the division took on overall responsibility for the BBC's General Office. Meanwhile, the workshops had to be moved and space for these was found in the attic-like rooms of the 5th floor of the Mansions buildings. The last floor to be brought into service comprised space at ground-floor level in the undamaged portion of the Mansions where offices for the drama department were allocated (plan 15).

Before the Mansions had been bombed it had been possible to enter at each end. With so many studios now located in the mansions the rebuilt entrance was the one used by artistes and became known as the "North Entrance" thereby avoiding confusion with the west entrance, already in existence at No. 2 Savoy Hill (plan 1).

Beyond the inner doors of the north entrance a short flight of steps led up

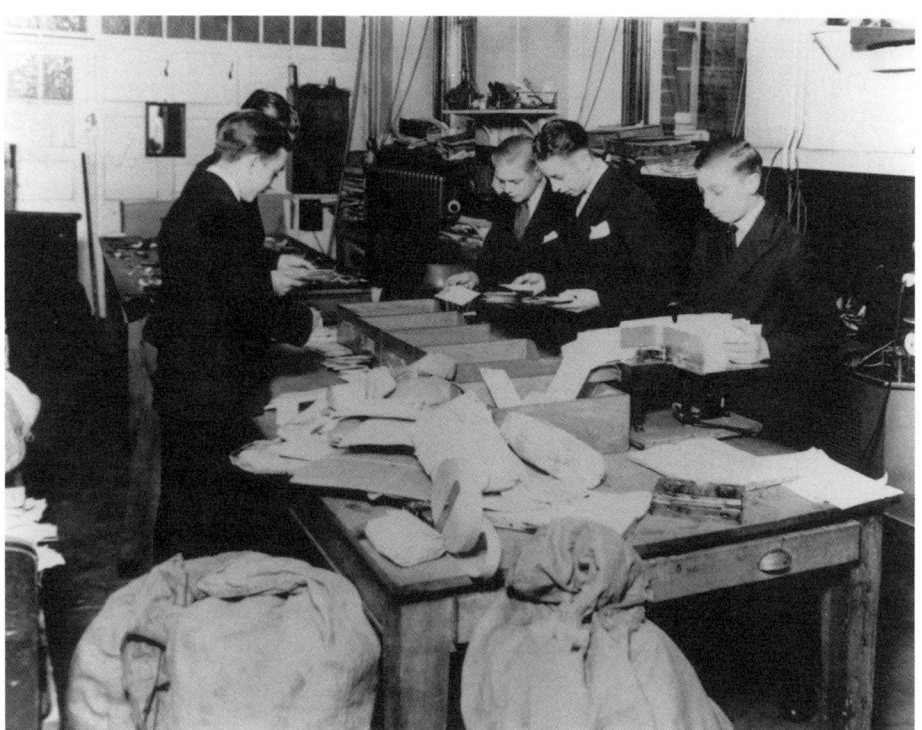

Reproduced by permission of the BBC

Messenger boys sorting the mail

to the corridor and to the main stairway (plan 14). Before going up, the artiste could enjoy the comfort of the drawing room. 'Outside Messenger Boys', in blue serge suits, stood ready to escort artistes and to call taxis. An artiste arriving at the old west entrance would now find a box sign, illuminated after dark, showing a hand pointing up the slope and carrying the words "TO THE STUDIOS - NORTH ENTRANCE". In September 1925 the historic "2 Savoy Hill" address was abandoned, becoming simply "Savoy Hill".

For much of the public, the BBC's headquarters presented a splendid sight, particularly at night when its many windows lit up like a hundred glowing valves. Compared to this, the IEE building paled into relative insignificance. But it was by no means redundant. Changing conditions in the Mansions and elsewhere now demanded a complete overhaul of the IEE accommodation.

On the third floor of the IEE building was the all-important control room; it now required four control desks to cope with the variety of programme sources and destinations. Programme departments had their own specialist studios; the dance floors of the Savoy Hotel and the Hotel Cecil constituted, in effect, additional studios; programmes could be relayed from provincial stations. In addition to these incoming programmes, new destinations now existed, namely the main and relay stations established in 1924.

Hitherto, the control room had been flanked at its north and south ends by Research and Development workshops (plan 8d). The space occupied by these workshops was now taken over, along with that of an adjoining corridor, so as to create an enlarged control room with ancillary space for batteries (plan 9). Against the southern wall, glass-fronted cabinets contained amplifiers and a relay board for Simultaneous Broadcasting. Against the northern wall was the master clock and Greenwich "Time Signal" apparatus. Beside that was a switchboard for controlling the battery system, the batteries and their generators being placed in a room behind this wall. The long east and west walls, against which the control desks were situated, carried illuminated boards with numbers representing the five in-house studios. These numbers glowed red when the studio was live or green when the studio wished to be "put on air" or "taken off".

The control room now possessed an impressive appearance. Rich mahogany contrasted with highlights of gleaming brass. Elegant cabinet work and rows of jack-strips reflected the influence of Post Office switchboards. The general effect was of Victorian solidity with, here and there, a touch of the impeccable style associated with the name Heath Robinson (Pawley, E., *BBC Engineering 1922 to 1972,* p50).

Reproduced by permission of the BBC
Enlarged Simultaneous Broadcast Switchboard, Savoy Hill, January 1927.

The floor below was the nerve centre for the BBC. Here were Reith's headquarters. Leading off from his room were the boardroom and offices for the Heads of the Secretariat and Finance Divisions. Beyond was the most impressive typing pool with its splendid views overlooking the Thames.

In contrast to this opulence was the north-west staircase where little passageways were cut through massive masonry to provide access to the Mansions block. Steps formed in the passageways brought the differing floor levels of the two buildings into alignment (plan 13a).

Something of the magical quality of Savoy Hill stemmed from the fact that so many varied jobs were concentrated in one location. Here questions of administration, policy and finance were settled. The nation's leading experts on broadcast music, education and drama developed their ideas. Technical research and development was carried out. BBC publications were prepared. Communication with listeners by means of programme and technical correspondence was maintained. Workshops dealt with calls for specialised equipment. Outside Broadcast engineers stood ready to rush off to any part of the country. Potential broadcasters poured in daily to take part in auditions;

artistes arrived to take part in rehearsals and programmes, and to discuss any plans for touring main and relay stations. This variety of activity and humanity made a deep impression on those whose who visited Savoy Hill (H L Chilman, *Wireless World*, 30 March 1927).

But the BBC's Savoy Hill staff never reached the point where relations became impersonal. It was possible, for instance, for Reith to be familiar with the names and jobs of those for whom he was responsible. It was equally possible for the complete, assembled staff to pose on the main steps of the IEE for a group photograph - such a photograph was in fact taken in November 1924 (*BBC Archives*).

Reproduced by permission of the BBC

BBC Head Office Staff, November 1924.

Even divisional and departmental heads could hardly have foreseen the remarkable future ahead as they arrived each morning in the early twenties to be greeted at the west entrance by the commissionaire, Arbuckle, with his sharply waxed moustache and dark eyes twinkling from beneath the peak of his cap. Perhaps only Reith had thought things through to their logical conclusion. For him the BBC could no longer function as a commercial company and it was unthinkable that it should become a department of government. A solution of an entirely new character would have to be found somewhere between these two extremes.

Royal Charter

In 1925, in anticipation of the expiration of the BBC's licence, a committee was formed under the chairmanship of the Right Hon. the Earl of Crawford and Balcarres:

> 'To advise as to the proper scope of the Broadcasting Service and as to the management, control and finance thereof after the expiry of the existing licence on 31 December 1926. The committee will indicate what changes in the law, if any, are desirable in the interests of the Broadcasting service.'

Reith had for some years been preparing his ground for such an inquiry. He had long been concerned that the BBC should not be conducted as a private commercial Company; neither should it be controlled by the government. When the Crawford Committee was formed he submitted a statement of 21 pages advocating "the adoption and maintenance of definite policies and standards and unity of control." (Allighan, Garry, *Sir John Reith*, p202). Reith advocated that the BBC:

> 'should bring into the greatest possible number of homes the fullest degree of all that is best in every department of human knowledge, endeavour and achievement (and so) become a world influence with immense potential for good'. (There should be) 'a high moral tone, the avoidance of the vulgar, for it must be remembered that children listen to almost every broadcast. ... Policy must be clear, consistent and courageous.'

Reith showed considerable courage in advocating the winding up of the Company and its replacement by a Corporation. He was a servant of the Company. In advocating a Corporation, Reith was putting himself out of a job with no guarantee of leading the new Corporation. Indeed, within the committee there were those who considered that the Company had not yet proved itself and that the Company's licence should simply be renewed until it had done so.

The Crawford report was published on 2 March 1926. The recommendations were largely those of Reith. It considered "not merely ...

scientific or mechanical aspects but also their ultimate impact on the education and temperament of the country." It rejected the United States system of free and uncontrolled transmission and reception, deciding that Broadcasting must remain a monopoly controlled by a single authority - a public corporation set up to act as a trustee for the national interest in broadcasting and invested with full authority. A Board of Governors would be formed, nominated by the Government. It suggested that the corporation be known as the "British Broadcasting Commission". The Commissioners would take over the entire property, interests and contracts etc of the Company and repay Company shareholders their capital; if it dispensed with the service of individuals it would compensate them on a scale to be approved by the Treasury. So as to command public confidence, the licence granted to the Commission by the Postmaster General should last for not less than 10 years, and be renewable.

The committee rejected the idea that the personnel of the Commission should represent various interests such as music, science, finance and manufacturing; it required, instead,

> 'persons of judgement and independence, free of commitments,   ... having no other interests to promote than those of the public service. ... They should be nominated by the Crown (and) number between five and seven persons.'

The committee was anxious that money should not be a limiting factor in the development of the Commission and commissioners should be paid

> 'such fees as will secure the best available service; ... outlay on bold experiment should not be meagre; ... research should be constant.'

It was recommended that the existing licence fee of 10 shillings should continue, in principle, indefinitely. It should be collected by the Postmaster General and, after he had deducted his expenses

> 'and when the adequate service has been assured, but not until then, it is expedient that the surplus should be retained by the State.'

Restrictions that had been placed on the British Broadcasting Company by the press and other interests should not continue. The committee declared that it could "see no adequate reason for withholding ... rights regarding the use of copyright material"; neither did they consider it necessary to invest the Commission with special privileges in this respect.

The committee felt the British Broadcasting Company had held the balance between conflicting tastes with discretion, providing both "highbrow" and "light" music for example. It was concerned that Broadcasting should never be used for the trite and commonplace; the Commission

> 'must try to improve the standard in each sphere of its activity, especially in music (and) religious services. ... Material should be of high quality, not too lengthy or insistent, and distributed with scrupulous fairness, ... but the discretion of the new Authority must be upheld.'

The committee accepted that Parliament had ultimate control and that the parliamentary spokesman on broad questions of policy would be the Postmaster-General. However, it emphasised that the Commission should not be subject to continuing ministerial guidance. Within well-defined limits, it

> 'should enjoy full liberty, (and be) elastic enough to permit variation according to technical developments and changes in public taste. (It) should therefore be invested with the maximum freedom which Parliament is prepared to concede. ... The Commission should present an annual report to Parliament.'

On 3 May 1926 a General Strike was called by the TUC, to be followed by the Declaration of a National Emergency. With no newspapers published, the Government's only means of communicating with the nation was through the BBC; crippling for the country but timely for Reith in his advocating a National Corporation rather than a Company linked to commerce. The strike brought it home to the government and the country that broadcasting was of key value in time of emergency; it was a national asset.

The recommendations of the Crawford Committee were, with some modifications, accepted (Allighan, Garry, *Sir John Reith,* p218). On 1 January 1927 the British Broadcasting Corporation was constituted under Royal Charter.

A ten-year licence was granted and a board of governors was formed, nominated by the government. Reith, no longer the managing-director of a Limited Company, became director-general of a royal chartered corporation.

His staff had increased from four, when he joined in December 1922, to 630 when chartered four years later.

Reith generally held himself aloof from critics. However, on one occasion, in response to American criticism, he gave a comprehensive defence of the charter. Parliament, Reith said, decided the type of constitution and terms of reference of the BBC, imposed certain obligations and limitations and required an annual account. Thus there was broad control of policy. However in management, there was freedom from interference; in administration, autonomy. Parliament had deliberately chosen a monopoly; central control produced concentration of effort, economical administration and the highest degree of efficiency in every sense of the term. Under the charter, Reith continued, technical work was controlled by the BBC, with the sole exception of telephone cables which were hired from the General Post Office. This unified policy facilitated the maintenance of a high standard of artistic reproduction and the ready expansion of technical facilities. The BBC could pursue the policy most suitable for listeners.

At the time the Charter was granted - 1 January 1927 - the British Broadcasting Company had 21 transmitting stations. 85 per cent of the population could receive a choice of programmes, both by day and night; 95 per cent could obtain at least one programme even with low quality receivers. It wasn't until April 1932 that the BBC headquarters in Savoy Hill Mansions finally burst its seams and the great move to the new purpose-built broadcasting house was made.

The changeover from Company to Corporation did nothing to stem the headlong growth of the BBC, but it did mark the limit in the capacity of Savoy Hill to cope with this growth. Within a few months the BBC's Head of Premises, Marmaduke Tudsbury, was instructed to think about a new headquarters and to find a suitable site. His task, and the design and construction of the new purpose-built Broadcasting House, would take 5 years. The great move from Savoy Hill to Broadcasting House took place in April 1932.

Transmitting stations at the time the Charter was granted, 1 January 1927.

station	call sign	start of regular broadcasting	power/type
London	2LO	14-Nov-22	3000W Main
Manchester	2ZY	15-Nov-22	3000W Main
Birmingham	5IT	15-Nov-22	3000W Main
Newcastle-on-Tyne	5NO	24-Dec-22	3000W Main
Cardiff	5WA	13-Feb-23	3000W Main
Glasgow	5SC	06-Mar-23	3000W Main
Aberdeen	2BD	10-Oct-23	3000W Main
Bournemouth	6BM	17-Oct-23	3000W Main
Sheffield	6SL	12-Nov-23	200W Relay
Plymouth		26-Mar-24	200W Relay
Edinburgh		01-May-24	200W Relay
Liverpool		11-Jun-24	200W Relay
Bradford		08-Jul-24	200W Relay
Leeds		08-Jul-24	200W Relay
Hull		15-Aug-24	200W Relay
Belfast		15-Sep-24	3000W Main
Nottingham		16-Sep-24	200W Relay
Stoke-on-Trent		21-Oct-24	200W Relay
Dundee		12-Nov-24	200W Relay
Swansea		12-Dec-24	200W Relay
Daventry, Northants		27-Jul-25	25000W High

Reith's Vision Shapes the Future

Much of our story has been concerned with practicalities - the development of satisfactory microphones, amplifiers, the provision of a national network of land-lines and radio links; the acquisition and allocation of office space. But it was a man who had no knowledge of wireless and none of the theatre or entertainment who was entrusted to bring broadcasting from its birth and, through turbulent times, to adulthood. A man dedicated to more than mere practicalities; a man of vision. Reith was that man, a paternalistic man of his time, but one with a vision based on his ideals - and the determination to carry it through against all opposition, no matter whence it came.

He saw that wireless would soon take continents in its stride, cast a girdle round the earth, with a message instantaneous and direct, surpassing all other means of delivery. Statesman of the home country and of the Dominions and Colonies would be enabled to listen to the pronouncements of policies and aspirations as they were expounded in the parliaments and great assemblies. Rural areas would be brought into direct contact with the institutions of Empire. The striking of Big Ben, chiming over the Mother of Parliaments, would be heard in the remotest villages of Britain and the farthermost parts of empire. Radio, Reith envisaged, would bring light to mankind.

But let Reith speak for himself. In 1924, Reith wrote, in his book *Broadcast over Britain*:

> 'No early popularity was sought ... for the ready appeal. ... Our responsibility (is) to carry into the greatest possible number of homes everything that is best in every department of human knowledge, endeavour and achievement ... it is occasionally indicated to us that we are apparently setting out to give the public what we think they need, and not what they want; but few know what they want, and very few what they need.
>
> 'There is no harm in trivial things ... entertainment unadulterated is good, and is required and demanded at different times and in different ways by all people, (but) it must be kept in its place ... We say, for instance, that the alleged humour which depends for its sustenance on drunkenness, mothers-in-law, and so on, can be dispensed with, and other sources tapped.

'The practical idealist ... looks to education as the hope of the nation ... for the practical idealist is he who, loving his kind, is willing to toil unremittingly on behalf (of boys and girls of today) ... and die without seeing the first fruits of his labour.

'I think ... wireless lessons will become, to the child mind, an integral part of its schooling, and it will be impossible to dissociate its immediate effect from the general effect of the school routine on each child's work. ... 'Special efforts have been made to interest children in music ... the next generation has every likelihood of being better equipped to understand and enjoy good music than its forerunners.

'Our thoughts are also turned to the poor, that vast majority whose children look on the streets as their playground and attend when they can the performances of the nearest picture house. ... one does not contemplate with equanimity the effect on the minds of young children of seeing ... films of a morbid, if not actually vicious, nature.

'(May) wireless broadcasting be taken as the expression of a new and better relationship between man and man; ... be shared by all alike, ... the wealthy and the poor listen(ing) simultaneously, and to the same extent.'

No matter that the Empire would fade, Reith's vision would shape broadcasting through the desperate days of the Depression. In the World War which followed, the BBC, on which Britain and so many conquered nations would depend, would be the voice of freedom.

'Let us see that our principles and ideals are worthy, and that the policy of service be clear, consistent and courageous.'

Pioneers Recall The "Great Days"

The great days that had been and were no more - the days chronicled in this book - were recalled with a certain wistfulness by one of the pioneers at the end of 1923:

> 'the microphone tied up with string, the switches falling to pieces, the gadgets that won't work unless coaxed by someone who knows how'. Days when 'something goes wrong and one has to step into the breach and talk nonsense for half-an-hour ... In those days it did not matter who handled anything, as long as it was handled and handled well. It was a democracy of young pioneers, doomed like all the pioneering of youth to come up against the rigidity of age, discipline and experience; doomed to be swept quickly into the inexorable mills of civilisation and organisation. We must content ourselves with the memory that once, for a very short time, it existed. ... Great days! Not easily forgotten.'

This is a remarkable statement by Lewis, bearing in mind the long journey the BBC had still to make and the fact that the Company was scarcely one year old when these words were written.

Lewis was not the first to reminisce in this way. The 'official organ of the BBC', the Radio Times, itself looked back, recalling those

> 'hectic but happy times ... a whole crowd of us herded together in one small room, all but the General Manager who had a cupboard to himself, so small that he had to sit like an Oriental at a bazaar. Uncle Arthur and Uncle Caractacus at different phones a yard apart; Captain Eckersley dictating a highly technical letter and an intensely humorous burlesque at the same time.'

These words were penned in September 1923; the scene they record lay only six months in the past but to all intents and purposes it could have been six millennia. Obviously you had to have been in the right place at exactly the right time to spot that 'Auntie' was young once.

This comes across best when one actually hears the pioneers reminiscing about the early days in the BBC Sound Archives. Here is Noel Ashbridge:

'So it was that we Engineers down there in Essex received instructions to start. Our equipment was primitive to say the least of it. We had one army hut which served both as studio and transmitter. We hurriedly hired a piano from the nearest shop, three-and a-half miles away, and in due course we went on the air, quite casually and without any cheering - Britain's first regular broadcasting station. Our microphones were like ordinary telephones ... we even put one inside the piano. Our concerts consisted mostly of records and impromptu items by the staff.'

Here is Peter Eckersley:

'This is Two Emma Toc Writtle testing! Can you hear me, 2LO? Hello Ash. Wave your arm if you can hear me.'

Now it is 2LO's turn and Burrows looking back to the historic beginning:

'To Stanton Jefferies I dispatched a memorandum, the most historic Order of the Day in the history of broadcasting. Jefferies has treasured it ever since and he will now read it to you.' Jefferies: "A R Burrows to L Stanton Jefferies, London Station Director. The British Broadcasting Committee has arranged to transmit the following programme each evening from the London Broadcasting Station 2LO: 6pm news bulletin; 8 to 9 music; 9 to 9.30 news; 9.30 to 10 music.'

Now Cecil Lewis recalling 2LO at Marconi House:

'a dingy room, 20ft square, with a faded green carpet, a grand piano, and a worn-out settee with the horse hair coming through. ... We hear, in the background, a man singing: it is Leonard Hawke, using an original microphone, singing with piano accompaniment "Drake goes West', the first item of entertainment the BBC ever put on for its listeners. We hear Stanton Jefferies playing the Westminster chimes on the studio's hired set of tubular bells; Kenneth Wright's voice is also heard recalling the early 2ZY Manchester programmes ... "We had a unique contrivance for adjusting the height of the microphone to the singer's mouth - the singer stood on a pile of books! One night a tenor, in taking a top note took a step backwards; there was a terrific crash as he slid under the piano.'

Marconi engineer E O P Thomas recalled the promise to get the Newcastle station in operation by Christmas 1922.

'A hitch arose and there was no hope of connecting studio and transmitter. As a last resort I had several empty horse drays wheeled into the stable yard, chairs were placed on them and microphones connected to the nearby transmitter.
'The inaugural programme of 5NO (Newcastle) was punctually carried out.'

Frank Hawke was in the 2LO (London) Orchestra ...

'I also acted as music librarian. The few sheets of music we had, I kept on an old kitchen range at Marconi House.'

Finally Burrows, once again concluding his good-night to listeners with lines from Longfellow:

'The night shall be filled with music,
And the cares that infest the day
Shall fold their tents like the Arabs
And as silently steal away.'

(Baily, L and Brewer, C. *Scrapbook for 1921, Scrapbook for 1922*).

In his anniversary broadcast on 14 November 1923 Reith recalled the start a year earlier when the BBC was represented 'by a staff of three in temporary possession of one small room.' He went on to speak of the sturdy one year old Company that he now led; it was now a 'large organisation' and an 'established institution'. It was ready to offer 'all that is best and most worthwhile in every department of human achievement, knowledge and endeavour'.

Despite this solemn pledge, the birthday party spirits spilled over during the evening broadcast and Eckersley's attempt to get good music out of the 2LO Wireless Orchestra rendered even the solemn Reith helpless with laughter. All the same, listeners recognised that Reith's words were not without foundation. The BBC had indeed become 'an established institution'.

What then happened in the short time between the first few weeks and the last few weeks of 1923 to make such a radical change, the change which created the BBC as we know it in our time? What brought their 'Great Days' to a close?

A centralising policy welded the BBC together. The isolation of the provincial stations began to diminish as their Directors were called to meetings in London and fed with material from the new HQ departments. Simultaneous Broadcasting of the news and other items reinforced this trend. Soon there were relay stations across the country, each in a major city. Fed from 2LO's studio, they became known as 'London's babies'.

Nevertheless, each of the provincial Stations had by then its own orchestra and its own Music Director. Stations began to appoint specialist full-time announcers and none was without its family of 'Uncles' and 'Aunties'. By the end of 1923 the Marconi-Sykes moving coil microphone had become the standard BBC microphone in all but one of the nine stations and leading instrumentalists in the provinces were happy with it; no more fiddling with the massive moving coil apparatus of Marconi House days or with the carbon microphones installed in Newcastle and Cardiff studios. The little Western Electric 'double button' and capacitor microphones of 1923 were now only used for outside broadcasts.

The older provincial stations severed some material links with the companies that had given them birth. In August 1923 2ZY Manchester left the Metrovick's factory at Trafford Park for a new location in the heart of Manchester. It was only a cotton warehouse with a goods hoist for a lift but at least artistes could get there. 5IT Birmingham likewise left the GEC works at Witton for a central location in New Street; 5WA Cardiff and 5SC Glasgow moved in 1924 to more spacious accommodation.

Another link with the founding companies was broken with the recruitment, in mid-1923, of BBC engineers. Until then, company engineers had serviced the BBC apparatus. By the end of 1923 the BBC had 46 engineers on its payroll.

The Sykes committee formed in April 1923 further loosened the links and the 'Big Six' companies represented on the Board knew their days of wet nursing were over. In October 1923 the flow of revenue was allowed to flood into the BBC coffers, the number of licences rising from 180,000 to 600,000 by the end of the year and continuing to rise rapidly. The BBC could hold its head high and contemplate a massive extension of its activities.

The Radio Times, which first appeared in September 1923 whilst stressing the friendly rivalry between the Stations, also reflected their similarity, thereby reinforcing links to headquarters. Initiatives of one tended to spread to the others. Many artistes simply did the rounds under contracts organised centrally.

The story of the emergence of broadcasting in this country was set down by one or two pioneers, in particular Lewis and Burroughs; these chatty volumes reflect the 'great days'. But in mid-1924, Reith wrote 'Broadcast over Britain'. It was an 'exposition of the ideals which animate the policy of the British Broadcasting Company'. Thenceforth all further books on the BBC by staff and ex-staff were, unless specifically approved, banned!

Lewis, who enjoyed long retirement in Corfu, had been in at the beginning –

> 'there we were, around half dozen people, with the whole Company's organisation to set in motion, … guardians and attendants of the most voracious creature ever created by man - a microphone, which clamoured daily to be fed. … It not only grew in the amount it wished to devour but became fastidious in the extreme'.
> (Lewis, Cecil, *Broadcasting from Within*, p26)

By 1924, with 20,000 hours of annual programme, 75 per cent of it original and 'live', the amateur approach of the early-days had necessarily been replaced by organised professionalism.

As the prestige of the BBC soared it could pick its staff with the utmost choosiness. You had of course to have a degree - only Oxford or Cambridge would do; you would have represented your university or county or country in some approved sporting capacity; you would naturally possess an outstanding musical ability. With such qualifications you might apply for an interview and meet the Head of Department. If found suitable he would lead you into the Controller's presence. Carpendale would then demand to know which public school you had attended and he would go on to explore your war record. In the event of your clearing these hurdles, you would be led in front of the Director General himself for some penetrating enquiries as to religious orthodoxy. If accepted, you learned the job on the job by hard experience.

But as the organisation grew and diversified, there came a new generation. From the energy of these early pioneers would spring new life. From the Savoy Hill days would come, in 1932, Portland Place and the great white edifice of Broadcasting House. Over its entrance is Prospero, a symbol of wisdom and benevolence, sending forth the young Ariel, the invisible spirit of the air serving as a personification of broadcasting.

It is ironic that the begetter of all this - Savoy Hill - is now a haven of peace and a place of almost ghostly character. If one were to brave now the east entrance in the late evening would the caretaker's dog be heard? Is the bison's head still inexplicably there on the wall of the dark passage giving the impression of a nightmare cowshed? And are the dramatists and educationists still upstairs, aloof in their secluded quarters? Is Reith still in his office staring out like a ship's captain on his bridge over the Thames and London?

The chimes still ring out from Westminster, but Savoy Hill is as quiet as it was before our story began 100 years ago; and as you walk back towards reality the soft rustle of the trees by the Savoy Chapel seems to mingle with the faint sound of gentle music - the Wireless Orchestra are playing still - a melody – 'A Perfect Day'.

FINIS

PLANS

Location and plans of accommodation in the
IEE building and Savoy Hill Mansions arranged
chronologically from March 1923 to May 1928

Compiled and Drawn by
Brian A Hennessy

List of plans

Location Map

Plan 1	*May 1928*		IEE and Savoy Hill Mansions Allocation of rooms to BBC
Plan 2	*March 1923*	IEE	2nd Floor: West and North Wings
Plan 3	*May 1923*		IEE 3rd Floor: West and North Wings
Plan 4	*September 1923*	IEE	Ground Floor: West Wing Entrance 1st Floor:　West Wing (South) 2nd Floor:　North Wing 3rd Floor:　West Wing (South)
Plan 5a	*January 1924*	IEE	1st Floor:　West Wing
Plan 5b	*January 1924*	IEE	2nd Floor:　South Wing 　　　　　　West Wing (South)
Plan 6	*February 1924*	IEE	Basement: West Wing (North)
Plan 7a	*April 1924*	IEE	2nd Floor:　North Wing 　　　　　　West Wing (North)
Plan 7b/c	*April 1924*	IEE	3rd Floor:　North Wing 　　　　　　West Wing (South)
Plan 8a/b	*May 1924*	IEE	Basement 1st Floor
Plan 8c/d	*May 1924*	IEE	2nd Floor 3rd Floor
Plan 9	*November 1925 – 1926* 	IEE	3rd Floor:　West Wing (South)
Plan 10	*February 1927*	IEE	Ground Floor: West Entrance
Plan 11	*June 1925*		Savoy Hill Mansions 5th Floor

Plan 12   *June/Sept 1925*   Savoy Hill Mansions
                                              3rd Floor
                                              4th Floor

Plan 13a   *September 1925*   Link of IEE to Savoy Hill Mansions

Plan 13b   *September 1925*   Savoy Hill Mansions
                                              Basement: North-West

Plan 14   *December 1925*   Savoy Hill Mansions
                                              Ground Floor: North-West
                                              1st Floor: North-West
                                              2nd Floor: North-West

Plan 15   *June 1926*   Savoy Hill Mansions
                                              Ground Floor

Plan 16   *June 1926 - January 1927*
                                    Savoy Hill Mansions
                                              1st Floor
                                              2nd Floor

Plan 17   *May 1927 - May 1928*
                                    Savoy Hill Mansions
                                              Basement
             May 1928   Savoy Hill Mansions
                                              2nd Floor: North-West

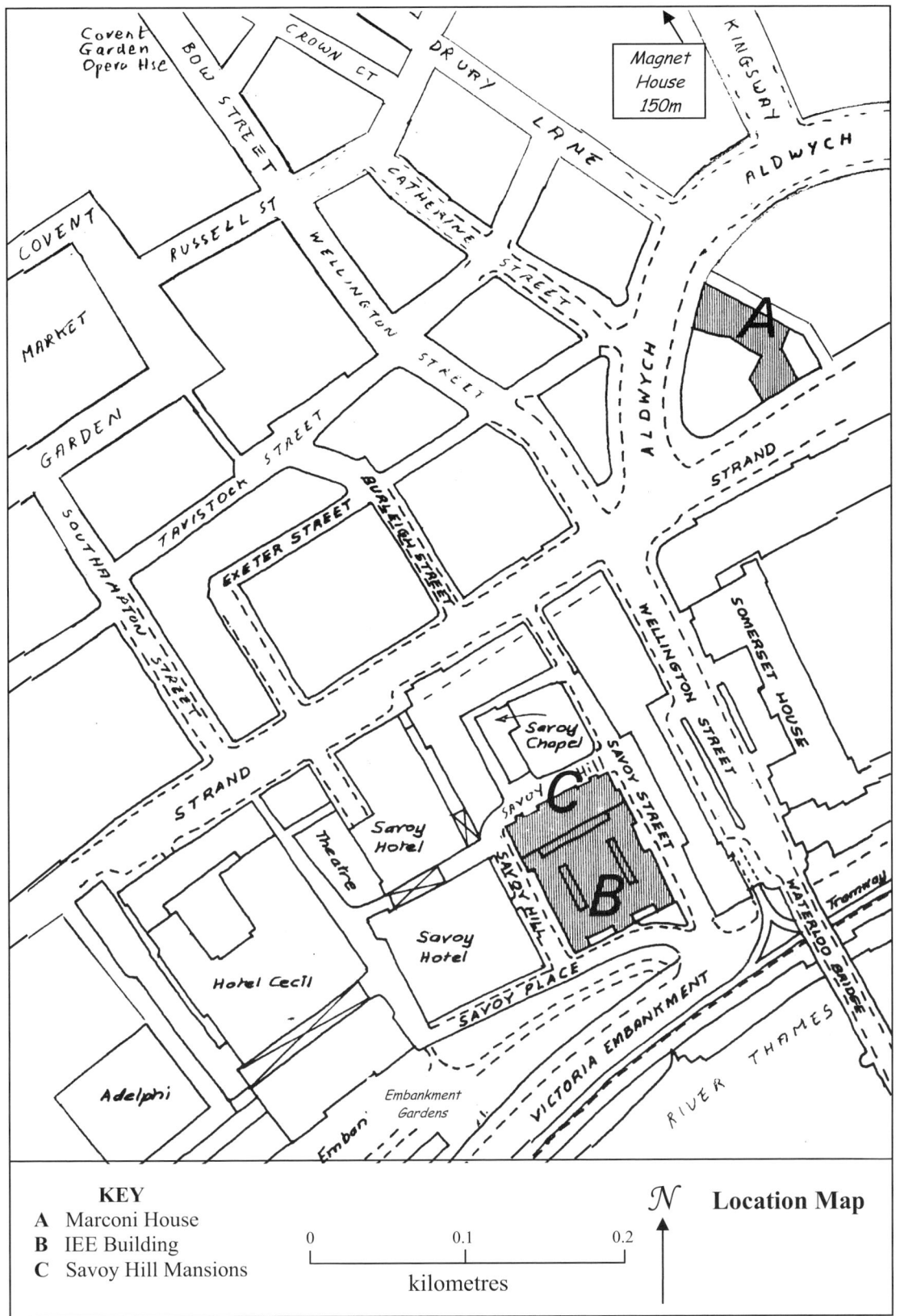

KEY
A Marconi House
B IEE Building
C Savoy Hill Mansions

Location Map

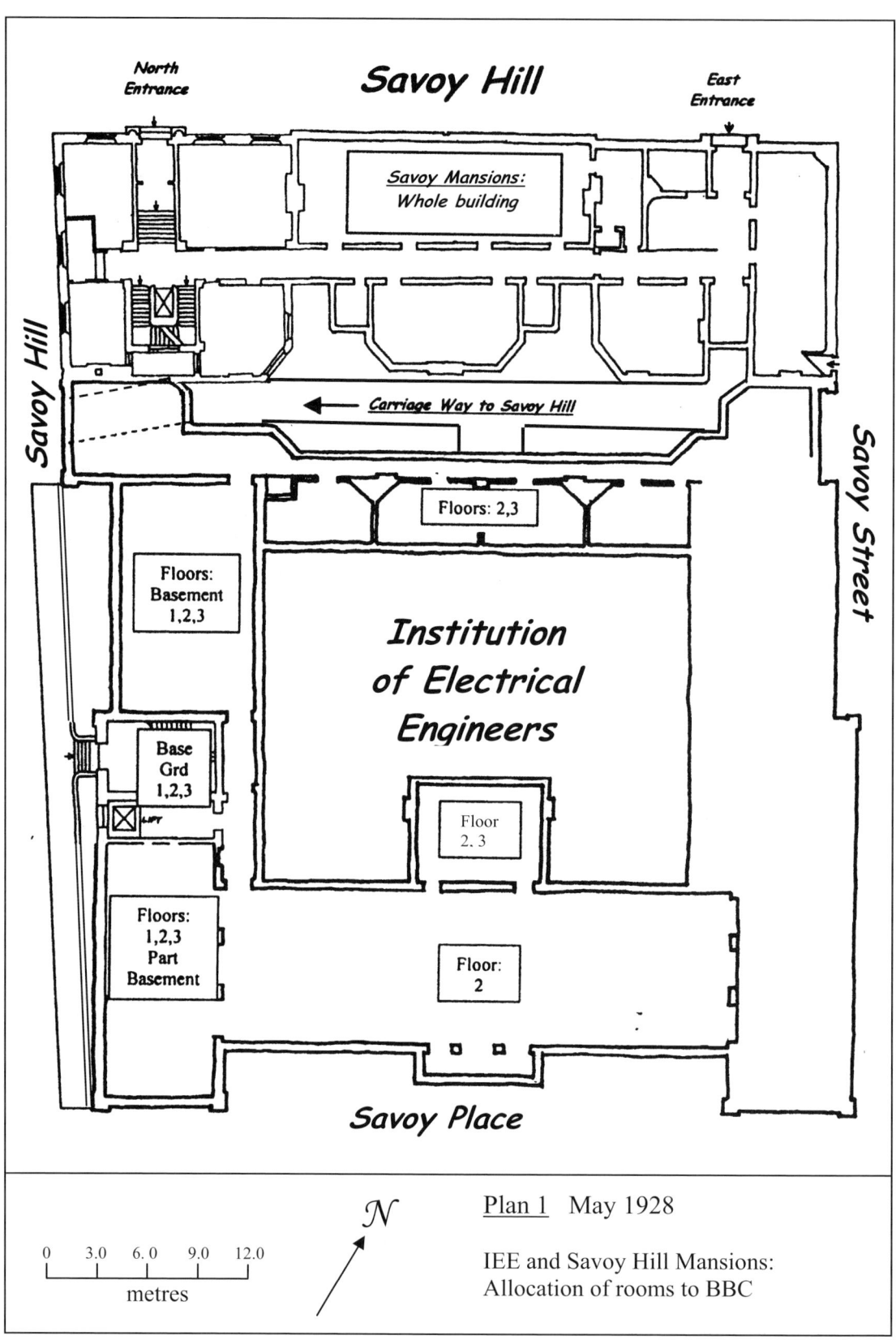

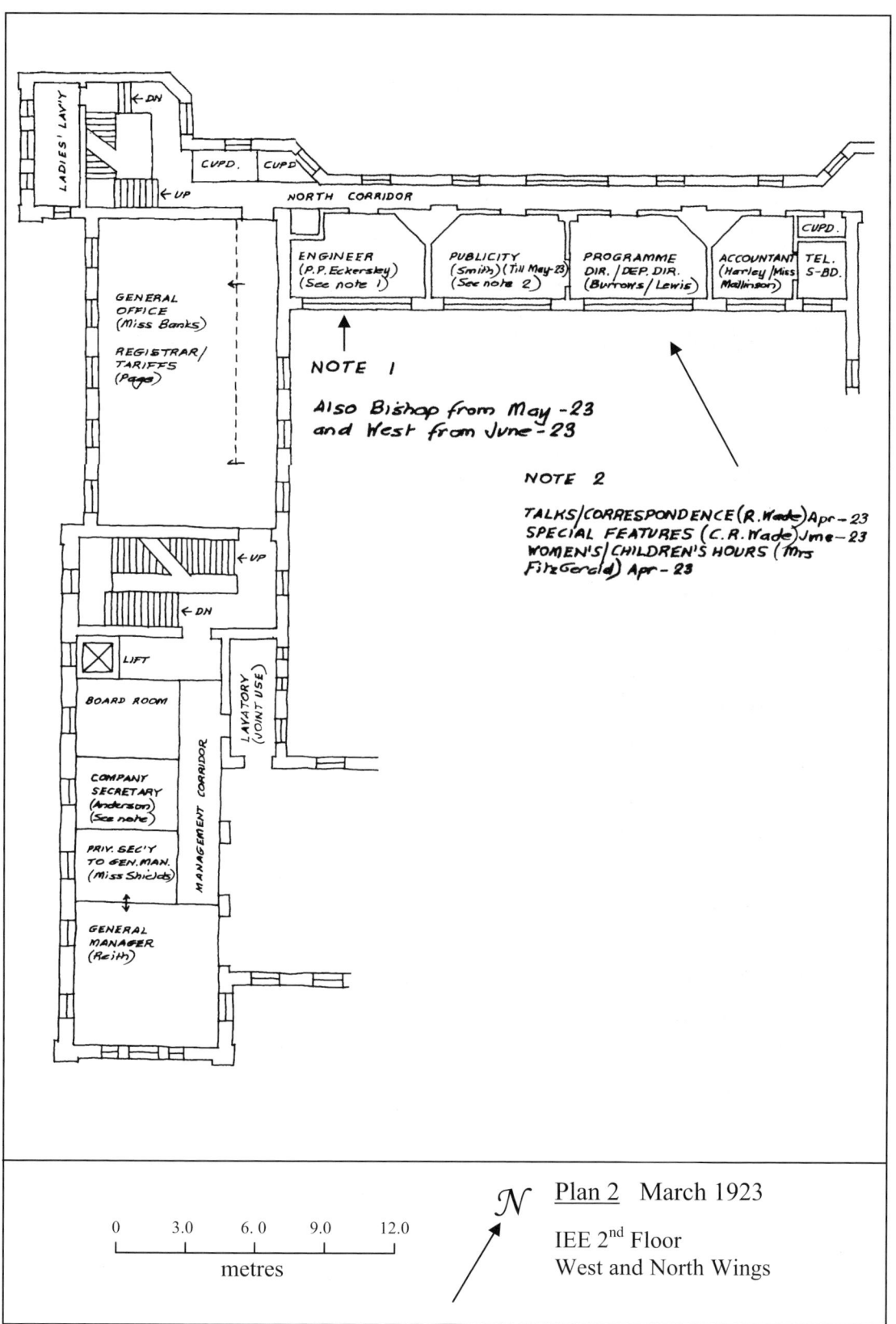

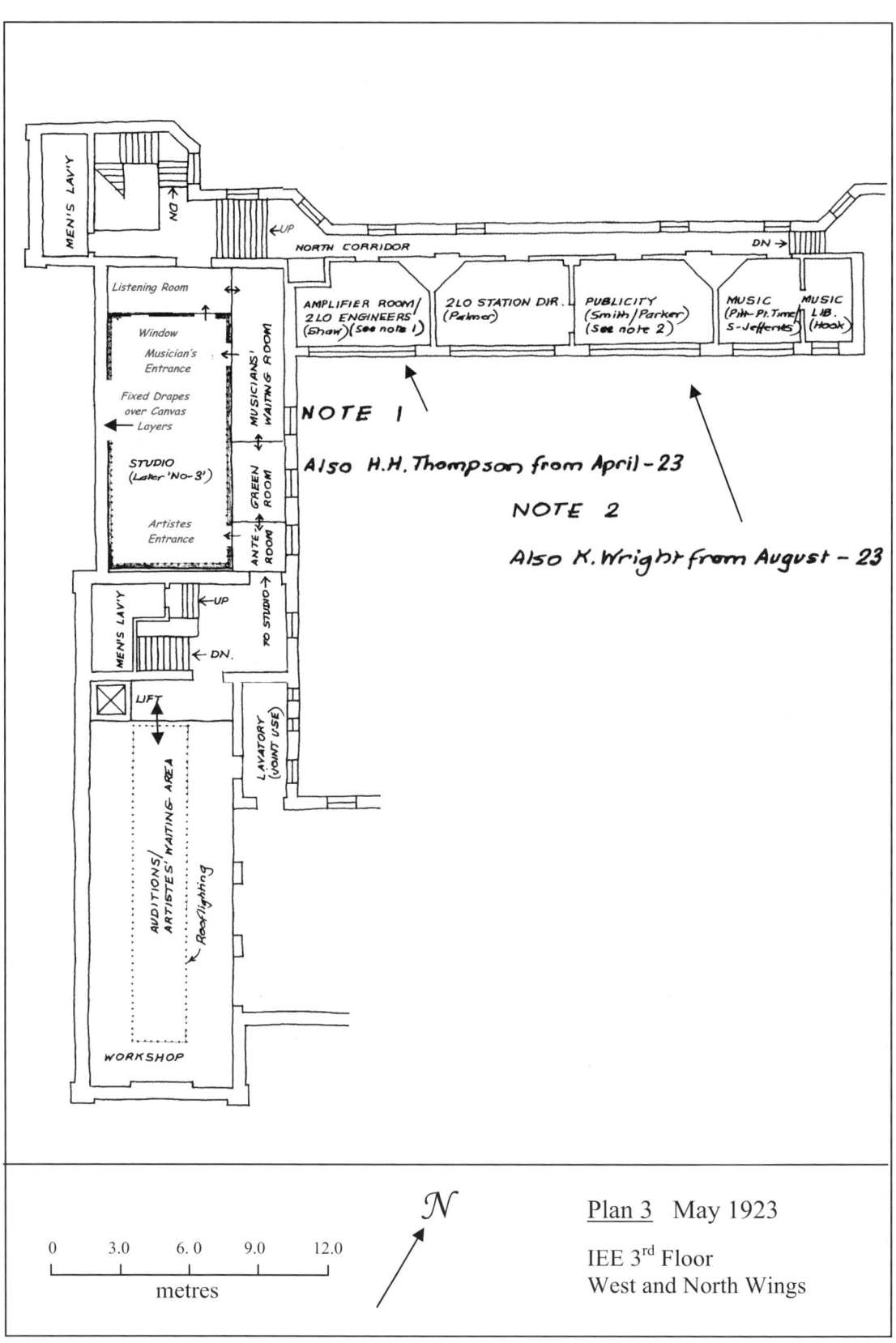

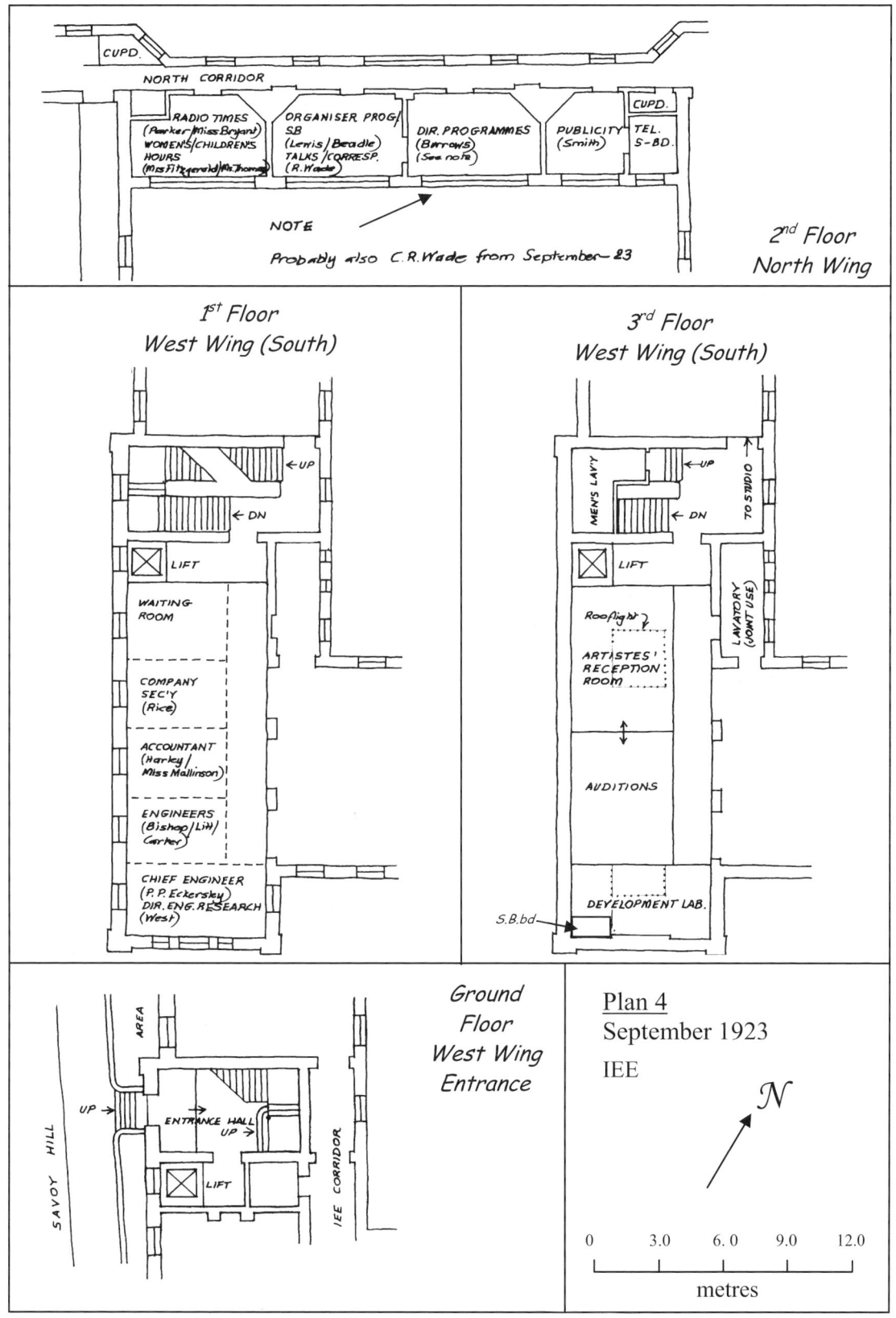

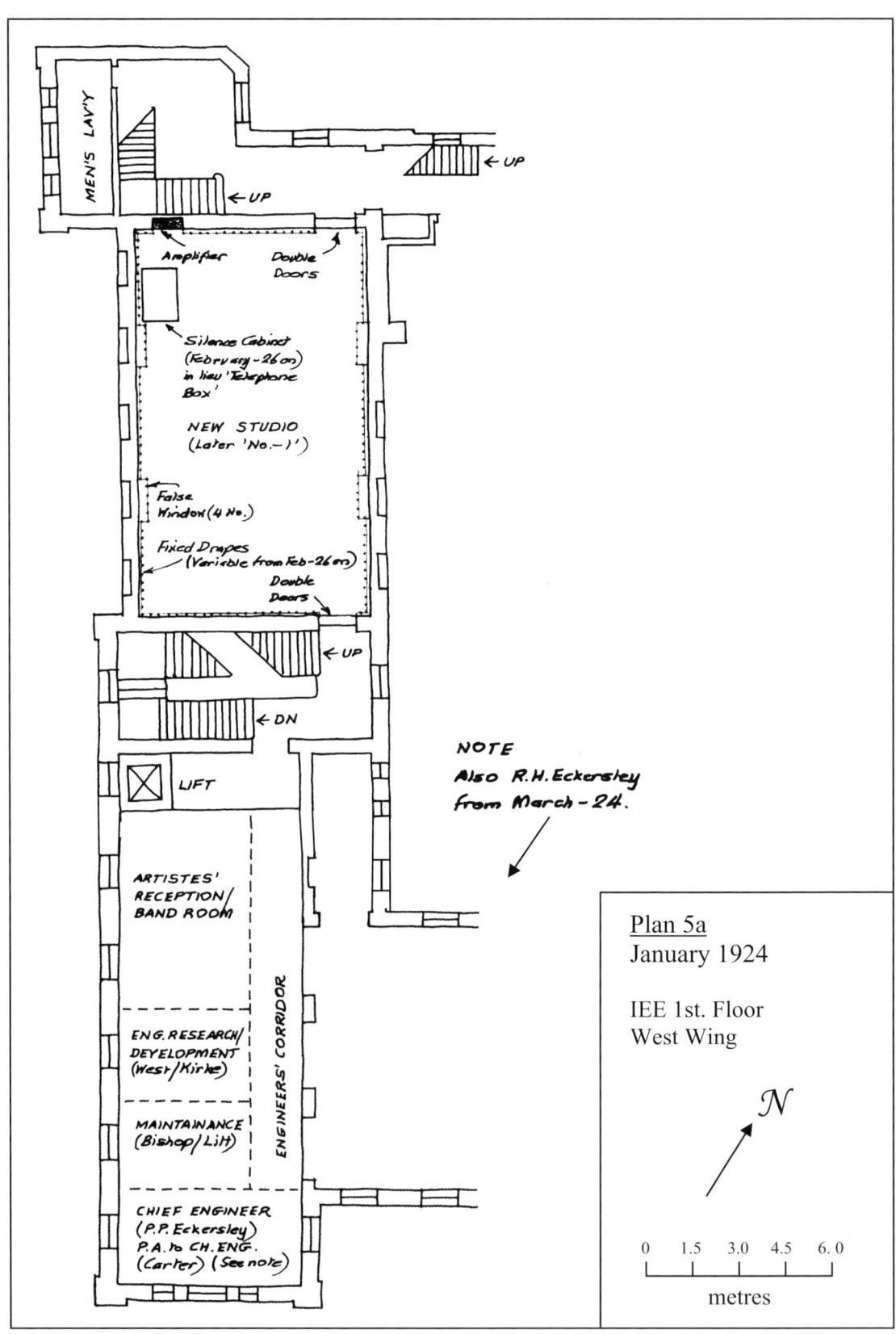

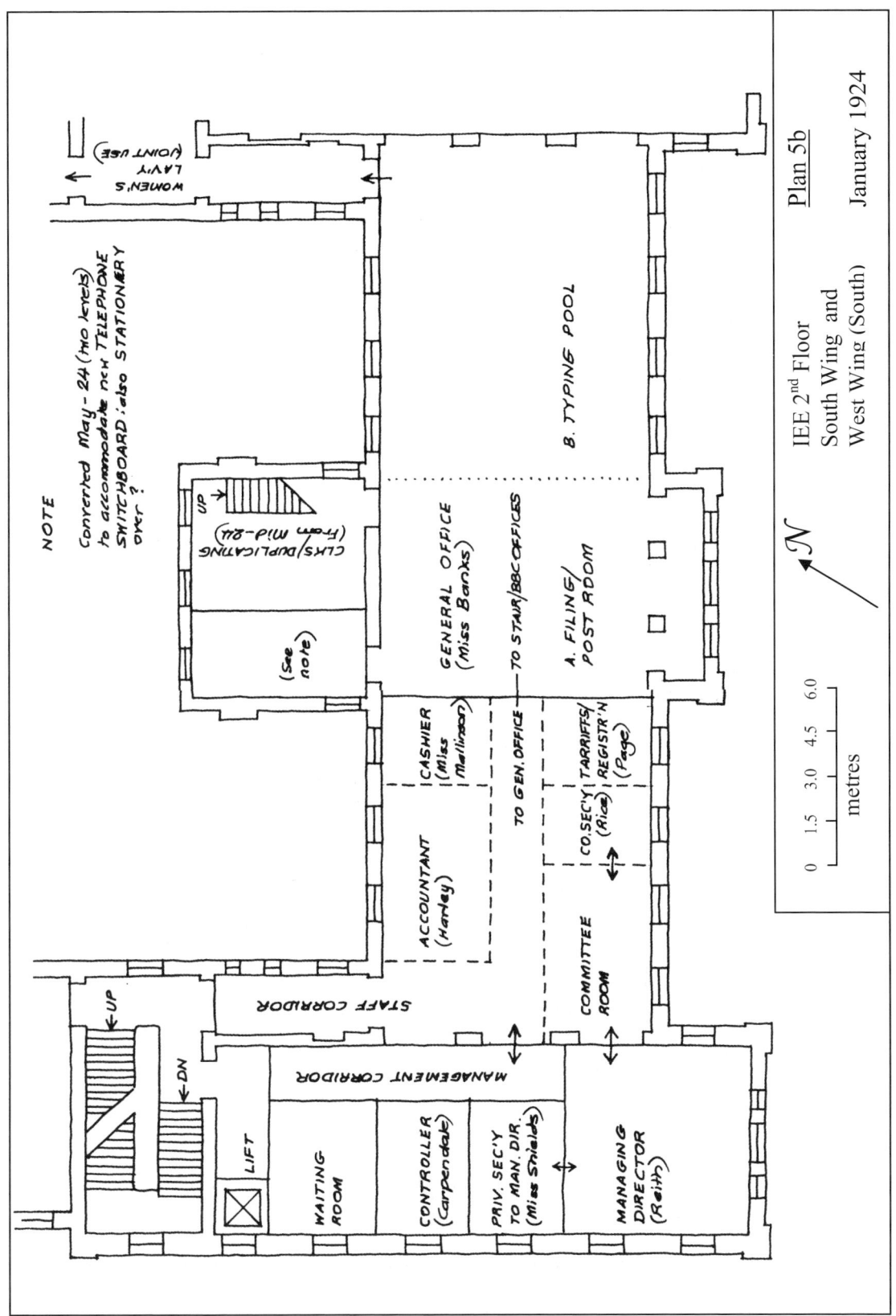

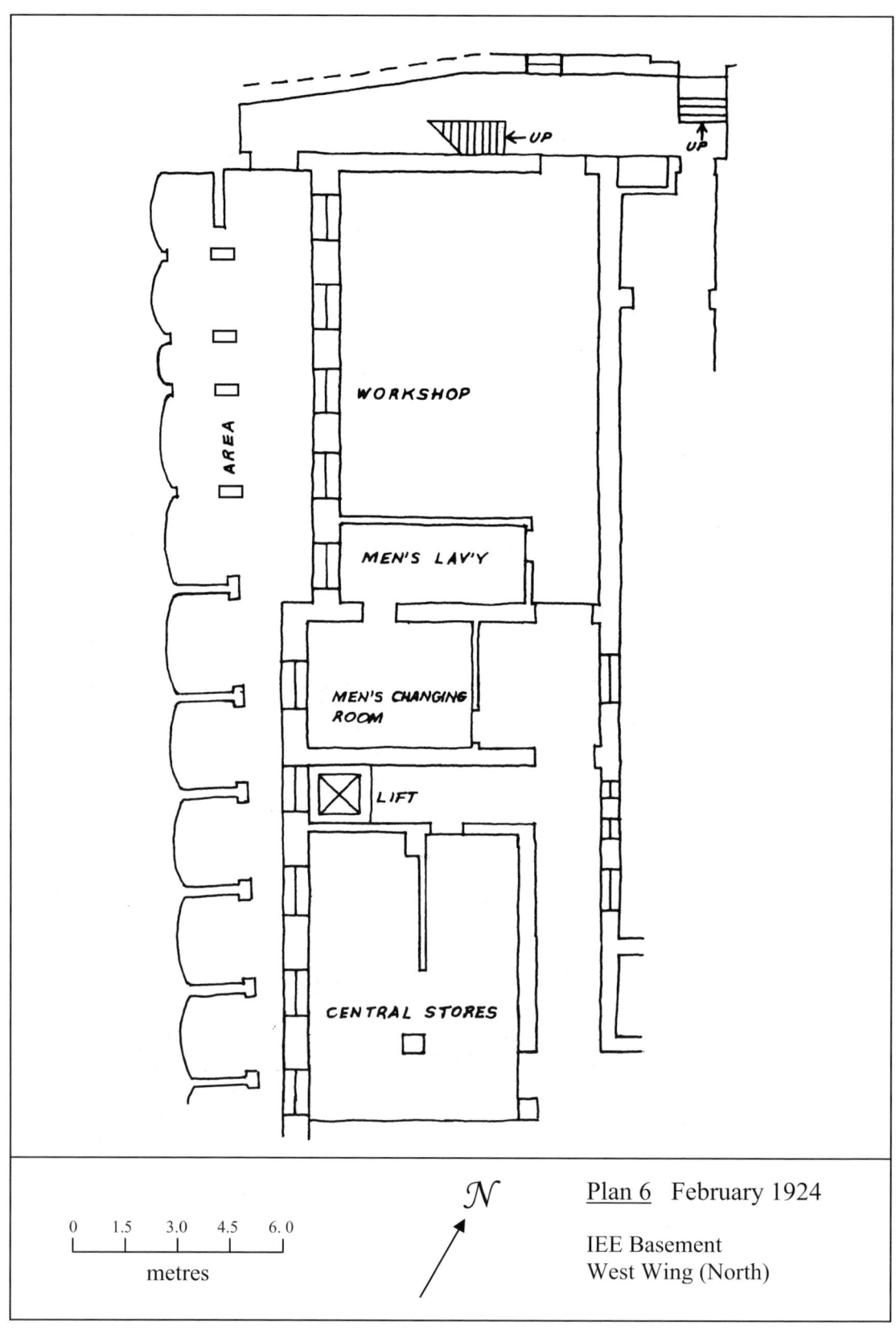

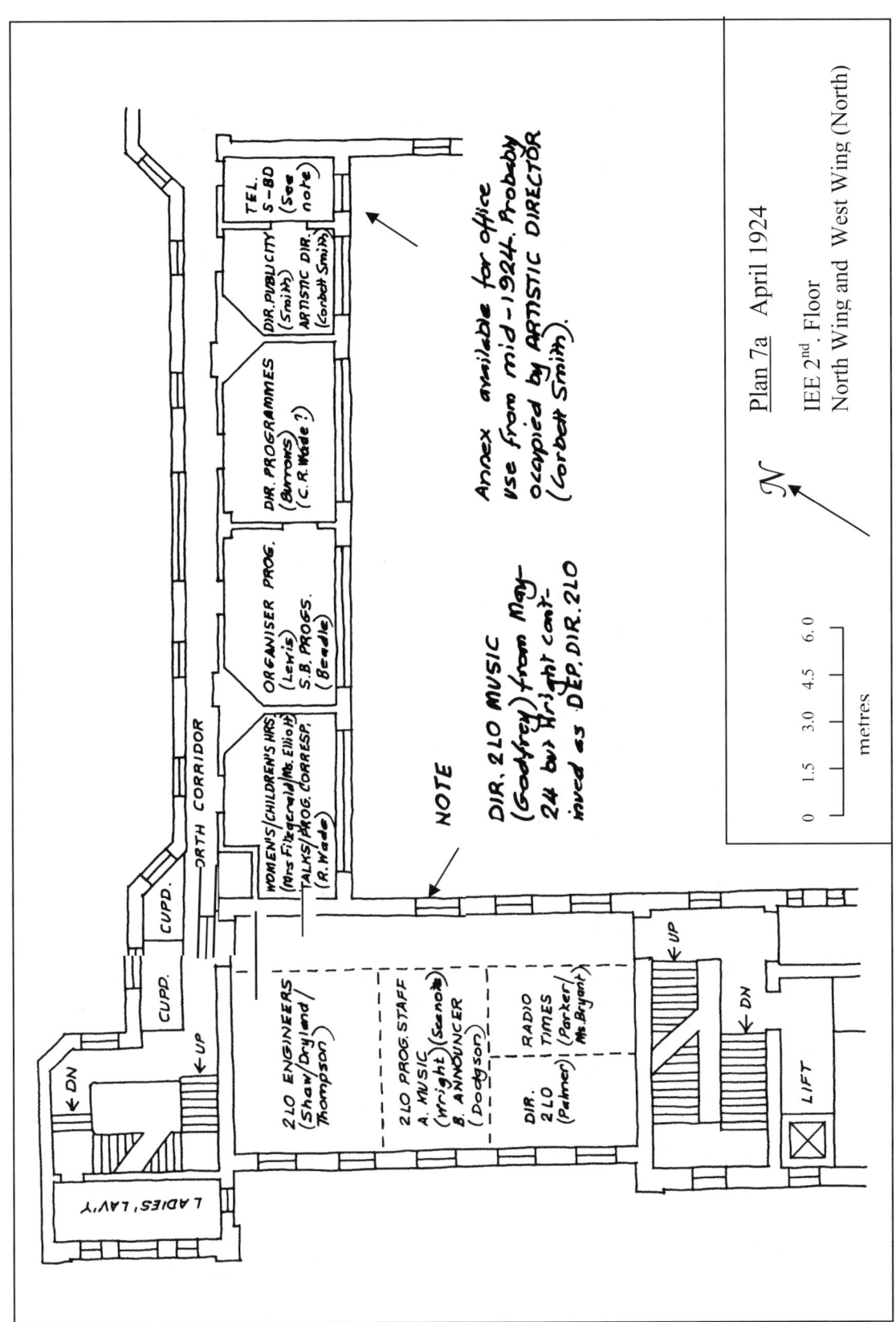

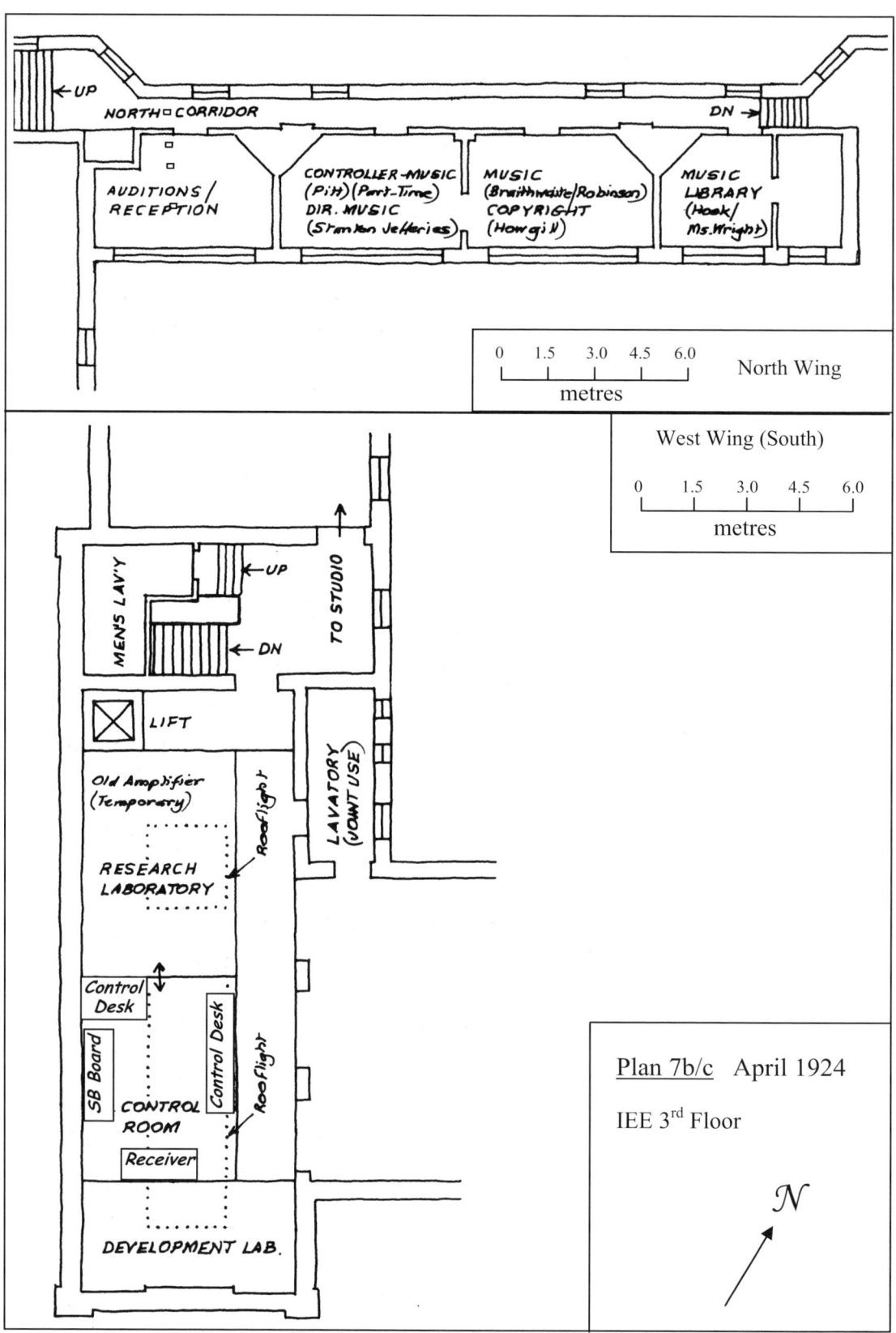

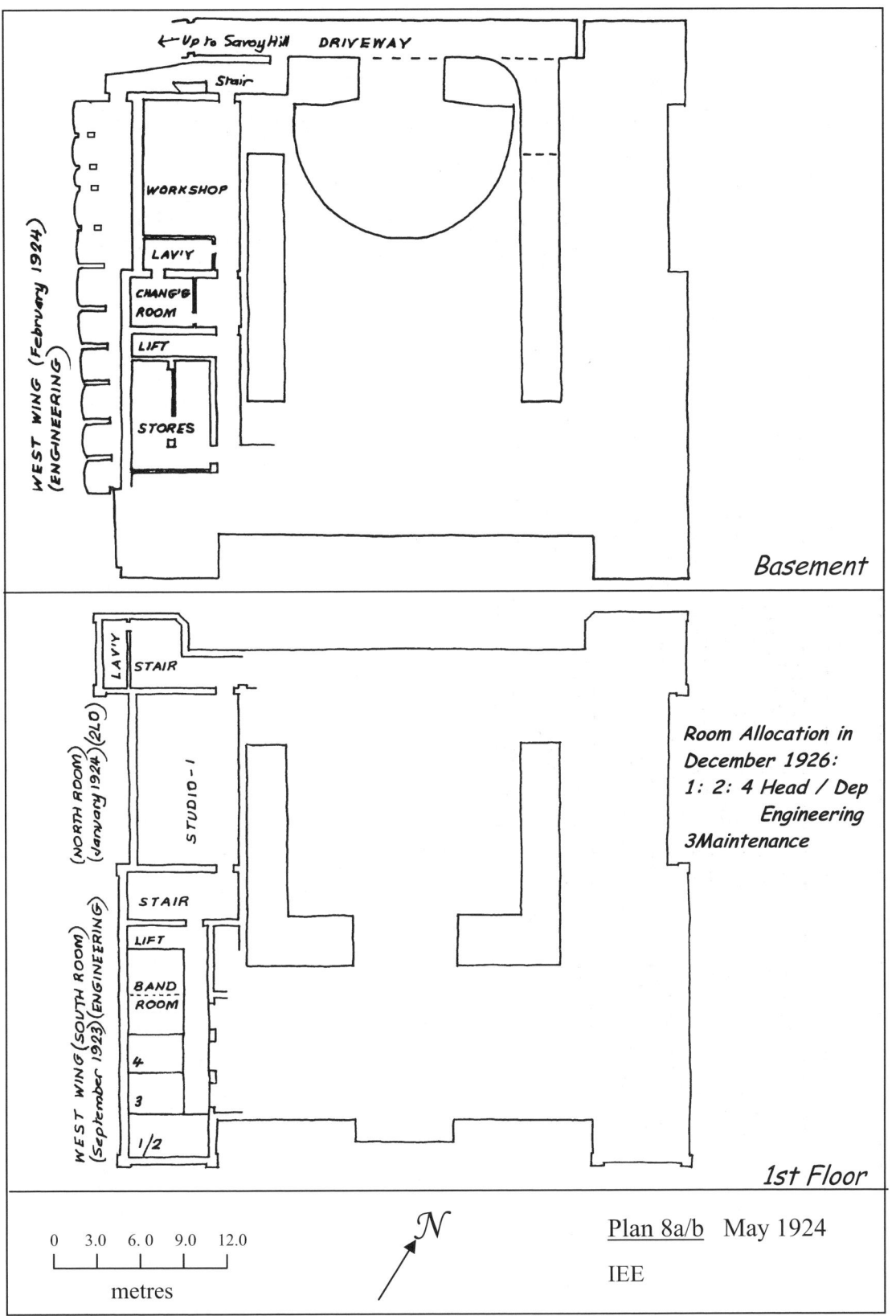

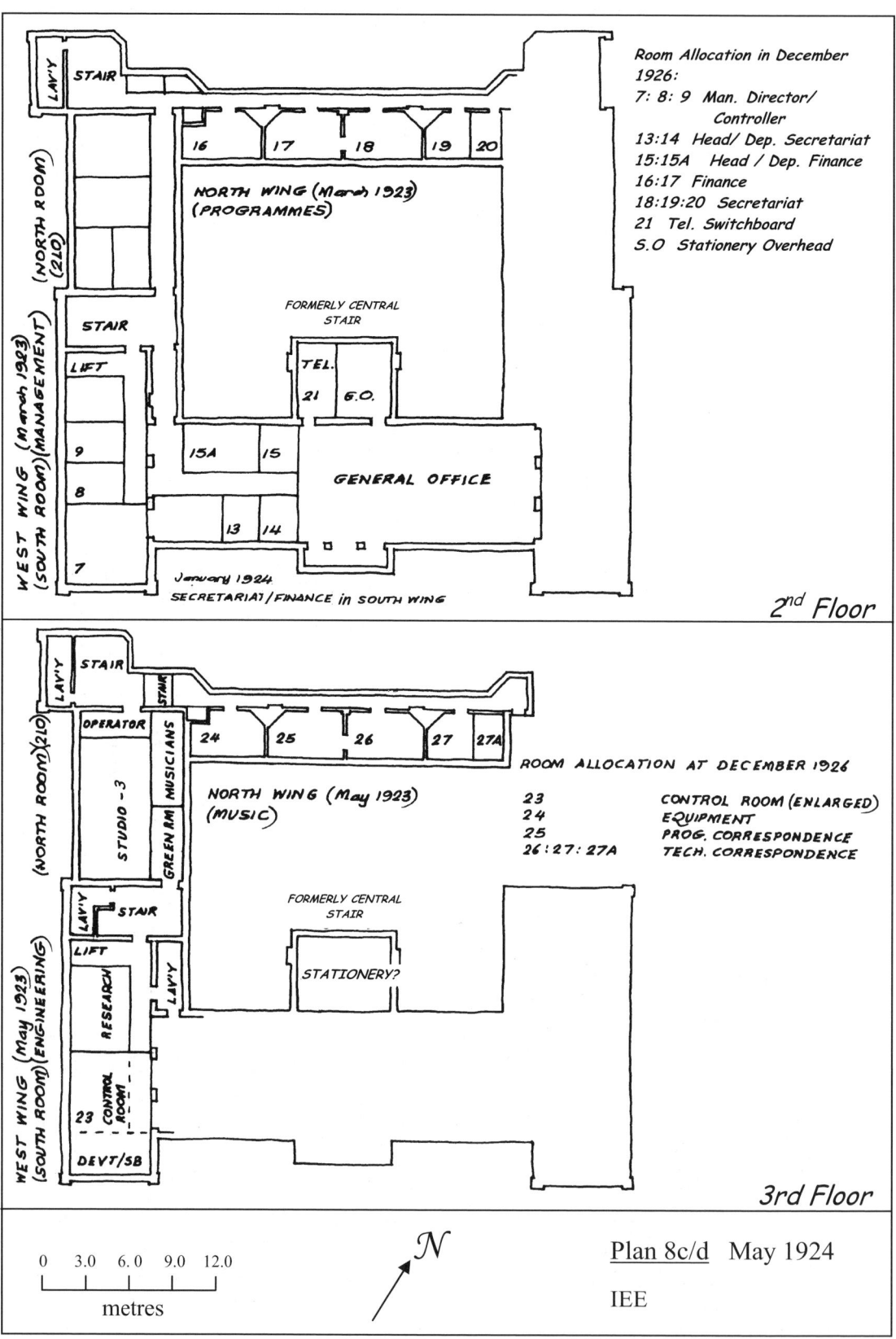

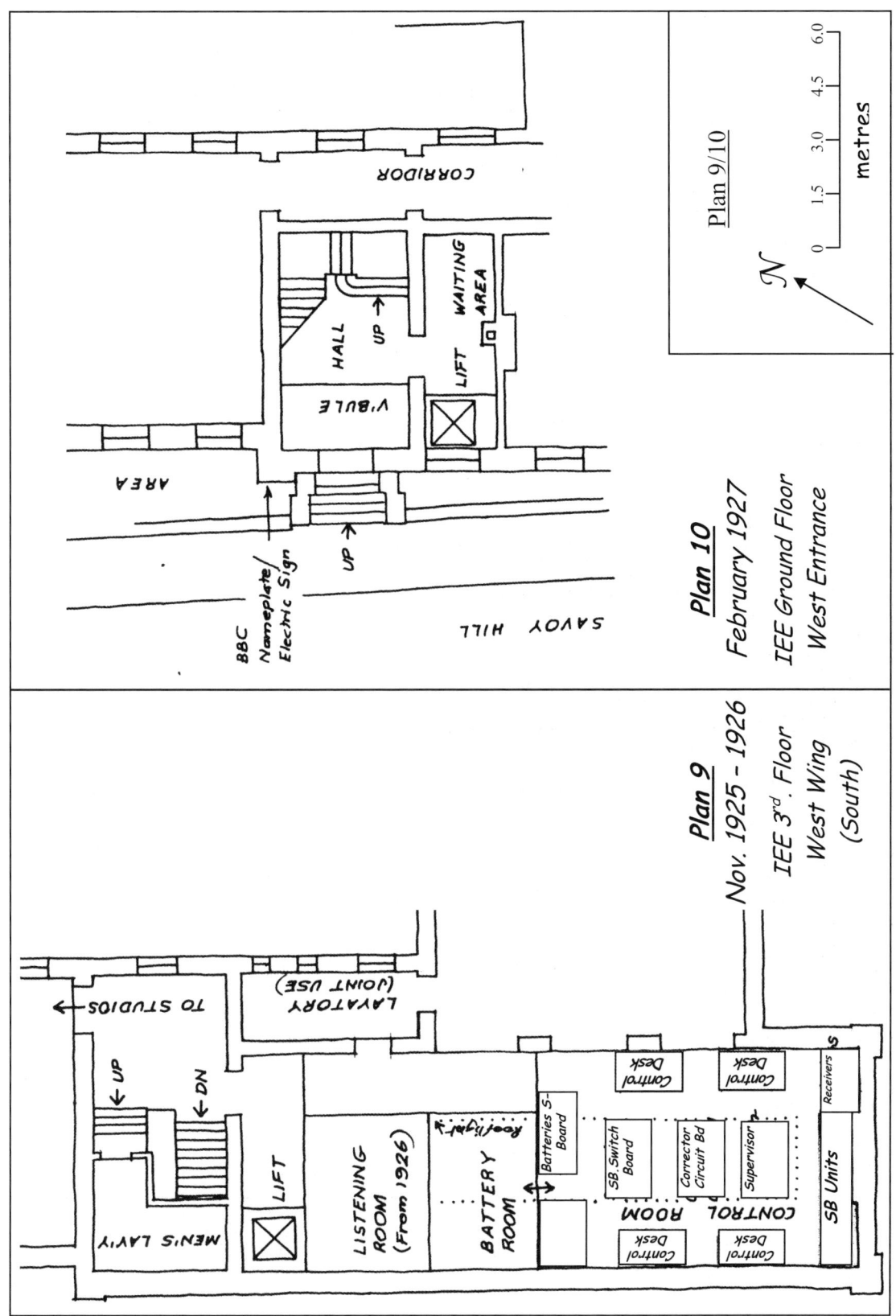

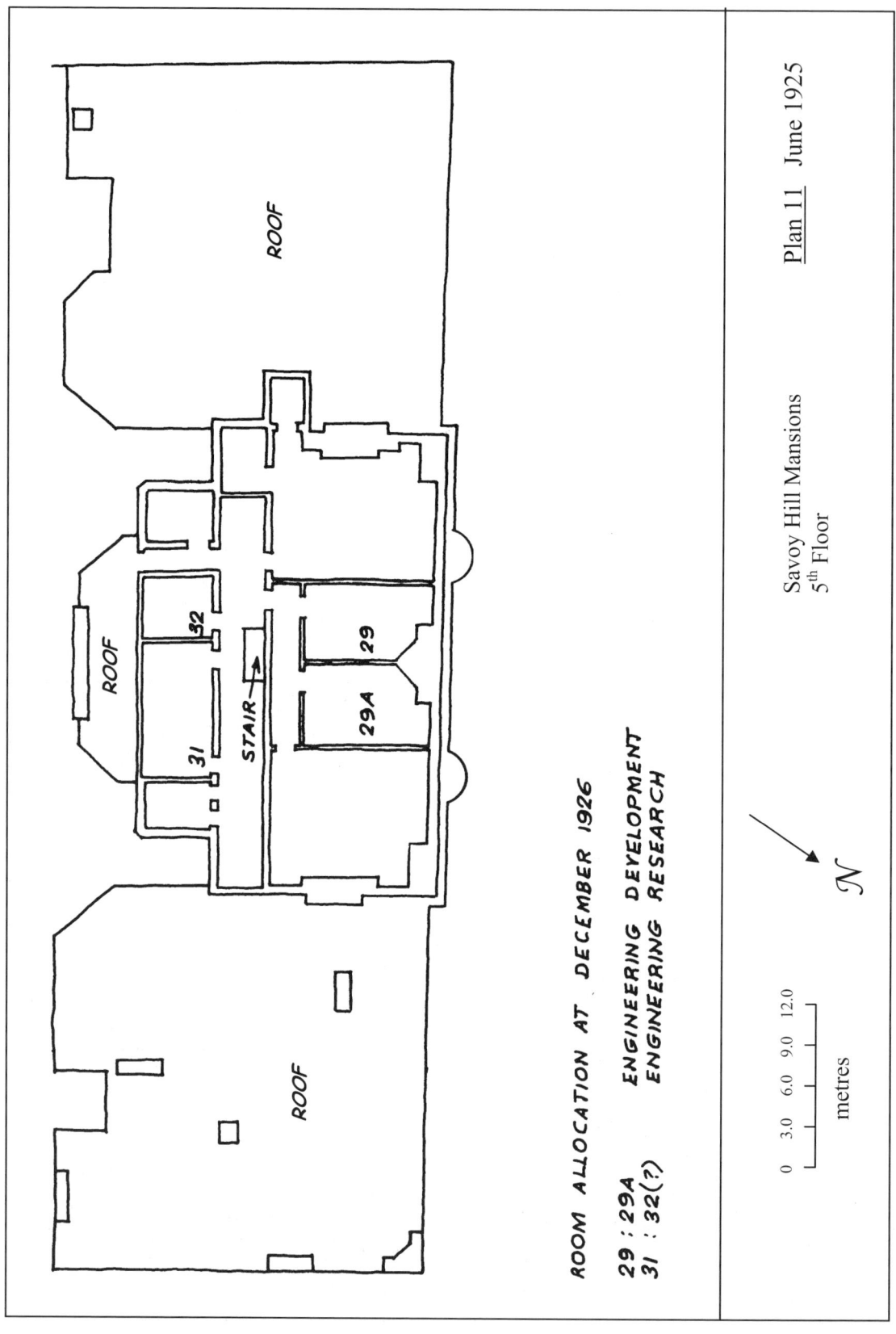

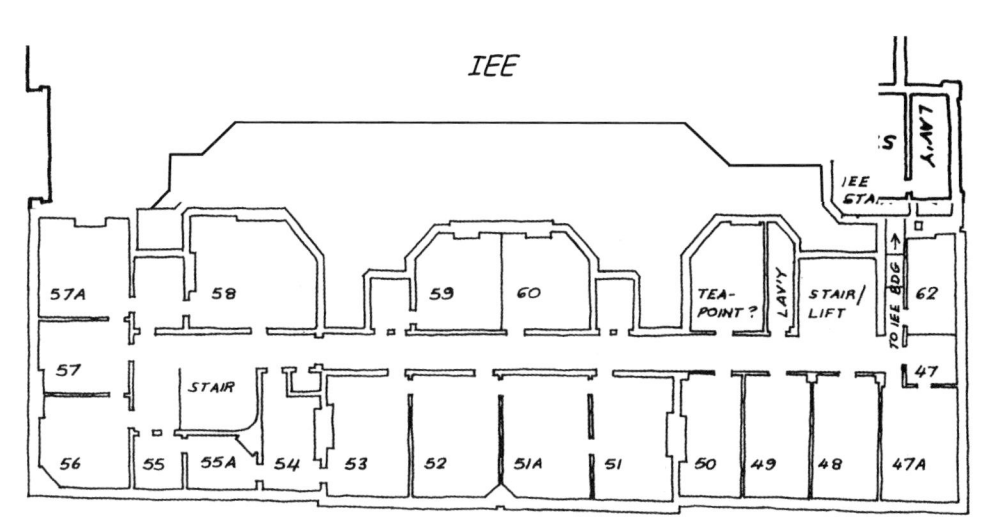

ROOM ALLOCATION AT DECEMBER 1926

Room	Allocation
47: 47A: 48	HEAD/DEP. PROGRAMMES
49	PROGRAMMES EXECUTIVE
51: 51A: 52	TALKS/LOCAL NEWS/EDUCATION
53: 54	2LO
55: 55A	OUTSIDE BROADCASTS – 2LO
56: 57: 57A: 58	MUSIC/CH. ANNOUNCER
59	CHILDREN'S HOUR
60	S.B./ANNOUNCER – 2LO
62	CONTROL ROOM ENGINEERS

3rd Floor

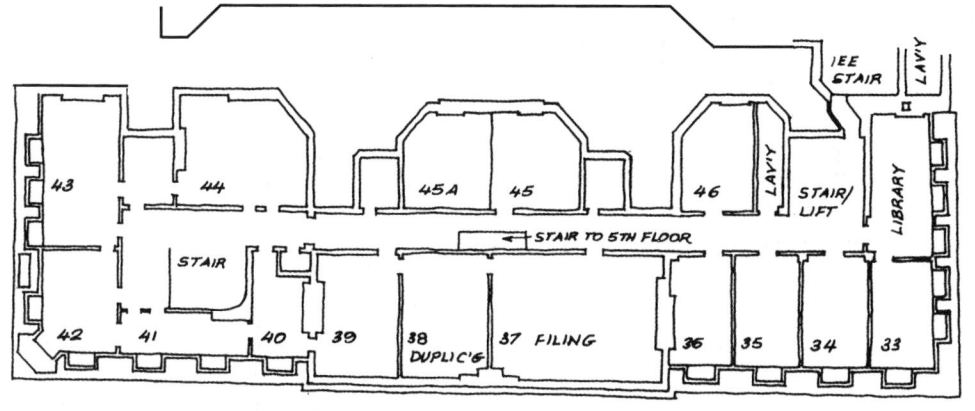

ROOM ALLOCATION AT DECEMBER 1926

Room	Allocation
33: 45	LIBRARY/PHOTO LIBRARY
34: 35	HEAD/DEP. INFORMATION
36	PRESS
37: 38	REGISTRY
39: 46	PUBLICATIONS
40: 44	INTERNATIONAL/'WORLD RADIO'
41: 42: 43	RADIO TIMES

4th Floor

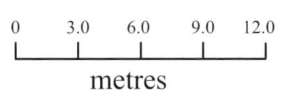
metres

N

Plan 12   June/September 1925

Savoy Hill Mansions

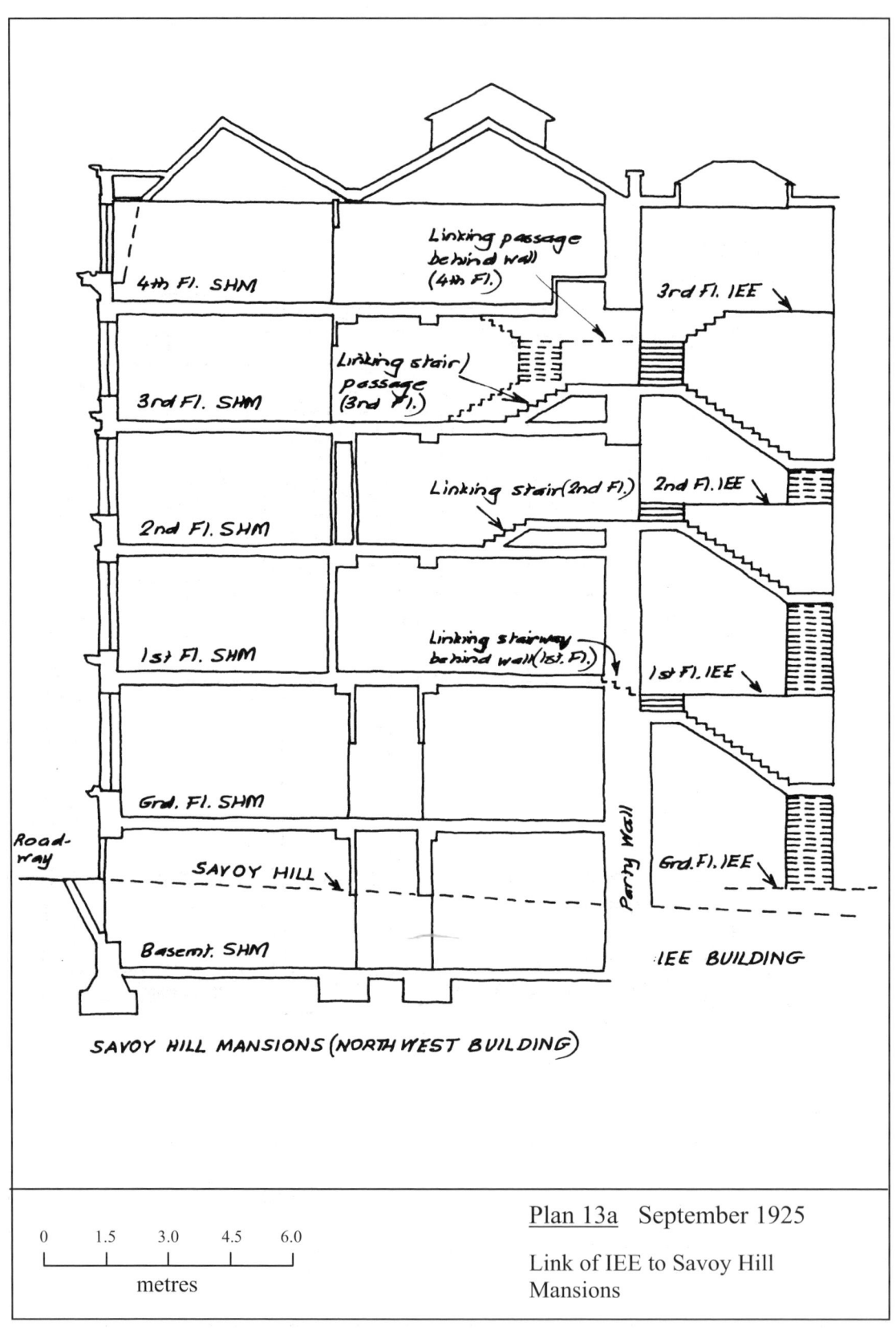

Plan 13a September 1925

Link of IEE to Savoy Hill Mansions

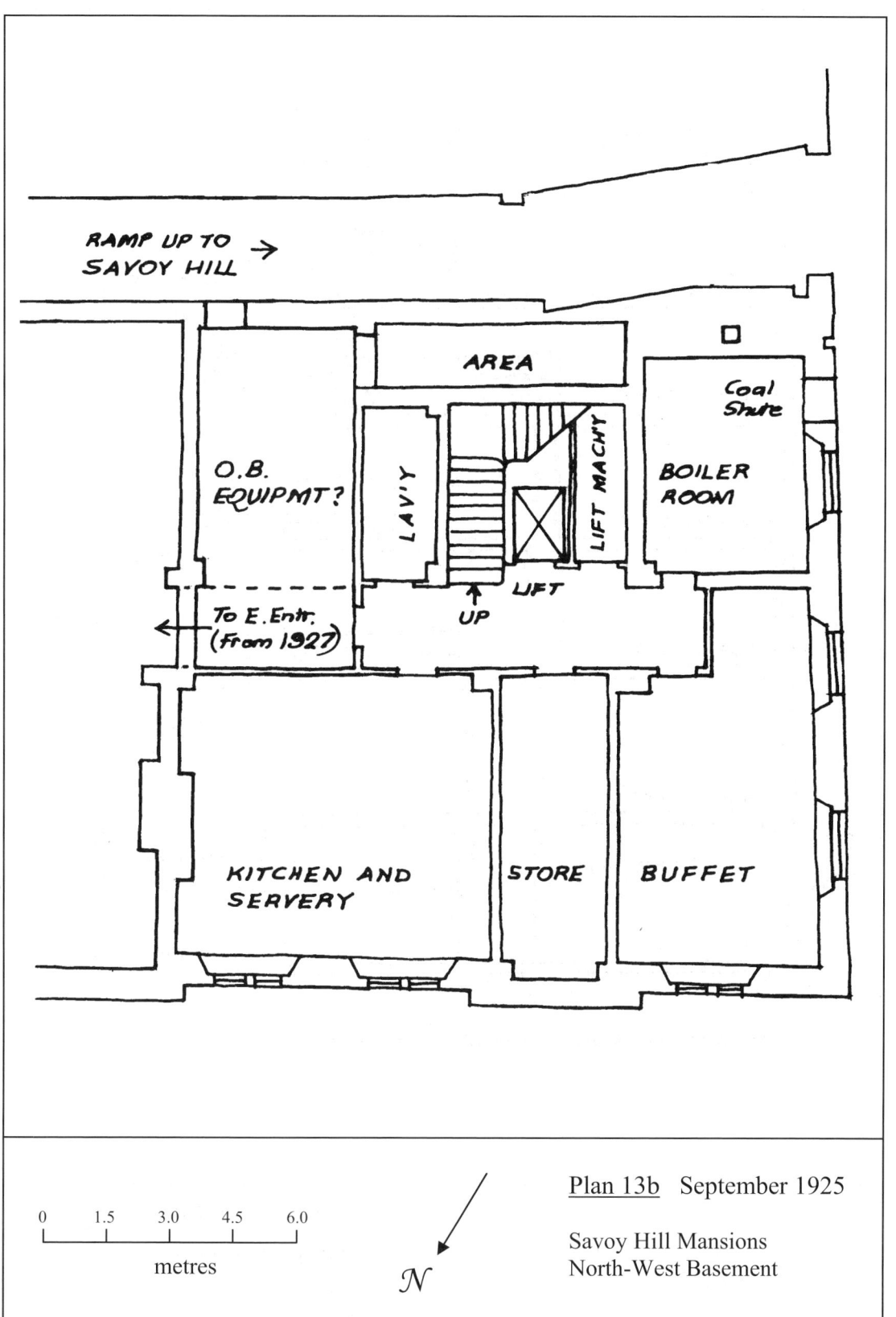

Plan 13b   September 1925

Savoy Hill Mansions
North-West Basement

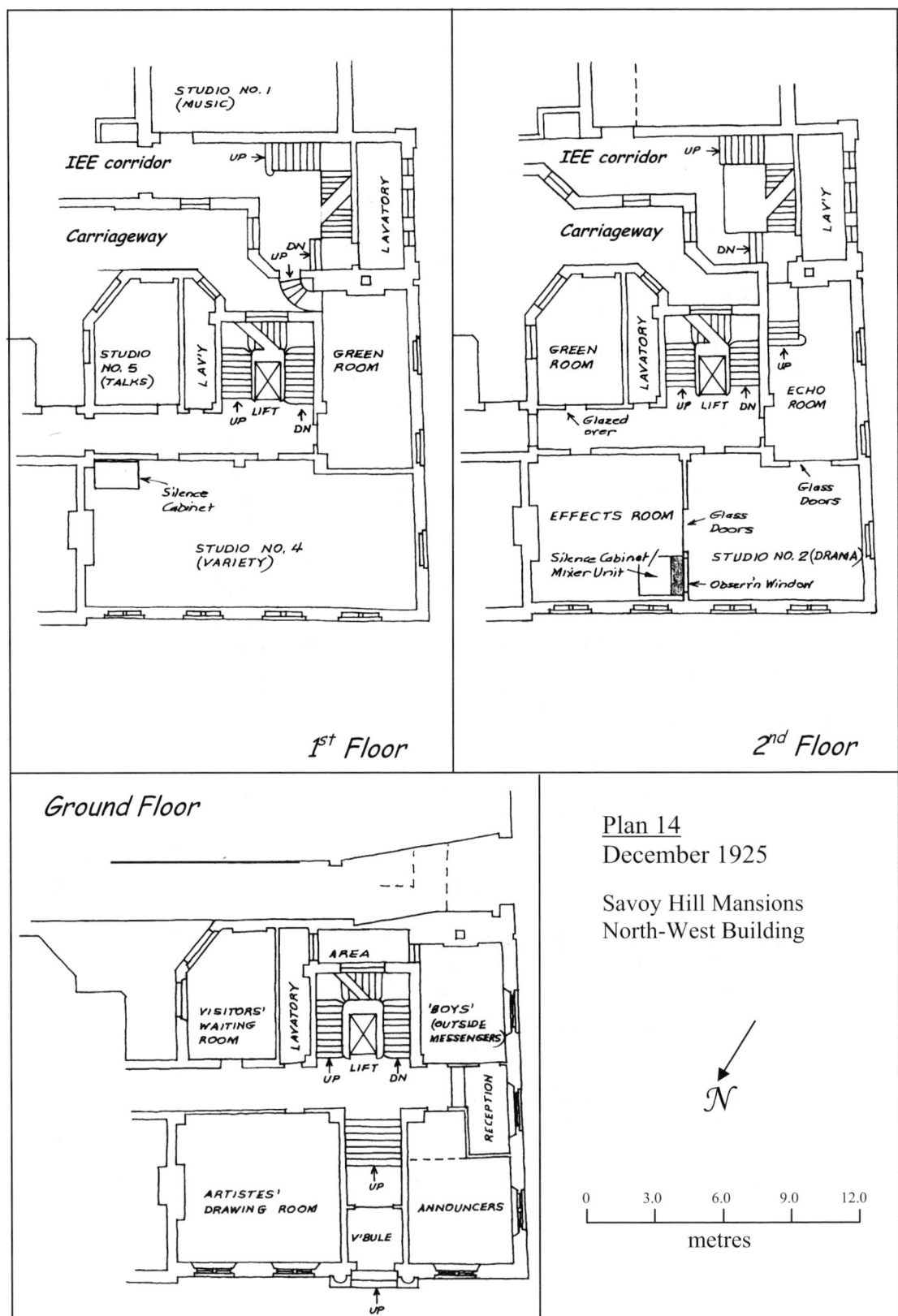

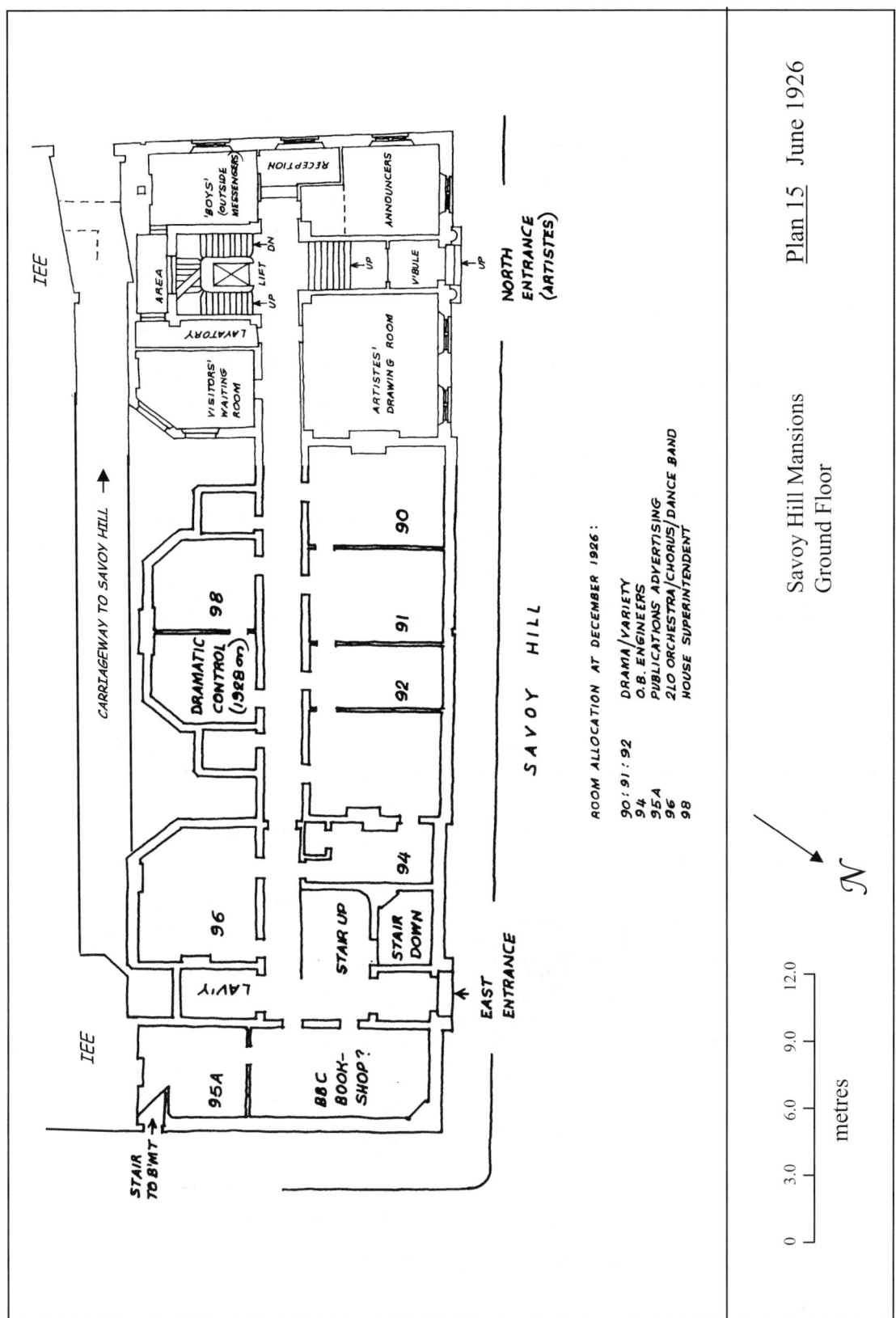

Plan 15 June 1926

Savoy Hill Mansions
Ground Floor

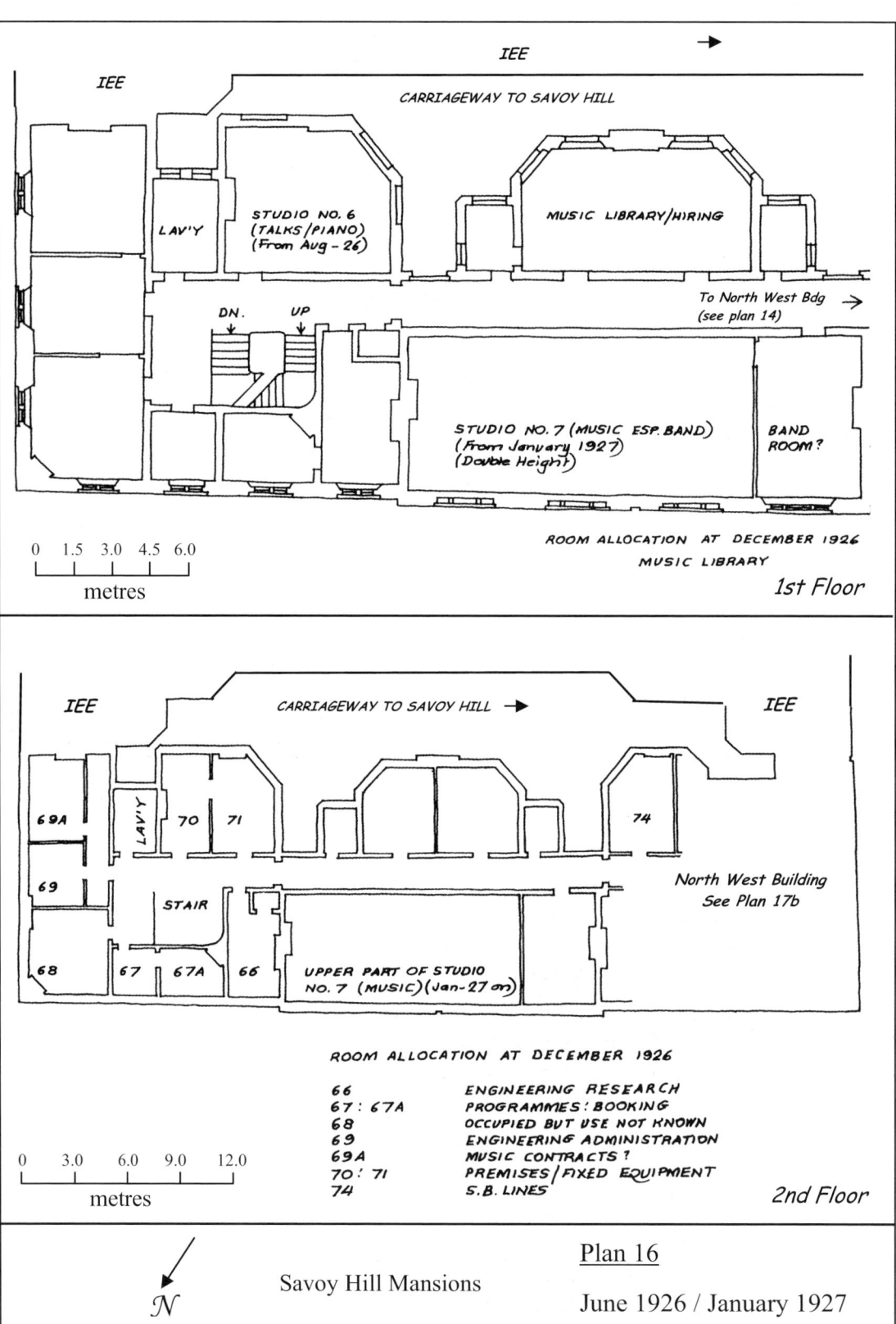

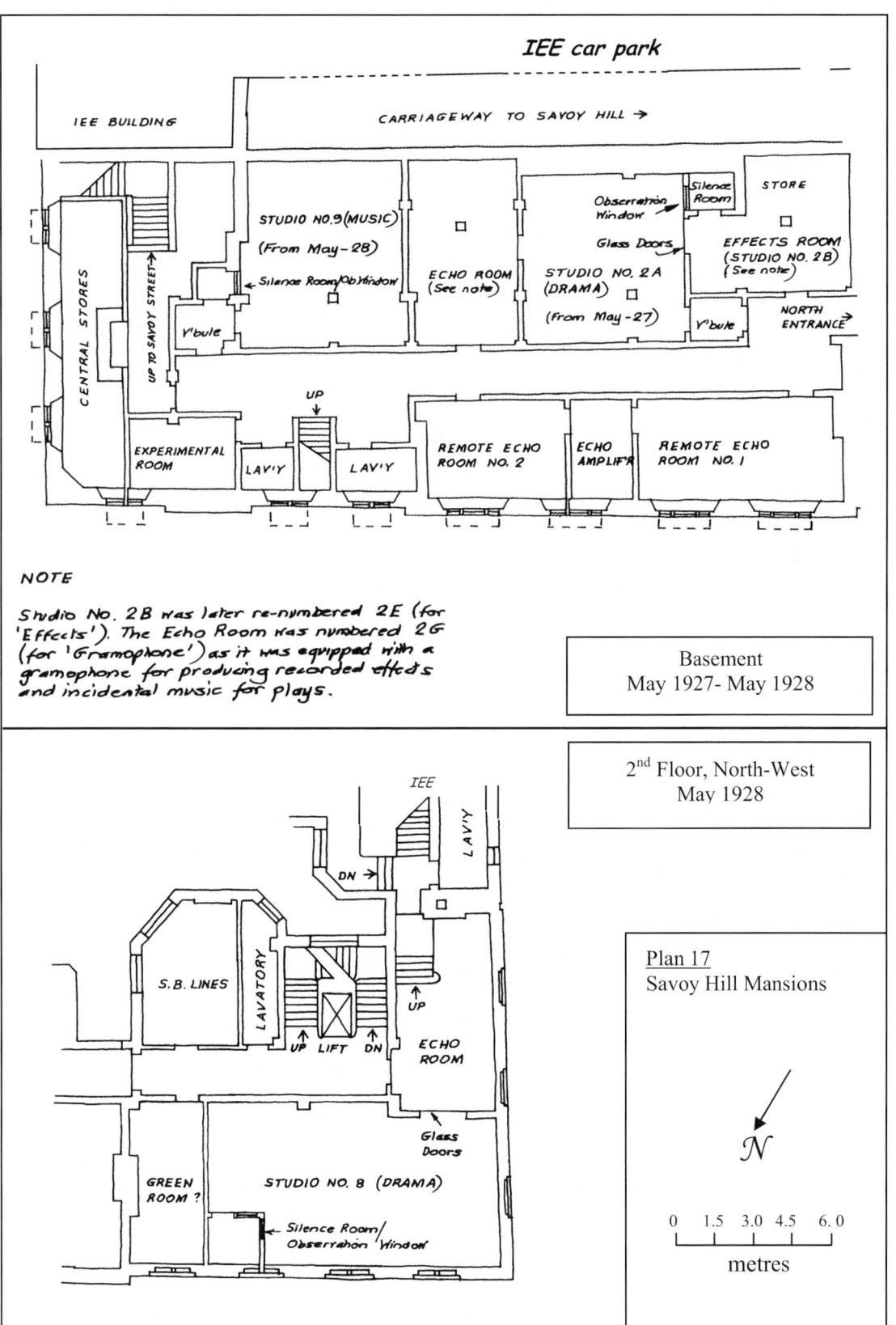

BIBLIOGRAPHY & SOURCES

Bibliography

2WP / 5IT: Midland Broadcasting News, November 1947, BBC.

50 Years of Broadcasting (Recordings), BBC, 1972.

A Historic Event: Souvenir of Prince of Wales' Broadcast to the Scout Movement, Marconi Wireless Telegraph Co., 7 October 1922.

All-British Wireless Exhibition and Convention: Programme of Concerts relayed from 2LO, RSGB Archives, BBC Archives, September 1922.

Allingham, Garry, *Sir John Reith,* Stanley Paul 1938.

Appleyard, R, *History of the Institution of Electrical Engineers,* IEE, 1939.

Appleyard, R, *How Broadcasting reached the Midlands,* Western Electric Co. (Standard Telephones and Cables Archives) 1924.

Art and Technique of Broadcasting, Marconi Wireless Telegraph Company, 1924.

Atkinson, Frank R, *GEC London HQ,* Architects Journal, 4 January 1922, (RIBA).

Baily, Leslie, *BBC Scrapbooks,* vol. 2, 1918-1939, George Unwin Alan and Unwin 1968

Baily, L and Brewer, C, *Scrapbook for 1920 (*BBC Sound Archives).

Baily, L and Brewer, C. *Scrapbook for 1921 (*BBC Sound Archives: Broadcast 12 February 1935)

Baily, L and Brewer, C. *Scrapbook for 1922 (*BBC Sound Archives: Broadcast 21 January 1937).

Baily, L and Brewer, C. *Scrapbook for 1924 (*BBC Sound Archives: Broadcast 27 May 1936).

Baily, L and Brewer, C, *The BBC Scrapbooks,* Hutchinson 1937.

Baker, W J, *H J Round: The Unrecognised Pioneer,* Electronics Weekly, 16,25 May 1966.

Barwell, E H G, *Death Ray Man: Life of Wireless Pioneer Grindell Matthews,* Hutchinson, 1946.

Beadle, Gerald, *Television: A critical review,* Allen & Unwin, 1963.

Binyon, Major Basil, *Papers (*BBC Archives).

Bishop, Harold, *Thirteen Years of Technical Progress,* World Radio, 15 November 1935.

Blake, G G, *History of Radio Telegraphy and Telephony,* 1926.

Boyle A, *Only the Wind Will Listen: Reith of the BBC,* Hutchinson, 1972.

Braillard, Raymond, *World Radio,* 30 March 1934.

Briggs Asa, *History of Broadcasting in the United Kingdom.*
- *Volume I: The Birth of Broadcasting,* Oxford University Press, 1961.
- *Volume II: The Golden Age of Wireless,* Oxford University Press, 1965

Briggs, Susan, *Those Radio Times,* Weidenfeld & Nicholson, 1981.

Broadcasting Committee Minutes (BBC Archives).

Broadcasting Committee's Advertisement, Morning Post, 13 October 1922, British Library.

Bull, Sir William, *Papers* (BBC Archives).

Burrows, Arthur R, *The Story of Broadcasting,* Cassell, 1924.

Burrows, Arthur R, *Looking Backwards: 10 years,* Article in World Radio, 13 June 1930.

Burrows, Arthur R to Stanton Jefferies, L, *Experimental and Pioneer Broadcasting* (BBC Archives).

Burrows, Arthur R, *Demonstration Lecture, London Rotarian,* 6 September 1922.

Burrows, Arthur R, *Letter to Reith,* 8 May 1937, BBC Archive.

Burrows, Arthur R, *Mysterious Voices in the Ether, Morning Standard,* December 1912.

Burrows, Arthur R, *Reflections at a Milestone,* World Radio, 11 November 1932.

Burrows, Arthur R, *The Peaceful Years: Arthur Burrows speaking into microphone,* Howard Thomas, Pathé Film, 1948 (British Film Institute).

Bussey, Gordon, *Wireless: The Crucial Decade,* History of the British Wireless Industry 1924 to 1934, IEE, 1990 (IEE library).

Cain, John, *BBC-70 Years of Broadcasting,* 17 September 1992 (British Library).

Call signs allocated, 1918 (Post Office Archives).

Caudrey, Jean, *Round's Diary* (British Vintage Wireless Society).

Chamier, J Daniel, *Percy Pitt of Covent Garden and the BBC,* Edward Arnold, 1938.

Clarke, D H, *The Old BBC,* BBC Yearbook 1930.

Clarke, Tom, *My Northcliffe Diary,* New York NY. Cosmopolitan Book Corp. 1931.

Clarricoats, John, *The World at the Fingertips,* (Video), RSGB, 1967.

Coase, R H, *British Broadcasting: A Study in Monopoly,* Longmans, 1950 (British Library).

Communication with the aeroplanes by means of public telephone service, 1920 (Post Office Archives).

Corbett-Smith, *My Year in Radio,* 1924,1925 (British Library).
Daily News, 24 March 1920.
Daily Programme Sheets, 14 November 1922, BBC Archives.
de Forest system, 1904 (Post Office Archives).
Demonstration Broadcasts by 2LO, 1 July 1922 to 21 December 1922, BBC Archives, Marconi Archives.
Development of Broadcasting at the Temporary Manchester Stations: Metropolitan-Vickers Electrical Co. A.E.I. (Manchester) Archives.
Dinwiddie, Melville, *The Scot and his Radio,* BBC, 1948.
Donaldson, Frances, *Anatomy of a Merger,* 1982 (British Library).
Donisthorpe, H de A, *Wireless at Home,* Percival Marshall and Co.
Dowsett, H M, *Wireless Telephony and Broadcasting,* (2 Volumes), Gresham Publishing, 1924.
Driver, David, *The Art of the Radio Times,* BBC, 1981.
Early Days of Radio, BBC Script, 1 August 1988.
Early Wireless Telephony, Wireless World, 27 April, 11 May 1932 (IEE Archives).
Eccles, *Wireless Telegraphy and Telephony,* 1918 (IEE Archives).
Eckersley, P P, *Lectures (*Sound Recordings).
Eckersley, P P, *List of records sent to Writtle,* BBC.
Eckersley, P P, *My Radio Career,* Popular Wireless, 13 June 1929.
Eckersley, P P, *The Early Days of Broadcasting,* Lecture to BBC Engineering Society, 16 February 1960 (GEC-Marconi Archives).
Eckersley, P P, *The Power behind the Microphone,* Cape 1941.
Eckersley, R., *BBC and All That,* Sampson Low, Marston, 1946.
Edgar, Percy, *Radio Times*, 10 September 1937
Edwards, Norman, *Broadcasting for Everyone,* Herbert Jenkins, November 1924.
Experimental Licences, 1912 (Post Office Archives).
Experimental licences. Conditions of issue. Fees reduced for Post Office servants, 1913 (Post Office Archives).
Experimental wireless stations suppressed during war. Custody of apparatus. 1916 (Post Office Archives).
Experiments by Marconi's Wireless Telegraph Company, 1920 (Post Office Archives).
Fortescue, C L *Wireless Telegraphy*, Cambridge University Press, 1913.
Gainford Papers, 22 August 1922 (Nuffield College, Oxford).
Geddes, Keith and Bussey, Gordon, *The Setmakers: A History of the Radio and Television Industry,* BREMA, 1991.

Geddes, Keith, *Broadcasting in Britain,* HMSO, 1972.
Gielgud Val, *British Radio Drama, 1922 to 1956,* Harrap, 1957.
Goatman, W, *By-ways of the BBC,* P S King & Son 1938.
Goldsmith, Alfred N, *Radio Telephony,* The Wireless Press Inc, USA.
Gorham, Maurice, *Sound and Fury,* Percival Marshall, 1948.
Grevatt, Wallace, *BBC Children's Hour,* Lewes; The Book Guild 1988.
Grindell Matthews Wireless Patent Syndicate Limited. Compensation claim for loss and damage due to stations being closed during war, 1915 (Post Office Archives).
Grindell Matthews-Ditcham Wireless Station, Letchworth Garden City Museum.
Grisewood, Freddie, *The World Goes By,* Martin Secker & Warburg, 1953.
Grisewood, Harmen, *One Thing at a Time,* 1968 (British Library).
Hadow, Sir Henry, *preface to* New Ventures in broadcasting, BBC 1928.
Hanker, Pat, *PCGG,* Electronics and Wireless World, February 1986.
Harrison, Beatrice, *The cello and the nightingales : the autobiography of Beatrice Harrison* ed. Patricia Cleveland-Peck, Murray, 1985.
Hartley, Ian, *Goodnight Children Everywhere,* Midas Books, 1983.
Hartley, Ian, *Origin of the Children's Corner,* Metropolitan-Vickers Archives, 1932.
He climbed our mast, Essex Chronicle, 14 April 1944.
Hibbard, Stuart, *Programmes recalling early days: '2LO Calling',* May/June 1942.
Hibberd, Stuart, *This - is London,* Macdonald & Evans, 1950.
Hill, Jonathan, *Radio! Radio!* 1986.
*IEE Building Coloured plans (*IEE Archives).
*It's on Record-Marconi 193*3 (BBC Library) (GEC-Marconi Archives).
Jessop, G R, *The Bright Sparks of Wireless,* RSGB, 1990.
Kavanagh, Ted, *Tommy Handley,* Hodder & Stoughton, 1949.
Kenyon, Nicholas, *The BBC Symphony Orchestra 1930 – 1980,* BBC, 1981.
Lambert, Richard S., *Ariel and all his Quality: an impression of the BBC from within,* Victor Gollancz, 1940.
Lazell, David, *What's on the wireless?* Evergreen, 1989.
Lea, Gordon, *Radio Drama and how to write it,* 1926 (British Library).
Lewis, Cecil, *Broadcasting from Within,* Newnes, 1924.
Lewis, Cecil, *Never Look Back,* Hutchinson, 1974.
Lewis, Cecil, *Sagittarius Rising,* Macmillan, 1936.
*Licence and Agreement (*BBC Archives).
Licences. Inter-Departmental Committee 1919, 1919 (Post Office Archives).

List of wireless telegraph stations opened or proposed for commercial, government or experimental purpose, 1907 (Post Office Archives).
Listening-In Articles, Daily News, 22 March / 21 April / 6 May / 30 May / 14 June 1922.
MacLarty, *Marconi, 2MT Writtle,* Wireless World, January 1963 (IEE Archives).
Manchester Station - 2ZY: Letter of 1922, AEI News, February 1948.
Marconi Invoices, 16 July, 13 October, 9 November, 17 November, 3 December (BBC Archives).
Marconi's Wireless Telegraph Co., experimental stations. Applications for permission to transmit, 1920-1931 (Post Office Archives).
Maschwitz, Eric, *No Chip on my Shoulder,* Herbert Jenkins, 1957.
McIntyre, Ian, *The Expense of Glory: a Life of John Reith,* Harper Collins, 1993.
Memorandum and Articles of Association (BBC Archives).
Minutes of the Broadcasting Committee / BBC Council and Committees, 1922/1923, BBC Archives.
Moore, S, *The Box on the Dresser,* Media, Culture and Society, Vol 10 No 1, 1988, (British Library).
*Move to Savoy Hill (*BBC Archives).
Northampton Chronicle, 1913 (Colindale Newspaper Library).
Northampton Herald, 29 August 1913 (Colindale Newspaper Library).
Northampton Independent, 8 March 1913 (Colindale Newspaper Library).
Palmer, Cecil, *'Hullo Boys!' The Wireless Uncles Annual,* November 1924.
Palmer, Cecil, *'Hullo Girls!' The Wireless Aunties Annual,* November 1924.
Patton, J S P, *Manchester Station at Trafford Park* (Metrovick Archives).
Pawley, E, *BBC Engineering 1922 – 1972 ,*BBC, 1972.
Payne, Jack, *This is Jack Payne,* Sampson Low, Marston 1932.
Pedrick, Gale, *These Radio Times,* 29 September 1951, 18 April 1952, 29 September 1953, 19 September 1954, 3 July 1955, 9 September 1956.
Photos of Magnet House, The Electrician, 29 December 1922 (IEE Archives)
Plans of Buildings Owned and Leased, BBC Archives.
Plans of Premises of BBC, BBC.
Poulsen arc system. Trials and reports, 1907 – 1913 (Post Office Archives).
Prince, C E, *Lecture as President of FHOSA,* Faraday House Journal, vol XIV, No 5, 1932.
Programme Details including Start of Children's Hour, Liverpool Daily Courier, 15 November 1922 to end 1922.
Proposed use for Press messages, 1920 (Post Office Archives).

Radio and Radiance: Testing of microphone prior to broadcast, 2LO Savoy Hill Film, 1925,1926 (British Film Institute).
Radio Society of Great Britain. Regulations for issue of licences, etc. 1913 (Post Office Archives).
Reith, J C W, *Article,* Wireless Magazine, February 1927 (British Library).
Reith, J C W, *Into the Wind,* Hodder and Stoughton, 1949.
Reith, J C W, *Picture Post,* 25 July 1942.
Reith, J C W, *- Broadcast over Britain,* Hodder & Stoughton, 1924.
Reith, J C W, *The Reith Diaries,* (ed. Charles Stuart), Collins, 1975.
Review of 'Savoy Hill', 1966 (IEE Archives).
Ridge, Pett, *Little Tales,* Broadcast on 2LO, *Daily News,* September 1922.
Robertson, Patrick, *Shell Book of Firsts,* Elbury Press and Michael Joseph, 1974.
Rodger, Ian, *Radio Drama,* Macmillan, 1982.
Round, H J, *Marconi-Sykes Magnetophone with details of the Amplifiers,* Wireless World, 26 November 1924.
Round, H J, *Letter with Diagram,* 1958, (Marconi Archives).
Round, H J, *Speech to Radio Club of America,* 1959 (GEC-Marconi Archives).
Round, H J, *Broadcasting Reminiscences,* World Radio, 21 October 1932 and 19 November 1932.
Sandeman, E K, *The Development of Simultaneous Broadcasting,* Wireless World, 21 May 1924.
Savoy Hill with the Lid Off, a series of five articles, Radio Times, 6 April, 20 April, 4 May, 25 May, 15 June 1928
Scannell, Paddy and Cardiff, David, *A Social History of British Broadcasting: Vol 1,* Blackwell, 1991.
Scott-Taggart, J, *55 Years of Radio,* International Broadcast Engineer, July 1968.
Scrapbook for 1922, Pathé Reel 2 (Pathé Archives),1947.
Scrapbook for 1922: 'Wireless for All' headline, Pathé Film, 1947.
Scrapbook for 1922: Arthur Burrows at microphone, Pathé Film, 1947.
Scrapbook for 1922: Buses and traffic in the Strand Pathé Film, 1947.
Scrapbook for 1922: Car with wireless and loudspeaker driving through the streets, Pathé Film, 1947.
Scrapbook for 1922: Exterior of studio in the Strand, Pathé Film, 1947.
Scrapbook for 1922: Extract from 'The Bathing Butler', Pathé Film, 1947.
Scrapbook for 1922: Singers on the air, Pathé Film, 1947.
Scrapbook for 1922: Transmitter at Writtle, Pathé Film, 1947.
Scrapbook for 1922: Transmitter masts, Pathé Film, 1947.
Scrapbook for 1922: Transmitting equipment, Pathé Film, 1947.

Scrapbook for 1922: Wireless on donkey cart and people dancing to the music, Pathé Film, 1947.

Scrapbook for 1922: Lady with crystal set on her garter, Pathé Film, 1947.

Shaw, A C, *Early Days of Broadcasting,* World Radio, 11 November 1932, 15 November 1935.

Shaw, A C, *The Battery Room at 2LO,* Wireless World, 24 March 1926.

Sieveking, Lance, *The Stuff of Radio,* Cassell 1934.

Snagge, John and Barsley, Michael, *Those Vintage Years of Radio,* Pitman, 1972.

Souvenir of an historical achievement, the first wireless telephone news service, Feb/March 1920, Marconi Archives.

Stanton-Jefferies, L, *Soap Box,* Popular Wireless, 5, 12, 19 October 1935.

Sturmey, S G, *Economic Development of Radio,* Duckworth, 1958.

Swierstra, N Tj, *The Birth of Broadcasting,* EBU Review, March 1969, Nos. 114B, 116, 117 and 120.

The Citizen (Letchworth), 17 July 1912 (Colindale Newspaper Library).

The High Power Radiophone Transmitter at Marconi House: Man speaking into microphone and aerials on roof, Film, 1922.

The Magic Doorway: BBC Aunts and Uncles, Partridge, 1927 (British Library).

The Voice from 2LO, Pathé Film, 1923 (GEC-Marconi Archives).

The Voice from 2LO: Studio with Children's Hour in progress – uncles and aunt, Pathé Film, 1923.

Thompson, A E, *The Silver Jubilee of Broadcasting,* Standard News, June 1948.

*Tour with plans, camera, including Savoy Hill House (*IEE Archives).

Twenty-Five Years of British Broadcasting, BBC, 1947.

Wade, Ralph, *Early Life in the BBC,* Unpublished Manuscript, Author's Collection.

Wander, Tim, *2MT Writtle, The Birth of British Broadcasting,* Capella, 1988.

Wander, Tim, *Birth of Airborne Wireless,* Radio Bygones, April, May 1990 (British Library).

West, A G D, Shaw, A C, Attkins, A S, and Chilman, H L, *A Tour round Savoy Hill,* Wireless World, 9 February to 30 March 1927.

West, P E F A, *The First Five Years,* BBC Engineering No.92, October 1972.

Who's Who in Engineering, 1920 Annual (British Library).

Wireless Telephony: Broadcasting (Cards 1-20), Sunripe Cigarettes, 1923.

Witton Broadcasting Station, Birmingham: The Manager's Notebook, 15 November 1922 to 3 March 1923, BBC Archives.

Wolfe, Kenneth, *The Churches and the BBC: 1922 – 1956,* SCM Press, 1984.

Wood, Robert H, *A World in your Ear,* Macmillan, 1979.

Wright to Smythe, Ariel (BBC Staff Magazine), 8 February 1923.
Wright to Smythe, Ariel (BBC Staff Magazine), 14 December 1924.
Wynn, R T B, *2MT Writtle,* London Calling, 10 October 1946.
Wynn, R T B, *Memories of Writtle etc. (*Sound Recording, BBC Archives).

Specialist Magazines

Amateur Wireless and Electrics, 10 June 1922 onward, weekly, Cassell.
Amplion Magazine, July 1925 to June 1927 (British Library).
Amplion Radio Annual, 1927 – 1928 (British Library).
BBC Annuals 1935 to 1937.
BBC Handbooks, 1928 to 1929 1938 to 1942.
BBC Staff Magazines, Ariel, June 1936-June 1939, quarterly (BBC Archives).
BBC Staff Magazines, Savaloy, 1928-1930 (BBC Archives).
BBC Staff Magazines, The Heterodyne, January 1930 onward (BBC Archives).
BBC Yearbooks 1930 to 1934, 1943 to 1952.
British Vintage Wireless Society Bulletin.
Broadcast Listeners' Year Book, 1924, Radio Press (British Library).
Broadcast Listeners' Year Book, 1925, Radio Press (British Library).
Modern Wireless, February 1923 onward, monthly, Radio Press (British Library).
Popular Wireless, 3 June 1922 onwards, weekly, Amalgamated Press.
Radio Bygones, bi-monthly (British Library).
Radio Magazine 1934 onward, (British Library).
Radio Monthly, April 1924 onward.
Radio Pictorial 1934 onward, (British Library).
Radio Press Year Book, 1926 (British Library).
Radio Times, 28 September 1923 onward, weekly, Newnes.
Radio Year Book, Pitmans, 1923 (British Library).
Radio, April 1924 onward, monthly Journal (British Library).
Radio, June 1930-May 1934 (British Library).
Savoy Hill Veterans Association (BBC Archives).
Sounds Vintage, January 1979 onward, bi-monthly, Stevens, Norman and Riches, Colin (Eds).
The Broadcaster – The Radiophone Monthly for the Listener-in, August 1922 onward, monthly, Odhams (British Library).
The Radiogram, 21 March 1923 onward, British Library.
Wireless Annual for Amateurs and Experimenters, 1924, Wireless Press.
Wireless Review and Science Weekly, 29 May 1923 onward, Amalgamated Press.
Wireless Weekly, 11 April 1923 onward, weekly, Radio Press.
Wireless World and Radio Review, April 1913 onward, weekly, Wireless Press.
Year-book of Wireless Telegraphy and Telephony, 1913 onward, annually, Wireless Press, (IEE Archives).

Archive Collections

Amberley Chalk Pits Museum, Sussex
BBC Photographic Library and Archives, London
BBC Sound Library, London
BBC Written Archive Centre, Reading, Berkshire
British Pathé News, Bucks
British Vintage Wireless Society, London
Chelmsford and Essex Museum, Chelmsford
Colindale Newspaper Library, British Library, London
Gainford Papers, Oxford
GEC, London
Hulton-Deutsch Collection, London
Institution of Electrical Engineers, London
Marconi Archives at GEC, Chelmsford
Metropolitan-Vickers (Metrovick) Electrical Co., at GEC Alsthorn Engineering Systems Ltd, Manchester
National Film and Television Archive, British Film Institute, London
National Monuments Record, London
National Sound Archive, London
Post Office Archives, London
Radio Society of Great Britain
Science Museum Reference Library, London
The British Library Humanities and Social Sciences, London
The Scientific Reference Library and Information Service, London
Vintage Wireless Museum, London
Western Electric, at Standard Telephones and Cables Ltd, London

INDEX

Photos shown in bold

2BD Aberdeen 360, 380
2LO London 99, 240, 380
   Marconi House ....
      .... **105**, 104–25, 165–89
     accommodation 166, **167**
     acoustics 110
     aerial .... *See aerial*
     artistes 111, 119
     broadcasts **118**, **121**
       Christmas 1922 179–81
       daily 99, 162, 165
       music 173–75, 178–79, 241, 246–47
       news 175, 177
       religous 181
       time signal 172, 175, **176**
       weather 177
     building 104, 105, 106
     control room 171
     microphone .... *See microphone*
     site 104
     Station Director ... *See Jefferies, S*
     studio . **107**, 171–73, 186, 187–88
     test transmissions . 109–16, 119, 131, 134, 135, 150, 157
     transmitter .... *See transmitter*
   Savoy Hill ....
     .. **260**, 249–60, **263**, 283–91, **372**, **374**, **375**
     accommodation ... **258**, 252–59, 287–91, 353, 356–57, 359, 363, 371–73
     broadcasts
       drama and features .. 323–27
       music 304–10
       news 311
       religious broadcasts 313, 314
       schools 315
       sound effects 324, **325**
       talks 311–16
       weather 311
     building .. **252**, 249–52, 254–55
     control room **250**, **251**, 363, 373
     Musical Director .... *See Pitt, P*
     official opening 264–66
     Savoy Hill Mansions ....
       .... 357, **358**, 371–73, 379
     staffing .... *See Reith, J C W*
     studio . **262**, 261–68, **305**, **355**, 354–56, **366**, 365–67, **368**
2MT Writtle .. 40, 79, 81, **84**, 81–103, 241
   aerial 91
   Ashbridge, N .... *See Ashbridge, N*
   Bangay, R D .... *See Bangay, R D*
   Beeson, B .... *See Beeson, B*
   Bubb, F .... *See Bubb, F*
   building 86, **87**, 89, 102
   Eckersley, P P ..... *See Eckersley, P P*
   Kirke, H L .... *See Kirke, H L*
   MacLarty, B N .. *See MacLarty, B N*
   Melchior .... *See Melchior, L*
   microphone 91, **96**
   Nora Scott .... *See Scott, Nora*
   plan **89**
   Russell, H J .... *See Russell, H J*
   transmissions 81, **96**, 97, 91–100
   transmitting equipment .. 90, **91**, 96
   Trump, E H .... *See Trump, E H*
   Wynn, R .... *See Wynn, R T B*
2WP/5IT Witton Birmingham ..... 159, 205–14, *See also 5IT New Street Birminghm*
   accommodation 207–9
   aerial 209
   microphone 206
   Station Director .... *See Edgar, P*
   studio 208, 210, 214
   transmitter **213**, 214

2ZY Dickenson Street Manchester
.... 273–76, 309, 386
  Station Director .... See Godfrey, D
2ZY Trafford park Manchester
  aerial **195**
  studio...**199**
2ZY Trafford Park Manchester 145,
  149–50, 157, 159–62, 166, 190–
  204, 227, 309, 380, 384, 386
  aerial 193
  building 190
  microphone...................... 198–203
  Station Director ..... See Wright, K A
  studio........................**192**, **201**, 203
  transmitting equipment..... 191–93,
    194, 200–203
  weather 177
5IT New Street Birmingham .. 276–78,
  309, 318, 380, 386, See also
  2WP/5IT Witton Birmingham
  Station Director .... See Edgar, P
5NO Newcastle ....
  .... 269–71, 274, 380, 385
  opening..................................... 270
  Station Director .... See Payne, T
5SC Glasgow ... 272–73, 309, 380, 386
  opening..................................... 273
  Station Director ....
    .... See Carruthers, H A
5WA Cardiff ... 271–72, 274, 380, 386
  opening..................................... 271
  Station Director See Smith, Corbett
6BM Bournemouth 360, **361**, 380
6SL Sheffield 380
Aberdeen station .... See 2BD Aberdeen
aerial
  2BD Aberdeen 360
  2LO Marconi House. 36, 108, 111,
    171, **172**, 249, 362
  2MT Writtle............................... 91
  2NO Newcastle 269
  2WP Witton Birmingham 209
  2ZY Manchester 193, **195**, 275
  5IT Birmingham....................... 276
  5SC Glasgow 272
  5WA Cardiff............................. 271
  aviation 38, 40

Day, G....................................... 11
Letchworth 23
Marconi New Street.................. 50
media... 67
Northampton 25
receiver 132
aircraft telephone........................... 38
Alan, A J.................... See Lambert, L H
All British Wireless Exhibition and
  Convention.. 120, **121**, 122, 126,
  130, 134–38
Allen, H W 91
American broadcasting ... 142–46, 190,
  191, 206
Amis, F H 207, 210, 211
amplifier..166, 182–86, 198–206, 213,
  241, 244
Anderson, Major P F 228–31, 234,
  237, 245, 257, 265, 284
arc generator.........See transmitter, spark
Armstrong, G 62
Army........................ 37, 43, 129, 228
  Donisthorpe 42
  Russian 36
Ashbridge, N **84**, 85
  2MT Writtle...................................
    ...40, 83, 85, 86, 89, 90, 101,
    383
  broadcasts 92, 93, 96, 98
  receiver 93, 95
  transmitter 85, 90, 188
Auntie ...247, 295, 317, 318, 319, 320,
  321, 331, 342, 386
  Birmingham 212
  Cardiff..................................... 272
  Glasgow.................................. 273
  London.................................... 246
  Manchester 161, 276
aviation 39
Backhouse, E................................. 10
Baillie, I................................. 198, 202
Baird, E....................................... 314
Bangay, R D........................... 84, 85
  textbooks 127
Banks, Sir D 186, 187
Beadle, G 288, 299, 342
Beer, B 163
Beeson, B **84**, 87, 89, 99, 101

426

Beeson, Mr 89
Beeson, Mrs 89
Beeton, A V 57, 70
Bell, Captain H G 162, 196, 204
Bemberg, H 62, 65
Bennett, R 135
Bennie, A 161, 196
Bennie, L 196
Big Ben. 125, 172, 175, 301, 309, 332, 337, 363, 381
Big Six 148–51, 252, 386
Biggin Hill 38, 85
Binyon, B
    British Broadcasting Committee
        .... 224, 230, 253
    engineer 145, 149, 196, 274
    WSL lecture 31
Birmingham station .... *See 2WP Witton Birmingham* and *5IT New Street Birmingham*
Black, D 196
Blackman, Colonel 321
Blake, E 91
Blake, G G 31
Boosey, W 296
Bournemouth station .... *See 6BM Bournemouth*
Braillard, R 15, 43, 329
British Broadcasting Committee ... 124, 150, 151, 156–66, 173–77, 182, 192–96, 210, 223, 227, 245, 254, 351, 384
    Noble, Sir W .... See Noble, Sir W
British Broadcasting Company.............
    . 83, 100, 124, 148–51, 157, 175, 181, 186, 223, 224, 254, 265, 331, 348, 352, **375**, 377–79
    Memorandum and Articles of Association **153**
    Share certificate **154**
British Broadcasting Corporation 83, 142, 249, 376–79
British National Opera Company 241, 284, 285, 295, 306
British Thomson-Houston 148
Broadcasting stations...................... 380
    Aberdeen .... See 2BD Aberdeen

Birmingham..... See 5IT New Street Birmingham, See 2WP Witton Birmingham
Bournemouth .... See 6BM Bournemouth
Cardiff .... See 5WA Cardiff
Glasgow .... See 5SC Glasgow
London .... See 2LO London
Manchester ......See 2ZY Dickenson Street Manchester, See 2ZY Trafford Park Manchester
Newcastle........ See 5NO Newcastle
Brown Brothers 131
Brown, F J 145, 147, 283
Brown, F V 79
Brown, S G................. 130, 132, 137
Brown, W J 162, 204
Brown, W V 196
Bubb, F **84**, 89, 90
Buckley, Major V W 196, 204
Buggins, Mrs 333
Bull, Sir W 222
    BBC Board 230, 266
Burman, A................................ 23, 26
Burnaby, D................................ 111, 247
Burnham and Co 76, 78
Burnham, W N 230
Burrows, A R 43–44, **45**, **291**, **317**
    2LO Marconi House........ 104, 125, 165, **176**, 196
    concerts 174
    daily broadcast..... 157–59, 162, 177, 384
    licence 124
    programmes 117–19, 123, 124, 174, 177–82
    studio 187
    test transmissions 110, 114, 116
    British Broadcasting Company....... 150, 165, 173, 174, 175, 182
    Director of Programmes 224, 227, 228, 229, 235, 241, 253, 270, 284, 286, 314–17, 326
    Magnet House............ 234, 237
    Savoy Hill accommodation 253–59, 357
    Marconi publicity officer..... 61, 62, 82, 125

S. S. Victorian **70**, **71**, 69–71
Writtle programmes ....
.... 81, 92–95, 99
Radio Times 341
Union Internationale de
    Radiodiffusion................. 187
call signs 28, 76, 108
1921 77
Cameron, J M A 278, 287
Cameron, V C 274
Cardiff station .... *See 5WA Cardiff*
Carpendale, Vice Admiral C D 231, 283, 284, 387
Carpentier, G 106
Carruthers, H A............273, **291**, 295
Carter, T G 288
Casey, H................................ 210–12
Casson, L................................ 323
Cassuto, Signor........................ 68
Chalmers, Dorothy 163
Chappell Piano Company...................
.... 92, 110, 172
Charles Hards........................... 175
Charles, David.......................... 68
Chatterton, V 120, 180
Chelmsford
    2MT Writtle........*See* 2MT Writtle
    Marconi Works..........*See* Marconi
        Company, Chelmsford
Chester, B............................. 111
Children's Hour 315, 317–20, 357, 364, 371
Childs, G............................... 111
Christie, Major 314
City of Birmingham Symphony
    Orchestra 299, 309
Clare, Lily............................. 163
Clarke, D.............................. 299, 342
Clarke, T 61–66, 67
Cliff, L................................ 111, 247
Coburn, C............................... 111, 327
Cochran, C B 296
Cock and Bell 81, 89, 93, 99, 101
Cockerell, A........................... 23, 26
Cockerell, Sir C 102
Colbourn, G............................ 212
Cole, M................................ 114
Collins, J 179, 180

Collins, Lottie 111
Collins, W................................. 119
components, radio................... 130–38
Constanduros, M 332, 333
continuous waves.... 11–14, 19, 26, 31, 35, 79
Cooper, E................................ 55, 57, 58
Co-Optimists 111, **112**, **113**, 295
Cormack, J.................... 198, 199, **201**
Corsham, B 76–78
Cory, C 135
Cosmos 137
Covent Garden Opera House 100, 240–44, 336
Cram, M 322
Crampton, W J 241
Crawford and Balcarres, Earl of 376
Crawford Committee 376–78
Crawford, Captain Q C A 17
Crocombe, L 126, 341–42
Croydon Aerodrome....................... **40**
CW .... *See continuous waves*
Daily Mail Ideal Home Exhibition ......
.... 295
Davies, B L............................. 29, **30**
Davies, Sir W 298, 315, 330
Davis, G................................ 14
Dawson, Sir T and Lady................ 110
Day, B 134
Day, G 10–13
de Forest, L 13, 14, 19, 30, 35, 43
De Groot............................... 307
Deloraine, E M 207, 210
Ditcham, W T 18–20, **56**, **69**
    Chelmsford.. 51–57, 63, 65, 66, 68
    Letchworth and Northampton ... 25
    multi-microphone............... 19, **20**
    quenched spark transmitter............
.... 19, **24**, 25, 26, 27
Dixon, C...................... 114, 246, **317**
Don Hyden Quartet.................... 309
Donisthorpe, H 42, 43
Dowell, G 163
Eckersley, Mrs S 90, 99

428

Eckersley, P P **82**, 83, 85, 90, 328, 342
   2MT Writtle .40, **84**, 81–101, 241, 328
      broadcasts 85, 94, 97–100
      aviation 38–40
      chief engineer, BBC ....
        . 101, 227, 230, 235–37, 304, 328, 329, 383–86
         accommodation 259
         appointment 100, 230
         microphones 183, 274
         provincial stations 277, 287, 360
Edgar, P .. 160, 163, 208–14, **215**, **291**
Edinburgh relay station 362
Edwards, N 295
Ellingford, R 89, 101
Esmond, E 177, 301, 311, 312
Eveline, B 110
Everett, P 116
experimenters .... *See* radio ham
Faithful, Rex .... *See* Palmer, R F
Felce, M 95
Fessenden, R A 12–14, 43
first soprano .... *See* Sayer, *Winifred*
Fitzgerald, E .. 266, 268, 286, 288, 314, 315, 318–22, 357
Fleming, Ambrose 35, 313
Fleming, Sir Arthur ....
   . 142–46, 149, 190, 191, 194–98, 204, 205, 213, 274, 289, 337
Forest, L .... *See* de Forest, L
Frankau, G 314
Franklin, C S 35, 49, 104, 106, 108
Fraser, Captain I 110, 114
Freeman, H 134
Frost, Captain W (Jack) 288
Fryer, B 270, **291**, 312
Gage, E 59
Gainford, Lord 229, 238, 264, 265, 271, 273, 283, 284
Gamage 234
Garner Schofield Band 309
Garratt, G R M 188
Garscadden, K 273
Gecophones **133**, 137

General Electric Company 144, 148, 150
   aviation 39
   components 137
   station 159, 166, 207
General Strike 378
Gideon, M 111
Gielgud, V 325
Gill, F 148, 149, 150, 252, 253
Gilman, J 188
Glasgow station .... *See 5SC Glasgow*
Godfrey, D ... 275, **291**, 305, 307, 309, 356
Goldschmidt 12, 31
Goodship, G 83
Goossens, E 306
Gordon, M 119
Great War 17, 25, 42, 75, 84, 207, 251
   Dick Sheppard 330
Grindell Matthews .... *See* Matthews, H Grindell
Hamilton Harty and the Hallé 309
Handley, T 331
Hankey, A 17, 18
Harley, W H B 236, 259, 353
Harrison, Beatrice 337–39
Hart, E 29
Hawke, F 385
Hawke, L 163, 384
Hawkhead, J C 127
Hay, W 119
Heaton-Smith, E 321
Henry, J 298, 331
Hibberd, S 308, 356
Higby, W 57
Hirst, H 229, 234
Holloway, S 111
Honey, S G 276, 318
Hopkins, G G 51–56
Hullo Boys! 319
Hullo Girls! **319**
Hunt, R 111
Huntingdon, D 259, 286
Idzerda, Hanso 78
IEE .... 148, 151, 166, 228, 232, **252**, 249–57, *See also 2LO London, Savoy Hill*
Imperial Airways **40**, 187

Imperial Communications Committee 146
   Wireless Sub-Committee.. 146, 147
Institution of Electrical Engineers ... *See IEE*
interference 75–80, 97, 329
   2LO London 108
   2MT Writtle 96
   2ZY Manchester 275
   aviation 72
   continuous waves 12
   crystal sets 132
   licences 152
   relay stations 361
   Simultaneous Broadcasting 281
International Radio Exhibition 134
Isaacs, G . 58, 62, **63**, 66, 97, 101, 141, 142, 149, 150, 177, 223, 224, 232, 252
jamming 72
Jefferies, L Stanton **185, 291**
   2MT Writtle 97, 98
   Marconi House 110, 114–20, 125–26, 162–68, 172–75, **176**, 179–88, 235
   Savoy Hill .. 240–48, 266–68, 285–89, 295, 296, 304, 305, 356, 384
   Uncle Jeff 317
Jeffrey, R E 303, 324, 359
Jell, J 111
Judd, H 95
Kellaway, F G 146–52, 155, 191
King's Cup Air Race 124
Kirke, H L .. 82, 83, **84**, 86, 87, 90, 92, 93, 95, **96**, 101, 103
   2MT Writtle 40
   mobile transmitter 364
Klein, R 29, 30
Knowles, C 110
Lambert, L H 333–35
Leeds/Bradford relay station 362
Lester, J 331
Letchworth station 20–27, 31
   aerial 23, **24**
   building 23
   Ditcham, W T .. See Ditcham, W T

licence 25
Matthews, H Grindell .... See Matthews, H Grindell
microphones 19, **20**, 26
   plan **22**
   site 20
   transmissions 23–26
   transmitter 19, 23, **24**
Lewis, C 226, 289, **291**
   BBC deputy Director of Programmes ... 177, 229, 234, 240–48, 254, 259, 270, 275, 280, 284–89, 299, 311, 323, 326, 357, 371, 383–85, 387
   Men's Hour 314
   Savoy Hill opening 266
   silence cabinets 366–67
   Uncle Caractacus 235, 317
   Metropolitan-Vickers 150
Lewis, J 276
Lewis, Kid 106
licence
   broadcasting 124, 155, 230, 376–79
   experimental 10, 11, 25, 28, 29, 75, 79, 106–8, 110, 117, 124, 152, 347
   Interim 350–51
   receiver 144, 145, 149, 151–56, 245, 329, 348, 349, 350, 377, 386
Lipscombe, G 127
Litt, H W 288
Liverpool relay station 362
Lock, Miss 287, 353
Lodge, Sir O 329
London Chorus 307
London station .... *See 2LO London*
Long, N 264, 331
Lord Mayor of Bristol 122, 279
Lord Mayor's Show 124
loudspeaker 132, 154
   Amplion Junior' 202
   Magnavox R2B 132
   poor man's 132
   S G Brown 132
   Western Electric 132, 206

Lupino, S 184, 320
Macfarlane, E 111
Macintosh, E 42
MacLarty, B N **84**, 87–89, 101
magazines .... 126–30, 423, *See also publications*
   Popular Wireless Weekly ....
        .... 123, 127, **128**, 163, 309
   Radio Times 126, 288, 298, 299, **343**, 341–44, 356, 372, 387
       launch 288
   The Broadcaster 127
   The Electrician 31
   The English Mechanic 31
   The Model Engineer 31
   Wireless World ....
        .... 17, 29, 31, 75, 127, 141
Magnet House BBC Head Office ....
    .... **225**, 230–39
   accommodation 233–35, 237
   liaison with 2LO Marconi House
        235
   staffing 237
magnetophone. *See microphone, moving coil, Marconi-Sykes*
Mallinson, Miss 236, 259, 287, 353
Manchester station ..... *See 2ZY Trafford Park Manchester* and *2ZY Dickenson Street Manchester*
Marconi Company, Chelmsford
   Hall Street 15, 35, 37, 49
   New Street **69**, 49–72
      aerial 50, 51
      buildings 49, **50**, 51, **53**, 54
      Butt, Dame Clara, broadcasts 55
      Ditcham, W T ....
          .... *See Ditcham, W T*
      Melba broadcasts ....
         .... *See Melba, Dame Nellie*
      Melchior broadcasts ....
          .... *See Melchior, L*
      microphone 62, **64**
      plan **51**, 54
      Sayer, Winifred .... 55, *See also Sayer, Winifred*
      site 49
      studio 54, 55

      transmissions 56–60, 67, 68, 69, 70, 71, 72
      transmitter 169
      transmitting equipment .. 54, 56
Marconi Company, London ....
   9, 12, 57, 58, 69–72, 79, 80, 94, 141–48, 174, 186, 190, 205, 227, 329, 350, 362–64
   aviation 39, 226
   equipment 26, 35, 83
   Managing Director .... *See Issac, G*
   Marconi House ..... *See 2LO London*
   radio receivers 131, 137
   stations .. 9, 49, 57, 67, 72, 81, 104, 150, 157, 206, 236, 269, 273, 277, 281, 360
Marconi Company, Writtle ... *See 2MT Writtle*
Marconi, Guglielmo 9, 15, **16**, 36
Marconigram 10, 68, 347
Marconiphone ....
   119, 131, 132, 137, *See also radio receivers, crystal sets*
Marconi-Sykes .. *See microphone, moving coil*
Mason, A G L 160, 207
Matthews, H Grindell 1, 18–27
   early experiments 18
   Letchworth and Northampton .. 18, 20, 23, **24**, 25, 26, 27
Mazarin, Mariette 14
McKinstry, A ....
   .... 149, 150, 191, 196, 205, 223, 224, 226
McMichael, L 28, 76
   call sign 76
   dealer 130, 138
      Hesketh 130
   licence 76
   transmitter 28
   WSL 29, 92
Meissner, A 35
Melba, Dame Nellie ....
   .... 51, 53, 54, 51–54, 55, 61, 62, 63, **64**, 65, 66, 61–66, 67, 68, 72, 243, 244

Melchior, L **69**
  2MT Writtle 95
  Marconi Company, Chelmsford 54, 55
  Memorandum and Articles of Association 150, 151, **153**, 155
Men's Hour 314
Menges, Isolde 198, **199**
Merson, B 119, 295, 320
Metropolitan Opera House 14
Metropolitan Symphony Orchestra .. 77
Metropolitan-Vickers ....
  .. 3, 125, 142, 148–50, 190, 191, 196, 198, 202, 206, 386
  components 137
  station ....
    145, 149, 150, 157–61, 166, 190, 192, 203–7, 274
Metrovick .... *See Metropolitan-Vickers*
microphone
  capacitor 277, 386
    McLachlan 123
  carbon granule ....
    13, 14, 62, **64**, 163, 172, 192
    de Forest 14
    double button 206, 213, 244, 272–80, 336, 360, 386
    Marzi 15
    multi-microphone 19, **20**, 26
    Peel Conner ....
    . 91, 173, 179, 182, 183, 193, 197, 200, 269, 271, 274
  electrodynamic .... *See moving coil*
  horn .62, **64**, 111, 173, **199**, 198–200, **201**, 203
  liquid 13
  magnetophone ...... See moving coil, Marconi-Sykes
  moving coil 202, 203, 213, 336
    Marconi-Sykes ... 264, **265**, 304, 337, 338, **339**, 360–67, 386
    Round. 173, **185**, 182–88, 245, 261, 304
    Round-Sykes 264
  photophone 198–200, 213, 274
Military Bands 308
Millais, H 124
Millican, Colonel 271

Monkman, P 111
Mr X .... *See Bell, Captain H G*
Mr Z .... *See Brown, W V*
music 304–10
Nesbitt, K 323
New Street Chelmsford ..... *See Marconi Company, Chelmsford*
Newcastle station .... *See 5NO Newcastle*
Newnes 341, 342
nightingale .... *See outside broadcast*
Nightingale, S 196, 200, **201**
Nitti, Signor 68
No. 2 Savoy Hill .... *See 2LO London*
Noble, Sir W .. 122, 124, 148–59, 174, 175, 210, 219, 223–32, 238, 241, 252–54, 271, 273, 311
North Atlantic Times **70**, **71**, 69–72
  equipment 69
Northampton station 20–27
  aerial 25, 27
  Ditcham, W T .. See Ditcham, W T
  licence 25
  Matthews, H Grindell .... See Matthews, H Grindell
  plan **21**
  site 20, 23
  transmissions 23–26
Northcliffe, Lord 62, 66
O'Brien, D 111
Old Vic 337, 364
Openshaw, J T 23
outside broadcast 122–24, 143, 144, 203, 205, 214, 244, 264, 285, 295, 296, 330, **339**, 336–40, 364, 371, 374, 386
  nightingale 337
Palm Court Orchestra 307
Palmer, R F 245, 271, **291**
  2LO 240, 245
  Station Director 267, 285, 289, 305, 333
  Rex Faithful 120, 245
  Uncle Rex 317
Partridge, J 76
Payne, T 232, 270
PCGG 78, 79, 97, 116, 126
Pease, H M 149

Peel, C S 322
Pells, G 126, 150, 229–30
Pennington, J 116, 180
Pettengill 51, 55, 67
Phillips, F 148
piezoelectric .... *See also radio receivers, crystals and crystal sets*
piezophone 193, 200
Pitt, P ...266, 267, 284, 287, **291**, 298, 304–7, 344, 356, 371
Plymouth relay station 361
Polar 137
Poldhu 9, 10, 16, 57, 69, 72
Popular Wireless Weekly. *See magazines*
Post Office trunk line ....
 ... 17, 122, 279–81, 306, 338, *See also Simultaneous Broadcasting*
Poulsen arc .... *See transmitter, spark*
press
  2LO broadcast 106
  announcements 151, 219
  collaboration 117, 126, 295
  first transmissions 68
  Grindell Matthews 18
  Melba broadcast 62
  PCGG broadcasts 97, 116, 126
  portable receiver 67
  reports 157
  Tom Clarke .... See Clarke, T
Price-Smith 39
Prince of Wales broadcast 120, 122
Prince, C 15, 37
  aviation 38, 39, 40
programmes
  centralisation 295
  organisation 295–303
publications 126–30, 423
  Elementary Textbook on Wireless Vacuum Tubes 129
  Hullo Boys/Girls! **319**, 319
  Radio Press 127, 129
publications .... *See also magazines*
Pullen, J G 23, 26
quenched spark transmitter .... *See Ditcham, W T*
Radio Communications Company .. *See RCC*

radio critics 315
radio ham ... 10, 16–18, 28–31, 41, 43, 58–62, 66, 75–81, 90–93, 97, 108, 115–17, 126, 132, 141, 227, 236, 328, 362
Radio Press .... *See publications*
radio receivers ..... **133**, 131–37, *See also licence*, *See also amplifiers*
  crystals and crystal sets .. 11, 13, 20, 28, 35, 38, 59, 67, 78, 97, 104, **133**, 130–38, 145, 152, 154, 168, 193, 206, 212, 276, 321
  valve sets .**36**, 42, 78, 97, 129, **133**, 132–38, 168
Radio Times .... *See magazines*
Ralton, Bert 308
RCC 125, 129, 145, 148, 150, 191, 193, 206
  components 137
  station 150, 159, 202–5, 274
receivers .... *See radio receivers*
Reith, J C W 220–23, **239**, 254
  2LO Marconi House 186
  studio 187
  finances 348–52
  General Manager, British Broadcasting Company .. 150, 181, 182, 234, 235, 264–67, 273, 284, 341, 342
  appointment.**221**, 219–24, 229
  Magnet House 228–31, 232, 233, 234, 235, 238
  Savoy Hill accommodation ....
   .... 251, 254–59, 287–91, 356
  Savoy Hill Mansions.. 357, 371, 374
  staffing 234, 236, 237, 245, 270, 283–89, 316
  talks 311–16
  Imperial Airways Chairman 187
  Managing Director, British Broadcasting Corporation
   .... 375, 387
  No. 2 Savoy Hill, IEE accommodation **354**
  Royal Charter 376–79
  Vision for the Future.......... 381–82

433

Rhodes, R 276, 318
Rice, G V 231, 288, 353
Richards, C S 226
Richards, W J 226
Roberts, F 314
Robey, G 295, 296
Robinson, Heath 314
Robinson, S 305, 307
Ronald, L 299, 306
Roosters, The 298, 331
Ross, H 359
Round, H J ....
.... 12, 15, 19, 35–39, 49, **54**, 55, 57, 104, 168, *See also microphone, moving coil*
    2LO transmitter 168, 169, 269
    amplifier 356
    Melba broadcast . 51–54, 55, 65, 66
    Melchior broadcast 54
    moving coil microphone ....
        173, **185**, 182–88, 245, 261, 264, 269, 360, *See also microphone, moving coil*
    North Atlantic Times 69
Round-Sykes .... *See microphone, moving coil*
Rouse, W 327, 331
Royal Air Force 38, 72, 108
Royal Charter 376–80
Royal Flying Corps 38
Royal Navy 9, 17, 30, 36
    Italian 36, 37
Royal Northern and Passmore Edwards Hospitals 116
Royal Signals Experimental Establishment 38
Rumford, K 55
Russell, H J **84**, 89, 90
Rutherford, Sir E 282
S. S. Victorian *See North Atlantic Times*
Savoy Hill Mansions .. *See 2LO London, Savoy Hill*
Savoy Orphaeans 297, 308
Sayer, Winifred **59**, **60**, 55–61, 65
Scholes, P 313
Scott, Nora 95, **96**, 103
Scott-Taggart, J 28, 129, 130, 135

Shakespeare 323
Sharman, J 331
Shaw, N 104
Shaw, W J 30
Sheffield relay station 361
Sheppard, Dick 316, 330
silence cabinet 366, 367, **368**, 371
Simpson, A 166
Simpson, Colonel 147, 253
Simultaneous Broadcasting .. 267, 279–82, 288, 297–99, 306, 309, 313, 315, 323, 361, **374**, 386
    control room **282**, 363–65, 373
    first broadcast 282
    programming 289, **300**
    test transmissions 279–81
Smale sisters 89
Smith, Corbett **291**
    Artistic Director 298, 357
      Feature Programmes 326
    Cardiff Station Director 272
Smith, M 160
Smith, W C .. 236, 259, 267, 288, 356, 357
Smythe, V 197–98, 275, 276, 318
Soap Box microphone .. 183, 188, 203, 304, *See also Round, H J, moving coil microphone*
Sockett, J 210
Somers, Debroy 252, 297, 308
sound effects 302, 324, **325**
Southney, W R 106
spark generator ...... *See transmitter, spark*
St Dunstan's 110, 114
St Leger, F 62–65
Stewart, J 85, 89
Stobart, J C 316, 371
Stuart, Sir C 62
Sturgess, O 135
Swinton, Viscount 187
Sykes Committee . 283, 287, 288, 349–51, 386
Sykes, Sir F 349
Taylor Tunnicliffe 27
telegraphy 9–14, 19, 36, 42, 72, 84, 205
The Broadcaster 127
thermionic valve .... *See valve*

Thomas, F W 314
Thompson, A E 159, 160, 207–12, **215**, 244, 272, 356
Thorndike, S 119
Thurlow, J 97
Thurlow, R 97
Tilley, Mr 117, 121
time signal 10, 131, 143, 151, 172, 363, 367–68, 373
   Hope-Jones Synchronome **366**, 367
   pips 367
   Pulsynetic 367
transmitter
   1914 transmitter/receiver **36**
   2BD Aberdeen 360
   2LO Marconi House 106, **109**, **170**, 166–71, 168–71, 188, 255, 362
   2MT Writtle 81, 85, 87, **91**, 90–93
   2ZY Manchester .... .192, **194**, 193–98, 201, 203, 274
   5IT Birmingham **213**, 276
   5NO Newcastle 269
   5SC Glasgow 272
   5WA Cardiff 271
   6BM Bournemouth 360
   aviation 39
   Donisthorpe 42
   Edinburgh relay station 362
   Franklin, C S 108
   Leeds relay station 362
   Letchworth station 19, 23, **24**
   Marconi New Street 51, 56
   McMichael 28
   outside broadcasts ... 108, 114, 143, 337, 364
   Plymouth relay station 361
   radio ham 29
   radio telephone 15
   Sheffield relay station 361
   simultaneous broadcasting 279
   spark 9, 11, 12, 19, **30**, 79
      Morse arc 78
      Poulsen arc 12, 14, 17, 19
      quenched spark .... *See Ditcham, W T*
   Western Electric Station 214
Travers, A 98
Tristram, C 341
Trost, O 68
Trump, E H **84**, 86, 89, 101, 102
   2MT Writtle 40
   aviation 39
Tudsbury, M 379
Twelvetrees, Captain 314
Twigg, Phyllis 181
Uncle ... 247, 266, 286, 295, 304, 317–21, 386
   Birmingham 211, 213
   Bournemouth 271
   Cardiff 272
   Glasgow 273
   London 235, 245, 342
   Manchester 196, 204, 276, 318
valve 12, 26, 35, 42, 129, 185, 203
   0/500 Mullard 193
   air-cooled silica 203, 274
   dull emitter 137
   Fleming diode 35
   low frequency amplifying 56
   Marconi 'C' type 35
   Marconi 'T' type 35
   MR2 .... 56, 170
   MR4 57
   MR9 170
   MT4 .... 57, 90, 170
   MT7B 170
   rectifier 90
   triode 35
   Wecovalve 206
Victorian experiment *See North Atlantic Times*
Wade, C R 287, 315
Wade, R .. 266, 285, 289, 312–16, 357
Walker, E 110
Walker, Major H S 28, 76, 230, 362
war .... *See Great War*
Warrander, F 212
Wecovalve 206
West, Captain A G D 281, 287, 338

Western Electric 125, 148, 150, 205
   radio receiver............ 132, 137, 206
   station... 150, 159–61, 205–7, 212, 214, 241, 244, 272–81, 336, 360, 363, 386
Westinghouse Company 142–45, 147, 190–91
White, G W 57, 68, **69**, 78
White, R H .. 104, 106, 123, 169, 207, 227, 228, 232, 253–55
Wilcockson, Captain A S 187
Wireless amateur .... *See radio ham*
Wireless Club 28
   Derby 77
   London 29, 30
Wireless Orchestra 125, 144, 173, 174, 179, 240, 246, 263, 304, **305**, 353, 385
wireless receivers .... *See radio receivers*

Wireless Society
   Croydon 29
   London (WSL) . 29, 31, 75, 76, 79, 80, 83, 92, 97, 134
Wireless World 17, 29, 31, 75, 127, 141
Women's Hour 266, 273, 287, 297, 298, 314, 315, 321, 322, 357
Wood, D 305
Wood, J A 314
Wood, R H 275
Wright, A 305
Wright, H 119
Wright, K A 161–63, 175, 194–98, 202, 204, 275, 289, 317, 384
Wright, S 199
Writtle .... *See 2MT Writtle*
Wynn, R T B ... 83, **84**, 85, 86, 89, 90, 98, 99, 101

Compiled by Jane Wardle